Paul has long been regarded as an early champion of sexual asceticism, but little account has hitherto been taken of the Stoic and Cynic discourse on marriage which formed the context of his writings. This study overturns the traditional interpretation, first by a critique of established theories about the influence of Jewish spirituality, "enthusiasm" and material dualism on Paul's theology, and then by a reconstruction, using the surviving philosophical "fragments," of the course of Stoic and Cynic thinking on marriage from early Greek precursors to late Roman and patristic authors – information which is then applied to Paul in a close exegesis of the text. The result is an illuminating reassessment of both Paul's understanding of marriage and his place in the history of Christian asceticism, providing new information for discussions of Christian sexuality and feminist evaluations of the Bible.

SOCIETY FOR NEW TESTAMENT STUDIES

*MONOGRAPH SERIES*

General Editor: Margaret E. Thrall

**83**

PAUL ON MARRIAGE AND CELIBACY

# Paul on marriage and celibacy

The Hellenistic background of 1 Corinthians 7

**WILL DEMING**

*University of Portland*

**CAMBRIDGE**
UNIVERSITY PRESS

Published by the Press Syndicate of the University of Cambridge
The Pitt Building, Trumpington Street, Cambridge CB2 1RP
40 West 20th Street, New York, NY 10011-4211, USA
10 Stamford Road, Oakleigh, Melbourne 3166, Australia

First published 1995
Reprinted 1996

Printed in Great Britain by Biddles Ltd, Guildford, Surrey

*A catalogue record for this book is available from the British Library*

*Library of Congress cataloguing in publication data*

Deming, Will, 1956–
Paul on marriage and celibacy: the Hellenistic background of
1 Corinthians 7 / Will Deming.
    p.    cm. – (Society for New Testament Studies Monograph Series: 83)
Originally presented as the author's thesis (doctoral),
University of Chicago, 1991.
Includes bibliographical references and index.
ISBN 0 521 47284 9 (hardback)
1. Bible. N.T. Corinthians, 1st, VII – Criticism, interpretation, etc.
2. Marriage – Biblical teaching.
3. Celibacy – Biblical teaching.
4. Cynics (Greek philosophy).   5. Stoics.   I. Title.
II. Series: Monograph series (Society for New Testament Studies); 83.
BS2675.6.M3D½6    1995    227'.206 – dc20    94–15915    CIP

ISBN 0 521 47284 9 hardback

CE

Maidee Elizabeth Coffman Deming and Andrew S. Deming

# CONTENTS

# PREFACE

In origin this book was my doctoral dissertation, which was accepted by the University of Chicago's Divinity School in August of 1991. In editing it for publication I have subjected it to a thorough revision, taking into account relevant scholarship that has appeared since that date.

For having reached this stage in my career as a teacher and scholar I am indebted to many people, but first of all to my parents, to whom this book is dedicated: to my mother, who taught me patience and curiosity, and to my father, who taught me to think logically and muster a good argument. Throughout the many years of my graduate education they generously supplied me with both financial support and encouragement, two of a scholar's most precious resources.

I am also indebted to my dissertation advisor Hans Dieter Betz for his exacting reading and rereading of this work, and to Elizabeth Asmis for her thoughtful criticisms of my Greek translations.

Beyond this I wish to express my gratitude to the many other teachers I have had at the University of Chicago and at Göttingen University in Germany. Among these are Wendy Doniger and Frank Reynolds, who initiated me into the study of symbolism and comparative religious ethics; the late David Wilmot, who imparted to me, and to all his students, a passion for reading Greek; and Hartmut Stegemann, Robert Hanhart, and Berndt Schaller, under whom I had the privilege of studying Hellenistic Judaism.

Finally, a special thanks is due to my wife, Lauren Wellford Deming, for reading through the manuscript as a non-specialist, offering suggestions regarding style and clarity, and to my good friend the Rev. Owen Guy for providing me with a quiet place to work while I wrote the last two chapters.

# ABBREVIATIONS

| | |
|---|---|
| AB | Anchor Bible |
| *ANRW* | *Aufstieg und Niedergang der römischen Welt* |
| *ARW* | *Archiv für Religionswissenschaft* |
| ATANT | Abhandlungen zur Theologie des Alten und Neuen Testaments |
| BHT | Beiträge zur historischen Theologie |
| BU | Biblische Untersuchungen |
| BWANT | Beiträge zur Wissenschaft vom Alten und Neuen Testament |
| *BZ* | *Biblische Zeitschrift* |
| *CBQ* | *Catholic Biblical Quarterly* |
| *CQ* | *Classical Quarterly* |
| CSCO | Corpus Scriptorum Christianorum Orientalium |
| *ERE* | *Encyclopædia of Religion and Ethics* |
| *EvT* | *Evangelische Theologie* |
| FRLANT | Forschungen zur Religion und Literatur des Alten und Neuen Testaments |
| HNT | Handbuch zum Neuen Testament |
| HNTC | Harper's New Testament Commentaries |
| *HR* | *History of Religions* |
| *HTR* | *Harvard Theological Review* |
| HTS | Harvard Theological Studies |
| ICC | International Critical Commentary |
| *IDB* | *Interpreter's Dictionary of the Bible* |
| *JAAR* | *Journal of the American Academy of Religion* |
| *JBL* | *Journal of Biblical Literature* |
| *JHS* | *Journal of Hellenic Studies* |
| LCL | Loeb Classical Library |
| MeyerK | H. A. W. Meyer (ed.), Kritisch-exegetischer Kommentar über das Neue Testament |
| *MTZ* | *Münchner Theologische Zeitschrift* |

| | |
|---|---|
| NICNT | New International Commentary on the New Testament |
| *NovT* | *Novum Testamentum* |
| *NRT* | *Nouvelle Revue Théologique* |
| NTAbh | Neutestamentliche Abhandlungen |
| *NTS* | *New Testament Studies* |
| NTTS | New Testament Tools and Studies |
| *PG* | *Patrologia Graeca*, ed. J. Migne |
| *PL* | *Patrologia Latina*, ed. J. Migne |
| *PW* | *Paulys Real-Encyclopädie der klassischen Altertumswissenschaft* |
| *RAC* | *Reallexikon für Antike und Christentum* |
| *RB* | *Revue biblique* |
| *Rh. Mus.* | *Rheinisches Museum für Philologie* |
| *RSR* | *Recherches de Science Religieuse* |
| SBLDS | Society of Biblical Literature Dissertation Series |
| SBLGRS | Society of Biblical Literature Graeco-Roman Religion Series |
| SBLMS | Society of Biblical Literature Monograph Series |
| SBLSBS | Society of Biblical Literature Sources for Biblical Study |
| SBLSPS | Society of Biblical Literature Seminar Papers Series |
| SBLTT | Society of Biblical Literature Texts and Translations |
| SNT | Studien zum Neuen Testament |
| SNTSMS | Society for New Testament Studies Monograph Series |
| SUNY | State University of New York |
| *SVF* | *Stoicorum Veterum Fragmenta* |
| *TDNT* | *Theological Dictionary of the New Testament* |
| *TLZ* | *Theologische Literaturzeitung* |
| *TQ* | *Theologische Quartalschrift* |
| *TRE* | *Theologische Realenzyklopädie* |
| TU | Texte und Untersuchungen |
| *VC* | *Vigiliae Christianae* |
| WMANT | Wissenschaftliche Monographien zum Alten und Neuen Testament |
| WUNT | Wissenschaftliche Untersuchungen zum Neuen Testament |
| *ZKG* | *Zeitschrift für Kirchengeschichte* |
| *ZNW* | *Zeitschrift für die neutestamentliche Wissenschaft und die Kunde der älteren Kirche* |
| *ZST* | *Zeitschrift für systematische Theologie* |
| *ZTK* | *Zeitschrift für Theologie und Kirche* |

# INTRODUCTION

The seventh chapter of Paul's first letter to the Corinthians is arguably one of the most influential discussions of marriage and celibacy in the entire Christian tradition. Not only does it represent the most extensive treatment of these topics in the New Testament, but in the centuries following its appearance its importance grew to such an extent that one leading church historian has called 1 Corinthians 7 "the one chapter that was to determine all Christian thought on marriage and celibacy for well over a millennium."[1] In recent times a resurgence of interest in this text has added still further to its prominence in the church. During the last century 1 Corinthians 7 has been the subject of innumerable articles on marriage, sexuality, gender issues, and feminism, as well as the focus of several book-length inquiries.[2]

One result of this recent and intense scholarship is that most interpreters today support a view of Paul similar to one advanced by some of his earliest interpreters in the patristic era. According to this view, the Apostle held a very low opinion of marriage and consequently encouraged his readers in the direction of sexual asceticism, which is the rejection of one's erotic nature in order to become more holy or closer to God. Yet as venerable and widely accepted as

[1] Peter Brown, *The Body and Society: Men, Women and Sexual Renunciation in Early Christianity*, Lectures in the History of Religions, n.s. 13 (New York: Columbia University Press, 1988) 54.

[2] Namely, Darrell J. Doughty, "Heiligkeit und Freiheit: Eine exegetische Untersuchung der Anwendung des paulinischen Freiheitsgedankens in 1 Kor 7" (Ph.D. diss., Göttingen, 1965); Werner Wolbert, *Ethische Argumentation und Paränese in 1 Kor 7*, Moraltheologische Studien, systematische Abteilung 8 (Düsseldorf: Patmos, 1981); Norbert Baumert, *Ehelosigkeit und Ehe im Herrn: Eine Neuinterpretation von 1 Kor 7*, Forschung zur Bibel 47 (Würzburg: Echter Verlag, 1984); O. Larry Yarbrough, *Not Like the Gentiles: Marriage Rules in the Letters of Paul*, SBLDS 80 (Atlanta: Scholars, 1985); and Vincent L. Wimbush, *Paul the Worldly Ascetic: Response to the World and Self-Understanding according to 1 Corinthians 7* (Macon, Ga.: Mercer University Press, 1987).

this picture of Paul is, it is open to serious question on the grounds that it leaves many important aspects of 1 Corinthians 7 unexplained or otherwise obscure. For some passages, for example, there is disagreement among scholars as to what issue Paul is addressing, or whether he is presenting his own view or quoting one supplied by the Corinthians. And more basic and telling than this is the fact that scholars have never reached a consensus regarding Paul's reasons for favoring asceticism over marriage.

Part of the difficulty is that Paul did not write 1 Corinthians 7 as a theological treatise. It is, rather, his response to a particular situation that arose among certain Christians in first-century Corinth, and as such represents only one part of a dialogue between Paul and this readership. But, with the possible exception of Romans, circumstances like these pertain to all of Paul's letters and therefore cannot be the whole problem with understanding the chapter. The main difficulty, in my opinion, is that interpreters have actually lost touch with much of the conceptual framework that undergirds Paul's discussion. Without the original context or world view for his ideas, or those of the Corinthians to whom he is responding, it has been impossible to second-guess his meaning. Many scholars, to be sure, have come to this same conclusion and have suggested contexts for Paul's words based on their investigations of various Christian and non-Christian groups within the Greco-Roman world. As I have indicated above, however, and will show more thoroughly in the next chapter, these solutions have not done justice to the information supplied to us by the text.

The goal of this study is to offer a new assessment of Paul's understanding of marriage and celibacy. I will base this assessment on a hypothesis that has, to date, gained only minimal acceptance among those working on 1 Corinthians 7. Beginning with the insight, often overlooked by scholars, that not all forms of celibacy stem from a theology of sexual asceticism, I will argue that in writing 1 Corinthians 7 Paul drew his basic concepts of marriage and its alternatives from a centuries-old debate on marriage that had been shaped by the political and intellectual vicissitudes of the Hellenistic world. In Paul's day the line that separated antagonists in this debate was drawn between a Stoic and a Cynic position, both of which presented married life as primarily a matter of duty and responsibility to a larger human community, not as the starting point of sexual activity in the life of an individual.

The Stoics and their supporters favored marriage, and for a

reason which, to us, might seem rather curious at first: they saw it as the salvation of the city-states. Marriage, they reasoned, was the one institution that could halt the decline of local autonomy and traditional life in the Hellenistic world: if more people would take seriously the responsibilities of marriage, concerned citizens and stable households would result, insuring the future of the city-states. The Cynics, by contrast, renounced the institutions of the city-state, including marriage. By avoiding wedlock, they argued, a person secured the free time necessary to pursue philosophy and achieve virtue and well-being. To complicate matters, there was also a certain amount of crossover between the Stoic and Cynic camps. Some Stoics took a hybrid position, holding that while under normal conditions it was one's moral obligation to marry, special considerations in one's life, such as poverty or the advent of war, could force a person to forgo marriage and concentrate on the philosophical life.

In using this marriage debate as the backdrop for Paul's discussion in 1 Corinthians 7, I will show that the dynamics of the two are remarkably similar. Paul, like the Stoics and Cynics, defines marriage principally in terms of responsibility, not sexual activity; and he takes the position, much like the Stoic hybrid view, that under certain circumstances the duties of married life interfere with one's allegiance to a higher cause – which, in Paul's case, was Christ. Beyond demonstrating that the dynamics of the Hellenistic debate and Paul's discussion are comparable, however, and that the former sheds considerable light on the latter, I will also show that 1 Corinthians 7 actually contains a number of Stoic and Cynic terms, phrases, and ideas. From this I will argue that Stoic and Cynic thought had a clear and decisive impact on how Paul and his readers conceived of marriage.

Implicit in this study, therefore, is a major theological statement, for what I am suggesting is that the understanding of 1 Corinthians 7 held by most scholars and church leaders today derives from an early Christian reinterpretation of Paul, and that this text has been essentially misunderstood almost since its composition. Briefly stated, the decisive moment appears to have been near the end of the first century CE. As this century passed into the second, intellectuals of the age turned their attention away from the city-state to notions of earthly and cosmic empires. With much searching and introspection they weighed the benefits of a purely spiritual life against the vagaries and evils of mere physical existence. In this context marriage became more than a means of involving oneself in the local community: it symbolized an ominous bond with the material world. In line with these developments, the fathers of the church began to view 1 Corinthians 7 with a new eye. Some of what Paul said became mysterious or unintelligible to these interpreters, while other statements were cast in an ascetic mold never intended by the Apostle. In the centuries that separate us from Paul, the world view from within which he wrote was all but forgotten. This state of affairs has left modern interpreters with little to go on, and has encouraged them to follow the lead of their patristic and medieval counterparts. As a consequence, they have explained Paul's position on marriage in terms of a vision of the world that may not have existed in his day, let alone informed his thought.

The implications of interpreting 1 Corinthians 7 from this perspective are nothing short of profound. No longer will it be possible to see Paul as one of Christianity's first champions of sexual asceticism. Instead, we will come to know him as a cautious and measured proponent of the single lifestyle, a form of celibacy characterized by freedom from the responsibilities of marriage and for which the absence of sexual fulfillment was no more than an unintended consequence and an inconvenience, never an end in itself.

# 1

## THE MOTIVATION FOR CELIBACY IN
## 1 CORINTHIANS 7: A REVIEW OF
## SCHOLARLY OPINION

As a preliminary step in our reassessment of Paul's understanding of marriage and celibacy, this chapter will present a critical review of the work of other scholars to help determine which options for interpretation are open to us and which are not. It will also reveal an extensive history of the misinterpretation of 1 Corinthians 7, which should be of interest both to scholars working on 1 Corinthians 7 itself and to those working on other parts of the Corinthian correspondence.

In all of the research that has been done on 1 Corinthians 7, the one aspect of this chapter that has both fascinated and perplexed biblical scholars and theologians more than any other is its characterization of Christian marriage as the necessary alternative to certain forms of celibacy. In 1 Corinthians 7.2, for example, Paul states, "because of sexual immorality, let each man have his own wife, and let each woman have her own husband." In 7.9 he advises, "it is better to marry than to burn"; and in 7.36 he tells a single man that if he is "over the limit" he should marry without delay. Without much exaggeration one could even say that Paul's topic in 1 Corinthians 7 is not so much marriage, but the benefits and limitations of celibacy. As one scholar lamented, "one looks in vain for a positive appreciation of love between the sexes or of the richness of human experience in marriage and family."[1]

Because celibacy looms so large in Paul's discussion, scholars have directed most of their efforts to determining the theological motivation for this celibacy – both for that which the Corinthians promote and which Paul, in part, seeks to restrain, and that which

---

[1] Günther Bornkamm, *Paul* (New York/Evanston, Ill.: Harper and Row, 1971) 208. Cf. Johannes Weiß, *The History of Primitive Christianity* (New York: Wilson-Erickson, 1937) 2.582; and Kurt Niederwimmer, *Askese und Mysterium: Über Ehe, Ehescheidung und Eheverzicht in den Anfängen des christlichen Glaubens*, FRLANT 113 (Göttingen: Vandenhoeck und Ruprecht, 1975) 66, 67.

Paul himself promotes. A few have argued for the influence of Stoic and Cynic thought. This is the theory for which there is the most evidence, and consequently the one that will guide the investigations in chapters two, three, and four of this study. As I will show here, however, the manner in which this theory has been presented until now is unacceptable for a number of reasons. The vast majority of scholars, by contrast, hold a very different view. They assume the importance of a theology of sexual asceticism in the thinking of Paul and the Corinthians, although there is little agreement as to its source. Some point in the direction of Hellenistic Judaism while others see it as arising from ascetic tendencies thought to be *sui generis* products of first-century Christianity. Still others contend that Paul and his readers were motivated by considerations similar to those which inspired Christians of the second, third, and fourth centuries. In reviewing the work of these scholars, I will argue that all such theories of an ascetic basis for the discussion in 1 Corinthians 7 are highly questionable since they rest on very little evidence indeed. I shall show, in fact, that most of what has been offered as evidence for these theories is both inconsistent with the information provided by 1 Corinthians 7 and poorly fits the context of the middle of the first century CE. In concluding this chapter I will return to this matter of insufficient evidence and offer other methodological observations as well.

## 1. Paul in the light of Stoic and Cynic materials

Perhaps the first to connect Paul's statements on marriage and celibacy with Stoic and Cynic thought was Clement of Alexandria in the second century CE. As we will see in the next chapter, Clement identified Paul so closely with the Stoics on this matter that he had considerable difficulty distinguishing Paul's arguments from theirs. Many centuries later the Dutch humanist and theologian Hugo Grotius picked up on this thread. He began his treatment of 1 Corinthians 7 by pointing out that the question of marriage was frequently debated among the Greek philosophers, and he mentioned two Stoics by name, Musonius Rufus and Hierocles. He further speculated that the faithful in Corinth were "really philosophers under the name of Christians (although nonetheless Christians)."[2]

---

[2] Hugo Grotius, *Annotationes in Novum Testamentum* (Paris: Pelé, 1646) 2.377–8.

In more recent times, especially since the publication of Johannes Weiß's commentary on 1 Corinthians, it has become commonplace for scholars to cite parallels between 1 Corinthians 7 and Stoic and Cynic authors, although the implications of these parallels are rarely explored.[3] An exception to this rule is the work of David Balch, Larry Yarbrough, and Vincent Wimbush. Despite the contribution these three scholars have made to our understanding of 1 Corinthians 7, however, their efforts to interpret this chapter with reference to Stoic and Cynic texts have left many stones unturned. This is because none of them has developed a clear picture of the central issues of Stoic and Cynic discourse on marriage. Balch's understanding of this discourse relies almost entirely on a topology that he finds in an anthology of ancient literature compiled by Johannes Stobaeus around the fifth century CE. In this anthology Stobaeus collected excerpts on marriage from a wide range of authors, including not only Stoics and Cynics, but also philosophers such as Thales, Socrates, and Plato, tragedians such as Euripides and Sophocles, comic poets such as Menander and Aristophanes, and orators such as Demosthenes and Lycurgus. These he arranged under seven general headings: (1) marriage is best (or most beautiful), (2) it is not good to marry, (3) for some marriage is helpful but for others the life of those who marry will produce inconvenience, (4) courtship, (5) in marriages one should give thought to the ages of those marrying, (6) in marriages one should not give thought to social standing or wealth, (7) the censure of women.[4] Stobaeus then follows these with sections on marriage precepts, children, parents, relatives, social status, and household management. Somewhat arbitrarily, Balch chooses Stobaeus' first three headings on marriage and uses them to define the parameters of what he calls the "Stoic debates about marriage." From the start, then, Balch's method for determining the issues is far too oblique. In consequence, he is able to recognize Stoic elements only in verses 32–5 of 1 Corinthians 7,

[3] E.g., Johannes Weiß, *Der erste Korintherbrief*, MeyerK 5 (Göttingen: Vandenhoeck und Ruprecht, 1925) 169–210 (passim); Alfred Juncker, *Die Ethik des Apostels Paulus* (Halle a. S.: Max Niemeyer, 1919) 2. 188–90, 209–11; Hans Conzelmann, *1 Corinthians: A Commentary on the First Epistle to the Corinthians*, Hermeneia (Philadelphia: Fortress, 1975) 114–46 (passim); Kümmel in Hans Lietzmann, *An die Korinther I·II*, HNT 9, 5th ed. (Tübingen: J. C. B. Mohr, 1969) 176.
[4] Stobaeus 4. 494–568 Wachsmuth and Hense.

and he presents a very abbreviated and confused picture of Stoic thinking.[5]

Like Balch, Yarbrough also comes short of adequately defining the concerns of Stoic and Cynic thinking on marriage, although with Yarbrough this is partly by design, for he makes clear that his interest lies with the sociological *function* of what Paul says on marriage, not its theological or philosophical basis.[6] From this methodological starting point Yarbrough draws a comparison between 1 Corinthians 7 and Paul's statements in 1 Thessalonians 4.3–8. According to Yarbrough, the first passage consists of general moral admonitions, or paraenesis, which serve to establish "boundaries" between Christians and non-Christians on the basis of sexual morality. This is its sociological function in the Christian community at Thessalonica. By contrast, Yarbrough sees 1 Corinthians 7 as Paul's adaptation of the paraenesis in 1 Thessalonians 4 to deal with actual problems at Corinth. While 1 Corinthians 7 also contributes to defining the distinctiveness of Christians over against "outsiders," Paul is mainly concerned here with the *internal* affairs of the community.[7]

From this Yarbrough concludes that the sociological function of 1 Corinthians 7 is similar to that of both rabbinic literature on sexual norms[8] and Greco-Roman discussions of marriage. Yarbrough's handling of the latter, however, is diffuse, moving thematically and somewhat freely between different chronological periods and philosophical contexts.[9] Moreover, he sees no need to focus specifically on Stoic or Cynic authors, and never ventures much beyond a very general comparison with their writings.[10] Due, then,

---

[5] David Balch, "1 Cor 7:32–35 and Stoic Debates about Marriage, Anxiety, and Distraction," *JBL* 102 (1983) 429–39. Aside from excluding consideration of the *Cynic Epistles* (ibid., 439 n. 35), Balch mistakenly concludes that Musonius held what was considered a "Cynic" position on marriage (ibid., 433 and n. 17; cf. 434, 439), and fails to see that Epictetus advocated both Stoic and Cynic positions (ibid., 435 and n. 25; 436; 439 n. 35). See my treatment of these authors below, pp. 78–87; and cf. Roy Bowen Ward, "Musonius and Paul on Marriage," *NTS* 36 (1990) 281–9.

[6] Yarbrough, *Not Like the Gentiles*, 3–5.

[7] Ibid., 7–18, 77–88, 92, 96–7, 114, 117–22; see also 5, 8, 28, 69. Cf. Wayne A. Meeks, *The First Urban Christians: The Social World of the Apostle Paul* (New Haven/London: Yale University Press, 1983) 100, 105.

[8] Yarbrough, *Not Like the Gentiles*, 18–29.

[9] Ibid., 31–63. Cf. 106 where he uses Antiphon (early fifth century BCE) to generalize how "many in the Hellenistic world referred to marriage."

[10] See, e.g., the conclusion to his thirty-page treatment of Greco-Roman literature on marriage: "We can only conclude from what we have seen that for many marriage and the stability of the home was indeed very important. We must, therefore, take

to his interest in the sociological function of 1 Corinthians 7 and the corresponding goals he has set for his investigation, the connections Yarbrough draws between Paul and Stoic and Cynic texts are too tangential for our purposes.

Finally, Vincent Wimbush has made use of Stoic and Cynic materials in an attempt to explain Paul's understanding of celibacy in the context of a general trend toward ascetic behavior that he sees arising in the Hellenistic world.[11] Beginning with the assumption that 1 Corinthians 7 is largely Paul's attempt to clarify his position on sexual asceticism in the face of misunderstanding at Corinth,[12] Wimbush isolates two passages as the essence of Paul's views on celibacy, arguing that they constitute a digression in Paul's discussion for the purpose of clarification. These passages are 7.29–31, where Paul discusses eschatological detachment from the world, and 7.32–5, where Paul contrasts married life with single-minded devotion to the Lord. The first passage is important because it seems to "represent a direct expression of Paul's understanding of the appropriate mode of Christian existence in the world," while the second is a "reinterpretation and application" of the first.[13] Thus in 7.32–5, according to Wimbush, Paul relativizes the importance of Christ's imminent return and offers a new basis for Christian detachment from the world. This is the ideal of "indifference" or "lack of concern," which Wimbush sees expressed in the Greek words ἀμέριμνος and ἀπερισπάστως in verses 32 and 35, and which he identifies with the philosophical notion of ἀπάθεια, "freedom from emotion," or as he translates it, "spiritual detachment."[14] Relying almost exclusively on Festugière's popular study, Wimbush traces the notion of detachment through Greek and Roman philosophical traditions, giving special attention to its use among the Stoics.[15] Then, following Balch, he points to the similarity between Stoic discussions on marriage and 1 Corinthians 7.32–5, and con-

---

this into account when we examine Paul's advice on marriage to the Thessalonians and Corinthians" (ibid., 63; see also 32, 105, 109–10).
[11] Wimbush, *Worldly Ascetic*, 3; cf. 10. Note that Weiß, *Korintherbrief*, 171 considers and rejects a similar view.
[12] Wimbush, *Worldly Ascetic*, 6–7, 9, 12–13; cf. 17 n. 14.
[13] Ibid., 7, 21, 44–7, 50; see also 10, 13, 73, 85, 95.
[14] Ibid., 50, 56, 69, 87.
[15] Ibid., 56–62, encompassing a grand sweep from Plato to Plotinus, with little concern for chronological issues (3 n. 9). See 59 n. 37 and cf. André-Jean Festugière, *Personal Religion among the Greeks*, Sather Classical Lectures 26 (Berkeley: University of California Press, 1954; repr., Westport, Conn.: Greenwood, 1984) 37–65.

cludes that Paul's model of celibacy in 1 Corinthians 7 derives from
a Panhellenistic spirit of detachment which both the Stoics and Paul
had brought to bear on the question of marriage.[16]

The problem with Wimbush's conclusion, aside from whether one
can accept his assumptions regarding the purpose of 1 Corinthians 7
or the centrality of 7.29–35, is that it depends on equating the notion
of living a life free from distraction, which Paul invokes in 7.32–5
and which some Stoics invoke in their discussions of marriage, with
the Stoic ideal of ἀπάθεια. Yet these are not analogous concepts.
The former has to do with the proper management of one's outward
routine, the result of which is a measure of freedom from civic,
social, and economic obligations, and access to leisure time. The
latter, by contrast, concerns release from mental and emotional
attachment to things and people, resulting in an inner freedom of
the soul. For this reason, too, the notion of ἀπάθεια plays no part in
the Stoics' discussions of marriage. Although some Stoics maintained that marital obligations could divert a philosopher's attention from his true purpose, none entertained the thought that marriage could endanger a philosopher's inner freedom.[17] Wimbush's
attempt to understand 1 Corinthians 7.29–35 in terms of a Hellenistic trend toward ascetic detachment by virtue of its similarity to
Stoic discussions on marriage is consequently without foundation.
Moreover, since Wimbush's understanding of Stoic and Cynic views
on marriage depends entirely on Balch's interpretation of the texts,
with Wimbush we advance little, if any, beyond Balch.[18]

Thus, while several scholars have examined 1 Corinthians 7 in
light of Stoic and Cynic marriage discussions, their efforts lack a
solid understanding of the main issues of these discussions. As a
result, no scholar has yet shown the full extent to which Stoic and
Cynic principles have shaped Paul's statements on marriage and
celibacy. This will be our task in the subsequent chapters of this
study. At present, however, we continue with our critical review of
scholarly theories.

[16] Wimbush, *Worldly Ascetic*, 62–9, 87.
[17] According to Diogenes Laertius Stoics held that the wise man was free from
emotion (ἀπαθής), and married and had children (D.L. 117, 121). See also Epict.
*Diss.* 2.14.8–12; Sen. *Ep.* 9.17–19; and Teles *frag.* 2.18.183–97 O'Neil.
[18] See, e.g., Wimbush, *Worldly Ascetic*, 64, 65. For a critical review of Wimbush's
work from another perspective see David R. Cartlidge, review of *Paul, the Worldly
Ascetic* by Vincent L. Wimbush, *JBL* 108 (1989) 355–7.

## 2. Motivations for celibacy from Hellenistic Judaism

### Asceticism and revelation

Let us now turn our attention to two scholars who suggest a Hellenistic Jewish context for the celibacy in 1 Corinthians 7. The first, curiously, is David Balch, who as we just saw also argues for a Stoic interpretation of some verses in this chapter. In the latter half of an article devoted to 2 Corinthians 3, Balch proposes that the Corinthian church practiced celibacy out of a desire to receive revelations from God.[19] His point of departure is a passage from Philo's *Life of Moses* in which Moses, in his role as priest and prophet, prepares himself to receive such divine revelations. As part of this preparation, Philo tells us, Moses abstained from sexual intercourse.[20] Because Philo's description (which follows Exod. 34.29–35) also states that when Moses descended from Mount Sinai his face shone with God's divine radiance, and because Paul emphasizes this same detail in his discussion of the new covenant in 2 Corinthians 3.4–18, Balch postulates a connection between the ascetic theology Philo attributes to Moses and the celibacy in evidence in 1 Corinthians 7. To strengthen his position, he notes further that Philo presents Moses as a divine man, or "ascetic θεῖος ἀνήρ," which Balch interprets as a sort of model or ideal that was imitated by many Jews, "including Corinthian Jewish-Christians."[21]

This theory has several questionable aspects. To begin with, Balch misunderstands the notion of divine men in antiquity. They are not ideals intended as "an actual possibility for all men," but rather ideal types. That is, they are rare human beings possessed of divine powers quite unattainable by normal men and women.[22] If

---

[19] David L. Balch, "Backgrounds of I Cor. vii: Sayings of the Lord in Q; Moses As an Ascetic ΘΕΙΟΣ ΑΝΗΡ in II Cor. iii," *NTS* 18 (1971/72) 351–64. Supporters of his theory include S. Scott Bartchy, *ΜΑΛΛΟΝ ΧΡΗΣΑΙ: First-Century Slavery and the Interpretation of 1 Corinthians 7:21*, SBLDS 11 (Missoula: University of Montana Press, 1973) 145–8; and Benedetto Prete, *Matrimonio e continenza nel cristianesimo delle origini: Studio su 1 Cor. 7,1–40*, Studi Biblici 49 (Brescia: Paideia, 1979) 74–86.

[20] Philo *De vita Mosis* 2.66–70.

[21] Balch, "Backgrounds," 358–61. On asceticism as characteristic of the divine man, see Ludwig Bieler, *ΘΕΙΟΣ ΑΝΗΡ: Das Bild des „göttlichen Menschen" in Spätantike und Frühchristentum* (Vienna: Oskar Höfels, 1935) 1.70–3. Cf. Balch, "Backgrounds," 356, where Balch discusses Noah as a divine man with ascetic tendencies.

[22] See the catalog of divine men in Greco-Roman antiquity collected in H. D. Betz, "Gottmensch II," *RAC* 12 (1983) 235–88.

Balch were correct in his thinking, we would expect to find many examples of divine men in Philo's writings, including Philo himself. But Balch has only the example of Moses, together with other glorified figures from Israel's past.[23] Beyond this, although Philo presents Moses as a divine man, it is primarily in his role as priest and prophet that Moses abstains from sexual intercourse in *Life of Moses* 2.66–70. The idea of priestly consecration for the purpose of receiving a revelation does not occur, however, in Paul's discussion in 1 Corinthians 7. Finally, we must question the appropriateness of Balch's attempt to connect ideas from Philo's *Life of Moses* with 1 Corinthians 7 via 2 Corinthians 3. Balch has not shown that any connection exists between *Life of Moses* and 2 Corinthians 3, other than the fact that both Philo and Paul have an Old Testament narrative in common and perhaps a similar haggadic tradition of interpretation. Regarding asceticism in particular, Paul makes no mention of ascetic practices in 2 Corinthians 3, nor may we safely posit any here on the basis of Balch's suggestion that *Life of Moses* 2.66–70 is representative of a larger haggadic tradition that reads an ascetic theology into Moses' actions at Mount Sinai.[24] Moreover, I do not think Balch has successfully demonstrated a connection between 2 Corinthians 3 and 1 Corinthians 7, for neither his claim that the interpretation of Exodus 34 was a "central part of the Corinthians' theology," nor his claim that this theology was "one source of the asceticism which appears in I Cor. vii" can be viewed as reliable.[25]

## Asceticism as marriage to Sophia

In contrast to Balch's theory that the Corinthians practiced asceticism for the purpose of receiving revelations, Richard Horsley proposes that the Corinthians had renounced physical marriage in

---

[23] Balch, "Backgrounds," 356. On Moses as divine man in Philo see Carl R. Holladay, *"Theios Aner" in Hellenistic Judaism: A Critique of the Use of this Category in NT Christology*, SBLDS 40 (Missoula, Mont.: Scholars, 1977) 103–98.

[24] For which he cites several late rabbinic sources, "Backgrounds," 360. His suggestion on p. 364 employs the same reasoning: "Moses' vision (Exod. xxxiii–xxxiv) as interpreted in Jewish exegesis [i.e., rabbinic sources] contained the notion that Moses was transformed to similarity with the divine 'image' seen by him ... Transformation into likeness with the divine Image might well have been supposed by the Corinthians to include the overcoming of sexual differentiation."

[25] Cf. the criticism of Balch's theory in Niederwimmer, *Askese und Mysterium*, 81–2 n. 6.

view of participating in a "spiritual marriage" between themselves
and the personification of divine wisdom, Sophia. Horsley, who has
written several articles demonstrating the importance of Hellenistic
Jewish wisdom traditions at Corinth,[26] bases this theory primarily
on material from the Wisdom of Solomon and from Philo, where he
finds several passages that speak of a marriage between Sophia (or
her equivalent) and the wise man's mind or soul.[27] In one particular
text, moreover, Horsley sees an instance of actual asceticism
stemming from this line of metaphorical thought. This is *On the
Contemplative Life*, in which Philo depicts a community of Jewish
mystics called Therapeutae, who live somewhere in the Egyptian
countryside around Alexandria.[28]

As supporting evidence, Horsley cites two other texts. One is
Philo's description of Moses in *Life of Moses* 2.66–9, which, as we
have seen, Balch also uses. The second is Apuleius' *Golden Ass*, or
*Metamorphoses*, chapter eleven. Here a devotee of Isis named
Lucius speaks of practicing sexual abstinence as part of his preparation to receive a vision from the Goddess. Noting that there are
certain similarities between Sophia and Isis, Horsley argues for
affinities with the wise man's marriage to Sophia, calling Lucius'
relation to his goddess a "spiritual marriage with Isis."[29]

Following the analysis of these texts from Wisdom, Philo, and
Apuleius, Horsley turns to 1 Corinthians 7. He contends that the
Corinthians' interest in wisdom, especially apparent in 1 Corinthians 1–4, resulted in a similar form of asceticism. Here he
considers the evidence of the Therapeutae particularly cogent. In his
opinion "extensive parallels" exist between this ascetic community
and the Corinthians, including an interest in the symbolic interpretation of Scripture, "ecstatic experiences and revelation of

[26] Richard A. Horsley: "Pneumatikos vs. Psychikos: Distinctions of Spiritual
Status Among the Corinthians," *HTR* 69 (1976) 269–88; "Wisdom of Word and
Words of Wisdom in Corinth," *CBQ* 39 (1977) 224–39; " 'How Can Some of You Say
That There Is No Resurrection of the Dead?': Spiritual Elitism in Corinth," *NovT* 20
(1978) 203–31; and "Gnosis in Corinth: I Corinthians 8.1–6," *NTS* 27 (1980/81)
32–51. For still other research on the influence of wisdom traditions in 1 Corinthians
see Gerhard Sellin, "Hauptprobleme des Ersten Korintherbriefes," *ANRW* 2.25.4
(1987) 3021–2.
[27] E.g., Wis. 8.2 and Philo *Posterity and Exile of Cain* 78, where Philo speaks of
Understanding as the spouse of wise men (τὴν σοφῶν σύμβιον ἐπιστήμην), and lauds
their betrothal to the *logos*. These and other passages are cited in Richard A. Horsley,
"Spiritual Marriage with Sophia," *VC* 33 (1979) 32–7.
[28] Horsley, "Spiritual Marriage," 39–40.
[29] Ibid., 43, 54.

wisdom," and a belief in the "dualistic division between body and soul."[30] The difficulty with Horsley's theory is twofold. First, it is doubtful he has proven that a form of asceticism based on the wisdom tradition's notion of spiritual marriage with Sophia was very widespread; and second, it is equally doubtful that he has identified this form of asceticism among the Corinthians. In reality, Horsley has only one clear instance of asceticism that can be understood as a spiritual marriage with Sophia, namely, among Philo's Therapeutae. Regarding his examples of the wise man's marriage to Sophia elsewhere in Philo and Wisdom, Horsley himself admits that this is no more than a metaphor, and carefully suggests that these texts are "tending toward a general asceticism," or "clearly a step in that direction."[31] He also proposes that we see an "ascetic inclination" in Philo's own religiosity, citing Philo's many prohibitions against illicit sexual practices and his insistence that sexual intercourse be engaged in only for the purpose of procreation.[32] But this is far from sexual asceticism, and these same injunctions are found elsewhere in texts that heartily endorse marriage – as does Philo.[33] As for Lucius' ascetic behavior in the *Metamorphoses*, this is described as preparation for a vision and modelled after the celibacy of the priests of Isis.[34] There is no evidence here of a spiritual marriage with the goddess, which, even if it did exist, might have little in common with a spiritual marriage to Sophia given the significant differences between Jewish wisdom and Greek mysteries.[35]

Thus the Therapeutae, we again stress, are Horsley's only clear example of asceticism described as spiritual marriage. But even here his treatment of the evidence is open to criticism. We must first object to Horsley's readiness to accept Philo's account at face value. While the Therapeutae may have been "an actual mystical ascetic

---

[30] Ibid., 49–51.
[31] Ibid., 35, 39; cf. 38.
[32] Ibid., 39.
[33] E.g., *Testaments of the Twelve Patriarchs*; on Philo see below, pp. 90–6. Horsley, "Spiritual Marriage," 36–7, also points to a Platonic estrangement from the body in Philo, from which he says Philo "draws ascetic conclusions." But these only concern Philo's description of the recovery by the soul or mind of its symbolic "virginity," not actual asceticism.
[34] Apuleius *Metamorphoses* 11.6, 19. The same is true of Horsley's reference to the priestesses of Ceres ("Spiritual Marriage," 46).
[35] Despite the similarities Horsley sees between Sophia and Isis. Cf. Helmut Koester, review of *Weisheit und Torheit* by Ulrich Wilckens, *Gnomon* 33 (1961) 594, who denies any close relation between the two.

group" – a matter open to *some* question, at least – Horsley surely overlooks Philo's apologetic tendencies when he reports summarily that Philo speaks of them as "almost typical of the devout Jews who 'pursue wisdom'."[36] In addition, Horsley generalizes Philo's account without sufficient cause: it is not, as he believes, *all* the Therapeutae who remain celibate for the sake of a spiritual marriage with Sophia, but only the women among them.[37] Finally, Horsley never considers the very real possibility that Philo has simply read his own wisdom tradition and metaphorical language onto the practices of the Therapeutae. Philo may have had little interest in reporting their actual motivation for celibacy. It is conceivable, in other words, that Horsley may not even have this one instance of spiritual marriage to point to.

Horsley's evaluation of the evidence from 1 Corinthians is likewise open to serious questioning. On the one hand, his "extensive parallels" between the Corinthians and the Therapeutae must all be taken with a grain of salt. The Therapeutae's fascination with symbolic and spiritual interpretation of Scripture as described by Philo really has no close counterpart at Corinth, and a passage such as 1 Corinthians 10.1–13, to which Horsley points to support this claim, is common enough in Paul's other letters, as well as elsewhere in the New Testament, that we need not account for it by postulating the influence of a certain brand of Jewish wisdom theology. As for the ecstatic forms of worship and the body–soul dualism that Horsley finds in both groups, these, too, are fairly common in the Mediterranean world in this period.[38] But by far the greatest difficulty Horsley has to overcome in extending his thesis of spiritual marriage to Corinth is the fact that a divine personification of wisdom is nowhere mentioned in either 1 or 2 Corinthians, and we find no mention of wisdom in any form in 1 Corinthians 7 – as Horsley himself admits.[39] To my mind this is no basis on which we

---

[36] Horsley, "Spiritual Marriage," 40, 41
[37] Ibid., 43; see Philo *De vita contemplativa* 68. Nor can we simply assume the men were included: e.g., in some orders of the Roman Catholic tradition nuns are thought of as "brides of Christ," but to assume that priests are also symbolically married to Christ would be a mistake. Horsley's claim that some Therapeutae women "are ascetically separated from husbands" ("Spiritual Marriage," 50 and n. 48) is equally unsupported by the text.
[38] E.g., on ecstatic speech see Johannes Behm, "γλῶσσα, ἑτερόγλωσσος," *TDNT* 1 (1964) 719–27.
[39] Horsley, "Spiritual Marriage," 49. 1 Cor. 7.32–5 does contrast the marriage relationship with devotion to Christ, but this is not marriage to Christ, nor is Christ a

can claim that the "vortex" of a "whole Corinthian pattern of religious thinking is the divine figure Sophia."[40]

## 3. Motivations for celibacy from first-century Christianity

### A sociological approach

In his recent book on sexuality in late antiquity Peter Brown has suggested a sociological explanation for the celibacy at Corinth. Rather than investigating influences or ideologies that outsiders may have exerted on the Corinthians, his analysis focuses on the dynamics within the church in Corinth, understood as a social group. He reasons that general disorder in the community, so evident in 1 Corinthians, has led directly to asceticism. Confusion at the Lord's supper, class problems, differing views on meat offered to idols, and the refusal of women to wear veils prompted some Corinthians to do away with the social structures they perceived to be causing this disorder, one of these structures being marriage.[41] While Brown makes a fascinating departure from the lines of research employed by other scholars, and while his engaging description of this "sociological beargarden" is a palpable lesson in eloquent prose, I question whether his notions of cause and effect really hold. In my mind, to make a convincing case for his theory Brown would either have to demonstrate from 1 Corinthians that the Corinthians did, in fact, consider marriage a source of their many problems, or he would need to offer other examples from this period showing how disruption within a small group brings about renunciation of marriage. He does neither.

### Fear and confusion as the cause of celibacy

An option pursued by a number of other scholars posits an ascetic theology among the Corinthians that arose from their confusion over Paul's teachings on holiness and eschatology. As Johannes Weiß explains, these "earnest, fearful, unfree souls" were frightened by the Apostle's condemnation of sexual sins, such as one finds in 1

---

personification of wisdom. On the latter point see Koester, review of *Weisheit und Torheit*, 593–5.
[40] So Horsley, "Spiritual Marriage," 48.
[41] Brown, *Body and Society*, 52–3.

Corinthians 6, and by the nearness of the End.[42] The most avid supporter of this view recently has been Kurt Niederwimmer. Adamant that the celibacy in 1 Corinthians 7 is to be derived from the basic, founding principles of the Corinthian church, he goes further than Weiß in identifying the puritanical, sexually negative paraenesis to which he thinks the Corinthians were exposed. Whereas Weiß had pointed specifically to 1 Corinthians 6.12–20, which he claimed was a fragment of a letter that preceded 1 Corinthians 7,[43] Niederwimmer defines a much broader base, citing Hellenistic catalogs of vices and Hellenistic Jewish wisdom literature as the source of both 1 Corinthians 6.12–20 and of Paul's baptismal teachings in general. Noting that a denunciation of illicit sex, or *porneia*, is prominent in all these traditions, he postulates a "thoroughly pessimistic character of the churches in Paul's time regarding sexuality."[44] At Corinth, therefore, it was a matter of course that marital relations should be viewed with suspicion, virginity seen "as an advantage," and believers gripped with the fear "that the hitherto 'pure' virgins could be profaned through marriage."[45]

The difficulty with this approach to 1 Corinthians 7 is clear. It confuses or requires that the Corinthians confused illicit sex with sex in general, and draws the conclusion, supposedly held by the Corinthians, that sexual abstinence equates to holiness. Yet this sort of confusion is highly unlikely on two counts. First, not one text from the extensive list cited by Niederwimmer gives any evidence of such a confusion between sex and *porneia*, let alone questions the propriety of marriage on this basis. A case in point is the *Testaments of the Twelve Patriarchs*, where we find abundant warnings against

[42] Weiß, *Korintherbrief*, 169. See also Yarbrough, *Not Like the Gentiles*, 120–1; Herbert Preisker, *Christentum und Ehe in den ersten drei Jahrhunderten: Eine Studie zur Kulturgeschichte der alten Welt*, Neue Studien zur Geschichte der Theologie und der Kirche 23 (Berlin: Trowitzsch und Sohn, 1927; repr., Aalen: Scientia, 1979) 129–30; and Heinrich August Wilhelm Meyer, *Critical and Exegetical Handbook to the Epistles to the Corinthians*, Critical and Exegetical Commentary on the New Testament 5 (Edinburgh: T. and T. Clark, 1892) 192–3, who cites earlier commentators.

[43] Weiß, *Korintherbrief*, 169.

[44] Niederwimmer, *Askese und Mysterium*, 67–74, 81–2.

[45] Ibid., 65, 80–1, 98 (where he states that the "fundamental question" facing couples at Corinth was "whether baptism abrogates marriage," and that behind 1 Cor. 7.10–11 stands the question "whether or not the new existence, into which they have come through baptism, demands divorce"), 108, 115; "Zur Analyse der asketischen Motivation in 1. Kor. 7," *TLZ* 99 (1974) 242–3. Cf. Doughty, "Heiligkeit und Freiheit," 178, 189.

*porneia*, yet marriage is never challenged: all twelve of the patriarchs are married, and they encourage their sons in this endeavor.[46] Second, there is no indication in 1 Corinthians 7, or anywhere else in the letter, that such a confusion took place. To the contrary, in 1 Corinthians 7.2 Paul promotes marriage as a protection against *porneia*, which rules out any identification between the two; and since Paul states his position here without further justification, we may assume that the Corinthians shared this basic (and common) understanding of marriage, sex, and *porneia*.[47]

Finally, a note on Gerhard Delling is in order here. In his oft cited book, "Paul's Stance on Woman and Marriage," Delling takes the position that the misunderstanding which Weiß, Niederwimmer, and others attribute to the Corinthians is actually no misunderstanding at all. The Corinthians, he maintains, have understood Paul correctly. For Paul, sex is an action against Christ that mixes Christ's members, which belong to the Spirit, with the flesh: in marriage a person is "ruled by a foreign power – as also in extramarital relations – instead of letting oneself be ruled by Christ." By practicing celibacy, therefore, the Corinthians have done nothing more than take Paul's theology to its logical conclusion. It is Paul, says Delling, who has not followed through with his views; his promotion of marriage and his stance against celibacy in 7.1–24 are clear evidence of his inability to think consistently on this matter.[48]

Against Delling, we may object simply that if it is difficult to comprehend the Corinthian position in terms of a misunderstanding of what Paul said it is all the more difficult to see their position as a valid reading of his theology. Indeed, Delling's treatment of Paul must be viewed as something of a curiosity for another reason as

---

[46] See, e.g., *Test. Levi.* 9.6–10.1.

[47] See also 7.14, where Paul argues that marriage with an unbeliever makes the latter "holy"; and Wolfgang Schrage, "Zur Frontstellung der paulinischen Ehebewertung in 1 Kor. 7 1–7," *ZNW* 67 (1976) 230 n. 65. In this context we may also note that Walter Schmithals proposed a similar theory of confusion, to which Conzelmann replied reasonably enough that such a position attributes to the Corinthians "a high degree of ignorance of language and morals – even to the point of stupidity" (Conzelmann, *1 Corinthians*, 115 n. 11, commenting on Walter Schmithals, *Gnosticism in Corinth: An Investigation of the Letters to the Corinthians* [Nashville/New York: Abingdon, 1971] 234–5, where the latter argues that the tendency toward celibacy in 1 Cor. 7.1–16 was motivated by the Corinthians' misunderstanding of Paul's denunciation of intercourse with prostitutes. His half-hearted reply to Conzelmann is found in the addendum to his work, 386.)

[48] Gerhard Delling, *Paulus' Stellung zu Frau und Ehe*, BWANT 4/5 (Stuttgart: W. Kohlhammer, 1931) 62–9, 80; cf. 78–9, 86. "Indeed, Paul says [in 7.5] that the Holy Spirit cannot be in people during sexual intercourse . . ." (65).

well. In 1923, eight years before Delling wrote, a clearly stated "corrective" to much of what he said about Paul appeared in a book bearing a title similar to his.[49]

## Secondary Christological motivations

Along with developing a theory explaining the Corinthians' motivation for celibacy from first-century Christian principles, Niederwimmer has made a similar proposal regarding Paul's own motivations. This theory defines three distinct sources for the Apostle's celibate tendencies.[50] The first may be seen in 1 Corinthians 7.1b, where he finds "a general ascetic motivation about which nothing more detailed is said," but behind which stands "a radical sharpening of the sexual taboo." It is neither theologically grounded nor even Christian, according to Niederwimmer, but represents a "taboo-asceticism" based on the "fear of ritual uncleanness" and hails from Paul's pre-Christian days.[51] Paul's second motivation for celibacy, for which Niederwimmer cites 1 Corinthians 7.26–31, is inspired by the nearness of the End. This, like the first motivation, is not specifically Christian, and actually holds little interest for Niederwimmer since, as he says, it "is obviously a secondary rationalization" of the first.[52] The third source of Paul's celibacy, according to Niederwimmer, stems from a "Christological justification of sexual asceticism," and is found in 1 Corinthians 7.32–5.[53] Like the second it is also a rationalization of Paul's taboo-asceticism[54]; but unlike the second it is completely Christian

---

[49] P. Tischleder, *Wesen und Stellung der Frau nach der Lehre des heiligen Paulus: Eine ethisch-exegetische Untersuchung*, NTAbh 10/3–4 (Münster: Aschendorf, 1923) esp. 95–7. Cf. the brief criticism of Delling in Yarbrough, *Not Like the Gentiles*, 3–4. One source of Delling's misunderstanding of 1 Cor. 7 is his reliance on Tertullian's exegesis (*Paulus' Stellung*, 64 n. 61; 65 n. 64; 66 n. 67).

[50] Niederwimmer: *Askese und Mysterium*, 122; "Zur Analyse," 243–4.

[51] Niederwimmer, "Zur Analyse," 243–4; and *Askese und Mysterium*, 122 and 84–5, where he also speaks of the "demonizing of the γυνή [woman] in 7.1" and reasons "that for Paul any manifestly sexual activity at all is inadvisable." Cf. Conzelmann, *1 Corinthians*, 115: "Paul's view has an ascetic stamp; he does not give reasons for it"; and Delling, *Paulus' Stellung*, 64: "deep in [Paul] lies the fear of pollution."

[52] Niederwimmer, *Askese und Mysterium*, 122. See also 108 n. 138; 109 and n. 144; and "Zur Analyse," 244. Here Niederwimmer may be following Weiß, *The History of Primitive Christianity*, 2.582.

[53] Niederwimmer, *Askese und Mysterium*, 113.

[54] Niederwimmer: "Zur Analyse," 244; and *Askese und Mysterium*, 84 n. 21 (where he is much less emphatic; cf. 83 n. 15).

in origin, coming "from the center of Paul's faith."[55] For this reason Niederwimmer ascribes particular importance to 7.32–5 as containing the "decisive motivation" of the chapter: "Taboo asceticism (sexuality is damaging to body and spirit) is here directly tied in with Christologically justified asceticism (Christ demands unconditional, undivided devotion)."[56]

In assessing the reasonableness of Niederwimmer's theory we may ask, first of all, whether he is justified in seeing three separate and distinct motivations behind Paul's understanding of celibacy. It is far from "obvious," for example, that Paul's eschatological argument in 7.26–31 and his Christological argument in 7.32–5 can be neatly categorized as independent rationalizations of taboo fear. It is even doubtful that such a sharp caesura should be placed between these two passages on any basis. While 7.26–31 and 7.32–5 may differ in emphasis, they are, in fact, juxtaposed and flow one into the other as part of the same discussion. Their differences, I would suggest, are better explained in terms of the development of Paul's argument than in terms of contradictory motivations, for there is no reason why the "idea of radical and undivided devotion to the Kyrios" need necessarily exclude an eschatological withdrawal from worldly obligations.[57] The end result of Niederwimmer's method, moreover, is that it rules out, without any apparent warrant, the possibility of identifying a coherent theology of celibacy in 1 Corinthians 7. For this reason it also runs the risk of psychoanalyzing Paul on the basis of these forty verses. It leads Niederwimmer, for instance, to talk of an "overdetermination" in Paul's thought, brought on by "contradictory" and "overlapping" ascetic motivations which the apostle is unable to reconcile in the course of the chapter. Paul's advice, we are told, is borne along by tides of "unconscious constraint," "unconscious taboo fears," and "unconscious defense mechanisms."[58]

---

[55] Niederwimmer: *Askese und Mysterium*, 112–13 (cf. 122 where he states that verses 32b–35 is the only passage where "specifically Pauline elements play a role"); "Zur Analyse," 244.

[56] Niederwimmer: "Zur Analyse," 244; *Askese und Mysterium*, 115; cf. 108: "*Here, here first and here only* ..." (his emphasis); and 113, where he reasons, "the person who is married cannot completely belong to Christ (according to the clear wording of the text)."

[57] See 7.26a, 28b, 32a. Cf. Niederwimmer's contention that verses 29–31 are in tension with the overall argument because they do not speak of the advantage of being single but of inner distance from the world ("Zur Analyse," 248 n. 20).

[58] Niederwimmer: "Zur Analyse," 244; *Askese und Mysterium*, 121–3. Cf. the psycho-phenomenological approach taken by Weiß, *Korintherbrief*, 170–1, where he

Aside from these considerations, Niederwimmer's contention that Paul's basic, driving motivation throughout chapter seven is "taboo-asceticism," and that this can be seen in 7.1b, has two serious weaknesses. First, there is nothing in 7.1b that specifically points to taboo fears; and second, there is still no consensus among scholars that this half-verse even represents Paul's opinion. Indeed, many scholars see 7.1b as the Corinthians' viewpoint, with which Paul, for the sake of argument, tacitly agrees[59] – an interpretation I shall attempt to substantiate below in chapter three. Finally, we may ask whether this hypothesis really explains very much. Even if we grant that "taboo-asceticism" is Paul's true (albeit unconscious) motivation for the stance he takes in 1 Corinthians 7, Niederwimmer still does not clarify why this motivation should come to expression Christologically – in terms of so radical a devotion to Christ – or why the Christological side should so outweigh the eschatological considerations of 7.26–31. Ultimately, I suspect, Niederwimmer's real reason for adopting this circuitous route stems not from anything he finds in the text, but from his own theological (and somewhat polemical) agenda of identifying a purely Christian origin for the church's asceticism in the first century.[60]

## Enthusiasm and realized eschatology

Yet another way in which scholars have argued for a first-century Christian origin for the celibacy in 1 Corinthians 7 is to trace it to the spiritual "enthusiasm" of the primitive church. The first to propose this theory was W. Lütgert in 1908. Challenging the widely held opinion of F. C. Baur that the various difficulties Paul faced at Corinth arose from the activities of a Jewish party, Lütgert suggested that Paul's opponents were "enthusiasts."[61] Under this

---

derives Paul's celibacy, in part, from the apostle's personal constitution, which he describes as characteristic of "very great, very inward looking personalities."

[59] For bibliography see John Coolidge Hurd, Jr., *The Origin of I Corinthians* (London: SPCK, 1965; repr., Macon, Ga.: Mercer University Press, 1983) 67–8, 163; and Yarbrough, *Not Like the Gentiles*, 93–6.

[60] See Niederwimmer, *Askese und Mysterium*, 10.

[61] W. Lütgert, *Freiheitspredigt und Schwarmgeister in Korinth: Ein Beitrag zur Charakteristik der Christuspartei*, Beiträge zur Förderung christliche Theologie 12/3 (Gütersloh: C. Bertelsmann, 1908) 43–62. "Enthusiasts" was popularized during the Reformation – see Gerhard Ebeling, "Der Grund christlicher Theologie: Zum Aufsatz Ernst Käsemanns über 'Die Anfänge christlicher Theologie'," *ZTK* 58 (1961) 230–1. This may be where Lütgert gets the term since he once says that Paul stood in the same relation to his opponents as Luther did to his (*Freiheitspredigt*, 86).

rubric he envisioned a group of Christians who had put undue emphasis on Paul's claim that they possessed God's Spirit. This led them to believe that they had access to knowledge, or "gnosis," which gave them a freedom of action even beyond what Paul taught or imagined.[62] It was this misinterpretation of Paul, according to Lütgert, that lay at the root of all the Corinthian problems: it caused the Corinthians to question the resurrection of the dead, it was the impetus behind their effort to emancipate women and slaves, it led to speaking in tongues and abuses at the Lord's supper, and it promoted, paradoxically, both licentiousness and asceticism.[63]

Regarding these last two problems, the fact that the same theology could spawn diametrically opposed attitudes toward sex was explained by Lütgert in the following way. Licentiousness, or sexual "libertinism" as he called it, was an inevitable product of the enthusiasts' zeal for freedom and their exaggerated emphasis on the spirit, the corollary of which was a complete devaluation of the physical body.[64] Their celibacy, on the other hand, was partly a reaction against this libertinism, as well as their former pagan lifestyles, on which this libertinism was modelled. But more importantly, according to Lütgert, it was grounded in the selfsame overemphasis of the spirit and subsequent deprecation of the body that produced libertinism.[65]

In one form or another Lütgert's explanation has received wide support. Scholars have been particularly enamored with the ability of his theory to derive both asceticism and libertinism from the same theology, since these facets of the Corinthian situation appear curiously juxtaposed in 1 Corinthians 5–7.[66] But Lütgert's theory has also undergone a major development. In the 1960s, expanding on ideas that C. H. Dodd had presented earlier in the century, Ernst Käsemann presented his thesis that Christianity in its earliest form in Palestine was thoroughly apocalyptic. On Greek soil, he argued further, this apocalypticism evolved into a theology of enthusiastic freedom similar to what Lütgert had described, but fueled by the

---

[62] Lütgert, Freiheitspredigt, 58, 67, 76, 86, 119–20. "Pneumatics must at the same time be gnostics" (105).

[63] Ibid., 124–35.

[64] "Everything belonging to nature," wrote Lütgert, "is, as such, free – that is, exempted from the moral canon 'good and evil' . . . For the pneumatic, the entire area of sexuality as well lies, with all of nature, outside of the opposition of good and evil" (ibid., 124; cf. 128–9).

[65] Ibid., 124–8, 135.

[66] See, e.g., Bornkamm, Paul, 207.

belief that Christians had come into possession of the eschaton.[67] As a result of this proposal scholars began to view the many problems at Corinth not only as the products of a theology of the spirit and freedom, but also as products of a "realized eschatology."[68] With regard specifically to 1 Corinthians 7, the notion of a realized eschatology opened up two new possibilities for more closely defining the Corinthians' practice of celibacy.

First, some scholars suggested that the Corinthians saw themselves as participating in a post-resurrection existence in which people no longer married but lived "like angels," a concept found in Mark 12.25. Here Jesus states, "For when they rise from the dead they neither marry nor are they given in marriage, but are like angels in Heaven." Luke's version of this tradition, moreover, is suggestive of ascetic practices in the here and now, and was interpreted in this way by several patristic authors, beginning in the second century. It reads: "The sons of this age marry and are given in marriage, but those counted worthy to receive that age and the resurrection from the dead neither marry nor are given in marriage" (Luke 20.34–5).[69]

---

[67] Ernst Käsemann, "On the Subject of Primitive Christian Apocalyptic," *New Testament Questions of Today* (Philadelphia: Fortress, 1969) 130–1. Cf. his "Sentences of Holy Law in the New Testament," *New Testament Questions of Today*, 72–3, 78–81. The idea of a realized eschatology in 1 Cor. 15 goes back as far as John Chrysostom – see Jack H. Wilson, "The Corinthians Who Say There Is No Resurrection of the Dead," *ZNW* 59 (1968) 95–7. On Käsemann's thesis generally see Jürgen Becker, "Erwägungen zur apokalyptischen Tradition in der paulinischen Theologie," *EvT* 30 (1970) 593–609, esp. 596–7; and A. J. M. Wedderburn, *Baptism and Resurrection: Studies in Pauline Theology against Its Graeco-Roman Background*, WUNT 44 (Tübingen: J. C. B. Mohr, 1987). Cf. C. H. Dodd, *The Apostolic Preaching and its Developments: Three Lectures* (Chicago/New York: Willett, Clark and Company, 1937) 93–108, although Käsemann never cites Dodd. For further information on Dodd, see Clayton Sullivan, *Rethinking Realized Eschatology* (Macon, Ga.: Mercer University Press, 1988).

[68] See, e.g., Anthony C. Thiselton, "Realized Eschatology at Corinth," *NTS* 24 (1977/78) 512: "distortions or imbalance in the area of eschatology stand in direct causal relationship to errors about the gifts and work of the Holy Spirit ... In specific terms, *an over-realized eschatology leads to an 'enthusiastic' view of the Spirit*" (his emphasis); cf. 523. See also Niederwimmer, *Askese und Mysterium*, 76. Lütgert himself seems to have entertained this view, but never explores it; see *Freiheitspredigt*, 118.

[69] On the ascetic "life of angels" in the patristic period see Peter Nagel, *Die Motivierung der Askese in der alten Kirche und der Ursprung des Mönchtums*, TU 95 (Berlin: Akademie, 1966) 34–48; and Jean-Paul Broudéhoux, *Mariage et famille chez Clément d'Alexandrie*, Théologie Historique 11 (Paris: Beauchesne et ses Fils, 1970) 105 n. 36. On Tatian, specifically, see G. Quispel, "The Syrian Thomas and the Syrian Macarius," *VC* 18 (1964) 228–9; D. Plooij, "Eine enkratitische Glosse im Diatessaron," *ZNW* 22 (1923) 13–16; and Arthur Vööbus, *History of Asceticism in the Syrian Orient*, CSCO 184 (Louvain: Secrétariat du CSCO, 1958) 42–3.

As for a link between this notion of angelic existence and 1 Corinthians 7, scholars have argued in one of two ways. On the basis of Paul's mention of "tongues of angels" in 1 Corinthians 13.1, some scholars suggest that the Corinthian practice of "speaking in tongues" is evidence they are living a life of angels.[70] Other scholars note that the rare causative γαμίζω occurs both in the gospel passages (in the passive "are given in marriage") and in 1 Corinthians 7.38. From this they conclude that a version of Jesus' statement, perhaps the Lukan version, was known at Corinth and used there in an ascetic theology.[71]

The second possibility scholars have seen for defining the Corinthians' celibacy in terms of a realized eschatology comes from the suggestion that the Corinthians saw their heavenly existence as beginning with baptism. While this was not Paul's understanding of baptism, it is argued that the enthusiasts interpreted Paul in this manner.[72] Pointing to Paul's claim in Galatians 3.26–8 that "in Christ" "there is no male and female," and noting that the bap-

---

[70] David R. Cartlidge, "1 Corinthians 7 as a Foundation for a Christian Sex Ethic," *Journal of Religion* 55 (1975) 230; see also Balch, "Backgrounds," 354 n. 4; Bartchy, *ΜΑΛΛΟΝ ΧΡΗΣΑΙ*, 149–51; and Wayne A. Meeks, *The First Urban Christians*, 121. Yarbrough, *Not Like the Gentiles*, 120 says that the mention of "gifts" in 1 Cor. 7.7 indicates a connection between speaking in tongues and the Corinthians' celibacy; and Adolf Hilgenfeld, *Die apostolischen Väter: Untersuchungen über Inhalt und Ursprung der unter ihrem Namen erhaltenen Schriften* (Halle: C. E. M. Pfeffer, 1853) 81 n. 9 suggested a connection between the spirit-filled Christians of 1 Cor. 14 and the celibates of chapter 7 on the basis of 7.40, where Paul grounds his authority in his possession of the Spirit. Both these theories are highly speculative.
[71] Balch, "Backgrounds," 357; cf. Cartlidge, "1 Corinthians 7 as a Foundation," 227, 229–30. See also Wayne A. Meeks, "The Image of the Androgyne: Some Uses of a Symbol in Earliest Christianity," *HR* 13 (1973/74) 202; and Wolbert, *Ethische Argumentation*, 117, who gives the unlikely view, "If the Corinthian enthusiasts knew a saying of the Lord in the manner of Luke 20.34–36 and appealed to it, it would also be understandable why Paul (verse 25) expressly emphasizes that he knows of no saying of the Lord regarding this topic." Confessions of ignorance in matters of law or moral argumentation are generally not a strong suit.
[72] E.g., Cartlidge, "1 Corinthians 7 as a Foundation," 228: "The Corinthians have taken a Pauline baptismal formulation – for example, Romans 6.1–10 – and have turned the future tense of the apodosis into a present tense: having died with Christ in baptism, we are already raised into the heavenly life." See also James M. Robinson, "Kerygma and History in the New Testament," *Trajectories through Early Christianity*, ed. James M. Robinson and Helmut Koester (Philadelphia: Fortress, 1971) 30–40; and Hans Conzelmann, "Zur Analyse der Bekenntnisformel I. Kor. 15,3–5," *EvT* 25 (1965) 10–11 n. 59. Cf. Käsemann, "Primitive Christian Apocalyptic," 125; and Hans von Soden, "Sakrament und Ethik bei Paulus: Zur Frage der literarischen und theologischen Einheitlichkeit von 1 Kor. 8–10," in *Urchristentum und Geschichte*, ed. Hans von Campenhausen (Tübingen: J. C. B. Mohr, 1951) 1.259.

tismal formula in Galatians 3.28 is reflected (although without this particular clause[73]) in 1 Corinthians 12.13 and, significantly, 7.17–24, these scholars suggest that the Corinthians' realized eschatology included the denial of sexual distinctions, and hence celibacy.[74] Thus, on the basis of Mark 12.25 par. and Galatians 3.28, scholars have posited two ways in which a realized eschatology at Corinth could have promoted ascetic practices there. As a final step, many have considered these to be complementary and have combined them.[75]

Although the theory of realized eschatology and enthusiasm has gained the approval of a great number of scholars, it is nonetheless open to criticism from several angles. We may begin by considering the eschatological aspects that were added to Lütgert's original theory of enthusiasm. First, it seems to me that those scholars who posit a connection between 1 Corinthians 7 and *both* Mark 12.25 par. and Galatians 3.28 have all too quickly assumed that these latter passages are supportive of the same realized eschatology. Mark, however, speaks of an existence devoid of marriage, while Galatians speaks of one in which there is "no male and female," and these are not necessarily compatible concepts. Thus in Mark 12.18–23 par., the Sadducees evidently assume that there will be sexual distinctions in the new age, for it is on this basis that they object to the notion of a bodily resurrection. On logical grounds, they argue, a bodily resurrection presented an impossible situation in light of the practice of levirate marriage: in the new age, who

---

[73] But see, e.g., Hans Dieter Betz, *Galatians: A Commentary on Paul's Letter to the Churches in Galatia*, Hermeneia (Philadelphia: Fortress, 1979) 200, who suggests that in 1 Cor. Paul retracted his Galatians position on the equality of women.

[74] E.g., Meeks, "Image of the Androgyne," 180–9, 202, 207; Bartchy, *ΜΑΛΛΟΝ ΧΡΗΣΑΙ*, 131; and cf. Käsemann, "Primitive Christian Apocalyptic," 126, 131. For use of the tradition "no male and female" in later ascetic groups see Niederwimmer, *Askese und Mysterium*, 177–9, 217; Gerhard Delling, "Geschlechter," *RAC* 10 (1978) 790–3; Nagel, *Motivierung der Askese*, 50–5; and Ton H. C. van Eijk, "Marriage and Virginity, Death and Immortality," *Epektasis: Mélanges patristiques offerts au Cardinal Jean Daniélou*, ed. Jacques Fontaine and Charles Kannengiesser (Paris: Beauchesne, 1972) 214–35.

[75] E.g., Nils A. Dahl, "Paul and the Church at Corinth According to 1 Corinthians 1:10–4:21," *Christian History and Interpretation: Studies Presented to John Knox*, ed. W. R. Farmer, C. F. D. Moule, and R. R. Niebuhr (Cambridge: Cambridge University Press, 1967) 333; Elaine H. Pagels, "Paul and Women: A Response to Recent Discussion," *JAAR* 42 (1974) 540. Cf. Käsemann, "Primitive Christian Apocalyptic," 130–1.

would be paired with whom?[76] Although Jesus overrules their objection, he does not attack their assumption that sexual differentiation continued in the resurrection. Rather, as Luke explains, he faults them for overlooking the fact that marriage is not needed in the hereafter, due to immortality: those participating in the resurrection do not marry "for they are no longer able to die"; they no longer take part in the human cycle of procreation but are "sons of God, being sons of the resurrection" (Luke 20.36). According to Luke's Jesus, therefore, it is not sexual distinction that is inconsistent with bodily resurrection but marriage and procreation, since resurrection implies immortality.[77]

If this is an accurate picture of the synoptic traditions,[78] there is no warrant for thinking of the angels in Mark 12.25 par. as "either asexual or bisexual,"[79] nor can these passages be closely tied to the notion in Galatians 3.28 of "no male and female." But perhaps this conclusion is not so surprising, for if we consider the relevance of Galatians 3.28 in its own right, apart from Mark 12.25 par., we find that it has nothing to do with a *future* existence. Paul's claim here is that there is in the *here and now* "no male and female" for those bap-

---

[76] Josephus also knew of a tradition that imagined marriage in the hereafter: Josephus *Antiquities* 15.69 (cf. *Jewish War* 1.441); and *Ant.* 17.349–53 (cf. *War* 2.116).

[77] See Lucien Legrand, *The Biblical Doctrine of Virginity* (London: Geoffrey Chapman, 1963) 46; and cf. Luke 7.28, where the participants of the Kingdom are contrasted with "those born of women."

[78] Since Luke is the only gospel to add this or any explanation to Jesus' statement about the resurrection and since his reasoning draws on ideas current in several ancient authors, I would argue, lacking any evidence to the contrary, that this same reasoning is also operative in Mark 12.25 and Matt. 22.30. See Cartlidge, "1 Corinthians 7 as a Foundation," 230; Richard A. Baer, Jr., *Philo's Use of the Categories Male and Female* (Leiden: E. J. Brill, 1970) 78 n. 1; and the excellent study, Eijk, "Marriage and Virginity," 209–35. Cf. the following texts: *1 Enoch* 15.3–7; *Sibyline Oracles* 2.327–9; *Sirach* 30.4; Clem. Alex. *Strom.* bk. 3, chap. 6.45.3 (2.217.5–10 Stählin) and parallels; bk. 3, chap. 6.49.3 (2.218.26–30 S.); bk. 3, chap. 9.63.2 (2.225.4–7 S.).

[79] The phrase is John G. Gager's in *Kingdom and Community: The Social World of Early Christianity* (Englewood Cliffs, N. J.: Prentice-Hall, 1970) 34. In fact, one piece of evidence from this period strongly indicates otherwise. A very famous, or infamous, group of angels, known as the "Watchers," receives mention in a wide variety of texts precisely because they, unlike God's other angels, made use of their sexual potential. See, e.g., Jude 6; Philo *Quaestiones et solutiones in Genesin* 1.92; *Test. Reub.* 5.5–7; and generally, Johann Michl, "Engel II (jüdisch)," *RAC* 5 (1962) 60–97. A much stronger case can be made for angels being only male: they bear masculine names such as Gabriel and Michael, and they appear on earth in the form of men (– although see Zech. 5:9). Cf. L. William Countryman, *Dirt, Greed, and Sex: Sexual Ethics in the New Testament and Their Implications for Today* (Philadelphia: Fortress, 1988) 182–3.

tized into Christ, just as there is neither "Jew nor Greek," "slave nor free," which are also claims for the present.[80] It remains to be seen, then, why the Corinthians would draw any connection between Paul's baptismal teaching in Galatians 3.28 and their realized eschatology.

But, returning to the synoptics, neither can we acknowledge that all is well for the theory that links Mark 12.25 par. to the Corinthians' realized eschatology. As we saw above, the only connections that scholars have been able to draw between the Corinthian situation and these passages are the mention of "tongues of angels" at 1 Corinthians 13.1 and the verb γαμίζω in 1 Corinthians 7.38. But 1 Corinthians 13.1 does not actually prove that the Corinthians saw angelic language as a sign of their new existence,[81] and furthermore, we have no reason to assume that angelic speech is part of the heavenly existence described in Mark 12.25 par., for these passages say nothing on the subject. In fact, the use of angelic language by human beings is a notion very poorly documented for this whole period. Our one and only clear instance is in the *Testament of Job*, where Job's daughters – three legendary figures from Israel's past – speak in various heavenly dialects by virtue of the power inherent in their father's phylacteries.[82] On the other hand, with regard to the presence of γαμίζω in both Mark 12.25 par. and 1 Corinthians 7.38, the following needs to be said. While it is true that this verb is extremely rare, it does occur in Matthew 24.38//Luke 17.27, which make no reference to either angelic existence or ascetic practices,[83] and in the second-century grammarian Apollonius Dyscolus, in a discussion of transitive and intransitive verbs.[84] Since Matthew 24.38 and Luke 17.27 are from the "Q" source of the synoptic tradi-

---

[80] These are all "accomplished facts" (Betz, *Galatians*, 189).

[81] See the discussion in Conzelmann, *1 Corinthians*, 221 n. 27.

[82] *Test. Job* 48–52. See the note in R. P. Spittler, "Testament of Job," *The Old Testament Pseudepigrapha*, ed. James H. Charlesworth (Garden City, N.Y.: Doubleday, 1983) 1.866 n. 48 f. *Test. Job* is dated ca. the first century BCE–first century CE, but the passage in question could be a Montanist gloss from the second century (Spittler, "Testament of Job," 833–4). If this is true, the case for speaking in angelic tongues in 1 Corinthians or the synoptic traditions becomes even weaker.

[83] Balch's attempt ("Backgrounds," 355–6) to see an ascetic bent in these passages based on Philo's description of Noah and his sons abstaining from sexual relations in the ark (*Quaest. et sol. in Gen.* 2.49) rests on extremely circumstantial evidence. Schrage, "Zur Frontstellung," 227, and Niederwimmer, *Askese und Mysterium*, 81–2 n. 6 both express misgivings regarding his logic. See also the critique of Balch's argument in C. M. Tuckett, "1 Corinthians and Q," *JBL* 102 (1983) 613–16.

[84] Apollonius Dyscolus *De syntaxi* 3.153.

tions, whereas Mark 12.25 par. is not, and since Apollonius Dyscolus has no apparent relation to the Gospels at all, it is clear that the verb γαμίζω had a wide enough currency apart from the tradition in Mark 12.25 par. that, lacking other evidence, there is no necessary connection implied between Mark 12.25 par. and 1 Corinthians 7.38 simply on the basis of this verb.

Beyond these two considerations, however, there is a final problem with drawing connections between Mark 12.25 par. and a realized eschatology at Corinth. For a long time scholars have had difficulty understanding how the Corinthians imagined themselves to be fully resurrected or fully part of a heavenly existence. Did this mean they considered themselves immortal? – and if so, how did they explain sickness or death in their community (see 1 Cor. 11.30)? Julius Schniewind, for example, went so far as to propose that the Corinthians explained away death as being only a mirage or mistaken "appearance."[85] More recently, complaining that the case for realized eschatology is "usually lost by sheer overstatement," Anthony Thiselton has contributed the following clarification:

> The question was *not* whether the Corinthians believed that their resurrection was past, but whether they placed such weight on the experience of transformation in the past and present that when they thought about resurrection the centre of gravity of their thinking was no longer in the future ... Paul is speaking to those who made too little of the future in their Christian outlook.[86]

Yet if Thiselton is correct – and his appears to be the most reasonable formulation to date – a connection between 1 Corinthians 7 and Mark 12.25 par. is again open to question. This is because the absence of marriage for those participating in the resurrection according to Mark 12.25 par. is predicated, as we just saw, on the very fact that these people *are* immortal, "no longer able to die."[87]

---

[85] Julius Schniewind, "Die Leugner der Auferstehung in Korinth," in *Nachgelassene Reden und Aufsätze*, ed. Ernst Kähler, Theologische Bibliothek Töpelmann 1 (Berlin: Alfred Töpelmann, 1952) 117–18, alluding to Wisdom 3–4 as his sole evidence.

[86] Thiselton, "Realized Eschatology," 523, 524 (his emphasis); cf. 510.

[87] One could avoid this discrepancy by claiming that those in Corinth who remained unmarried did so out of anticipatory imitation of the celestial existence depicted in Mark 12.25 par. – cf. Herbert Preisker, "Ehe und Charisma bei Paulus," *ZST* 6 (1928/29) 94 – but we should at least be clear that this entails yet one more layer of speculation: it is an assumption as to how the Corinthians might have interpreted a tradition we are not even sure they knew.

Having now examined the central elements of the argument that a realized eschatology promoted asceticism at Corinth, we may question its validity from two additional perspectives. The first involves asking if this understanding of 1 Corinthians 7 is compatible with the notion, held almost universally by advocates of realized eschatology, that this same realized eschatology also promoted libertinism at Corinth, as seen in 1 Corinthians 5–6. Even if we grant, as Lütgert maintained, that the Corinthians' exaggerated emphasis on freedom and the spirit could produce the diametrically opposed attitudes of asceticism and libertinism, it is much less obvious that these initial attitudes could then play themselves out so fully in the life of a community that opposing *visions of salvation* – a marriageless angelic life and a life of complete dissipation – could result and coexist. It should come as no surprise that supporting this view has, for some scholars, resulted in projecting a dubious schizophrenia onto the Corinthians.[88]

The second additional perspective from which we may question whether a realized eschatology promoted sexual asceticism in Corinth concerns Paul's use of apocalyptic language in 1 Corinthians 7. It is often maintained, for the letter as a whole, that the presence of a realized eschatology at Corinth can be measured by Paul's reaction to it in the form of apocalyptic ideas, since these ideas emphasize that the eschaton still lies in the future.[89] Yet while

[88] So Cartlidge, "1 Corinthians 7 as a Foundation," 230, who writes, "The encratic practices of the Corinthians are a bold statement by these Christians that they have fully achieved the heavenly reality. We should perhaps see their sexual libertinism in the same light (6.12–20)" – having written six pages earlier, "It is even quite possible that it is the same people in Corinth who are celibate in marriage, or, within the Christian community, yet relieve their sexual drives with a πόρνη [prostitute] (6.15)" (ibid., 224). Likewise Gordon D. Fee, *The First Epistle to the Corinthians*, NICNT (Grand Rapids, Mich.: William B. Eerdmans, 1987) 12, 276. Cf. his "1 Corinthians 7.1 in the *N.I.V.*," *Journal of the Evangelical Theological Society* 23 (1980) 314. Hurd, *The Origin of 1 Corinthians*, 164, favors avoiding this problem by taking the position that 1 Cor. 6.12–20 does not reflect the existence of actual libertinism at Corinth, but represents only a theoretical discussion about freedom and its misuse (cf. 277–8). Similarly, Yarbrough, *Not Like the Gentiles*, 96–7, also denies that there were libertines at Corinth, reasoning that the problems there were not caused by disputes between ascetics and libertines, but by ascetics who had arrogated themselves above married Christians (cf. 119–20, 124).

[89] Käsemann, "Primitive Christian Apocalyptic," 125, 132, 133. Käsemann is followed, among others, by Wolfgang Schrage, "Die Stellung zur Welt bei Paulus, Epiktet und in der Apokalyptik: Ein Beitrag zu 1 Kor 7,29–31," *ZTK* 61 (1964) 150–1; Thiselton, "Realized Eschatology," 514–15, cf. 519, 520; and Wayne A. Meeks, "Social Functions of Apocalyptic Language in Pauline Christianity," *Apocalypticism in the Mediterranean World and the Near East*, ed. David Hellholm (Tübingen: J. C. B. Mohr, 1983) 699.

this theory may explain the apocalyptic elements in other parts of 1 Corinthians, notably chapter fifteen, it does not work for 1 Corinthians 7. This is because, as several scholars have noted, the apocalyptic traditions in 1 Corinthians 7 are emphatically in the present tense: Paul says that the frame of the world *is* passing away, the time *has* been shortened, and he speaks of the *present* distress.[90] If the usual understanding of apocalyptic material in the rest of the letter carries any weight, then this is certainly not the tack one would expect from Paul if chapter seven represents his efforts to fight an enthusiastic asceticism stemming from a realized eschatology. And this, moreover, is doubly apparent when we consider that Paul is using the apocalyptic material in 7.26–31 in order to *promote* celibacy, not refute it, a fact that has been almost completely overlooked in this context.[91]

Having now considered the eschatological elements that scholars have added to Lütgert's thesis of enthusiasm, let us return to his original formulation of this thesis. Lütgert, as I noted above, specified two ways in which he considered it possible for ascetic behavior to arise from an enthusiastic theology that emphasized freedom in the spirit. First, he saw asceticism as a reaction to libertinism, and second, he proposed that asceticism was inspired by a narrow focus on the spirit and a consequent disregard for the body, the same narrow focus, in fact, that also inspired libertinism. Despite their popularity, neither of these suggestions fare well under close scrutiny.

[90] 1 Cor. 7.26–31. See, e.g., Doughty, "Heiligkeit und Freiheit," 209–11; Gottfried Hierzenberger, *Weltbewertung bei Paulus nach 1 Kor 7,29–31: Eine exegetisch-kerygmatische Studie*, Kommentare und Beiträge zum Alten und Neuen Testament (Düsseldorf: Patmos, 1967) 65–6, cf. 99; Baumert, *Ehelosigkeit und Ehe*, 192–255; Wimbush, *Paul the Worldly Ascetic*, 34–44; Fee, *The First Epistle*, 336; and see below, pp. 185–6.

[91] Schrage, "Die Stellung zur Welt," 151 suggests that Paul is not promoting celibacy in 7.26–31, but relativizing the "definitive character" of marriage. Yet this is a rather fine distinction, and the larger context (7.25–38) tells against it. It should be noted that a growing number of scholars question the notion of realized eschatology in 1 Corinthians altogether. See, e.g., Wilson, "The Corinthians Who Say," 90–107; Wayne G. Rollins, "The New Testament and Apocalyptic," *NTS* 17 (1970/71) 454–76; Klaus Koch, *The Rediscovery of Apocalyptic: A Polemical Work on a Neglected Area of Biblical Studies and its Damaging Effects on Theology and Philosophy*, Studies in Biblical Theology 2/22 (Naperville, Ill.: Alec R. Allenson, 1972) 73–93; Horsley: "How Can Some of You Say," 203–4; "Spiritual Marriage with Sophia," 47; and cf. J. Christiaan Beker, *Paul's Apocalyptic Gospel: The Coming Triumph of God* (Philadelphia: Fortress, 1982) 66–9. Even supporters of the theory now express some hesitancy: see Thiselton, "Realized Eschatology," 514–15; and Yarbrough, *Not Like the Gentiles*, 119.

As for the first, Lütgert never explains why it is reasonable to think that those who were appalled by the libertine activities of their fellow Christians would react, or overreact, with asceticism. There is nothing logically compelling about this argument, nor can we cite other instances of such a phenomenon from antiquity. To the contrary. Many Greek and Roman moralists were also outraged at the licentiousness of their compatriots, but they never resorted to asceticism to counteract it. The same can be said of Hellenistic Jews, who criticized the sexual promiscuity of the surrounding gentile peoples at great length. In fact, it is just as logical, or illogical, to suppose the reverse – that the Corinthians' libertinism was a reaction to the asceticism of certain Christians there.[92] Apart from these considerations, however, it must also be said that the idea of asceticism as the opposite number of libertinism smacks of the old argument that asceticism at Corinth came about as a reaction to the dissipation for which that port city was famous. While this argument was popular in Lütgert's time and before, and still has some supporters even today, it is now generally rejected as completely unfounded.[93]

With regard to Lütgert's second suggestion, that asceticism derives from the same spiritual freedom and enthusiastic devaluation of the body that produced libertinism, there is again the problem of finding comparative materials. Darrell Doughty, for example, cites several models of behavior from the Hellenistic world which he believes are equivalent to the Corinthian situation. These include practices associated with Greek and Roman religious observances, mystery religions, Jewish apocalyptic sects, and Cynic philosophy.[94] In none of these, however, do we have an instance of both asceticism and libertinism stemming from the same source.

---

[92] Schrage, "Zur Frontstellung," 219 asks, if libertine and ascetic attitudes come from the same source, how can one be a reaction to the other?

[93] See, e.g., Peter Brown, "The Notion of Virginity in the Early Church," *Christian Spirituality: Origins to the Twelfth Century*, ed. Bernard McGinn and John Meyendorff, World Spirituality: An Encyclopedic History of the Religious Quest 16 (New York: Crossroad, 1985) 441, speaking of early Christian ascetic practices generally. For supporters of this discredited theory, past and present, see F. F. Bruce, *Paul: Apostle of the Heart Set Free* (Grand Rapids, Mich.: William B. Eerdmans, 1977) 249; the authors cited in Schrage, "Zur Frontstellung," 219 n. 21; and the lucid description of Johann Lorenz von Mosheim, *Erklärung des Ersten Briefes des heiligen Apostles Pauli an die Gemeinde zu Corinthus*, 2nd edn., ed. Christian Ernst von Windheim (Flensburg: Kortem, 1762) 275, who compares the hot and passionate temperate zones of Greece to the cooler, more rational climes of his native Germany.

[94] Doughty, "Heiligkeit und Freiheit," 132, 141–3.

Indeed, this dearth of comparative materials is no small problem for supporters of Lütgert's thesis, since his principal argument for associating the celibacy in chapter seven with the other enthusiastic phenomena of the letter is precisely this proposed "dialectic" of asceticism and libertinism which he sees at work in the Corinthians' attempts to actualize their spiritual freedom. Realizing this, scholars have tended to press a comparison between the Corinthians and second-century gnostics, who, according to patristic writers, also derived ascetic and libertine practices from the same theology. Lütgert himself may have used these patristic reports in formulating his theory, since he often refers to the Corinthian enthusiasts as "gnostics" and sees Paul's struggles with them as a forerunner of the church's fight against gnosticism in the second and third centuries.[95] Yet this comparison is flawed by the facile manner in which it understands gnosticism as a unified entity. It is not one "gnosticism" that the church fathers describe as practicing both asceticism and libertinism, but individual gnostic groups that practiced either one or the other. Thus, there is no evidence even in gnosticism that one religious community could derive opposing sexual practices from the same theological principles.[96]

This lack of supporting evidence for Lütgert's supposed dialectic of asceticism and libertinism at Corinth does not, of course, rule out his theory altogether. But it is worth stressing once again that the ability of his theory to establish an enthusiastic motivation behind the Corinthians' celibacy hangs essentially on this one point. Since Lütgert and his following contend that all the other problems Paul addresses in 1 Corinthians are explicable in terms of an enthusiastic *libertinism*, 1 Corinthians 7 stands out as an anomaly. His proposal of a libertine-ascetic dialectic has thus been defended by his followers as the key to setting chapter seven in an enthusiastic context as well. Without this key, the inclusion of chapter seven makes little sense.[97]

[95] Lütgert, *Freiheitspredigt*, 8, 79–80, 95–6, 105, 109, 111, 118, 126, 128, 134.

[96] See the discussion of gnosticism later in this chapter.

[97] It is telling that several scholars who propose an enthusiastic explanation for the issues addressed in 1 Corinthians "hesitate" noticeably when it comes to treating 1 Cor. 7. A good illustration of this is Bornkamm. In a preliminary sketch of the various problems caused by enthusiasts at Corinth he discusses all but those found in chap. 7 (Bornkamm, *Paul*, 71–4).

Ben Witherington III, *Women in the Earliest Churches*, SNTSMS 59 (Cambridge: Cambridge University Press, 1988) 39–40 suggests that enthusiasm behind the celibacy in 1 Cor. 7 is apparent at 7.40, where Paul appeals to his own possession of the

## 4. The use of second-, third-, and fourth-century sources

### General considerations

Rather than looking solely to the primitive church for clues that would explain the celibacy in 1 Corinthians 7, several scholars have formulated theories based on ascetic practices from second-, third-, and fourth-century Christianity. Working backward through the evidence, they identify Paul and the Corinthians as precursors of these later forms of Christian asceticism.[98] Niederwimmer, for example, despite his interest in first-century ascetic motivations, maintains that the Corinthians practiced abstinence after baptism in observance of a usage that some church fathers associated with Marcion and Tatian in mid-second-century Rome, and which is otherwise documented in Syria in the third century.[99] Other scholars suggest that Paul's denial in 1 Corinthians 7.28 and 7.36 that marriage is a sin indicates that certain Corinthians had taken a solemn vow of virginity which they felt would be sinful to break – our first certain information on such vows coming from the second or third century.[100] Again, based on what appears to be Paul's begrudging preference for marital relations over fornication, still others maintain that Paul understood marriage as a "necessary evil" after the

Spirit. He interprets this verse as an ironic criticism of the Corinthian "spiritualists." Yet this overlooks the fact that Paul's remark here *favors* celibacy. Cf. Adolf Hilgenfeld, *Die Glossolalie in der alten Kirche, in dem Zusammenhang der Geistesgaben und des Geisteslebens des alten Christenthums: Eine exegetisch-historische Untersuchung* (Leipzig: Breitkopf und Härtel, 1850) 135. Regarding the syntax of 7.40, see chapter 3, n. 419.

[98] On this generally, see Weiß, *Korintherbrief*, 204, followed by E.-B. Allo, *Première épitre aux Corinthiens*, Études Bibliques, 2nd edn. (Paris: Librairie Lecoffre, 1934) 183.

[99] Niederwimmer: "Zur Analyse," 242–3; and *Askese und Mysterium*, 98, cf. 124. For Marcion see Vööbus, *History of Asceticism*, 1.53–4, and for Tatian see ibid., 1.36, 42–3. For the later history of the practice see Niederwimmer, *Askese und Mysterium*, 176–86.

[100] E.g., Weiß, *Korintherbrief*, 194; Helmut H. Rex, "Das ethische Problem in der eschatologischen Existenz bei Paulus" (Diss., Tübingen, 1954) 85; and Wimbush, *Paul the Worldly Ascetic*, 20. On vows of virginity see Hugo Koch, *Virgines Christi: Die Gelübde der gottgeweihten Jungfrauen in den ersten drei Jahrhunderten*, TU 31/2 (Leipzig: J. C. Hinrichs, 1907) 63–4, 109–11; Broudéhoux, *Mariage et famille*, 103–4; Georg Kretschmar, "Ein Beitrag zur Frage nach dem Ursprung frühchristlicher Askese," *ZTK* 61 (1964) 29–30; Robert Schilling, "Vestales et vierges chrétiennes dans la Rome antique," *Revue de Sciences Religieuses* 35 (1961) 117–21; and Bernhard Lohse, *Mönchtum und Reformation* (Göttingen: Vandenhoeck und Ruprecht, 1963) 27–8.

manner of St. Jerome. According to these scholars, Paul defended the institution of marriage solely as a "lesser evil," to prevent "worse evils from breaking out in their midst."[101]

Aside from displaying a disregard for matters of chronology and geographic location, however, these theories involve a more serious methodological problem. This manner of using materials from the second century and beyond to clarify 1 Corinthians 7 completely overlooks the theological contexts of the ascetic practices involved. As several scholars have pointed out, even practices that outwardly appear to be identical may in reality have nothing in common with one another in terms of motivation or theological justification.[102] Thus, the practice of sexual abstinence following baptism finds its justification in an encratitic understanding of the world,[103] while perpetual virginity, vows of chastity, and the claim that marriage is a necessary evil presuppose either a dualistic view of the world that understands physical existence as morally deficient,[104] the related notion that moral purity is achieved through sexual abstinence,[105] or the belief that Christian women can be joined to Christ in spiritual wedlock.[106] In 1 Corinthians 7, however, we find no evi-

---

[101] E.g., Jerome Adv. Jovin. 1.7, 9. The phrases are from Ethelbert Stauffer, "γαμέω, γάμος," TDNT 1 (1964) 648–57; and David L. Dungan, The Sayings of Jesus in the Churches of Paul: The Use of the Synoptic Tradition in the Regulation of Early Church Life (Philadelphia: Fortress, 1971) 86. Rudolf Bultmann, Theology of the New Testament (New York: Charles Scribner's Sons, 1951) 1.202 says that for Paul marriage is "an unavoidable evil." For other examples, see the authors cited in Doughty, "Heiligkeit und Freiheit," 5 n. 3; and Wolfgang Schrage, Die konkreten Einzelgebote in der paulinischen Paränese: Ein Beitrag zur neutestamentlichen Ethik (Gütersloh: Gütersloh, 1961) 218.

[102] David Ray Cartlidge made this insight a major emphasis of his Harvard dissertation: "Competing Theologies of Asceticism in the Early Church" (Th.D. Diss., Harvard University, 1969), esp. 22. Karl Rahner observed that only in his day were scholars making the necessary distinctions between different types of asceticism: Marcel Viller and Karl Rahner, Aszese und Mystik in der Väterzeit: Ein Abriß (Freiburg: Herder, 1939) vi. See also the careful studies by Kretschmar, "Ein Beitrag zur Frage"; and Eijk, "Marriage and Virginity."

[103] See, e.g., Martin Elze, Tatian und seine Theologie, Forschungen zur Kirchen- und Dogmengeschichte 9 (Göttingen: Vandenhoeck und Ruprecht, 1960) 88–100, 108–18.

[104] See, e.g., Bornkamm, Paul, 208; Tischleder, Wesen und Stellung, 4, 9, 23–4; Weiß, Korintherbrief, 581; Bultmann, Theology, 1.202; and cf. Schrage, Die konkreten Einzelgebote, 25.

[105] See, e.g., Niederwimmer, Askese und Mysterium, 108, 115; and Weiß, Korintherbrief, 194, 195.

[106] Cf. Niederwimmer, Askese und Mysterium, 80. Tertullian is the first on record to use the phrase "brides of Christ" for Christian women; see Schilling, "Vestales," 116; and Niederwimmer, Askese und Mysterium, 186–98. On the "anticosmic" perspectives of the second-, third-, and fourth-century church fathers, see the

dence for any of these. In our search for the motivations that stand behind this chapter, therefore, these comparisons are of little value.[107]

Two further comparisons of this sort have been put forth, one involving gnostic ascetic practices, the other involving an institution known as *virgines subintroductae*. Since both of these have been accorded considerable credence by the scholarly community, we shall examine them here in detail.

## 1 Corinthians 7 as a case of gnostic asceticism

Several scholars have attempted to understand the Corinthians' celibacy as a reflection of gnostic thought, arguing that it was motivated by gnostic ideas of material dualism and devaluation of the physical existence. In order to be convincing, however, this theory needs to overcome a series of difficulties. The central difficulty, of which the others are extensions, is that 1 Corinthians 7 contains no evidence whatsoever that supports such an interpretation. One scholar who has been particularly outspoken on this point is Walter Schmithals, who rejects the whole notion of gnostic asceticism here. Indeed, the only connection with gnosticism that Schmithals has detected in 1 Corinthians 7 is in verse 40, which he understands as Paul's polemic against gnostics at Corinth who *oppose* ascetic practices.[108] This judgement, it seems to me, is especially noteworthy when we consider that no scholar in this century has done more than Schmithals to promote the idea of gnostic influence at Corinth.

Faced with this complete lack of direct evidence from within the chapter, those who support a gnostic explanation for the Corinthians' celibacy base their argument entirely on what we have

insightful study by Rosemary Radford Ruether, "Misogynism and Virginal Feminism in the Fathers of the Church," *Religion and Sexism: Images of Women in the Jewish and Christian Traditions* (New York: Simon and Schuster, 1974) 150–83.

[107] This was seen as early as Martin Luther: *Commentaries on 1 Corinthians 7, 1 Corinthians 15, Lectures on 1 Timothy*, ed. Hilton C. Oswald, in *Luther's Works*, vol. 28, ed. Jaroslav Pelikan and Helmut Lehmann (Saint Louis: Concordia, 1973) 47–54. See also C. F. Georg Heinrici, *Das erste Sendschreiben des Apostle Paulus an die Korinthier* (Berlin: Wilhelm Hertz, 1880) 205, 209, 211–17, 216–17; Juncker, *Ethik*, 2.183–91; Meyer, *Critical and Exegetical Handbook*, 226, 231, and 192 n. 3; and Doughty, "Heiligkeit und Freiheit," 6, who objects to the "unqualified claim to a general self-explanatory nature" that usually accompanies this use of second-, third-, and fourth-century materials.

[108] Schmithals, *Gnosticism in Corinth*, 234, 236, 387.

termed the "dialectic" between ascetic and libertine attitudes that one finds in second-century gnostic thought.[109] For this reason they assign great importance to the fact that chapter seven immediately follows a passage in which many scholars, including Schmithals, have identified a form of gnostic libertinism. 1 Corinthians 7 is thus seen as the logical "companion piece" to the gnostic libertinism of 6.12–20: it is the "ethical counter-pole" in a gnostic "bipolarity of libertinism and asceticism," a system which supports both these attitudes toward sexuality from the same "radical devaluation of everything bodily and worldly."[110] Of course, this sounds much like Lütgert's theory of enthusiasm, which is not surprising when we remember that Lütgert, too, seems to have relied on second-century gnostic models. As a consequence, this theory is open to some of the same criticisms as Lütgert's, as well as some new ones.

To begin with, it is now generally recognized that first-century gnosticism differed from the second-century phenomenon in many important ways.[111] Wolfgang Schrage and others have attempted to address this problem by speaking of a "nascent" gnosticism in Corinth, which implies a gradual and predictable development; and Schrage has pointed out that the later gnostic mythologies and metaphysical speculations are not prerequisite for the development of ascetic and libertine tendencies within the movement.[112] Luise Schottroff has lent some credibility to this latter claim inasmuch as her analysis of 1 Corinthians 1, 2, and 15 concludes that, while there

---

[109] On this ascetic-libertine dialectic in gnosticism see the treatments in Henry A. Green, *The Economic and Social Origins of Gnosticism*, SBLDS 77 (Atlanta: Scholars, 1985) 216–38; Hans Jonas, *Gnosis und spätantiker Geist*, vol. 1: *Die mythologische Gnosis*, 3rd edn. (Göttingen: Vandenhoeck und Ruprecht, 1964) 233–8, 313–15; and cf. Niederwimmer, *Askese und Mysterium*, 200–19; Erhardt Güttgemanns, *Der leidende Apostel und sein Herr: Studien zur paulinischen Christologie*, FRLANT 90 (Göttingen: Vandenhoeck und Ruprecht, 1966) 226–40; and John Ernest Leonard Oulton and Henry Chadwick, *Alexandrian Christianity*, Library of Christian Classics 2 (London: SCM, 1954) 22–33.

[110] Schrage, "Zur Frontstellung," 217–18; cf. 219–20.

[111] E.g., Koester, review of *Weisheit und Torheit*, 595; Hans-Friedrich Weiß, "Paulus und die Häretiker: Zum Paulusverständnis in der Gnosis," *Christentum und Gnosis*, ZNW Beiheft 37 (1969) 116–28; Carsten Colpe, "Vorschläge des Messina-Kongresses von 1966 zur Gnosisforschung," *Christentum und Gnosis*, ZNW Beiheft 37 (1969) 129–32; and George W. MacRae, review of *Gnosticism in Corinth* by Walter Schmithals, *Interpretation* 26 (1972) 489–91.

[112] Schrage, "Zur Frontstellung," 220 n. 26; cf. Conzelmann, *1 Corinthians*, 15 and 108.

is no evidence for a gnostic redeemer myth in 1 Corinthians, Paul's opponents do seem to have promoted a gnostic dualism.[113] Yet this does not necessarily settle the matter, for once we entertain the possibility that the Corinthians' gnosticism was a gnosis in its initial stages, our ground for assuming parallels between it and later, fully developed gnostic systems becomes potentially very tenuous. As Jack Wilson reminds us, "It is methodologically incorrect to call one group at one time Gnostic, another at another time Gnostic, then assume that since both are Gnostic their attributes can be interchanged!"[114] The entire problem is further complicated by the fact that even those scholars who entertain a gnostic interpretation for parts or all of 1 Corinthians vary greatly in their conceptions of this gnosticism. Robert Grant, for example, speaks of a gnosticizing "tendency" at Corinth deriving (à la Käsemann) from the experience of the Spirit and a "fully-realized eschatology,"[115] while John Painter sees the influence of mystery religions. Gerhard Sellin, in turn, detects the presence of a dualistic spiritualism which he also finds in Philo; and Horsley argues that the Corinthians' form of gnosis is close to Jewish wisdom literature.[116]

---

[113] Luise Schottroff, *Der Glaubende und die feindliche Welt: Beobachtungen zum gnostischen Dualismus und seiner Bedeutung für Paulus und das Johannesevangelium*, WMANT 37 (Neukirchen-Vluyn: Neukirchen, 1970) 115–227. Christian Maurer, "Ehe und Unzucht nach 1. Korinther 6,12–7,7," *Wort und Dienst*, n.s. 6 (1959) 166 suggests that the libertinism in 1 Cor. 6 was based on a gnostic anthropology and a docetic Christology. With regard specifically to 1 Cor. 7, however, Sellin, "Hauptprobleme," 3003 has pointed out that there is no evidence for an "anthropologic-dualistic" gnostic asceticism here.

[114] Wilson, "The Corinthians Who Say," 99. Cf. Dahl, "Paul and the Church at Corinth," 333. Even Schmithals has had to admit that there are difficulties in correlating the Corinthians' gnosticism with second-century examples. To explain the discrepancies he had argued for a "certain lack of correctness in Paul's train of thought," suggesting that Paul was not really aware that his opponents in Corinth were gnostics (*Gnosticism in Corinth*, 233). The pitfalls inherent in this sort of reasoning are obvious – see R. McL.Wilson, "How Gnostic Were the Corinthians?" *NTS* 19 (1972/73) 71.

[115] R. M. Grant, *Gnosticism and Early Christianity*, 2nd edn. (New York/London: Columbia University, 1966) 157–8. Gerhard Sellin, "'Die Auferstehung ist schon geschehen': Zur Spiritualisierung apokalyptischer Terminologie im Neuen Testament," *NovT* 25 (1983) 221 notes the indiscriminate use of "enthusiasm" for both gnosticism and realized eschatology; cf. Thiselton, "Realized Eschatology," 516–26, who attempts to distinguish between the two. Jörg Baumgarten, *Paulus und die Apokalyptik: Die Auslegung apokalyptischer Überlieferungen in den echten Paulus-briefen*, WMANT 44 (Neukirchen-Vluyn: Neukirchen, 1975) 199–200 questions the usefulness of the term "enthusiasm" altogether precisely because of its duplicity.

[116] John Painter, "Paul and the Πνευματικοί at Corinth," *Paul and Paulinism: Essays in Honour of C. K. Barrett* (London: SPCK, 1982) 237–50; Gerhard Sellin, *Der Streit um die Auferstehung der Toten: Eine religionsgeschichtliche und exegetische*

Given, therefore, the potential for differences between first- and second-century forms of gnosticism, and the difficulty of defining gnosticism at Corinth, it is far from clear that the same dynamics responsible for producing the second-century "dialectic" of libertinism and asceticism are operative behind 1 Corinthians 6–7, especially since chapter seven supplies no support at all for this theory.[117]

Finally, two further difficulties arise from this attempt to see 1 Corinthians 7 as reflecting one half of a gnostic dialectic of sexuality. The first we have already addressed in the context of Lütgert's theory of enthusiasm, namely, that it is problematic to attribute both asceticism and libertinism to the Corinthians on the basis of second-century gnostic models since we know of no one gnostic group in that or any following centuries that embraced both these extremes. What we find, rather, are ascetic gnostics on the one hand, and libertine gnostics on the other.[118] Reconciling himself to these facts, Schrage has attempted to show that the texts speak for a "double front" – a libertine front in chapter six and an ascetic front in chapter seven.[119] What his argument overlooks, however, is that

*Untersuchung von 1 Korinther 15*, FRLANT 138 (Göttingen: Vandenhoeck und Ruprecht, 1986) 54–63; Horsley, "Gnosis in Corinth," 33–4, referring to Bultmann, *Theology*, 1.692–6, 709–10.

[117] Recent research on possible gnostic influence in 1 Corinthians has, in fact, tended sharply away from seeing close parallels to the second-century phenomenon. See Sellin, "Hauptprobleme," 3020–1; Edwin M. Yamauchi, *Pre-Christian Gnosticism: A Survey of the Proposed Evidences* (London: Tyndale, 1973) 39–43, 173–86; Sasagu Arai, "Die Gegner des Paulus im I. Korintherbrief und das Problem der Gnosis," *NTS* 19 (1972/73) 430–7, esp. 436–7; Bernhard Spörlein, *Die Leugnung der Auferstehung: Eine historisch-kritische Untersuchung zu I Kor 15*, BU 7 (Regensburg: Friedrich Pustet, 1971) 174–81; R. McL. Wilson: "Gnosis at Corinth," *Paul and Paulinism: Essays in Honour of C. K. Barrett* (London: SPCK, 1982) 102–44; "Gnosis/Gnostizismus II," *TRE* 13 (1984) 535–50; Birger Albert Pearson: *The Pneumatikos-Psychikos Terminology in 1 Corinthians: A Study in the Theology of the Corinthian Opponents of Paul and its Relation to Gnosticism*, SBLDS 12 (Missoula, Mont.: SBL, 1973); "Philo, Gnosis and the New Testament," *The New Testament and Gnosis: Essays in Honour of Robert McL. Wilson*, ed. A. H. B. Logan and A. J. M. Wedderburn (Edinburgh: T. and T. Clark, 1983) 73–89; cf. Carsten Colpe, "Gnosis II (Gnostizismus)," *RAC* 11 (1981) 602–7.

[118] Schmithals has recognized the seriousness of this problem and comes to the following emphatic conclusion: "I deny that the same Pneumatics *at the same time* demand asceticism and libertinism, for reasons of logic as well as the lack of religio-historical parallels for such a procedure, and for the Corinthian situation moreover on the basis of the texts, which neither require nor suggest such an interpretation" (*Gnosticism in Corinth*, 387–8, his emphasis); cf. Niederwimmer, "Zur Analyse," 242.

[119] Schrage, *Die konkreten Einzelgebote*, 217 n. 141, in reply to Schmithals' declaration as cited in the previous note. Schmithals stands by his position, however:

the opposing forms of sexual conduct that we find in gnosticism are not merely the result of different gnostic groups drawing conflicting conclusions from one basic gnostic doctrine – "simply different forms of degradation of the body that comes with dualism."[120] Rather, they also reflect divergent views of the world. This is a point Brown has recently highlighted, stressing "the great diversity of the radical groups that had emerged in the course of the second century."[121] Thus, Schrage's explanation of 1 Corinthians 6–7 in terms of gnostic libertinism and gnostic asceticism, respectively, implies the coexistence of two distinct systems of thought. This in itself seems unlikely, and nothing that Paul says in these chapters speaks in its favor.

Finally, a very serious difficulty with appealing to a gnostic dialectic to interpret 1 Corinthians 7 stems from the recent conclusion reached by a wide consensus of scholars that gnostic libertinism was never widespread.[122] Based on information from the newly edited Coptic texts discovered at Nag Hammadi, scholars now understand gnostic libertinism as largely an invention of the leaders of the orthodox church for the purpose of discrediting their opponents. As Grant observed, "Earlier the Christians, now the Gnostics, were being accused of actions harmful to marriage and the family."[123] What this means for our investigation is that the libertine-ascetic

*Neues Testament und Gnosis*, Erträge der Forschung 208 (Darmstadt: Wissenschaftliche Buchgelsellschaft, 1984) 30, 32. On "two front" hypotheses in the research on 1 Corinthians see Sellin, "Hauptprobleme," 3018–19.

[120] Schrage, "Zur Frontstellung," 219, cf. 220.

[121] Brown, *Body and Society*, 86; cf. xiv, where he speaks of "the range of options faced by Christians in the remarkable fifty years that stretched from the generation of Marcion, Valentinus, and Tatian to that of Tertullian and Clement of Alexandria." Even attempts at grouping gnostic theologies of asceticism into one unified phenomenon using a broad psychological interpretation (e.g., Niederwimmer, *Askese und Mysterium*, 208–19, esp. 218–19) distorts this diversity – see, e.g., Brown, *Body and Society*, 65–139.

[122] See R. van den Broek, "The Present State of Gnostic Studies," *VC* 37 (1983) 49–50; and Klaus Berger, "Gnosis/Gnostizismus I," *TRE* 13 (1984) 522.

[123] Robert M. Grant, "Early Christians and Gnostics in Graeco-Roman Society," *The New Testament and Gnosis: Essays in Honour of Robert McL. Wilson*, ed. A. H. B. Logan and A. J. M. Wedderburn (Edinburgh: T. and T. Clark, 1983) 180; the quote continues: "A glance at A. Berger's *Encyclopedic Dictionary of Roman Law* immediately shows how offenders would be subject not only to social condemnation but also to legal penalties: Adulterium, Incestus, Stuprum, not to mention Homicidium. Beyond that came the general social attitudes which supported marriage and the family, notably under the Antonine emperors ... We conclude that the charges against the Gnostics are intended to show that they were outcasts from Graeco-Roman society ..."

dialectic, which is the sole basis for a gnostic interpretation of 1 Corinthians 7, appears to have been an extremely rare phenomenon even between different groups of gnostics, let alone within one religious community. In sum, the attempt to interpret 1 Corinthians 7 in terms of an asceticism based on a gnostic theology draws its inspiration from a model of gnosticism that is dated, rare, and poorly fits the information provided by 1 Corinthians.

### Spiritual marriages

In 1902 Hans Achelis, following the suggestion of two scholars at the end of the nineteenth century, sought a solution to the enigmatic 1 Corinthians 7.36–8. He attempted to prove that the relationship between a man and "his virgin" which Paul describes here was a "spiritual marriage," an arrangement in which a couple lived together, sharing all the responsibilities and benefits of a normal marriage, with the important exception of the sexual relationship. The man's virgin in 7.36–8, according to Achelis, was thus one of the *virgines subintroductae* spoken of by later church fathers.[124]

Beginning with "more certain" evidence and venturing backward in time to "questionable" cases of this institution, Achelis opens his analysis with the church father Cyprian, who, around 249 CE, writes with concern about several Christian men known to him (one being a deacon) who were cohabiting with virgins vowed to chastity.[125] His next instance is Eusebius' account of Paul of Samosata, a bishop of Antioch who was deposed in 268 CE. Paul, it seems, along with his presbyters and deacons, lived in chastity with women whom the people of Antioch had nicknamed συνείσακτοι, the Greek equivalent of the later *subintroductae*.[126] Following this, Achelis cites

---

[124] Hans Achelis, *Virgines Subintroductae: Ein Beitrag zum VII. Kapitel des I. Korintherbriefs* (Leipzig: J. C. Hinrichs, 1902); preceded by Carl Weizsäcker, "Die Anfänge christlicher Sitte," *Jahrbücher für Deutsche Theologie* 21 (1876) 33, cf. idem, *Das apostolische Zeitalter der christlichen Kirche*, 1st edn. (Freiburg im Breisgau: J. C. B. Mohr, 1886) 675–6; and Eduard Grafe, "Geistliche Verlöbnisse bei Paulus," *Theologische Arbeiten aus dem rheinischen wissenschaftlichen Predigerverein*, n.s. 3 (1899) 57–69. Achelis was the first to research a full history of spiritual marriage; Grafe had only alluded to possible occurrences in *Hermas*.

[125] Achelis, *Virgines Subintroductae*, 7–8, citing Cyprian *Epistle* 4, *To Pomponius*. Achelis also cites *Ep.* 13.5 and 15.3 (*Virgines Subintroductae*, 9), but these speak only of general promiscuousness in the church.

[126] Achelis, *Virgines Subintroductae*, 9–11, citing Eusebius *Church History* 7.30.12. Our first evidence for the Latin *subintroductae* is from Atticus of Constantinople in 419 CE in his Latin trans. of the Council of Nicea – cited by Pierre de Labriolle, "Le

Origen's stay with the virgin Juliana (235–7 CE),[127] and Tertullian's proposal (ca. 210 CE) that those who wished to marry after the death of their first wife take a "spiritual wife," by which he meant an aged widow who could offer a man chaste companionship and housekeeping.[128]

Achelis then turns to five cases of spiritual marriage from the late to middle second century. The one on which he spends the most time is the *Shepherd of Hermas, Similitudes* 9.10.6–11.8, where the seer Hermas encounters twelve virgins with whom he spends the night, but "as a brother, not as a husband."[129] Achelis' other cases involve: followers of Valentinus; the Montanist Alexander and a prophetess; Marcion's disciple Apelles, a woman called Philumene, and another woman who is not named; and several followers of Tatian.[130] Finally, Achelis arrives at 1 Corinthians 7.36–8. Challenging the church's traditional explanation of this passage, which envisioned a father agonizing over whether he should marry off his daughter, and discounting the idea that the virgin here is an orphan who was raised by a patron and is now being threatened by his sexual advances, Achelis proposes that we "assume with Paul the institute of the *subintroductae* in its fully developed form."[131]

«mariage spirituel» dans l'antiquité chrétienne," *Revue Historique* 137 (1921) 214 n. 4.

[127] Achelis, *Virgines Subintroductae*, 12, citing Palladius *Lausiac History* 147. Achelis is unsure as to whether this is really a spiritual marriage, however.

[128] Achelis, *Virgines Subintroductae*, 12–14, citing Tertullian *De exhortatione castitatis* 12 and *De monogamia* 16.

[129] ὡς ἀδελφός, καὶ οὐχ ὡς ἀνήρ; Achelis, *Virgines Subintroductae*, 14–19.

[130] Ibid., 19–20, citing Irenaeus *Aganist Heresies* 1.6.3, Eusebius *Church History* 5.18.6, Tertullian *De praescriptione haereticorum* 30, and Epiphanius *Haereses* 47.3.1, respectively. He also surveys possibilities from later periods (34–59, 63, 69).

[131] Achelis, *Virgines Subintroductae*, 26. Achelis' theory, with some modification, has achieved a fairly wide acceptance among scholars. See the bibliography in Werner Georg Kümmel, "Verlobung und Heirat bei Paulus (I. Cor 7 36–38)" *Neutestamentliche Studien für Rudolf Bultmann*, ZNW Beiheft 21 (1954) 275–6 n. 1 and 278 n. 11. See also Roland H. A. Seboldt, "Spiritual Marriage in the Early Church: A Suggested Interpretation of 1 Cor. 7:36–38," *Concordia Theological Monthly* 30 (1959) 113–19, 176–89; and Niederwimmer, *Askese und Mysterium*, 117–20.

Some scholars have even argued for extending the notion of spiritual marriages over the entire section 7.25–38. This was actually the brainchild of Weizsäcker in 1876, when he first proposed a connection between 1 Cor. 7 and spiritual marriages (Weizsäcker, *Anfänge*, 32–3), a fact overlooked in Albrecht Oepke's polemic, "Irrwege in der neueren Paulusforschung," *TLZ* 77 (1952) 450–1. Weizsäcker, in turn, was followed by Johannes Weiß in his influential commentary on 1 Corinthians (*Korintherbrief*, 194–6), and by Rudolf Steck, "Geistliche Ehen bei Paulus? (I. Kor. 7,36–38.)," *Schweizerische Theologische Zeitschrift* 34 (1917) 185–9. Yet as Adolf

A major, although by no means the only problem with this interpretation of 1 Corinthians 7.36–8 is, in fact, the passage itself, for nothing in these verses points distinctly to a spiritual marriage.[132] Indeed, Achelis openly conceded this much, and underscored the tenuous nature of his interpretation, as did Carl Weizsäcker and Eduard Grafe before him.[133] Beyond the absence of any clear evidence from 1 Corinthians 7.36–8, however, the most obvious difficulty with the work of Achelis is chronological. Even if we accept his analysis of the materials from Cyprian to *Hermas*, his earliest case of *subintroductae* before we reach Paul is in the middle of the second century, almost one hundred years after the Apostle writes.[134] The anachronism of Achelis' theory is further indicated by

Jülicher has shown, this proposal raises more problems than it solves ("Die Jungfrauen im ersten Korintherbrief," *Protestantische Monatshefte* 22 [1918] 114–15; see also Juncker, *Ethik*, 2.192–200).

Other scholars have sought to reinstate the traditional father-daughter understanding of this passage, an interpretation that goes back at least to Clement of Alexandria (*Strom.* bk. 3, chap. 12.79.2 [2.231.21–3 S.]), but which is impossible on philological grounds. See Kümmel, "Verlobung," 279–86, and 276 nn. 2–3. Still other scholars have developed interpretations based on comparisons with late rabbinic sources, a methodology that is suspect for several reasons. For these theories see Kümmel, "Verlobung," 289–95; Seboldt, "Spiritual Marriage," 107–13; Niederwimmer, *Askese und Mysterium*, 116–17; and J. Massingberd Ford, the Philogamist (I Cor. vii in Early Patristic Exegesis)," *NTS* 11 (1964/65) 326–48; and J. Duncan M. Derrett, "The Disposal of Virgins," *Studies in the New Testament* (Leiden: E. J. Brill, 1977) 1.184–92.

[132] See Plooij, "Eine enkratitische Glosse," 4; Adolf von Schlatter, *Paulus der Bote Jesu: Eine Deutung seiner Briefe an die Korinther* (Stuttgart: Calwer, 1934; repr., 1956) 246; and Franz Fahnenbruch's apt characterization of the elusiveness of the passage in his "Zu 1 Kor 7,36–38," *BZ* (Freiburg i. B.) 12 (1914) 392 – which parrots Achelis' own (*Virgines Subintroductae*, 22).

[133] A fact most present-day supporters of the *subintroductae* theory choose to overlook. See Achelis: *Virgines Subintroductae*, 26 n. 1; "AGAPĒTÆ," *ERE* 1 (1926) 179; Weizsäcker, *Das apostolische Zeitalter*, 675–6; Eduard Grafe, "Geistliche Verlöbnisse bei Paulus," *Theologische Arbeiten aus dem rheinischen wissenschaftlichen Predigerverein*, n.s.3 (1899).

[134] See Richard Kugelmann, "1 Cor. 7:36–38," *CBQ* 10 (1948) 66; Kümmel, "Verlobung," 289; P. Ladeuze, review of *Virgines Subintroductae* by Hans Achelis, *Revue d'Histoire Ecclésiastique* 6 (1905) 61; and Roger Gryson, *Les origines du célibat ecclésiastique: Du premier au septième siècle*, Recherches et synthèses, section d'Histoire 2 (Gembloux: J. Duculot, 1970) 36–8. Cf. Conzelmann, *1 Corinthians*, 135 n. 45; and Koch, *Virgines Christi*, 59–112. Even those who support Achelis are obliged to concede that "the historical gap is great" (Seboldt, "Spiritual Marriage," 189).

Some scholars have sought to close this gap by proposing that *Didache* 11.11, a text which may come from the late first or early second century, also speaks of spiritual marriages – e.g., Preisker, *Christentum und Ehe*, 158–60. But there is really nothing in this passage that points to spiritual marriages. It speaks of strange practices of itinerant prophets, which, the text says, are not to be imitated by the congregation as a whole. These could be almost anything. Further, the text never mentions proph-

the fact that no Greek or Latin church father ever interprets 1
Corinthians 7.36–8 as referring to spiritual marriage, although
many discuss it. Even in the church's many debates on the propriety
of *subintroductae*, this passage is never used as a proof text, even
though these debates lasted from the third to the seventh century
and employed many biblical proof texts.[135]
  Well aware of these shortcomings to his argument, Achelis
attempted to explain the silence of the fathers in light of two
developments within the church: beginning in the third century,
spiritual marriage fell into disrepute; and already in the second
century (*sic*), the marriage of a virgin vowed to a life of continence
was regarded a serious sin. According to Achelis, the church fathers
found it impossible to interpret Paul in a manner that would have
given either of these practices an air of legitimacy. While Henry
Chadwick and others have seconded Achelis' suggestion, it is
unclear how much this argument from silence can explain. If we
grant that the Greek and Latin fathers rejected a *subintroductae*
interpretation for 1 Corinthians 7.36–8, does it then follow that not
one of them would have ventured to refute it by showing how it was
in error?[136]

etesses or female companions to these prophets, nor does it refer to their associating
with women of the local congregations. Indeed, the only thing that even *remotely*
connects *Didache* 11.11 with spiritual marriages is an exegesis of this passage
developed by certain fathers in the Syrian church. On this see Alfred Adam, "Erwägungen zur Herkunft der Didache," *ZKG* 68 (1957) 20–37; Conzelmann, *1 Corinthians*, 136 n. 45; Kümmel, "Verlobung," 278 n. 9; and Niederwimmer, *Askese und
Mysterium*, 191–2. Achelis, we should note, never mentions the passage. He was,
however, prepared to consider Philo's Therapeutae in the historical trajectory of
spiritual marriage, and even compares the dancing of Hermas' virgins with the
religious activities of the female Therapeutae ("AGAPĒTÆ," 179; *Virgines Subintroductae*, 71; 29, 32). Cf. Kirsopp Lake, *The Earlier Epistles of St. Paul: Their Motive
and Origin*, 2nd edn. (London: Rivingtons, 1914) 188–9.
  [135] See Joseph Sickenberger, "Syneisaktentum im ersten Korintherbriefe?" *BZ* 3
(1905) 49–57; and Kugelmann, "1 Cor 7:36–38," 67. Cf. Kümmel, "Verlobung," 276
n. 2, and 289. On the nature of the church's debates see Achelis, *Virgines Subintroductae*, 34–5, 42–3. Achelis (23 n. 2) attempted to argue that John Chrysostom's use of
ἀσχημοσύνη and ἀσχημονεῖν in his two treatises on *subintroductae* had reference to 1
Cor. 7.36, but this is not at all compelling; cf. Sickenberger, "Syneisaktentum," 58 n.
1. It is only in the Syrian church, in St. Ephraem's commentary on Paul from the
middle of the fourth century (extant in Armenian), that 1 Cor. 7.36–8 is interpreted in
light of spiritual marriages – see Kugelmann, "1 Cor 7:36–38," 67–8; and Franz
Herklotz, "Zu 1 Kor 7, 36ff.," *BZ* (Freiburg i. B.) 14 (1916/17) 344–5. On spiritual
marriage in the Syrian church see Vööbus, *History of Asceticism*, 78–83.
  [136] See Achelis, *Virgines Subintroductae*, 28 n. 3; H. Chadwick, "'All Things to All
Men' (I Cor. ix. 22)" *NTS* 1 (1954/55) 267; and Seboldt, "Spiritual Marriage," 105–6,
who offers the unlikely theory that some mss. of 1 Cor. 7.38 read ἐκγαμίζων in place

Thus far we have assumed that Achelis accurately construed his patristic sources, but this, too, is problematic. Let us consider his evidence for the second century. Regarding the followers of Valentinus, Achelis' source, Irenaeus, tells us only that these gnostics proposed ascetic cohabitation with women as a ruse, in order to lure them away from their husbands.[137] As for the Montanist Alexander, Eusebius' informant Apollonius states that the former had a relationship with a prophetess, but leaves the actual nature of this relationship poorly defined. He says only in passing that the woman lived or "cavorted" with Alexander, for his real concern was to discredit this Montanist as a thief.[138] With Tatian's followers the matter is different. Here we learn from Epiphanius that they were found among women, led them astray, traveled with them, lived with them as companions, and let themselves be served by these women.[139] But whether this corresponds to spiritual marriage or simply an ascetic community, Epiphanius does not say. Concerning Marcion's disciple Apelles, by contrast, Tertullian states specifically that his first relation with a woman involved *leaving* the ascetic regiment of his teacher (*desertor continentiae Marcionensis*), while his second relationship began when he "forced himself" (*impegit*) on the virgin Philumene, who thereafter became a prostitute.[140]

Of Achelis' five examples of spiritual marriage from the second century this leaves us with only *Hermas, Similitudes* 9.10.6–11.8.[141]

---

of γαμίζων to prevent someone from interpreting the latter as the equivalent of γαμῶν, and thus as referring to spiritual marriages.
[137] Irenaeus *Against Heresies* 1.6.3.
[138] The expression used is συνεστιάω τινί, Eusebius *C.H.* 5.18.6.
[139] Epiphanius *Haereses* 47.3.1.
[140] Tertullian *De praescr. haer.* 30.5–6. One could argue, of course, that in their zealous opposition to the heretics, the church fathers distorted some of these reports for polemic reasons. But it would be precarious to speculate on this basis that the heretics practiced spiritual marriages.
[141] Achelis also cites *Hermas, Visions* 1.1.1, in his *ERE* article ("AGAPĒTÆ," 179), to which we may add *Visions* 2.2.3, which Plooij cites ("Eine enkratitische Glosse," 4–6). In these passages Hermas enters into a new relationship with two women: with Rhoda, whose servant Hermas once was, and with his wife. In *Hermas, Vis.* 1.1.1, however, Hermas says only that after many years he reacquainted himself with his former mistress and began to love her as a sister (ἠρξάμην αὐτὴν ἀγαπᾶν ὡς ἀδελφήν). He does not say that he took up residence with Rhoda and thus initiated a spiritual marriage (cf. Kugelmann, "1 Cor 7:36–38," 66–7). *Hermas, Vis.* 2.2.3, on the other hand, depicts Hermas receiving instructions that he should continue to live with his wife but cease sexual relations with her. Yet here we must ask whether this represents the beginning of a spiritual marriage or simply the application of Hermas' rigorism to an already existing marriage. In any case, Hermas' wife is not a *virgo subintroducta*.

Here Hermas is left by his spiritual guide, the Shepherd, to spend the night with twelve virgins who are watching over a tower (πύργος). Initially Hermas is reluctant, but after some persuasion he eventually gives in. Further on in the narrative we learn that these virgins are holy spirits and powers of God (δυνάμεις). The Shepherd instructs Hermas that he must clothe himself with these spirits and receive their power in order to please God, and he contrasts them with ten women dressed in black, who lead people astray. We also learn the names of the twelve virgins: Faith, Temperance, Power, Patience, Simplicity, Innocence, Holiness, Joyfulness, Truth, Understanding, Concord, and Love.

Achelis, of course, realized that this passage reported a vision. Even so, he argued, the author relates the incident of staying overnight in such a matter-of-fact manner that we must presuppose familiarity with spiritual marriages in *Hermas*. Robert Schilling has supported this view, adding that the scene with the virgins could hardly be an invention of Hermas' imagination.[142] Other scholars, however, object. Pierre Labriolle, for example, finds it difficult to compare Hermas' one night mystical experience with the practice of spiritual marriage; and noting the simple logistics of Hermas' lodging arrangements, J. Massingberd Ford remarks, rather wryly one hopes, that "polygamous *subintroductae* relationships would hardly be possible."[143]

But quite apart from these considerations is the fact that *Similitudes* 9.10.6–11.8 appears to be fashioned after the erotic scenes one finds in ancient novels. Novelistic elements that occur here include Hermas' overnight stay with the virgins as well as the suggestive exchange that takes place just before this, regarding the propriety of these arrangements.[144] Achelis had taken note of this, but denied any *risqué* intent on Hermas' part, explaining that the naivety and

142 Achelis, "AGAPĒTÆ," 179; Schilling, "Vestales," 115. See also Lietzmann, *An die Korinther*, 36. Cf. Niederwimmer, *Askese und Mysterium*, 196; and Bultmann, *Theology*, 1.103.
143 Labriolle, "Le «mariage spirituel»," 210; J. Massingberd Ford, *A Trilogy on Wisdom and Celibacy*, Cardinal O'Hara Series 4 (London/Notre Dame, Ind.: University of Notre Dame, 1967) 135 n. 39. See also Kümmel, "Verlobung," 278 n. 9; and cf. Kugelmann, "1 Cor 7:36–38," 66–7. As early as 1905 scholars had raised doubts about the inclusion of the *Hermas* passage in Achelis' survey – see G. Ficker, review of *Virgines Subintroductae* by Hans Achelis, *Theologische Rundschau* 8 (1905) 117–18.
144 *Hermas, Sim.* 9.11.3–6. As part of this scene the virgins kiss and embrace Hermas and begin to play with him, dancing, gavotting, and singing. Cf. Martin Dibelius, *Der Hirt des Hermas*, HNT Ergänzungsband: Die Apostolischen Väter 4 (Tübingen: J. C. B. Mohr, 1923) 618–19.

innocence of the middle of the second century toward sex – whatever that means – ruled out giving this scene so bawdy a reading.[145] Yet in another piece of literature from this period, which also displays novelistic influence, we find many important similarities. This is the story *Joseph and Aseneth*, dated somewhere between the first century BCE and the early second century CE.[146] Here Joseph and Aseneth, like Hermas and his virgins, address each other as "brother" and "sister" on the basis of their chaste behavior toward one another; they engage in suggestive banter; and Aseneth is accompanied by seven virgins who live with her in a tower (πύργος), just as those in *Hermas* are associated with a tower.[147] This last similarity is particularly intriguing when we consider that Hermas knows of yet another group of women who are stationed by a tower, this time seven in number. These women, moreover, are a variation on the twelve with whom Hermas spends the night: they have "powers" (δυνάμεις); those who serve them will be counted among God's saints; and their names are Faith, Continence, Simplicity, Innocence, Knowledge, Reverence, and Love.[148]

Given these parallels between *Hermas* and *Joseph and Aseneth*, it is an open question as to how much of *Similitudes* 9.10.6–11.8 we may reasonably attribute to actual practices in Hermas' church in Rome, and how much to the influence of novelistic topoi. In all, it is clear that we cannot take Achelis' assessment of the patristic materials at face value, for neither he nor those who accept his theory have succeeded in producing a clear instance of spiritual marriage before the third century.

Finally, Achelis' hypothesis must be criticized from the perspective of theological context. We may ask, namely, whether it is

[145] Achelis, *Virgines Subintroductae*, 15–19. Steck proposed that the scene reflected a testing of Hermas' continence (*Keuschheitsprobe*), since "Christians felt themselves so secure in their blameless purity that they found it a pleasure to be tested through intimate fellowship between persons of the opposite sex" ("Geistliche Ehen bei Paulus?" 185) – even though Achelis had denied that any such test was involved (*Virgines Subintroductae*, 66–7).
[146] See C. Burchard, "Joseph and Aseneth," *The Old Testament Pseudepigrapha*, ed. James H. Charlesworth (Garden City, N.Y.: Doubleday, 1985) 2.186–7; and Richard I. Pervo, "Joseph and Asenath and the Greek Novel," *SBL 1976 Seminar Papers*, SBLSPS 10 (Missoula, Mont.: Scholars, 1976) 171–81.
[147] *Joseph and Aseneth* 2.1 [2.1–2]; 7.1–8.7; 14.5; 19.10–21.1 [19.3; 19.11–20.10] (brackets indicate alternate versification).
[148] *Hermas, Vis.* 3.8.1–8. While it is true that these seven are not virgins, this is only because they are daughters of one another, symbolizing the fact that faith, continence, etc. give birth to one another. On this aspect of the women cf., e.g., Rom. 5.1–5.

meaningful to call an asceticism based on the Montanists' apocalyptic expectations, one inspired by Tatian's encratitic theology, a third inspired by Hermas' rigorism, and still others motivated by Marcion's or Valentinus' dualism all forms of the same practice.[149] Has Achelis, in other words, given sufficient consideration to the vast theological differences that separate his various cases of spiritual marriage? Although he was, in part, aware of this problem, the answer must be no. According to Achelis, spiritual marriage was the "natural product of two opposing tendencies in ancient Christianity," intimate brotherly love and a "strong aversion, based on religious feelings, to sexual intercourse."[150] But even if Achelis were to establish this as the motivation behind the relationship in 1 Corinthians 7.36–8, which he cannot, the simplistic notion of an asceticism based on "religious feelings" is so vague and all-encompassing that it provides no real explanation for any ascetic practice, let alone that of spiritual marriage.

This same confusion about motivation, moreover, is also found among the proponents of Achelis' theory. Thus, Jean Héring suggests "eschatological enthusiasm" as a motivating force, while Käsemann and John Hurd maintain that spiritual marriages developed out of a desire to live like angels in anticipation of the eschaton. Schmithals and Roland Seboldt contend that anticipation of apocalyptic times of distress played a part; and Chadwick suggests that Paul may have accidently created spiritual marriage by advising the Corinthians not to form new marriages, while at the same time insisting that they honor the relationships established by their wedding engagements.[151] As with Achelis, none of these scholars argues for a motivation that convincingly links this passage to any other putative case of spiritual marriage. Conversely, the motivations responsible for these other cases shed no light on 1 Corinthians 7.36–8.

### 5. Conclusion

With the analysis of Achelis our review of the secondary literature comes to a close. It began with an examination of several authors

---

[149] So also Adolf Jülicher, "Die geistlichen Ehen in der alten Kirche," *Archiv für Religionswissenschaft* 7 (1904) 378–80.

[150] Achelis, "AGAPĒTÆ," 178; cf. *Virgines Subintroductae*, 61.

[151] Jean Héring, *The First Epistle of Saint Paul to the Corinthians* (London: Epworth, 1962) 64 (cf. Weizsäcker, *Anfänge*, 33: "Frucht einer krankhaften

who argue for Stoic or Cynic influence on 1 Corinthians 7. Their work, as we saw, is both imprecise, in that it poorly represents Stoic and Cynic discussions on marriage, and incomplete, in that it deals with only small sections of Paul's discussion. The remainder of this chapter was then devoted to reviewing the many and diverse theories that interpret 1 Corinthians 7 in light of a theology of sexual asceticism. These theories argue for influences from Hellenistic Judaism or first-century Christianity, or from attitudes toward sexuality similar to what we find in the later church. In all, none of them stands out as particularly convincing, the reason for this being twofold. First, none of the authors we have examined offers any decisive comparative material. Texts from Philo, Wisdom, or Apuleius, Hellenistic catalogs of vices, reports of gnostic groups, and possible second-century examples of *subintroductae* all fall short of providing close parallels to the celibacy attested in 1 Corinthians 7. Second, and rather surprisingly, no author deals extensively with the text of 1 Corinthians 7 itself. Apart from Niederwimmer's psychological approach to 1 Corinthians 7.1b, 26–31, and 32–5 – passages which he examines in isolation from one another – all of these theories stand or fall on the interpretation of only a few of the chapter's forty verses.

Approaching this from another direction, I would suggest that the common, fundamental fault of these latter theories is their assumption, stated or otherwise, that 1 Corinthians 7 is best comprehended within a "trajectory" of Judeo-Christian thinking on sexuality that leads directly into the asceticism of the later church. This text is seen either as the starting point of such a trajectory or as part of some vaguely defined continuum that began earlier with ascetic practices in Hellenistic Judaism or primitive Christianity. But attempting to make sense of the data in this way does justice neither to 1 Corinthians 7 nor to the comparative materials, for as our survey has made abundantly clear, theories of this sort have essentially neglected the information provided by the former and misinterpreted the latter.

In the pages that follow I will pursue the hypothesis that Paul's discussion of marriage and celibacy is best understood against the backdrop of Stoic and Cynic discourse on these topics. I will first

Schwärmerei"); Käsemann, "Primitive Christian Apocalyptic," 130–1; Hurd, *The Origin of 1 Corinthians*, 276–8; Schmithals, *Gnosticism in Corinth*, 235, 387; Seboldt, "Spiritual Marriage," 187–8; Chadwick, "'All Things to All Men'," 268 n. 1 (cf. Schmithals, *Gnosticism in Corinth*, 235 n. 159).

examine the entire range of Stoic and Cynic positions on the marriage question, and then I will demonstrate, point for point, how this material relates to specific statements in 1 Corinthians 7, and how Stoic and Cynic traditions have shaped the thinking of both Paul and the Corinthians. In the end I will have made clear that Paul's discussion cannot be fitted into any presumed trajectory of ascetic thought. Rather, his words draw on a reservoir of ideas about marriage and celibacy that is neither ascetic, nor Judeo-Christian in origin, nor confluent with much of the later church's thinking, but one in which the basic anxieties of Greek culture in the Hellenistic age lay restlessly submerged.

# 2

## THE STOIC–CYNIC MARRIAGE DEBATE

In the Hellenistic world there existed several conceptions of marriage and celibacy quite different from the ones advanced by the fathers of the church. In this chapter we will explore those which were commonly held by Stoics and Cynics, our goal being to establish an appropriate context for interpreting 1 Corinthians 7.

One reason scholars have not satisfactorily pursued a comparison between Stoic and Cynic discussions on marriage and Paul is the fragmentary state in which the former have come down to us. From the beginning these discussions seem to have been mostly an oral affair. It is telling, for example, that two of our most important witnesses, the moral lectures of Musonius Rufus and Epictetus, survive only as the class notes of devoted students.[1] What Stoics, Cynics, and their followers did manage to write down, moreover, received rough treatment at the hands of the church fathers. Willing conduits for the works of Aristotle, Plato, Philo, Josephus, and many other authors from antiquity, the fathers balked when it came to Stoic and Cynic writings on marriage. Preferring their own, Christian treatments of the subject, they tended either to adopt Stoic and Cynic ideas as their own or ignore them completely. They saw no reason to pass the works of these pagan moralists on to future generations. In consequence, it fell to a relatively obscure anthologist, Johannes Stobaeus, to preserve some of our most valuable sources. Stobaeus, however, offers only excerpts or "fragments," not complete texts, and much has been lost altogether.

The course of Stoic and Cynic thinking on marriage must, therefore, be reconstructed. We will begin this task with an overview of their respective positions – as I have pieced these together from the

---

[1] See Cora E. Lutz, "Musonius Rufus 'The Roman Socrates'," *Yale Classical Studies* 10 (New Haven: Yale University, 1947) 5–8; and Arrian's dedication to Lucius Gellius, which prefaces his publication of Epictetus' *Discourses*.

extant materials – for the purpose of identifying the central issues and tensions in their considerations of marriage. The bulk of this chapter will then be given over to an examination of the extant materials themselves. Here I will chart the development of Stoic and Cynic arguments for and against marriage, starting with antecedents in early Greek philosophy and ending several centuries later in the patristic period. This chronological survey will not only serve to demonstrate the long-standing popularity and extensive influence that Stoic and Cynic ideas on marriage had in the ancient world, but it will also provide a considerable amount of comparative material with which to interpret Paul. This interpretive venture will take place in chapters three and four.

## 1. Issues and dynamics in the Stoic–Cynic marriage debate

Stoic and Cynic discussions on marriage are available to us from the second century BCE to the second century CE.[2] While none of them

---

[2] The classic survey of the Stoic discussions, often referred to as the περὶ γάμου topos, is Karl Praechter, *Hierokles der Stoiker* (Leipzig: Dieterich, 1901) 121–50, as well as 4–6, 66–90. See also Ernestus Bickel, *Diatribe in Senecae philosophi fragmenta*, vol. 1: *Fragmenta de matrimonio* (Leipzig: B. G. Teubner, 1915); Yarbrough, *Not Like the Gentiles*, 33–46; Lise Henrion, "La conception de la Nature et du rôle de la Femme chez les philosophes cyniques et stoïciens" (Ph.D. diss., Université de Liège, 1942/43) 36–62, 125–81; Claude Vatin, *Recherches sur le mariage et la condition de la femme mariée à l'époque hellénistique*, Bibliothèque des Écoles Françaises d'Athènes et de Rome 216 (Paris: E. de Boccard, 1970) 17–40; O. Hense, "Zu Antipatros von Tarsos," *Rh. Mus.*, n.s. 73 (1920–24) 300–2; and Albrecht Oepke, "Ehe I," *RAC* 4 (1959) 651–5. For general discussions of precursors to the περὶ γάμου material in the classical and archaic periods see Marylin B. Arthur, "Early Greece: The Origins of the Western Attitude Toward Women," *Women in the Ancient World: The Arethusa Papers*, ed. John Peradotto and J. P. Sullivan, SUNY Series in Classical Studies (Albany: SUNY, 1984) 7–58; Sarah B. Pomeroy, *Goddesses, Whores, Wives, and Slaves: Women in Classical Antiquity* (New York: Schocken, 1975) 18–23, 33–8, 48–9; Yarbrough, *Not Like the Gentiles*, 32–3; Walter Erdmann, *Die Ehe im alten Griechenland*, Münchener Beiträge zur Papyrusforschung und antiken Rechtsgeschichte 20 (Munich: C. H. Beck, 1934) 139–47, 155–61; and W. K. Lacey, *The Family in Classical Greece*, Aspects of Greek and Roman Life (London: Thames and Hudson, 1968) 9, 176. See also Stobaeus 4.532–49 W.-H.

Scholars are correct in pointing to a relationship between the περὶ γάμου and the περὶ ἔρωτος literature: see Praechter, *Hierokles*, 148–50; Friedrich Wilhelm, "Zu Achilles Tatius," *Rh. Mus.*, n.s. 57 (1902) 55–75; Daniel Babut, *Plutarque et le Stoïcisme* (Paris: Presses Universitaires de France, 1969) 108–115. But this is taken to an extreme in Lisette Goessler, "Plutarchs Gedanken über die Ehe" (Ph.D. diss., Basel, 1962), e.g., 31–2. Michel Foucault, *The Care of the Self*, History of Sexuality 3 (New York: Pantheon, 1986) 191–277, is right to discuss Plutarch *Amatorius*, Achilles Tatius *Leucippe and Clitophon* 2.35–8, and [Lucian] *Amores* as a category of literature in its own right. See also Hubert Martin, Jr., "Amatorius

individually can be thought of as a "debate" in the strict sense of the word, two considerations allow us to treat them collectively as the products of a larger, unified debate, rather than simply the writings of two schools of thought quite isolated from one another. First, there are enough correspondences between the arguments used by Stoics and Cynics, respectively, to warrant the conclusion that these two camps stood consciously in dialogue with one another on the subject of marriage. And second, arguments identified specifically as "Cynic" were adopted by certain Stoics. This resulted in an *inner-*Stoic debate on marriage based on the opposition between "Stoic" and "Cynic" positions, a phenomenon we can document as early as Cicero, and which comes into full bloom in the *Discourses* of Epictetus.[3]

The starting point for this "Stoic–Cynic marriage debate," as we shall refer to it, was the recognition of a basic datum of free Greek society: marriage involved a man in weighty responsibilities. To begin with, marriage joined a man socially and financially to another human being, his wife. To a greater or lesser extent her cares and concerns now became his as well. But marriage also meant accepting the responsibilities of a father, a householder, and a citizen.[4] This is because marriage in the ancient world almost always resulted in the birth of children. In marrying, a man thus obligated himself to providing for a family. He would need to raise and educate children; he would need to establish a household (οἶκος, οἰκία), a financial endeavor that was the ancient world's ideal of a small business; and he would need to become active in the social, political, and economic life of his hometown, since a household could not survive without the political protection and economic environment provided by the Greek city-state (πόλις). The effect was cumulative: marriage was the equivalent of leaving the freedom of one's bachelor days behind and beginning the settled life of a responsible citizen with all its cares and concerns.

(Moralia 748E–771E)," *Plutarch's Ethical Writings and Early Christian Literature*, ed. Hans Dieter Betz, Studia ad Corpus Hellenisticum Novi Testamenti 4 (Leiden: E. J. Brill, 1978) 443–9.

Vettius Valens' περὶ γάμου κτλ. and ἄλλως περὶ γάμου μετὰ ὑποδείγματος (second century CE), in which the author speaks of his subject as ὁ περὶ γάμου τόπος (bk. 2, chap. 37; 114.22, 24 Kroll), has nothing to do with the περὶ γάμου literature; the same applies to the fifth chap. of Maximus Astrologus' περὶ καταρχῶν (second century CE or later), also entitled περὶ γάμου.

[3] See the remarks in Praechter, *Hierokles*, 69, and the discussion below.
[4] Cf. Michel Foucault, *The Use of Pleasure*, History of Sexuality 2 (New York: Pantheon, 1985) 150–1.

There were, to be sure, various means by which a married man in antiquity could avoid children and thereby alleviate some of the responsibilities of married life. These included abortion, exposure, and several forms of contraception.[5] But aside from the fact that abortion and exposure were dangerous or otherwise unattractive, and contraceptives were unreliable, Stoics and Cynics alike ruled out the option of family planning on the basis that it was "contrary to nature."[6] Thus, Antipater of Tarsus, [Ocellus Lucanus], Musonius Rufus, and Hierocles the Stoic implicitly condemn all of these methods with their insistence that the goal of sexual intercourse was the producing of children; and Musonius condemns abortion and exposure outright. Hierocles, moreover, speaks of a wife being "worn out by pregnancies"; Dio Chrysostom maintains in a treatise on household management that "the begetting of children is a work of necessity"; and in the *Cynic Epistles* the birth of a child is referred to as "what had to come."[7] The inevitability of raising children is emphasized among these authors, finally, by the set phrase "marrying and having children," which recurs

[5] In general, see Emiel Eyben, "Family Planning in Graeco-Roman Antiquity," *Ancient Society* 11/12 (1980–81) 5–82; and David Michael Feldman, *Birth Control in Jewish Law* (New York: New York University Press/London: University of London Press, 1968). On contraception, see also John T. Noonan, Jr., *Contraception: A History of Its Treatment by the Catholic Theologians and Canonists*, rev. edn. (Cambridge: Harvard University Press, 1965); M. K. Hopkins, "Contraception in the Roman Empire," *Comparative Studies in Society and History* 8 (1965) 124–51; Norman Edwin Himes, *Medical History of Contraception* (London: Geo. Allen and Unwin/Baltimore: Williams and Wilkins, 1936; repr. New York: Gamut, 1963). On abortion, see also R. Crahay, "Les moralistes anciens et l'avortement," *L'Antiquité Classique* 10 (1941) 9–23; P. A. Brunt, *Italian Manpower: 225 BC–AD 14* (Oxford: Clarendon Press, 1971) 147–8; and J. H. Waszink, "Abtreibung," *RAC* 1 (1950) 55–60. On exposure, see also John Boswell, *The Kindness of Strangers: The Abandonment of Children in Western Europe from Late Antiquity to the Renaissance* (New York: Pantheon, 1988) 53–179; Averil Cameron, "The Exposure of Children and Greek Ethics," *Classical Review* 46 (1932) 105–114; and W. W. Tarn and G. T. Griffith, *Hellenistic Civilization*, 3rd edn. (London: Edward Arnold, 1959) 100–4 (inscriptional evidence).
[6] See, e.g., Paul Veyne, "La famille et l'amour sous le Haut-Empire romain," *Annales: Économies, Sociétés, Civilisations* 33 (1978) 48–9.
[7] Hierocles 63.26 von Arnim (in Stobaeus 5.699.9–10 W.-H.), τετρυμένη κυοφορίαις – cf. Aline Rousselle, *Porneia: On Desire and the Body in Antiquity* (New York: Basil Blackwell, 1988) 34–5, 39; Dio Chrys. *frag.* 9 Cohoon-Crosby (vol. 5), τὸ μὲν γὰρ τίκτειν ἀνάγκης ἐστὶν ἔργον; *Cynic Epistle of Crates* 33 (82.20 Malherbe), ὅπερ ἐχρῆν ἥκειν; on Musonius, see below, p. 79.

throughout their discussions,[8] often as a synonym for "marrying."[9]

Marriage and all that it implied thus spelled responsibility in the eyes of both Stoics and Cynics, and it is around this realization that their discussions on marriage revolve. The basic question they asked was: Should the intelligent, informed, morally upright person take on such responsibility? They often framed this question in terms of what the wise man would do, since the *sophos*, acting on the basis of an absolutely good disposition, was seen as the model for human behavior. The Stoics based their answer on the belief that the universe was governed by a divine principle, and that it was not only in a man's best interests to conduct his life in harmony with this principle, but he was morally obligated to do so. From this they argued in favor of marriage by pointing out that various gods patronized marriage, or that the Creator, or nature, seen as a divine entity, had decreed that men and women should come together in marriage for the purpose of populating and re-populating the earth. The real backbone of the Stoic discussions, however, was provided by two more complex lines of argumentation. Although these were often used in conjunction with one another, they were nonetheless distinct and, at times, even in conflict with each other.

The first of these focused on the presumed structure of the universe, or *kosmos*, and the place of marriage within it, this structure reflecting the divine will, variously, of nature, the Creator, God, or "the gods." The *kosmos*, the Stoics contended, consisted of a plurality of city-states, for men were designed by nature to be political beings and their existence – that is, their meaningful, civilized existence – required that they organize themselves into city-states. These city-states, in turn, consisted of citizens organized into a plurality of households; and households, finally, had their beginnings in the union of men and women in marriage. From this understanding of the structure of the *kosmos*, the Stoics argued that marriage was indispensable. Not only did it hold a key position in the divine plan, but more than any other element, it insured the future of the whole. It was only through marriage that succeeding

---

[8] Preachter, *Hierokles*, 67, notes that these terms are "readily joined"; see, e.g., Hierocles 55.22 v.A. (Stob. 4.603.9 W.-H.); Epict. *Diss.* 3.22.67, 68; D.L. 6.16; 7.121; cf. 10.119.

[9] E.g., Musonius *frag.* 14.96.3–6 L. (76.11–14 H.). Theon *Progymnasmata* 120.30 Spengel, by contrast, speaks simply of "having children" as an abbreviation for marrying and having children. See my note to this text in Will Deming, "Paul on Marriage and Celibacy: The Hellenistic Background of 1 Corinthians 7" (Ph.D. diss., University of Chicago, 1991) 363.

generations of householders could arise, guaranteeing a continuous supply of responsible citizens, and thus insuring the future of the city-states and of the *kosmos*.[10] In origin this line of argumentation draws on Aristotelian thought, a fact made clear by the first book of Aristotle's *Politics*. Here Aristotle also assumes a progression from marriages to households to city-states, insisting that this is the work of nature.[11] In advancing this schema he even parts company with his teacher Plato, who had characterized the household as a kind of miniature city-state. The household, Aristotle stresses, is an entity in its own right; it is the step in the natural progression that allows one to see the dependence of the city-state on the institution of marriage.[12] In adopting this vision of human existence, the Stoics made an important change. Whereas Aristotle had understood nature as that which prompted a thing to realize its full, inherent potential, the Stoics went a step further, identifying nature as a divine principle. As A. A. Long explains:

> Aristotle does not conceive nature as a rational agent; nature for him is that factor within each individual organism which accounts for its efforts to perfect itself. Though Aristotle sometimes speaks of nature as "divine" he cannot in his mature system identify God and nature, since God is not "in the world" ... The Stoics, by setting Nature/God within the world, have united under a single

[10] See Hense, "Zu Antipatros," 299, and the discussion below.
[11] Aristotle *Politics* 1.1252a 17–1253a 39; cf. *Nicomachean Ethics* 8.1162a 16–19; and Arius Didymus in Stobaeus 2.147.26–150.13 W.-H., translated in David Balch, "Household Codes," *Greco-Roman Literature and the New Testament: Selected Forms and Genres*, ed. David E. Aune, SBLSBS 21 (Atlanta: Scholars, 1988) 41–4. See also R. G. Mulgan, *Aristotle's Political Theory: An Introduction for Students of Political Theory* (Oxford: Clarendon Press, 1977) 18–25, 30–8, 140–1; Manfred Riedel, *Metaphysik und Metapolitik: Studien zu Aristoteles und zur politischen Sprache der neuzeitlichen Philosophie* (Frankfort: Suhrkamp, 1975) 73–80; and Elisabeth Schüssler Fiorenza, *Bread Not Stone: The Challenge of Feminist Biblical Interpretation* (Boston: Beacon, 1984) 73: "Aristotle, in contrast to the Sophists, stressed that the patriarchal relationships in household and city ... are based not on social convention but on 'nature.' He, therefore, insisted that the discussion of political ethics and household management begin with marriage."
[12] Arist. *Pol.* 1.1252a 7–16; 2.1260b 36–1261a 29. See Günther Bien, *Die Grundlegung der politischen Philosophie bei Aristoteles*, 3rd edn. (Freiburg/Munich: Karl Alber, 1985) 303–13; Erwin R. Goodenough, *The Politics of Philo Judaeus: Practice and Theory* (New Haven: Yale University Press, 1938) 49 n. 28; and Mulgan, *Aristotle's Political Theory*, 21: "[Aristotle] gives especial emphasis to the naturalness of the household as if this were the most solid part of the argument."

principle functions which Aristotle kept apart. Stoic Nature
resembles the Aristotelian Prime Mover in being a rational
agent which is the ultimate cause of all things.[13]

The upshot of this Stoic innovation was that it put a moral edge on
Aristotle's schema. The Stoics could now set the city-state in a
divine *kosmos* and argue that marriages, households, and city-states
not only came about naturally, but in fact *ought* to come about.[14] As
for marriage in particular, they maintained that any man who
respected the divine will would count it as his moral duty to marry
and have children.

The second major line of argumentation used by the Stoics was
more indigenous to their own school of philosophy, deriving from
their work in systematic ethics. For this reason it was also more
cosmopolitan, for instead of envisioning the *kosmos* primarily as a
collection of individual city-states, it stressed that the *kosmos* itself
was a grand city-state or "cosmopolis."[15] This difference in emphasis meant that the actions of an individual were assigned ethical
value first in terms of their impact directly on the whole, rather than
through the intermediary of the city-state. The starting point for this
second line of argumentation was the Stoics' assumption that virtue
(ἀρετή) was the sole requisite for happiness and well-being (εὐδαι-
μονία), and that a person could become virtuous through actions
done in accordance with nature. These they termed "preferred"
(προηγούμενον) and "fitting" (καθῆκον) actions. Actions absolutely in accordance with nature, they reasoned, were virtuous in

[13] A. A. Long, *Hellenistic Philosophy: Stoics, Epicureans, Sceptics*, 2nd edn.
(Berkeley: University of California Press, 1986) 151–2. See also F. H. Sandbach,
*Aristotle and the Stoics*, Cambridge Philological Society, suppl. 10 (Cambridge:
Cambridge Philological Society, 1985) 38–40; and Maximilian Forschner, *Die stoische Ethik: Über den Zusammenhang von Natur-, Sprach- und Moralphilosophie im
altstoischen System* (Stuttgart: Klett-Cotta, 1981) 17–24.
[14] Regarding the absence of this moral edge in Aristotle himself, see D. W.
Hamlyn, *A History of Western Philosophy* (Harmondsworth: Penguin, 1987) 74: "On
certain conceptions of morality there is little about morality in what Aristotle has to
say. He is simply clear that there is such a thing as the good life in some sense of those
words and that a man is thought εὐδαιμῶν, happy, to the extent that he attains it."
[15] On the Stoic idea *oikeiōsis*, which denoted the natural affinity between human
beings in this world community, see S. G. Pembroke, "Oikeiōsis," *Problems in
Stoicism*, ed. A. A. Long (London: University of London Athlone Press, 1971)
114–49; Margherita Isnardi Parente, "Ierocle Stoico: Oikeiosis e doveri sociali,"
*ANRW* 2.36.3 (1989) 2201–26; and Troels Engberg-Pedersen, *The Stoic Theory of
Oikeiosis: Moral Development and Social Interaction in Early Stoic Philosophy*,
Studies in Hellenistic Civilization 2 (Aarhus: Aarhus University Press, 1991). All
three authors see the possibility of tracing this idea back into the early Stoa.

themselves, while those simply in accordance with nature were natural advantages in the quest for virtue. Actions that were contrary to nature, on the other hand, were either directly in opposition to virtue or represented natural disadvantages, and were to be avoided. Beyond this basic dichotomy the Stoics reasoned further that some actions classified as preferred and fitting – namely, those that were simply in accordance with nature – could also be disadvantageous if performed under adverse circumstances. These, which in themselves were morally neither good nor bad, they called "intermediate" (μέσον) and "indifferent" (ἀδιάφορον) actions.[16] It is into this category, ultimately, that marriage falls, with the consequence that Stoics could argue that marriage, being in accordance with nature, was incumbent upon a man unless special circumstances stood in his way.

These, then, were the two basic lines of argumentation employed by the Stoics in their discussions of marriage. What they make clear is that Stoics did not evaluate marriage as an entity in itself, but as an important component in a larger system of morality. The act of marrying was a sign of allegiance to a higher metaphysical order; it was the equivalent of acquiescing to the divine will. We may gain some insight into why the Stoics took such an aggressive position if we now inquire into the historical impetus that gave rise to their discussions, for, in fact, the Stoic marriage discussions reflect one of the great issues that faced intellectuals in the Hellenistic period, namely, whether the Greek city-state could continue as the social, economic, and political center of a person's life.

From the time of Alexander the Great's conquests near the end of the fourth century, the Greek city-state lost ground as an important political unit. It was obliged to accept an ever diminishing role in the minds of its citizens due to the attention now focused on the successive empires of Alexander, his generals, and finally Rome. The gradual disappearance of local autonomous rule from the political map of Greece, and the tendency toward cosmopolitan thinking, whereby a man considered himself a citizen of the world rather than of any one city-state, were both the cause and the end of this development. As a consequence of these dramatic changes, many intellectuals of the time feared that citizens would find partici-

---

[16] On these aspects of Stoic ethics see Long, *Hellenistic Philosophy*, 179, 187, 189–205, 213–16; and I. G. Kidd, "Stoic Intermediates and the End for Man," *Problems in Stoicism*, ed. A. A. Long (London: University of London Athlone Press, 1971) 150–72.

58    *The Stoic–Cynic marriage debate*

pation in local politics and the responsibility associated with establishing a household and raising future generations of citizens increasingly unattractive, and would abandon their loyalty to the city-states altogether.[17] Several even maintained that the new cosmopolitan spirit proved the underlying cause of a severe depopulation of the Greek city-states.[18] As proof they pointed to the fact that authorities in some areas had found it necessary to pass measures requiring citizens to marry and have children under penalty of law.[19]

[17] See Pomeroy, *Goddesses*, 120; Otto Kiefer, *Sexual Life in Ancient Rome* (London: George Routledge and Sons, 1938) 35; Paul Veyne, "The Roman Empire," *A History of Private Life*, vol. 1: *From Pagan Rome to Byzantium*, ed. Paul Veyne (Cambridge: Harvard University Belknap Press, 1987) 38; and Gustave Glotz, *The Greek City and its Institutions* (New York: Alfred A. Knopf, 1951; repr., Ann Arbor: University Microfilms, 1965) 295–6 (cited by Richard J. Devine, "Holy Virginity: A study of the New Testament Teaching on Virginity and Celibacy" [Ph.D. diss., University of Fribourg, 1964] 70); Yarbrough, *Not Like the Gentiles*, 36–7, 41–6, 60; Max Pohlenz, *Freedom in Greek Life and Thought: The History of an Ideal* (Dordrecht, Holland: D. Reidel/New York: Humanities Press, 1966) 116–19; Eduard Zeller, *Die Philosophie der Griechen in ihrer geschichtlichen Entwicklung*, 5th edn. (Leipzig: Fues [O. R. Reisland], 1922/23) 3.1.1–22, 283–92; Long, *Hellenistic Philosophy*, 3–4; Emile Bréhier, *Chrysippe* (Paris: Félix Alcan, 1910) 262–70; Tomas Hägg, *The Novel in Antiquity* (Berkeley: University of California Press, 1983) 88–90, who traces this development through epic, tragedy, and the novel; Pál Csillag, *The Augustan Laws on Family Relations* (Budapest: Akadémiai Kiadó, 1976) 39–40; and Wayne A. Meeks, *The Moral World of the First Christians*, Library of Early Christianity (Philadelphia: Westminster, 1986) 26–31.

[18] The most famous example is perhaps Polybius 36.17. On this passage see Praechter, *Hierokles*, 84–6. See also L. P. Wilkinson, *Classical Attitudes to Modern Issues: Population and Family Planning, Women's Liberation, Nudism in Deed and Word, Homosexuality* (London: William Kimber, 1978) 22; Martin P. Nilsson, *Geschichte der griechischen Religion*, Handbuch der Altertumswissenschaft 5.2, 2nd edn. (Munich: C. H. Beck, 1961) 2.310–11; Pierre Salmon, *Population et dépopulation dans l'Empire romain*, Collection Latomus 137 (Brussels: Latomus, 1974); Vatin, *Recherches*, 228–40; Tarn and Griffith, *Hellenistic Civilization*, 100–4; Brunt, *Italian Manpower*, esp. 131–55; and Cameron, "Exposure of Children," 113.

[19] On the marriage laws enacted by Augustus Caesar, the *Lex Iulia de adulteriis* and the *Lex Iulia de maritandis ordinibus* (18 BCE), and the *Lex Papia Poppaea* (9 CE), see Csillag, *Augustan Laws*, 24–5; Brunt, *Italian Manpower*, 558–66; James A. Field, Jr., "The Purpose of the Lex Iulia et Papia Poppaea," *Classical Journal* 40 (1944/45) 398–416; Michel Humbert, *Le remariage á Rome: Étude d'histoire juridique et sociale*, Università di Roma: Pubblicazioni dell' Istituto di diritto Romano e dei diritti dell' oriente mediterraneo 44 (Milan: A. Giuffrè, 1972) 138–80; Leo Ferrero Raditsa, "Augustus' Legislation Concerning Marriage, Procreation, Love Affairs and Adultery," *ANRW* 2.13 (1980) 278–339; Richard I. Frank, "Augustus' Legislation on Marriage and Children," *California Studies in Classical Antiquity* 8 (1975) 41–52; Max Kaser, *Das römische Privatrecht*, vol. 1: *Das altrömische, das vorklassische und klassische Recht*, Handbuch der Altertumswissenschaft: Rechtsgeschichte des Altertums 10.3.3.1, 2nd edn. (Munich: C. H. Beck, 1971) 318–21, cf. 328–9; Diana E. E. Kleiner, "The Great Friezes of the Ara Pacis Augustae: Greek Sources, Roman

It is in this traditionalist reaction to the changing social and political climate of the Hellenistic world that the Stoic marriage discussions have their place.[20] Given the various social responsibilities that marriage implied in the ancient world, the Stoics' support of marriage was the equivalent of promoting active involvement in the life of the city-state. This is evident particularly in their insistence that marriage was linked via the household to the city-state, and that the *kosmos*, that entity for which all actions are ultimately performed, was no less than the sum total of all city-states.[21] What was really at stake in their "marriage discussions," in other words, was not marriage *per se*, but the promotion of a traditional view of human society.[22] In posing the question of whether a man should

Derivatives, and Augustan Social Policy," *Mélanges de l'École Française de Rome: Antiquité* 90 (1978) 772–6, 778–81; and J. P. verse D. Balsdon, *Life and Leisure in Ancient Rome* (New York: McGraw Hill, 1969) 82–90.

On the precursors of Augustus' marriage laws, see Field, "The Purpose," 404–5; Cicero *Laws* 3.3.7 (cf. *Pro Marcello* 23, and *Pro Caelio* 18.42); Dionysius of Halicarnassus *Roman Antiquities* 2.15 and 9.22.2; Plutarch *Vitae* 129D-E (*Camillus*); 451B-C (*Lysander*); Gellius *Attic Nights* 1.6.1–2; Suetonius *Augustus* 89; and Dio Cassius *Roman History* 56.6.4.

[20] Similarly, Adolf Bonhöffer, *Die Ethik des Stoikers Epictet* (Stuttgart: Ferdinand Enke, 1894; repr., Stuttgart-Bad Connstatt: Friedrich Frommann, 1968) 87 describes the high value the Stoics placed on marriage as part of their "conservative perspective" on the communal nature of human beings. See also Brent D. Shaw, "The Divine Economy: Stoicism as Ideology," *Latomus* 44 (1985) 16–54; Long, *Hellenistic Philosophy*, 3; and the older treatment in André Baudrillart, *Moeurs païennes, moeurs crétiennes*, vol. 1: *La famille dans l'antiquité païenne et aux premiers siècles du christianisme* (Paris: Bloud et Gay, 1929) 63–70.

[21] Cf. Meeks, *Moral World*, 61: "It seems to us in retrospect that the fundamental issue of the [Hellenistic] times must have been how the humane values achieved in the classical polis and the Roman Republic could be made effective in the vastly enlarged and transformed political and social world of the empire"; and Lacey, *The Family*, 9. On the importance of the city-state in Stoic ethical theory see Max Pohlenz, *Die Stoa: Geschichte einer geistigen Bewegung*, 2nd edn. (Göttingen: Vandenhoeck und Ruprecht, 1959) 1.139–40, 165–6; Zeller, *Philosophie der Griechen*, 3.1.300–2; Arnold Ehrhardt, *Politische Metaphysik von Solon bis Augustin*, vol. 1: *Die Gottesstadt der Griechen und Römer* (Tübingen: J. C. B. Mohr, 1959), 180–5; and Eleuterio Elorduy, *Die Sozialphilosophie der Stoa*, Philologus suppl. 28/3 (Leipzig: Dieterich, 1936) 135–9. Cf. Arthur W. H. Adkins, *Merit and Responsibility: A Study in Greek Values* (Oxford: Oxford University Press, 1960) 197, 226–32, 348–51.

[22] These discussions are thus correctly understood as "propaganda" for a larger apologetic – see Emiel Eyben, "De latere Stoa over het huwelijk," *Hermeneus: Tijdschrift voor antieke Cultuur* 50 (1978) 21; cf. Johannes Stelzenberger, *Die Beziehungen der frühchristlichen Sittenlehre zur Ethik der Stoa* (Munich: Max Hueber, 1933) 440–1 and n. 7; and Holger Thesleff, *An Introduction to the Pythagorean Writings of the Hellenistic Period*, Acta Academiae Aboensis, Humaniora 24/3 (Åbo, Finland: Åbo Akademi, 1961) 72. The larger apologetic is aptly brought out by Hans Jonas' description of Stoic popular philosophy in the time of the Empire:

"To play one's part" – that figure of speech on which Stoic ethics dwells so much –

take on the responsibilities of marriage, the Stoics were actually asking a much more profound question: should a man affirm the traditional Greek understanding of human society and consequently become involved in the life of his city-state, beginning with marriage, procreation, and the establishment of a household?[23]

Turning now to the Cynic side of the marriage debate, we observe that while the Stoics met this question with an affirmative response, the Cynics answered with an abusive no. Theirs, too, was a position fostered by the social and political developments of the Hellenistic age, but in contrast to the traditionalism of the Stoics, the Cynics denied the importance of the Greek city-states, promoting instead a radical cosmopolitanism. They held that the social structures of marriage, household, and city-state had their origin in mere human convention, not divine purpose, and in their place they demanded individualism and self-sufficiency.[24]

At the center of their philosophy was the idea of freedom, both freedom for something and freedom from something. It was freedom *for* the pursuit of philosophy, since they believed that it was only through living a life guided by philosophy that an individual could achieve the ultimate goal of happiness and well-being. Indeed, the Cynics considered philosophy a full-time profession, on the order of a "calling," and consequently insisted on devoting all of their "free time" (σχολή) to it – that is, all of the time not taken up with providing for the necessities of life. This meant that the Cynic idea of freedom necessarily also included freedom *from* the responsibilities of conventional existence: "from all care about food, clothing,

unwittingly reveals the fictitious element in the construction ... In the phrase of playing one's part there is a bravado that hides a deeper, if proud, resignation ... To be sure, the strained fervor by which man's integration in the whole was maintained, through his alleged affinity to it, was the means of reserving the dignity of man and thereby of saving a sanction for a positive morality. This fervor, succeeding that which had formerly been inspired by the ideal of civic virtue, represented a heroic attempt on the part of intellectuals to carry over the life-sustaining force of that ideal into fundamentally changed conditions. But the new atomized masses of the Empire, who had never shared in that noble tradition of *areté*, might react very differently to a situation in which they found themselves passively involved: a situation in which the part was insignificant to the whole, and the whole alien to the parts. [*The Gnostic Religion*, 2nd edn. (Boston: Beacon, 1963) 249.]

[23] Veyne, "La famille," 39, says of the Stoics in the first century CE, "one no longer forms wise men, one confirms and conforms men in their role as good citizens." Cf. Yarbrough, *Not Like the Gentiles*, 41–6.

[24] I. G. Kidd, "Cynics," *Encyclopedia of Philosophy* (ed. Paul Edwards) 2 (1967) 284–5; cf. Zeller, *Philosophie der Griechen*, 2.1.324–6; 3.1.306–7.

house, home, marriage, children, etc.; freedom from all ties which morality, law, state, and community life in general may put upon the individual."[25] For this reason they resolutely excluded marriage from their sphere of moral concern. The marriage and all that it implied – the duties of husband, father, householder, and citizen – represented for the Cynics a burden of responsibility that involved them in a vision of the world for which they had no sympathy, and reduced the time available to them for the practice of their true profession, the philosophical life.

In sum, the Stoic–Cynic marriage debate was essentially a forum for defining an individual's allegiances to a higher cause. It pitted Stoic dedication to traditional Greek life in the city-state against the Cynic calling to the philosophical life. One could even say that marriage became the central issue in this debate unwittingly, due to the claims it made on an individual regarding one of these two causes, for no participant in the debate ever evaluates marriage solely on its own merits.[26]

Having now defined the basic issues of the Stoic–Cynic marriage debate, let us proceed to a chronological examination of the evidence from antiquity. The first period we will treat stretches from the middle of the fifth century to the beginning of the third century BCE. This will bring us up to the start of the marriage debate, affording us glimpses of several of its antecedents.

## 2. The fifth to the third century BCE

### Anaxagoras, Antiphon, Democritus

The first examples we have of the conflict that lies at the heart of the Stoic–Cynic marriage debate come from the middle of the fifth

[25] Ragnar Höistad, "Cynic Hero and Cynic King: Studies in the Cynic Conception of Man" (Inaugural diss., Uppsala, 1948) 15. See also Rudolf Helm, "Kynismus," *PW* 12.1, half-vol. 23 (1924) 10–12, although he does not adequately distinguish between Epictetus and the Cynics.

[26] Musonius' eulogy of marriage in *frag.* 13A, *What is the Chief Aspect of Marriage?*, is often misunderstood in this respect. Its proper context, as *frag.* 13B and the similar discussions in Antipater and Hierocles indicate, is the Stoic understanding of marriage as a natural advantage for the wise man in his effort to live in accord with nature. Kurt Deißner, *Das Idealbild des stoischen Weisen: Rede anläßlich der Reichsgründungsfeier der Universität Greifswald am 18. Januar 1930*, Greifswalder Universitätsreden 24 (Greifswald: L. Bamberg, 1930) 10–11, is quite correct in seeing this "deepest and most noble appraisal of marriage" as stemming from the Stoics' sense of duty toward the *kosmos*.

century. If we can believe the later accounts, it is at this time that the philosopher Anaxagoras (ca. 500–ca. 428 BCE) gave up his patrimony – and with it presumably his marriage – and abandoned all concern for his city-state in order to devote his energies to the study of physical theory.[27] As Plutarch describes it, he chose the life of a theoretical philosopher over that of a man active in the affairs of his city-state.[28] Similarly, two other philosophers in this early period criticize the constraints of married life. Antiphon of Athens, an early fifth-century sophist, complains of the manifold burdens brought on by a wife and children in his treatise *On Harmony*; and the atomist Democritus (b. ca. 470 BCE) advises against having children due to the trouble of providing for them.[29] Later reports have it that Democritus, like Anaxagoras, abandoned both private and public responsibilities in order to pursue philosophy.[30]

### Xenophon

Anaxagoras, Antiphon, and Democritus are examples of an attitude that Cynic authors would later espouse. A very different viewpoint is presented in the first half of the fourth century by the philosopher and statesman Xenophon (ca. 430–ca. 354 BCE). In his treatise *Household Management*, in a dialogue between Socrates and the successful, if somewhat childlike, householder Ischomachus, Xenophon outlines the purpose of marriage, the instruction

---

[27] D.L. 2.7.
[28] Plut. *Vit.* 162B-D (*Pericles*), θεωρητικοῦ φιλοσόφου βίος versus πολιτικοῦ. For a popular treatment of the idea of philosophical retirement among the Greeks see Festugière, *Personal Religion*, 53–67.
[29] Antiphon *frag.* 49 (87 B49 Diels-Kranz); Democritus *frags.* 275–6 (68 B275–6 D.-K.) and *frag.* 170 (68 A170 D.-K.). On these authors see W. K. C. Guthrie, *A History of Greek Philosophy*, vol. 3: *The Fifth-Century Enlightenment* (Cambridge: Cambridge University Press, 1969) 287 n. 3; 288–9, and 491–2.
[30] Cicero *Tusculan Disputations* 5.39.115; Horace *Epistle* 1.12.12; Philo *De vita contemp.* 14. See also the story of the philosopher Epaminondas (late fifth century–362 BCE), who forgoes marriage for philosophy and the single life due to poverty: Plutarch *Vit.* 279E-F (*Pelopidas*); cf. Epict. *Diss.* 3.22.78. Stobaeus preserves a tradition in which Epaminondas is questioned on the advantage of not marrying and having children. He responds, "Not hesitating to die for the fatherland" (Stob. 4.520.19–22 W.-H.). Foucault, *Care of the Self*, 156, speaks of the "incompatibility between the goal of philosophy (the care of one's own soul, the mastery of one's passion, the search for peace of mind) and what was traditionally described as the agitation and troubles of married life," as being a perennial problem in Greek philosophy.

of one's wife, and the proper division of labor within the house-hold.[31] Far from being a burdensome and time consuming responsibility, marriage is depicted here as that which affords Ischomachus his life of leisure. Because he has a wife adept at household management he is able to "enjoy free time" (σχολάζειν),[32] which he spends in the pursuit of activities outside the home, such as civic affairs and philosophy. It is this attitude toward a wife and household that most Stoics would promote, evincing a similar interest in the details of establishing and managing households.[33]

### Early Cynics

About the time of Xenophon's *Household Management* we find evidence for the first Cynic positions on marriage, although in this early period there is no consensus. The reputed founder of the movement, Antisthenes (ca. 445–ca. 360 BCE), argued in favor of marriage, citing the need for men to procreate.[34] This is similar to one of the arguments used in the later Stoic discussions, and it may be that the contents of Antisthenes' treatise *On Procreation, or on Marriage*, of which only the title survives, resembled these. In support of this conjecture, his treatise on household management,

---

[31] Xenophon *Oeconomicus* 7.4–9.19. See the discussion in Foucault, *Use of Pleasure*, 152–65.
[32] Xen. *Oec.* 7.1.
[33] Some Stoics even show familiarity with Xenophon's dialogue, directly or otherwise – see Antipater *SVF* 3.256.2–17 von Arnim (Stob. 4.509.19–510.16 W.-H.); and Praechter, *Hierokles*, 122 n. 2 (re: Hierocles and Musonius). In the first century BCE Xenophon's *Oec.* was made available in Latin by Cicero (*De officiis* 2.24.87).
On the relation between the περὶ γάμου literature and the οἰκονομικός literature see Albrecht Dihle, "Ethik," *RAC* 6 (1966) 657; Peter Fiedler, "Haustafel," *RAC* 13 (1986) 1067; Friedrich Wilhelm, "Die Oeconomica der Neopythagoreer Bryson, Kallikratidas, Periktione, Phintys," *Rh. Mus.* 70 (1915) 162–4, cf. 182, 222; and Klaus Thraede, "Ärger mit der Freiheit," *"Freunde in Christus werden ...,"* ed. Gerta Scharffenort and Klaus Thraede (Gelnhausen: Burckhardthaus, 1977) 67, cf. 63. The best survey and discussion of the οἰκονομικός literature is now Ernst Dassmann and Georg Schöllgen, "Haus II (Hausgemeinschaft)," *RAC* 13 (1986) 801–906. Although the authors intend to be comprehensive (816), they overlook certain texts. The most obvious omission is [Arist.] *Oeconomica* 3; for others, see the discussion below. On the history of the *topos* περὶ οἰκονομίας see also David L. Balch, *Let Wives Be Submissive: The Domestic Code in I Peter*, SBLMS 26 (Chico, Calif.: Scholars, 1981) 23–62.
[34] D.L. 6.11. See the discussion in J. M. Rist, *Stoic Philosophy* (Cambridge: Cambridge University Press, 1969) 56–7.

also lost, seems to indicate his concern for the efficient operation of the business end of marriage.[35]

A position close to that taken by the later Cynics was championed by Antisthenes' contemporary and the movement's most colorful figure, Diogenes of Sinope (ca. 400–ca. 325 BCE). Diogenes rejected the duties of a citizen and took a stand against conventional marriage, offering two alternatives. He suggested that men take joint responsibility over several women and their children, and define marriage simply as intercourse between the "man who persuades" and the "women who is persuaded";[36] and he also appears to have advocated the practice of masturbation in place of all forms of sexuality that demanded a partner,[37] being accredited with the remark that sexual love is "an activity of those who have time to waste" (τὸν ἔρωτα σχολαζόντων ἀσχολίαν).[38] Finally, a third Cynic of this period, Diogenes' disciple Crates (ca. 365–ca. 285 BCE), may have stood somewhere between Antisthenes and Diogenes on the marriage issue, at least as far as his personal life was concerned. While he married, it was no marriage in the conventional sense, for though he raised a daughter, he seems neither to have founded a household nor carried out the duties of a citizen, from which, as a foreigner, he was excluded in any case.[39]

## The Academy, the Peripatetics, and Epicurus

Neither Plato (ca. 429–347 BCE) nor his student Aristotle (384–322 BCE) seems to have given much credence to the notion of an inevitable conflict between the duties of a married man and the call of a philosopher, although at one point Plato demands that the philosopher–guardians of his ideal state hold their wives in

---

[35] D.L. 6.16, περὶ παιδοποιίας ἢ περὶ γάμου, and περὶ νίκης οἰκονομικός. The latter, rather odd name is evidently not (?) to be separated into περὶ νίκης (*On Victory*) and οἰκονομικός (*Household Management*) – see Fernanda Decleva Caizzi, ed., *Antisthenis Fragmenta*, Testi e Documenti per lo Studio dell'Antichitá 13 (Milan: Istituto Editoriale Cisalpino, 1966) 81.

[36] D.L. 6.72.

[37] See Zeller, *Philosophie der Griechen*, 2.1.322–3.

[38] D.L. 6.51. See also Rist, *Stoic Philosophy* (Cambridge: Cambridge University Press, 1969) 59–61; and cf. D.L. 6.54. It may be noted here that no Cynic or Stoic author advocating celibacy explicitly demanded abstinence from all forms of sexual activity.

[39] See Rist, *Stoic Philosophy*, 61–2.

common, similar to what Diogenes suggested.[40] Both do, however, recognize the necessity of marriage for the prosperity of the city-state.[41] Further, Aristotle and another of Plato's students, Xenocrates, who headed the Academy from 339–314 BCE, wrote on the topic of household management,[42] and Aristotle seems to have addressed several related topics in other tractates as well.[43]

The situation changes significantly with two of Aristotle's students, Theophrastus (ca. 370–285 BCE) and his contemporary Dicaearchus, who championed the "theoretical" and the "practical" life, respectively.[44] In these authors we are already able to make out the basic polarities that characterized the later Stoic–Cynic debate.[45] Similar to the later Cynic position, Theophrastus held that married life and philosophy were incompatible with one another due to the cares and responsibilities imposed on a married man by his wife. He also criticized the notions that a wife was the best of all helpers and companions, and that marriage was necessitated by the need to raise

[40] E.g., Plato *Republic* 5.449A-465C. See Mulgan, *Aristotle's Political Theory*, 38; Susan Moller Okin, *Women in Western Political Thought* (Princeton: Princeton University Press, 1979) 31–45; and cf. *Phaedo* 66B; *Theaetetus* 172C-76A. On Aristotle see Adkins, *Merit and Responsibility*, 347; on Plato's teacher Socrates see Zeller, *Philosophie der Griechen*, 2.1.166–71.

[41] On Plato see, e.g., *Republic* 5.460A, 461A-C; and W. K. C. Guthrie, *A History of Greek Philosophy*, vol. 5: *The Later Plato and the Academy* (Cambridge: Cambridge University Press, 1978) 354–6. On Aristotle see, e.g., *Pol.* 7.1334b 29–1336a 2; see also Arius in Stob. 2.152.18–22 W.-H.

[42] Arist. *Pol.* 2.1253b 1–1260b 24; D.L. 4.12. [Arist.] *Oeconomica* 1, the anonymous work of an early Peripatetic, is also devoted to household management; on its date, authorship, and relationship to Xen. *Oec.*, see Dassmann and Schöllgen, "Haus," 818. These authors (816–17) maintain that philosophical reflection on household management begins with Plato's teacher Socrates (citing Xen. *Memorabilia* 1.2.48, 64; 4.1.2); the selection of an appropriate terminology, at least, seems to begin with Aristotle (*Pol.* 1.1253b 8–11).

[43] I.e., in his περὶ συμβιώσεως ἀνδρὸς καὶ γυναικός, his νόμοι ἀνδρὸς καὶ γαμετῆς, and his ὑπὲρ τοῦ μὴ γεννᾶν. On these see Fritz Wehrli (ed.), *Die Schule des Aristoteles: Texte und Kommentar*, vol. 4: *Demetrios von Phaleron*, 2nd edn. (Basel/Stuttgart: Schwabe, 1968) 60. Cf. the discussion in Praechter, *Hierokles*, 121–31. St. Jerome held that Aristotle also wrote a book entitled *On Marriage* (*Adversus Jovinianum* 1.49, "scripserunt Aristoteles et Plutarchus et noster Seneca de matrimonio libros")." Bickel, *Diatribe*, 16–28 thinks that Jerome has reference to Aristotle's περὶ συμβιώσεως ἀνδρὸς καὶ γυναικός known to him from a Neoplatonic collection of Aristotle's writings by Porphyrus, but this intriguing theory is only speculation.

[44] See Cicero: *Ad Atticum* 2.16.3; *De finibus* 5.4.11; Zeller, *Philosophie der Griechen* 2.2.858–9, 862–4, 891–3; and Alberto Grilli, *Il problema della vita contemplativa nel mondo greco-romano*, Filologia e Letteratura Classiche 1 (Milan/Rome: Fratelli Bocca, 1953) 125–33.

[45] Praechter, *Hierokles*, 129–31, and Konrad Graf Preysing, "Ehezweck und zweite Ehe bei Athenagoras," *TQ* 110 (1929) 93–4 think that Theophrastus may have been writing against Zeno or another early Stoic, but this is conjecture.

children.[46] In sharp contrast to this, and anticipating later Stoic discussions, Dicaearchus is reported to have argued that marriage was properly understood as one of the philosopher's true tasks in life.[47]

Whether Demetrius of Phaleron, a Peripatetic philosopher, statesman, and close associate of Theophrastus, supported the latter's views about marriage in his treatise *On Marriage* is not known, as only its title survives.[48] Concerning yet another con-

[46] Our source for this information is his work *On Marrying*, from which St. Jerome preserves an excerpt: *Adv. Jovin.* 1.47 (*PL* 23.289–90). Jerome's knowledge of this tractate may go back to a translation or partial translation made by Seneca; see Marion Lausberg, *Untersuchungen zu Senecas Fragmenten*, Untersuchungen zur antiken Literatur und Geschichte 7 (Berlin: Walter de Gruyter, 1970) 1 n. 2; Winfried Trillitzsch, "Hieronymus und Seneca," *Mittellateinisches Jahrbuch* 2 (1965) 43–4; and H. B. Gottschalk, "Aristotelian Philosophy in the Roman World from the Time of Cicero to the End of the Second Century AD," *ANRW* 2.36.2 (1987) 1140–1 n. 297. Bickel questions whether the original name was *De nuptiis*. He suggests, rather, that Jerome's excerpt was part of a book entitled περὶ βίων (*On Lifestyles*), for three reasons: the list of Theophrastus' works in D.L. 5.42–50 does not contain a περὶ γάμου, but it does contain three volumes entitled περὶ βίων (5.42); Philon of Larissa (160/159–ca. 80 BCE) demonstrates that εἰ γαμητέον τῷ σοφῷ is a topic handled by tractates entitled περὶ βίων (Stob. 2.41.7–11 W.-H.); and the Academic Eudoros of Alexandria (fl. ca. 25 BCE) names ὁ περὶ γάμου [λόγος] as part of ὁ περὶ βίων λόγος (Stob. 2.44.26–45.1, 6 W.-H.). See Bickel, *Diatribe*, 214–5; and Robert Philippson, "Hierokles der Stoiker," *Rh. Mus.*, n.s. 82 (1933) 110, who sees influence of the Middle Stoa on Eudoros. On the Theophrastus excerpt in Jerome generally, see Bickel, *Diatribe*, 129–220; Zeller, *Philosophie der Griechen* 2.2.858–9, 862–4; and Stelzenberger, *Beziehungen*, 432–3 n. 122.

[47] Dicaearchus *frag.* 31 Wehrli:

> Nor does it seem to Dicaearchus that these things behove wise men, for [he contends] neither did the ancients philosophize with mere discourse. Rather, back then wisdom was in fact devotion to good works, but in time it became an art of popular discourses. Thus at present, the one who engages persuasively in dialectic is thought to be a great philosopher, whereas in ancient times the good man alone was a philosopher, even if he could not craft celebrated and crowd pleasing sayings. For these men did not investigate whether in fact one should practice politics or how, rather they practiced politics well – nor if one had to marry, rather, having married in the manner that one should marry, they shared a common life with their wives. These things, he says, are works of men and pursuits of wise men, but these clever sayings are a tiresome matter.

This is *Codex Vaticanus* 435, which is attributed to "the *Roman Sayings* of Plutarch or Caecilius [first century BCE]"; see Hans von Arnim, "Ineditum Vaticanum," *Hermes* 27 (1892) 120, lines 13–14. Cf. Plut. *Mor.* 797D (*An seni respublica gerenda sit*), and Epict. *Diss.* 3.21.4–6.

[48] D.L. 5.81. Menander, the acclaimed poet of New Comedy, student of Theophrastus and friend of Demetrius, may also have been influenced by Theophrastus' dark view of marriage. See T. B. L. Webster: *Studies in Menander*, 2nd edn. (Manchester: Manchester University Press, 1960) 214–17; and *An Introduction to Menander* (Manchester: University of Manchester Press/New York: Barnes and Noble, 1974) 46–8. Stobaeus preserves two sayings from Menander that point in this direction: "To have

temporary, however, we are better informed. According to two late sources, the philosopher Epicurus (341–270 BCE) held a position very similar to that of Theophrastus. Diogenes Laertius, for example, has this report: "Nor, again, will the wise man marry and rear a family: so Epicurus says in the *Problems* and in *De Natura*. Occasionally he may marry owing to special circumstances (περίστασιν) in his life. Some too will turn aside from their purpose [by marrying]."[49]

## Early Stoics

What we know of the early Stoics makes it clear that the topic of marriage was discussed from the inception of this school, and in terms not unlike what we find in the later Stoic–Cynic debate.

a wife and to be a father of children, Parmenon, entails many cares in life" (Stob. 4.517.12–14 W.-H.; *frag.* 575 Körte); "To marry, if one would examine the truth, is an evil, but a necessary evil" (Stob. 4.527.5–7 W.-H.; *frag.* 578 K.). Cf. Menander *Sent.* 141 Jaekel, "For a wife is bane and salvation to a household." On the theme of marriage in New Comedy generally, see Ph. E. Legrand, *Daos: Tableau de la comédie grecque* (Lyon: A. Rey, 1910) 148–84.
   [49] D.L. 10.119, trans. R. D. Hicks, *Diogenes Laertius: Lives of Eminent Philosophers*, LCL (London: William Heinemann/Cambridge: Harvard University Press, 1925) 2.645; "[by marrying]" is my addition. Other editors read μὴν καὶ γαμήσειν instead of μηδὲ καὶ γαμήσειν, i.e., "the wise man *will indeed* marry . . ." See, e.g., H. S. Long, ed., *Diogenis Laertii: Vitae Philosophorum*, Scriptorum Classicorum Bibliotheca Oxoniensis (Oxford: Clarendon Press, 1964) 2.549. But given the next sentence, this would not change the sense significantly. The other source is Seneca *De matrimonio*, in Jerome *Adv. Jovin.* 1.48:

Epicurus, the patron of pleasure . . . says that a wise man can seldom marry, because marriage has many drawbacks. And as riches, honors, bodily health, and other things which we call indifferent, are neither good nor bad, but stand as it were midway, and become good and bad according to the use and issue, so wives stand on the border line of good and ill. It is, moreover, a serious matter for a wise man to be in doubt whether he is going to marry a good or a bad woman.

[trans. W. H. Fremantle, *A Select Library of Nicene and Post-Nicene Fathers of the Christian Church*, 2nd ser., vol. 6: *St. Jerome: Letters and Select Works*, ed. Philip Schaff and Henry Wace (New York: Christian Literature Co., 1893; repr., Grand Rapids: William B. Eerdmans, n.d.) 385.]
   Regarding Epicurus' views on marriage, see Vatin, *Recherches*, 32 and n. 1; Meeks, "Image of the Androgyne," 173–4; and Grilli, *Il problema della vita contemplativa*, 59–84. See also *Vatican Sayings* 41 and 58. After Epicurus, the Epicureans voice little opinion on marriage. In his critique of non-Epicurean theories of household management, Philodemus of Gadara (ca. 110–ca. 40 BCE) questions simply whether it is necessary to have a wife (*On Household Management* coll. 2–3, 9). Cf. Diogenes of Oenoanda 22S Long-Sedley. Epictetus seems to have encountered some Epicureans who revived their founder's teachings on marriage, see below pp. 83–4. On Epicurean communities in this late period, see Meeks, *The First Urban Christians*, 83–4 (lit.).

Diogenes Laertius tells us that Zeno (335–263 BCE), the school's founder, held that the wise man will marry and have children. Significantly, he cites Zeno's *Politics* as his source, which suggests that the relationship between marriage and the well-being of the city-state posited by later Stoics was part of Zeno's understanding of marriage as well.[50] After Zeno, his student Persaeus, and Chrysippus (ca. 280–207 BCE), the third in line as head of the Stoa, wrote about marriage. Whereas only the title of Persaeus' treatise *On Marriage* survives,[51] our information on Chrysippus is somewhat better. According to Plutarch, Chrysippus always discussed the topics of marriage and raising children under the assumption that these activities formed part of a larger cosmic order under the sway of a divine principle, which Chrysippus described variously as "Good Fortune," "Zeus," "Destiny," "Providence," or "the Common Nature."[52] Plutarch's report, moreover, receives support from Seneca's remark that "Chrysippus ridiculously maintains that a wise man should marry, that he may not outrage Jupiter Gamelius and Genethlius."[53]

But to this picture of early Stoic views on marriage we must add one more consideration. Citing from Chrysippus' *On Politics* and again from Zeno's *Politics*, Diogenes Laertius reports that both these philosophers also advocated the idea of holding wives in common, as had Diogenes of Sinope and Plato.[54] This seeming disparity in their teachings on marriage may reflect a distinction that Zeno and Chrysippus drew between utopian vision and practical reality.[55] It may also point to Cynic influence on their thinking, however, for as Diogenes Laertius says elsewhere, Zeno, a onetime follower of Crates, wrote his *Politics* while still a Cynic.[56]

[50] D.L. 7.121.

[51] D.L. 7.36.

[52] Plut. *Mor.* 1035B-C (*De Stoicorum repugnantiis*).

[53] That is, Zeus in his role as divine patron and guardian of marriage and the human race; Sen. *De mat.*, in Jerome *Adv. Jovin.* 1.48, trans. Fremantle in Schaff and Wace (eds.), *Select Library*, 385.

[54] D.L. 7.33, 131.

[55] So Pohlenz, *Die Stoa*, 1.137–9. On the utopian concept of "community of wives" in the ethnographic writers see John Ferguson, *Utopias of the Classical World* (London: Thomas and Hudson, 1975) 19–21.

[56] D.L. 7.4. Cf. A. A. Long and D. N. Sedley, *The Hellenistic Philosophers*, vol. 1: *Translations of the Principal Sources with Philosophical Commentary* (Cambridge: Cambridge University Press, 1987) 435. On Zeno's view of marriage see also Rist, *Stoic Philosophy*, 65–7; H. C. Baldry, "Zeno's Ideal State," *JHS* 79 (1959) 9–10; and Praechter, *Hierokles*, 128–9, who suggests that the *Cynic Ep. of Diogenes* 47 (To Zeno) might reflect Zeno's position. In this connection we should also note that

## 3. The second to the first century BCE

### Antipater of Tarsus and [Ocellus Lucanus]

The Stoic–Cynic marriage debate, as we have described it in the introduction to this survey, appears to have its beginning in the second century BCE. At least, it is not until this period that we have texts complete enough to define clearly the respective Stoic and Cynic positions on marriage. One of these is the treatise *On Marriage* by the Stoic philosopher Antipater of Tarsus (fl. middle of the 2nd century BCE).[57] In this text Antipater begins his discussion with the conviction that men are political beings destined by nature and the gods to play a part in a cosmic order composed of households and city-states. The institution of marriage, he maintains, serves as the foundation of this order, being the source of households and thus city-states. From this he concludes that all morally upright youths, in an effort to fulfill their obligations to the gods and express their allegiance to the divine plan, will consider marriage "to be among the primary and most necessary of those things which are fitting (τῶν ἀναγκαιοτάτων καὶ πρώτων καθη-κόντων)."[58]

Having thus identified marriage as a "fitting action," Antipater eulogizes its natural benefits. It is superior to all other "friendships and affections of life," he says, for in marriage the partners express their dedication to one another by sharing not only possessions and children, and their souls, but also their bodies. From this praise, Antipater proceeds to criticize those who see a wife as a burden, saying that this misconception arises from the inability of some men to select an appropriate mate – a matter to which he devotes another

Zeno's student Ariston is said to have held that both πατρίς and οἶκος were products of civilization not nature (Plut. *Mor.* 600E [*De exilo*]), and that the early Stoics in general were said to have favored the contemplative over the active life (D.L. 7.130). On Ariston see Rist, *Stoic Philosophy*, 74–7. For Chrysippus see ibid., 79; Zeller, *Philosophie der Griechen* 3.1.302–3 n. 6; D.L. 7.121; and Plut. *Mor.* 1033D (*De Stoic. repug.*). On the early Stoics generally see also Grilli, *Il problema*, 89–99.

[57] *SVF* 3.254–57 (Stob. 4.507–12 W.-H.); a complete translation is provided in appendix A. For a summary and discussion of this text see Hermann Cohn, "Antipater von Tarsos: Ein Beitrag zur Geschichte der Stoa" (Ph.D. diss., University of Giessen, 1905) 15–18, 80–3; and André-Jean Voelke, *Les rapports avec autrui dans la philosophie grecque: D'Aristote à Panétius*, Bibliothèque d'histoire de la philosophie (Paris: J. Vrin, 1961) 149–52. For Panaetius, Antipater's disciple and successor as head of the Stoa (129–109 BCE), see Pohlenz, *Die Stoa*, 1.202–7.

[58] Antipater *SVF* 3.255.5–6 (Stob. 4.508.2–4 W.-H.).

treatise[59] – and to instruct her in the art of managing a household and living piously. A wife who is properly chosen and instructed, he asserts, offers several advantages essential to anyone who "loves the good." She becomes a help to her husband, like a second pair of hands, affording him "leisure time" (σχολή)[60] to pursue philosophy or politics. It is through her diligence in matters pertaining to the household that he can give his full attention to these pursuits, remaining "undistracted" (ἀπερίσπαστος)[61] by concern for the necessities of life.

A text similar to this is *On the Nature of the Universe* 43(end)-51, mistakenly ascribed to the Pythagorean Ocellus Lucanus. Its provenance is Stoic and it stems from perhaps around 150 BCE, making its author a contemporary of Antipater.[62] Here we find a view of the *kosmos* identical to Antipater's, being a system that reflects the divine will and consists of households and city-states, the foundation of which is marriage.[63] Unlike Antipater, however, its author does not argue the case for marrying *per se*, but assuming marriage, proceeds to show that the married man must carry out the divine plan of the *kosmos* through the proper procreation of children. In his words, if a man wishes to protect his ancestral hearth, the altar of his city-state, and the altar of God, he is "obligated" (ὀφείλει) to replace each person whom death takes from his household and city-state.[64]

In a manner similar to Antipater, the author then criticizes those who have chosen wives badly, either for wealth or status, or a wife too old to bear children. Stressing once again the importance of marriage as a part of the larger system, he complains that the disharmony which results from these marriages is detrimental to the whole. Households are but the constituent parts, he states, and thus "whatever happens to characterize the parts also characterizes the whole and the entirety that is composed of such parts."[65]

---

[59] Antipater's περὶ γυναικὸς συμβιώσεως in *SVF* 3.254.3–22 (Stob. 4.539.5–540.6 W.-H.). Hense has argued that this fragment is actually part of Antipater's περὶ γάμου (Hense, "Zu Antipatros," 300–2), a theory made plausible by Nicostratus' περὶ γάμου, which contains similar material (Stob. 4.536–9, 593–9 W.-H.).

[60] Antipater *SVF* 3.256.34 (Stob. 4.511.16 W.-H.); cf. *SVF* 3.257.5, 10 (Stob. 4.512.2,7 W.-H.).

[61] Antipater *SVF* 3.257.3–4 (Stob. 4.511.20–512.1 W.-H.).

[62] *De universi natura*, see Praechter, *Hierokles*, 138–41. A translation of these sections is provided in appendix B.

[63] See Praechter, *Hierokles*, 140 n. 1, and 141. Cf. [Ocellus Lucanus] *De legibus*.

[64] [Ocellus] *De univ. nat.* 45, cf. 47.

[65] [Ocellus] *De univ. nat.* 50–51.

The Cynic Epistles

The next documents we need to consider come from a collection known as the *Cynic Epistles*. These are pseudepigraphic writings attributed to Greek philosophers of the classical and early Hellenistic periods, but which scholars have assigned to Cynic authors of the late Hellenistic period, situating them in the neo-Cynic revival that began in the second or first century BCE.[66] The particular letters in which we are interested, the *Cynic Epistles of Diogenes* 21, 35, 42, 44, 47 and the *Cynic Epistle of Heraclitus* 9, have been dated variously by scholars between the first century BCE and the second century CE, without the benefit of any true consensus.[67] Thus, while the dates of composition of some of them may extend beyond the first century BCE, it will be convenient for us to consider them all here, rather than divide them up on some basis and treat some later. These letters contribute greatly to our understanding of the Stoic–Cynic marriage debate since they present a fairly uniform position against many of the Stoic teachings. In other words, they give us a glimpse of the other side of the debate.

In the *Cynic Epistle of Diogenes* 47 the author opens his discussion by flatly denying the position emphasized so strongly by Antipater, that a man should marry because a wife's partnership serves to make her husband's life easier. In his opinion a wife and children are a burden that the philosopher can and should avoid by living self-sufficiently and without passion. The author then challenges the Stoic position that marriage is necessary because it guarantees the future of the human race. To his mind the majority of people in the world are largely "uninformed as to the true nature of things" and therefore no more worth worrying about than the races of various insects.[68] In a similar vein, two other letters take issue with Stoic views on the purpose of sexual intercourse and the necessity of

[66] On this revival see Margarethe Billerbeck, *Der Kyniker Demetrius: Ein Beitrag zur Geschichte der frühkaiserzeitlichen Popularphilosophie*, Philosophia Antiqua 36 (Leiden: E. J. Brill, 1979), esp. 1–11.

[67] These texts have been edited and translated in Abraham J. Malherbe (ed.), *The Cynic Epistles*, SBLSBS 12 (Missoula, Mont.: Scholars, 1977). For a summary of the various theories on dating the *Cynic Epistles of Diogenes* see ibid., 14–17; on the *Cynic Epistles of Heraclitus* see Harold W. Attridge, *First-Century Cynicism in the Epistles of Heraclitus*, HTS 29 (Missoula, Mont.: Scholars, 1976) 12.

[68] On this disdain for "non-philosophical" persons among the Cynics see Zeller, *Philosophie der Griechen* 2.1.314–16; and Abraham J. Malherbe, *Paul and the Thessalonians: The Philosophic Tradition of Pastoral Care* (Philadelphia: Fortress, 1987) 21 and n. 59.

72    The Stoic–Cynic marriage debate

procreation. The *Cynic Epistle of Diogenes* 21 tacitly denies the
Stoic claim that sexual intercourse must be performed solely for the
sake of procreation; and the author of the *Cynic Epistle of Heraclitus* 9 suggests that the feared depopulation of the city-states could be
halted by simply defining citizens on the basis of virtue rather than
birth.[69]

Still another perspective on marriage is afforded by the *Cynic
Epistle of Diogenes* 44. Starting with the assumption, also held by
the Stoics, that sexual desires are natural and the satisfaction of
these desires both natural and necessary,[70] its author argues that
sexual relations in general, let alone marriage, are too time consuming for the philosopher in his pursuit of happiness and well-being.
To solve this dilemma he promotes the practice of masturbation,
which both conserves a Cynic's precious free time (σχολή) and helps
him put his life in order as a teacher of moderation and endurance.[71]
From two other letters, the *Cynic Epistles of Diogenes* 35 and 42, we
learn that Cynics considered masturbation fully in accord with
nature, the latter employing a comparison between satisfying one's
sexual appetite and satisfying one's hunger.[72]

If we combine the information of these letters and place it against
the backdrop of what we know about the Cynics of this period more
generally,[73] the following picture of their position on marriage
emerges. First, the Cynics rejected the Stoic claim that a man is
morally obligated to marry, have children, and establish a household, thereby providing a constant supply of citizens for the city-
states. This rejection is consistent with the Cynic concept of radical
cosmopolitanism, and it is grounded in their more basic rejection of
the notion that "civilized life," or the life most worth living, is
dependent on the prosperity of the city-state.[74] Second, in place of
the Stoic concept of allegiance to this cosmic order, the Cynics

[69] Cf. Dio Chrysostom *Oration* 34.21–3.
[70] Cf. Zeller, *Philosophie der Griechen* 2.1.321–2; and Arthur O. Lovejoy and
George Boas, *Primitivism and Related Ideas in Antiquity* (Baltimore: Johns Hopkins
University Press, 1935; repr., New York: Octagon Books, 1973) 121.
[71] Cf. Dio Chrys. *Or.* 6.16–20; Galen *De locis affectis* 6.5 (8.419 Kühn); and
Agathias Scholasticus *Greek Anthology* 302 (sixth century CE). On the Cynic concern
for σχολή, see also *Cynic Ep. of Anacharsis* 5, and *Cynic Ep. of Heraclitus* 1.
[72] Similarly, Plut. *Mor.* 1044B (*De Stoic. repug.*); and D.L. 6.46, 69.
[73] On this see Meeks, *Moral World*, 52–6; and the description of "austere Cynicism" in Abraham J. Malherbe, "Self-Definition among Epicureans and Cynics"
*Jewish and Christian Self Definition*, vol. 3: *Self-Definition in the Greco-Roman World*,
ed. Ben F. Meyer and E. P. Sanders (London: SMC Press, 1982) 50–9, and 195 n. 30.
[74] Cf. *Cynic Ep. of Crates* 5.

proposed a different ideal and a different set of allegiances. They maintained that the true nature of a man was best served by a life devoted exclusively to a philosophy that promoted self-sufficiency and inner freedom. This, in turn, excluded marriage inasmuch as marriage introduced responsibilities that encroached on a wise man's self-sufficiency and made demands on his free time. The importance of marrying for the Stoic wise man is thus mirrored by the importance of rejecting marriage for the Cynic wise man. Shunning sexual relations with women altogether was, in fact, one of the things that distinguished the latter from the non-philosophical men of the world, earning him the title "Cynic."[75]

### Arius and Cicero

From the end of the first century BCE comes the epitome of Stoic ethics compiled by Arius Didymus, friend and teacher of Augustus Caesar.[76] Its importance lies in the fact that it details efforts within Stoicism to apply a systematic theory of ethics to the marriage debate. To some extent we have already seen this reflected in Antipater, both in his statement that marriage is the most necessary of those things which are "fitting," and in his discussion of the natural advantages of married life. Arius' treatment, however, allows us to see the fuller implications of these efforts.

Arius tells us that Stoics classified marriage as an "indifferent" (ἀδιάφορον), that is, a "fitting" action under normal circumstances.[77] He says further, they held that the wise or "good" man (σπουδαῖος) would correctly administer a household, and that they saw participation in the affairs of one's city-state as something "preferred" (προηγουμένον).[78] This much dovetails nicely with the

[75] *Cynic Ep. of Diogenes* 44 (174.11–15 M.). On the meaning "non-philosophical" for ἰδιώτης here, see Musonius *frag.* 3.40.35 Lutz (11.13 H.), and Epictetus *Diss.* 3.16 passim. Cf. *Diss.* 3.7.1 where an Epicurean calls himself a "layman" (ἰδιώτης) with respect to Epictetus.
[76] For a summary and discussion of Arius' epitome, see Charles H. Kahn, "Arius as a Doxographer," *On Stoic and Peripatetic Ethics: The Work of Arius Didymus,* ed. William W. Fortenbaugh, Rutgers University Studies in Classical Humanities 1 (New Brunswick: Transactions, 1983) 3–13.
[77] Arius in Stob. 2.86.12–16 W.-H. Cf. Eudoros of Alexandria (fl. ca. 25 BCE), who classifies ὁ περὶ γάμου [sc. λόγος] as one of the "fitting actions" (καθήκοντες, cited by Arius in Stob. 2.44.24 W.-H.). Cf. also Cic. *De fin.* 3.17.58–19.64; 3.20.68–21.69; and D.L. 7.107–21.
[78] Arius in Stob. 2.95.9–23 and 2.109.10–18 W.-H. See also 2.100.5 and 2.103.9–23 W.-H.

assertions of Antipater and [Ocellus] that the *kosmos* is a hierarchy
of marriages, households, and city-states. But Arius tells us one
more thing – that the Stoics saw all of these activities, including
marriage, as ethically "missing the mark," or "sin" (ἁμάρτημα),
when performed in a manner detrimental to one's well-being.[79] With
this he raises the possibility, not considered by Antipater or
[Ocellus], that the morally upright man will not marry if the circumstances of his life prove marriage to be impractical or disadvantageous.

Approaching this matter from another angle, we may isolate an
even more profound difference between Arius and Antipater and
[Ocellus]. All three emphasize an individual's allegiance to
"nature," and hence to the *kosmos*, the embodiment of nature's will.
In Antipater and [Ocellus], however, this *kosmos* is pictured as the
sum total of all city-states. This has the result that a man's place in
the *kosmos* is defined in terms of his identity as a citizen of one of
these city-states, leading to the conclusion that the role nature has
destined a man to play is identical to his roles as husband, householder, and citizen. By contrast, the Stoic position that Arius describes pictures the *kosmos* as a single world community. In consequence, a man's obligation to marry and establish a household is
less evident. It no longer derives primarily from his allegiance to a
city-state, but from his identity as a citizen of the world who is first
and foremost concerned for a community whose affairs sometimes
take precedence over those of the city-state.

Thus, somewhat ironically perhaps, the ethical system described
by Arius, which Stoics pressed into service in support of marriage,
breathes the same cosmopolitan spirit that the Stoics' promotion of
marriage originally sought to quell. The moral obligation to take on
the responsibilities of married life has now been relativized in light
of an allegiance higher than one's allegiance to the city-state. Not
surprisingly, this ethical system becomes the means by which some
Stoics were able to incorporate Cynic views into their thinking on
marriage, leading to what I have termed an "inner-Stoic" marriage
debate. Our first substantial evidence for this development is in
Cicero's *De finibus*, written not long before Arius composed his
epitome. Here Cicero tells us that the Stoics believed "the Wise Man
should desire to engage in politics and government, and also to live
in accordance with nature by taking to himself a wife and desiring to
have children by her," adding, "As for the principles and habits of
the Cynics, some say that these befit the Wise Man, if circumstances

[79] Arius in Stob. 2.86.11 W.-H. See also 2.99.8 and 2.109.16–18 W.-H.

should happen to indicate this course of action; but other Stoics reject the Cynic rule unconditionally."[80] With this the door swings wide for those Stoics who would shun the marital duties of a citizen in pursuit of the higher calling of philosophy.

As an additional note to Cicero, we should mention that our information concerning his own interest in the Stoic–Cynic marriage debate is intriguing, but slight and mixed. We know he held that a proper youth entered into mature life by taking on the responsibilities of domestic and civic affairs;[81] that he was familiar with Stoic views on the structure of the *kosmos*;[82] and that he translated Xenophon's *Oeconomicus* into Latin, which suggests he had more than a passing interest in the theory of household management.[83] On the other hand, he was familiar with certain philosophers who distanced themselves from civic affairs in order to have sufficient time for study,[84] and at certain points in his career Cicero chose the contemplative life over the active.[85]

[80] Cicero *De finibus* 3.20.68, ... *Cynicorum autem rationem atque vitam alii cadere in sapientem dicunt, si qui eiusmodi forte casus inciderit ut id faciendum sit, alii nullo modo*; trans. H. Rackham, *Cicero: De finibus bonorum et malorum*, LCL (London: William Heinemann/New York: Macmillan, 1914) 289. Cf. D.L. 7.121, where Diogenes Laertius, immediately after citing Zeno's position in favor of marriage, cites Apollodorus on Stoics acting like Cynics. Depending on how we read back into the arrangement of Diogenes' source material, this idea of a Stoic taking a Cynic position on marriage could possibly be dated as early as Apollodorus, a contemporary of Antipater.

On the idea that some Cynics of this period are "radical Stoics," see Donald B. Dudley, *A History of Cynicism* (London: Methuen, 1937; repr., Hildesheim: Georg Olms, 1967) 96–103, 117–124, 137, and esp. 189–99; Miriam T. Griffin, *Seneca: A Philosopher in Politics* (Oxford: Clarendon Press, 1976) 297–314; Abraham J. Malherbe, "Cynics," *IDB* suppl. (1962) 202; Cicero *De off.* 1.35.128; Arius in Stob. 2.114.22–5 W.-H.; Sen. *De brev. vit.* 14.2; *De ben.* 7.1.3; 8.2; and Epict. *Diss.* 3.22. Cf. Juvenal *Sat.* 13.122, and Ramsay MacMullen, *Enemies of the Roman Order* (Cambridge: Harvard University Press, 1966) 305 n. 2.

[81] *Rei domesticae ... reique publicae*, Cicero *Pro Caelio* 42.

[82] See Cicero: *Laws* 3.1.2–3; *De off.* 1.17.54; *De fin.* 3.19.62–64; *De natura deorum* 2.51.128; and Pohlenz, *Die Stoa*, 1.269–70. On his knowledge of the Stoic concept of *oikeiosis* see Pembroke, "Oikeiōsis," 121–2.

[83] Cicero *De off.* 2.24.87. It is also about this time that the Epicurean Philodemus writes his περὶ οἰκονομίας, a critical discussion of Xen. *Oec.*, [Arist.] *Oec.* 1343a–1345b, and various Cynic views on household management; see Dassmann and Schöllgen, "Haus," 819.

[84] Cicero *De off.* 1.9.28; 1.20.69–21.70.

[85] See Cicero *De fin.* 5.4.11 and *Ad Atticum* 2.16.3; cf. *Topica* 82; *De oratore* 3.29.112; *De off.* 1.20.69–21.73; and Plut. *Vit.* 862A (*Cicero*). See also Neal Wood, *Cicero's Social and Political Thought* (Berkeley: University of California Press, 1988) 122–3; and Grilli, *Il problema*, 192–200. According to an anecdote passed on by Seneca, Cicero chose not to remarry after his divorce from Terentia so as to devote himself to philosophical studies (Sen. *De mat.* in Jerome *Adv. Jovin.* 1.48, cited below, p. 76). Yet this divorce took place in 47 BCE, and by the next year Cicero had married Publilia, although their union lasted only until 45 BCE.

## 4. The first to the middle of the second century CE

### Seneca

By the beginning of the first century CE the basic parameters of the Stoic–Cynic marriage debate had been established. Over the next century and a half the focus would sharpen on one particular issue already familiar to us from Antipater and the *Cynic Epistles of Diogenes*, namely, whether the responsibilities of married life are compatible with the pursuit of philosophy. This period is also noteworthy in that it supplies us with our richest cache of materials. The marriage debate enjoys great popularity, attracting the attention of a variety of authors, many of whom were contemporaries of the apostle Paul.

Some of our first information on the marriage debate in the first century comes from the Stoic philosopher and statesman Seneca (ca. 5 BCE–65 CE). Here, as with Cicero, we encounter something of a mixed picture. On the one side, Seneca is the author of a treatise devoted entirely to marriage. This is his *On Marriage*, parts of which are preserved by St. Jerome in his polemical tractate *Against Jovinian*. While Jerome does not cite enough of Seneca's work for us to determine its full intent, it clearly dealt with the issue of whether marriage and philosophy were compatible, and two of the anecdotes it contains offer the sharply negative assessments of Epicurus and Cicero.[86] Regarding Cicero, for example, Seneca claims, "when Cicero after divorcing Terentia was requested by Hirtius to marry his sister, he set the matter altogether on one side, and said that he could not possibly devote himself to a wife and to philosophy."[87]

This negative attitude toward marriage seems inherent in several of Seneca's other writings as well. In two of his letters he portrays

[86] Jerome *Adv. Jovin.* 1.41–9. The fragments of Seneca's *De matrimonio* have been edited by Bickel, *Diatribe*, 382–94, and by Winfried Trillitzschi, *Seneca im literarischen Urteil der Antike: Darstellung und Sammlung der Zeugnisse* (Amsterdam: Adolf M. Hakkert, 1971) 2.370–5. For critical problems associated with this text see Bickel, *Diatribe*, 288–372; Trillitzsch: *Seneca im literarischen Urteil*, 1.145–51; "Hieronymus und Seneca," *Mittellateinisches Jahrbuch* 2 (1965) 42–54; and Marion Lausberg, *Untersuchungen zu Senecas Fragmenten*, Untersuchungen zur antiken Literatur und Geschichte 7 (Berlin: Walter de Gruyter, 1970) 1 n. 2. (The discussion in Lise Henrion, "La conception," 146–53 is uninformed by Bickel.) Zeller, *Philosophie der Griechen* 3.1.750, believes that this treatise, nonetheless, gave a positive evaluation of marriage.

[87] Sen. *De mat.*, in Jerome *Adv. Jovin.* 1.48, trans. Fremantle in Schaff and Wace (eds.), *Select Library*, 384; cf. Sen. *De otio* 3.2. On Epicurus see above, n. 49.

the wise man as favoring a cosmopolitan approach to public life that excludes participation in the affairs of any one community or city-state, and he comments on the philosopher's need for free time, maintaining that other aspects of life should be allotted to whatever time is left over from the pursuit of philosophy, not the other way around.[88] In one of his dialogues he even complains of how much of a man's life is wasted in dealing with a mistress and arguing with a wife, stating that this time should be dedicated to philosophy.[89] But Seneca can also take a clear stand against the Cynic notion that philosophy and marriage are mutually exclusive. In his ninth *Epistle*, arguing on the basis of the advantages that accrue from marriage, he maintains that the self-sufficiency required to give a man the time and the peace of mind to pursue philosophy is fully compatible with the responsibilities involved with marriage and raising children, relationships to which the philosopher is drawn by natural impulse.[90] Consistent with this, in his ninety-fourth *Epistle* Seneca demonstrates a knowledge of the theory of household management, which he assigns to an important category of philosophical precepts.[91]

In the final analysis, what we see reflected here is an ambiguity in Seneca's thought to which scholars have drawn attention especially in regard to his political theory.[92] In our terminology, Seneca's ambivalence displays the dynamics of the inner-Stoic debate on marriage. He is being drawn in two directions, one "Stoic" and one "Cynic" – options made possible by the very dissonance in Stoicism itself. On the one hand, Seneca is mindful of his civic responsibilities, including marriage; on the other, he lists to the higher calling of the philosophical life, a life which identifies him as a citizen of the world, responsible only to the world community.[93]

[88] Sen. *Epistles* 72.3–4; 53.9; cf. 64.6.
[89] Sen. *De brev. vit.* 3.2; 7.2; 14.2.
[90] Sen. *Ep.* 9.17–19.
[91] Sen. *Ep.* 94.1, 3, 15; on this see Balch, *Let Wives Be Submissive*, 51. Another Latin work from this period that shows knowledge of the literature on household management is Columella *On Agriculture* 1.4.8–9.9 (ca. 60–5 CE).
[92] E.g., Griffin, *Seneca*, 315–66; Pohlenz: *Die Stoa*, 1.313–15; *Freedom*, 147–9; and Grilli, *Il problema*, 217–78. While the dialogues are earlier than the letters, there does not seem to be a consistent development in Seneca's thought on participation in either politics or marriage; see Griffin, *Seneca*, 316–17, 334, 339.
[93] Seneca's anecdote involving Epicurus (cited above, n. 49) suggests that he was aware of the classification of marriage as an "indifferent." See also Sen. *De otio* 6.4–6; 8.1–4; *Ep.* 68.2; *De brev. vit.* 13.8–14.5.

Musonius Rufus

The ambiguities apparent in Seneca are completely absent from his contemporary and fellow Stoic philosopher Musonius Rufus (fl. middle to late first century CE). This is because, unlike Seneca, Musonius is untouched by cosmopolitan ideals in his thinking on marriage. As with Antipater and [Ocellus] before him, Musonius defines a man's allegiances and loyalties against the backdrop of a *kosmos* that is a collectivity of city-states. Man's nature, he maintains – his divinely sanctioned place in the *kosmos* – is that of a citizen, morally obligated to look after the affairs of his city-state. He must live with a wife, raise children, and establish a household. And for Musonius this rule would seem to have no exceptions.[94]

In line with these beliefs, Musonius devotes an entire treatise to refuting the (Cynic) claim that the philosopher cannot marry. His thesis is that a philosopher is no more and no less than a teacher and example of what is in accordance with nature's divine will, and if anything is in accordance with nature, and thus the business of the philosopher, it is marriage.[95] As an example, Musonius cites the early Cynic philosopher Crates, who, despite hardships, fulfilled this philosopher's duty. He also presents several arguments for the "naturalness" of marriage. He maintains that the Creator formed men and women with the intention that they join together in marriage; he claims that men's gregarious nature urges them to live together in city-states and act as responsible citizens, insuring stability and growth through stable households and procreation; and he points out that major gods of the Greek pantheon patronize the institution of marriage.[96] Beyond this, Musonius also makes use of the ethical categories outlined in Arius. He refers several times to marriage as something "appropriate" and "fitting,"[97] and he praises a wife's love for her husband as one of life's natural advantages.[98] In another treatise he develops the kindred notion, seen

[94] Musonius *frag*. 14.92.33–8; 94.33–96.4; *frag*. 15.96.12–26 L. (73.8–15; 76.1–11; 77.6–78.6 H.).
[95] Mus. *frag*. 14, *Is Marriage an Impediment to the Pursuit of Philosophy?*; see 14.92.6–9; 94.32–96.8 L. (71.7–11; 75.20–76.17 H.); cf. *frag*. 11.82.34–7 L. (60.19–61.2 H.).
[96] Mus. *frag*. 14.90.26–92.4 L. (70.14–71.5 H.); *frag*. 14.92.9–94.32 L. (71.11–75.20 H.).
[97] προσήκειν, Mus. *frag*. 14.92.17; 94.32, 33; 96.3, 4, 7 L. (72.4; 75.20, 21; 76.10, 12, 15 H.); προσῆκον, *frag*. 14.92.8 L. (71.10 H.); πρέπει, *frag*. 14.96.6 L. (76.15 H.).
[98] Mus. *frag*. 14.94.2–19 L. (73.17–75.5 H.).

already in Antipater, that marriage is a beautiful relationship, characterized by the uncommon closeness of its partners.[99]

Finally, Musonius' conviction that a man is morally obligated to marry, whether he is a layman or philosopher, is reflected in several writings devoted to the topics of choosing a capable wife,[100] family planning, and household management. As for family planning, Musonius maintains that sexual intercourse should be practiced only within marriage and only for the purpose of procreation, arguing further that all children who are born should be raised.[101] According to him, children are natural advantages to the wise man,[102] while abortion and the exposure of infants are an affront to the divine plan.[103] As for household management, in his treatise *That Women, Too, Should Pursue Philosophy* he again argues that there is no contradiction between marriage and philosophy, saying that household management is a "virtue" (ἀρετή), and that women who study philosophy can only become better guardians of the home.[104]

## Quintilian, Theon, and Dio Chrysostom

Contemporary with Musonius are three orators who give us a sense of the considerable popularity that the Stoic–Cynic marriage debate had achieved by the end of the first century CE.[105] Their works bear witness to the fact that both Greek and Roman rhetorical schools

[99] Mus. *frag.* 13A; see the discussion in Foucault, *Care of the Self*, 151–3.
[100] Mus. *frag.* 13B.
[101] Mus. *frag.* 15 L. (15A-B H.).
[102] Mus. *frag.* 15.98.1–17; 100.2–16 L. (78.14–79.13; 80.11–81.13 H.).
[103] Mus. *frag.* 15.96.12–98.1 L. (77.4–78.14 H.). See the suggestion in Keith Hopkins, "A Textual Emendation in a Fragment of Musonius Rufus: A Note on Contraception," *CQ*, n.s. 15 (1965) 72–4 that Musonius' denunciation of childlessness (ἀτοκία) at *frag.* 15.96.20 L. (15A.77.13 H.) should be read as a condemnation of "contraceptives" (ἀτόκια).
[104] Mus. *frag.* 3.40.8–42.29 L. (9.17–13.3 H.). Concerning division of labor in the household, see *frag.* 4.44.13–14; 46.13–31 L. (14.9–11; 16.15–17.17 H.). Cf. Philodemus' report that under the effects of Cynic philosophy wives desert their husbands and go off with whom they choose (Philodemos Περὶ Στωϊκῶν, *P. Herculaneum* 339, col. IX, lines 5–12 Crönert [64]). Similarly, Lucian *Fugitivi* 18 satirizes philosophers who seduce wives of others under the pretense of making them philosophers.
[105] Plutarch is a possible fourth writer from this period who may know something about the debate, especially on the issue of the compatibility of philosophy and marriage. See Plut. *Mor.* 750C; 751E; 770A (*Amatorius*); 138B-C (*Coniugalia praecepta*); 493C, E (*De amore prolis*); 1035B-C (*De Stoic. repug.*); and Dicaearchus *frag.* 31 W. (*Codex Vaticanus* 435), attributed to "the *Roman Sayings* of Plutarch or Caecilius" (cited above, n. 47). See also above, n. 2.

had taken account of the debate in their discussions of the different strategies of argumentation common to philosophers and statesmen.[106] Thus, the standard rhetorical manuals of Quintilian (ca. 35 CE–ca 95) and Theon of Alexandria (fl. middle to late first century?) make frequent use of the question "Should one marin their treatments of *theses*, and they discuss civic responsibility, procreation, and marriage in terms reminiscent of Stoic and Cynic authors.[107] The third orator, Dio Chrysostom (ca. 40 CE–ca. 120), gives much the same picture in his now fragmentary discourse *On Peace and War*. Introducing marriage, the establishment of a household, and participation in local politics under the Stoic heading of "fitting actions,"[108] he reviews the way in which philosophers, as opposed to rhetoricians, handle these matters, describing strategies identical to what we find in Theon.[109] Dio also shows knowledge of

---

[106] On this development see Praechter, *Hierokles*, 141–8.

[107] On this development see Pohlenz, *Die Stoa*, 1.246. See, e.g., Theon *Progym.* 123.6–10; 125.9–20 S.:

> For the sake of a model, let us take some beginning *thesis* from the category of practical *theses,* such as whether a wise man engages in politics. Now the person preparing to argue that it is necessary to engage in politics should say first that it is possible for the wise man to engage in politics; second, that it is in accordance with nature ... It is possible to bring to bear on the proposed *thesis* arguments based on examples of these things which are prior to the matter at hand, and which are contemporaneous with the very matter, and which come after the matter; but they will be clearer when brought to bear on other *theses*, such as whether one should have children. For taking marriage and generally everything that must exist prior to having children, we will commend them, showing them to be good (καλά), and beneficial (συμφέροντα), and pleasant, and whether, next, they go hand in hand with having children; then, after these, the positive consequences of having children, such as care and attention in one's old age, and the benefits and pleasures of children, and the like. For the refutation of this *thesis* we have at our disposal the opposites of these points.

See also 120.12–121.17 and 128.3–21 S.; and Quintilian 2.4.24–5; 3.5.8, 12, 13, 16. On the *progymnasmata* literature and Theon see Roland F. Hock and Edward N. O'Neil (eds.), *The Chreia in Ancient Rhetoric*, vol. 1: *The Progymnasmata*, SBLTT 27/ SBLGRS 9 (Atlanta: Scholars, 1986) 10–22, 63–6. Willy Stegemann, "Theon, 5," *PW* 2nd ser., 5.2, half-vol. 10 (1934) 2047 wrongly maintains that the *theses* εἰ γαμητέον and εἰ παιδοποιητέον are out of place in the *progymnasmata* literature. For a correct assessment see H. I. Marrou, *A History of Education in Antiquity*, Wisconsin Studies in Classics (Madison: University of Wisconsin Press, 1982) 201; and John Barns, "A New Gnomologium: With Some Remarks on Gnomic Anthologies," *CQ*, n.s. 1 [mistakenly 45] (1951) 13. Concerning the question of the compatibility of philosophy and marriage in Quintilian see 12.1.5, 8; 11.1.35; 12.2.7; 1.6.36. A translation of Theon is available in James R. Butts, "The Progymnasmata of Theon: A New Text with Translation and Commentary" (Ph.D. diss., Claremont Graduate School, 1986).

[108] Dio Chrys. *Or.* 22.1–3, περὶ τοῦ προσήκοντος; cf. 26.8.

[109] Dio Chrys. *Or.* 22.3–4.

several arguments in favor of marriage used by Stoics,[110] and he is the author of a treatise titled *Household Management*.[111]

### Hierocles the Stoic and Epictetus

Around the end of the first and the beginning of the second century CE, two further authors supply us with substantial materials from the Stoic–Cynic marriage debate. These are Hierocles the Stoic and Epictetus, the latter being a student of Musonius Rufus. For the most part, Hierocles (fl. early second century) stands squarely in the tradition of Antipater, [Ocellus], and Musonius. He holds the conviction that a man has a moral obligation to a higher order, and that this obligation is defined by the fact that a man is a citizen of a city-state. There is no one, he claims in his *Elements of Ethics*, who is not part of a city-state.[112] As for marriage, it is the beginning of the city-state, being the "first and most elementary" partnership, since marriages produce households and households constitute city-states.[113] A man's moral duty is thus clear: he must marry, establish a household, and thereby insure the future of his city-state.[114] This is nature's will,[115] and consequently what is "fitting"[116] for a man. Quite in accord with this perspective, a large portion of Hierocles' treatise *On Marriage* is devoted to reviewing the natural advantages of marriage – a wife, children, and the marriage relation itself. A wife and children, he states, lighten a man's burdens and make his

[110] Dio Chrys. *Or.* 7.135; cf. 7.34, 50 (on the depopulation of the city-states).

[111] Dio Chrys. *frags.* 4–9, assembled from Stobaeus in J. W. Cohoon and H. Lamar Crosby (eds.), *Dio Chrysostom*, LCL (London: William Heinemann/ Cambridge: Harvard University Press, 1951) 5.348–51. Cf. Dio Chrys. *Or.* 69.2. On the possibility that Dio was a student of Musonius, see Pohlenz, *Die Stoa*, 2.146.

[112] οὐδεὶς γὰρ ἄνθρωπος ὃς οὐχὶ πόλεώς ἐστι μέρος, Hierocles ἠθικὴ στοιχείωσις, col. 11, lines 15–16 (p. 43) von Arnim. On the contrasting notion of *oikeiosis* in Hierocles see Pembroke, "Oikeiōsis," 125–7; and Parente, "Ierocle Stoico."

[113] Hierocles 52.15–21 v.A. (Stob. 4.502.1–7 W.-H.). This is from his treatise *On Marriage*, the frags. of which have been assembled from Stobaeus by Hans von Arnim, *Hierokles ethische Elementarlehre*, Berliner Klassikertexte 4 (Berlin: Weidmann, 1906) 52–6. An English translation is available in Abraham J. Malherbe, *Moral Exhortation: A Greco-Roman Sourcebook*, Library of Early Christianity (Philadelphia: Westminster, 1986) 100–4.

[114] Hierocles 56.21–32 v.A. (Stob. 4.604.27–605.16 W.-H.).

[115] Hierocles 52.28–53.12; cf. 54.20–1 v.A. (Stob. 4.502.15–503.10; 4.505.12–14 W.-H.).

[116] Hierocles 52.26–7; 53.3, 11 v.A. (Stob. 4.502.13–14; 4.502.22, 503.9 W.-H.).

life safer and more pleasant.[117] Like Antipater and Musonius, Hierocles also praises the extraordinary partnership by which husband and wife agree to hold all things in common, even each other's body and soul.[118] Again, like Antipater, he marvels at those who consider a wife or married life burdensome. They only seem so to those who marry for the wrong reasons and find themselves unprepared for the responsibilities of being a husband,[119] a situation he seeks to rectify in a treatise on household management.[120]

Thus far there is little new in Hierocles. But Hierocles deviates from his predecessors in two respects. First, unlike Musonius, he does not insist that every child that is born must be raised. Rather, he says simply that it is in accord with nature to raise "all *or at least most*" of one's offspring.[121] Second, Hierocles gives attention to an aspect of Stoic systematic ethics that is passed over by Antipater and Musonius. As we have seen, this ethical program describes marriage as a "preferred" and "fitting" action for human beings, but which, depending on circumstances, engenders either advantages or disadvantages in one's life. Antipater and Musonius, however, spoke only of the advantages arising from married life, giving no indication that there might be circumstances in which it would be disadvantageous to marry. In fact, Musonius may have excluded this possibility altogether, for he insists that even extreme poverty is not a circumstance which impedes marrying.[122] By contrast, Hierocles discusses such adverse circumstances with respect to both the layman and the philosopher. In a treatise entitled "On Households" he states that marriage is to be preferred by the wise man "except in special circumstances (κατὰ περίστασιν)"; and, he continues, "since

---

[117] Hierocles 53.20–54.14; 55.16–20, 27–8 v.A. (Stob. 4.503.20–505.4; 4.506.26–507.5; 4.603.15–18 W.-H.).

[118] Hierocles 54.14–27 v.A. (Stob. 4.505.5–22 W.-H.).

[119] Hierocles 54.27–55.20 v.A. (Stob. 4.505.22–507.5 W.-H.).

[120] Hierocles 62.21–63.30 v.A.; cf. 52.23 v.A. (Stob. 4.696.21–699.15; 4.502.9 W.-H.). English trans. in Malherbe, *Moral Exhortation*, 98–9. On this treatise see Praechter, *Hierokles*, 64–6; on its original title see Robert Philippson, "Hierokles der Stoiker," *Rh. Mus.*, n.s. 82 (1933) 101, 103; and for a comparison between Hierocles and Sen. *Ep.* 94, see ibid., 107–9.

[121] Hierocles 55.22–4 v.A. (Stob. 4.603.9–12 W.-H.).

[122] Mus. *frag.* 15.98.17–27 L. (79.13 H. (as in n. 244) only the very beginning of this passage appears in the Hense edn.); cf. 14.92.1–4 L. (71.1–5 H.). For a comparison between Musonius and Hierocles, see Praechter, *Hierokles*, 5–6. On the issue of poverty and marriage, see also the two maxims attributed to Menander: "O thrice ill-fated, whoever being poor marries and has children!" (Stob. 4.514.11–12 W.-H.; *frag.* 335 Körte); "Whoever, being poor, wants to live pleasurably, let him keep away from marriage while others marry" (Stob. 4.519.7–9 W.-H.; *frag.* 576 K.).

we should imitate the man of intellect in those things we can, and marriage is preferred by him, it is evident that it would also be fitting for us except some circumstance prevent us."[123] Similarly, the Suidas lexicon reports that in book two of his *Philosophical Topics* Hierocles "says with regard to the philosophers: 'Which of them did not marry, raise children, and manage property *when there was no obstacle?*'"[124]

In Hierocles, then, the moral duty of a man to marry and raise children has been relativized in comparison with the positions taken by Antipater and Musonius. Here, once again, we sense the dynamics of the inner-Stoic debate on marriage, for as Cicero explained, it was precisely on this matter of "circumstances" that some Stoics made the decision to follow Cynics in the rejection of marriage. Just how far a Stoic could relativize the importance of marriage on this basis will be made clear by our examination of Epictetus.

With the Stoic philosopher Epictetus (ca. 50–ca. 135) we reach a new level of sophistication in the Stoic–Cynic marriage debate. Like others in this debate, he addresses the question of whether a man should take on the responsibilities of married life in the context of his moral obligations to a higher, divine order. Unlike them, however, Epictetus chooses to argue both for and against marriage, depending on whether he understands a man's primary allegiance as being to the individual city-state or to the *kosmos* as a whole. In this way, his writings develop both sides of the inner-Stoic marriage debate, integrating Stoic and Cynic positions on marriage into one philosophical system.

The Stoic vision of a *kosmos* consisting of city-states, households, and marriages is very much in evidence in Epictetus' thinking, and as a consequence he, like Stoics before him, comes to the conclusion that human existence as ordained by nature derives its meaning from men identifying themselves as citizens of city-states. Accordingly, Epictetus counts marriage and having children as part of the "purpose" or "business at hand" in a man's life, since these contribute to the fundamental well-being of the city-state.[125] This comes

---

[123] Hierocles 52.23–7 v.A. (Stob. 4.502.9–14 W.-H.), trans. Malherbe, *Moral Exhortation*, 100. See the discussion in Balch, "Stoic Debates," 434.

[124] μηδενὸς ἐμποδὼν ὄντος, Suidas, s.v. "ἐμποδών (1)" (my emphasis). This text is available in Praechter, *Hierokles*, 318; and in von Arnim, *Elementarlehre*, 64. On the *Philosophical Topics*, see Philippson, "Hierokles," 107–12, 113; and Praechter, *Hierokles*, 10.

[125] ἡ πρόθεσις and τὸ προκείμενον, respectively; Epictetus *Diss.* 2.23.37–8. See also 3.21.5–6.

out, for example, in his criticism of the Epicurean vision of the city-state, in which marriage and the raising of children are absent. "Where are the citizens [for this city-state] to come from?," he chides, maintaining that these two activities are among the "preferred actions" of life.[126] Epictetus seems to have been relatively well-known for holding this position, moreover, for he is thus depicted in an anecdote that circulated not long after his death. As the satirist Lucian recounts, Epictetus once confronted the Cynic Demonax with the admonition to marry and raise children, saying, "this also is fitting for a man who pursues philosophy, namely, to leave behind for nature another in his place."[127]

But scratch Epictetus and you will not find his teacher Musonius. Like Hierocles he recognized that certain conditions made it impossible for a man to marry and at the same time meet his moral obligations to nature and the gods.[128] He names two instances of this in passing in his On the Cynic Life, one of his longest discourses. They involve situations in which a man's energies are taken up by scholarship or the fulfillment of military duty.[129] A third instance, to which he devotes nearly a sixth of this discourse, involves a figure Epictetus calls the Cynic, whom he envisions as something of a philosopher's philosopher, called for a special mission by God.[130]

In this discussion of the Cynic's position on marriage, the initial question Epictetus seeks to answer is, Should the Cynic, like other men, regard marriage as a "preferred course of action?"[131] Here, as

---

[126] Epict. Diss. 3.7.19–28, τὰ προηγούμενα. At 3.7.20 he says that Epicurean beliefs are "disruptive of the city-state, destructive of households" (ἀνατρεπτικὰ πόλεως, λυμαντικὰ οἴκων). See also 1.23.3–7; 2.20.20; and Heinrich Greeven, Das Hauptproblem der Sozialethik in der neueren Stoa und im Urchristentum, Neutestamentliche Forschung, 3rd ser. 4 (Gütersloh: C. Bertelsmann, 1935) 121.

[127] Lucian Demonax 55, πρέπειν γὰρ καὶ τοῦτο φιλοσόφῳ ἀνδρὶ ἕτερον ἀντ' αὐτοῦ καταλιπεῖν τῇ φύσει.

[128] E.g., Epict. Diss. 4.5.6. On this passage see Bonhöffer, Ethik, 86. See also Long, Hellenistic Philosophy, 199; and Michel Spanneut, "Epiktet," RAC 5.606–10.

[129] Epict. Diss. 3.22.79.

[130] Epict. Diss. 3.22.67–82. Too often the position on marriage Epictetus attributes to his Cynic is taken to be normative for Epictetus, e.g.: William Klassen, "Musonius Rufus, Jesus, and Paul: Three First-Century Feminists," From Jesus to Paul: Studies in Honour of Francis Wright Beare, ed. Peter Richardson and John Coolidge Hurd (Waterloo, Ontario, Canada: Wilfrid Laurier University Press, 1984) 196, cf. 190–1; Balch, "Stoic Debates," 430–1; cf. Greeven, Das Hauptproblem, 123; and Bernhard Lohse, Askese und Mönchtum in der Antike und in der alten Kirche, Religion und Kultur der alten Mittelmeerwelt in Parallelforschungen 1 (Munich/Vienna: R. Oldenbourg, 1969) 66.

[131] Epict. Diss. 3.22.67: γάμος δ' ἔφη, καὶ παῖδες προηγουμέμως παραληφθήσονται ὑπὸ τοῦ κυνικοῦ; Cf. 3.22.76 and 3.14.7.

earlier, we see clear reference to the categories of Stoic ethics. But as Epictetus proceeds, using further categories from this system, it is not without violence to these categories. In order to prove that a Cynic cannot marry, he essentially flips everything on its head. What holds true for the common man is wrong for the Cynic, and vice-versa. Thus, Epictetus claims, the Cynic can marry *only* under "special circumstances."[132] In an ideal city-state, in which all are wise men and women, marriage is possible,[133] or when a Cynic falls passionately in love with a woman who is herself a Cynic. This was the case with Crates, Epictetus admits,[134] but Crates was a rare exception, not the rule, as Musonius had supposed.[135] Under "usual circumstances" the Cynic cannot view marriage as a "preferred" course of action.[136]

The key to Epictetus' curious logic is his perception of society in his day. To his mind it was "like a battlefield," a chaotic state of affairs in which common people were in need of moral guidance.[137] For this purpose God calls forth the Cynic, whose task it is to oversee society, showing people which things are good and which are bad.[138] This even includes monitoring the doings of the dutiful householder, checking up on "those who have married, those who have had children."[139] By the same token, however, the Cynic himself cannot marry. The very same adverse conditions that make his calling necessary require him to forgo the responsibilities of a

[132] Epict. *Diss.* 3.22.76. In this Epictetus comes very close to the positions held by Theophrastus and, especially, Epicurus.

[133] Epict. *Diss.* 3.22.67–8. Early Stoics, as we saw, envisioned a community of wives in the ideal state. By the second century CE, however, this notion, popularized through Plato's *Republic*, had come under strong criticism from many quarters: Epict. *Diss.* 2.4.8–10; *frag.* 15 Oldfather; Lucian *Vitarum auctio* 17; *Fugitivi* 18; *Verae historiae* 2.19 (on this last see Ferguson, *Utopias*, 174–6); Sextus Empiricus *Outlines of Pyrrhonism* 3.205; Clem. Alex. *Strom.* bk. 3, chap. 2.10.2 (2.200.16–20 Stählin); bk. 3, chap. 2.5.1 (2.197.16–18 S.). This last has reference to a gnostic treatise *On Righteousness* by Epiphanes (fl. early second century). On Clement see Paul Wendland, *Quaestiones Musonianae: De Musonio Stoico Clementis Alexandrini Aliorumque Auctore* (Berlin: Mayer und Mueller, 1886) 14–15.

[134] Epict. *Diss.* 3.22.76. Cf. the *Cynic Ep. of Crates* 1 and 28–33; and *Greek Anthology* 7.413 (attributed to Antipater of Sidon, fl. 120 BCE).

[135] Praechter, *Hierokles*, 5 n. 1, calls Epictetus' use of Crates "almost like a polemic against his teacher." But cf. *Diss.* 4.1.159, where Epictetus is very close to Musonius.

[136] Epict. *Diss.* 3.22.76, τῶν κοινῶν γάμων καὶ ἀπεριστάτων.

[137] Epict. *Diss.* 3.22.69, ὡς ἐν παρατάξει. Cf. Philo's description of a "peacetime war" (κατ' εἰρήνην πόλεμος) in *Quod omnis probus* 34.

[138] Epict. *Diss.* 3.22.72, 77. On the Cynic's divine appointment see Epict. *Diss.* 3.22.2, 23, 53, 69; 4.8.31; *Enchiridion* 7.

[139] Epict. *Diss.* 3.22.72, τοὺς γεγαμηκότας, τοὺς πεπαιδοποιημένους.

86    *The Stoic–Cynic marriage debate*

husband, father, and householder. "In these present circumstances," Epictetus explains, marriage presents the Cynic with too
many disadvantages – obligations to his in-laws and to his wife,[140]
and the endless responsibilities involved in raising children, which
Epictetus recounts at length: "he must get a kettle to heat water for
the baby, for washing it in a bath-tub; wool for his wife when she has
had a child, oil, a cot, a cup (the vessels get more and more
numerous); not to speak of the rest of his business, and his distraction (τὴν ἄλλην ἀσχολίαν, τὸν περισπασμόν)." "Where, I beseech
you," he despairs, "is left now ... the man who had leisure for the
public interest (ὁ τοῖς κοινοῖς προσευκαιρῶν)?"[141]
   In better times a wife and in-laws would also have the Cynic's
wisdom, children would be raised accordingly,[142] and there might
not even be a need for the Cynic's profession.[143] But "given such
conditions as prevail," Epictetus argues, the Cynic must keep
himself "free from distraction" (ἀπερίσπαστος) and "wholly
devoted to the service of God."[144] Can there be any free time
(σχολή), he asks, for the man tied down to his own wife, children,
and household affairs? While these things are "fitting" for the
common man, they are nonetheless private affairs,[145] and the
Cynic's task involves grander issues.[146] He must show the common
man where to look for true happiness and serenity precisely by *not*
being married.[147] As opposed to Musonius' ideal of a philosopher,
Epictetus' Cynic has much more of a "do as I say not as I do"
attitude: "'Look at me,' he says, 'I am without a home, without a
city, without property ... I have neither wife nor children ... Yet
what do I lack? ... am I not free?'"[148] In this way, the Cynic's
calling takes precedence over the responsibilities of married life.
Rather than concerning himself with raising a few "ugly-snouted"

---

140 Epict. *Diss.* 3.22.70, 76.
141 The tirade continues, peppered with belittling diminutives: "Come, doesn't he
have to get little cloaks for the children? Doesn't he have to send them off to a
school-teacher with their little tablets and writing implements, and little notebooks;
and, besides, get the little cot ready for them?"; Epict. *Diss.* 3.22.70–2, 74, trans. W.
A. Oldfather, *Epictetus: The Discourses as Reported by Arrian, the Manual, and
Fragments*, LCL (Cambridge: Harvard University Press/London: William Heinemann, 1959) 2.155, 157.
142 Cf. *Cynic Ep. of Crates* 33.
143 Epict. *Diss.* 3.22.67–8; cf. Long, *Hellenistic Philosophy*, 205.
144 Epict. *Diss.* 3.22.69; cf. *Ench.* 15.
145 Epict. *Diss.* 3.22.74, καθήκουσιν ἰδιωτικοῖς.
146 Cf. Sen. *De otio* 4.1–2; 6.4–5.
147 τὴν εὐδαιμονίαν καὶ ἀταραξίαν, Epict. *Diss.* 4.8.30–1.
148 Epict. *Diss.* 3.22.47–8, trans. Oldfather, *Epictetus*, 2.147.

children of his own, he must look upon all of society as his household – they are his children and he is their father.[149] And that is
responsibility enough.[150]

Epictetus' presentation of his ideal philosopher includes much
that we have identified as belonging to the Cynic attitude toward
marriage. It speaks of marriage as impeding the work of the philosopher (the philosopher *par excellence*), and advocates his need for
"free time"; it expresses something of the Cynic disdain for the
non-philosophical population of the world in its remarks that be-
little the rearing of children; and, above all, it employs the name
"Cynic" for this extraordinary philosopher. But it is not Cynic. In
the final analysis we must regard it as a compromise between Stoic
and Cynic positions on marriage, between allegiance to the traditional values of the Greek city-state and the total rejection of these
values in favor of philosophy.[151] While Epictetus has succeeded in
alleviating his ideal philosopher – and himself, evidently[152] – of the
responsibilities of marriage, he has not made this into a general
principle. Unlike the Cynics, he has not espoused a radical cosmopolitanism that promotes complete freedom from all social institutions.[153] Rather, he continues to affirm the Stoic belief that the
civilized world reflects a divine plan and that every man is morally
obligated to lend his support to the divine plan through marriage
and raising children. The one exception to this rule is the "Cynic,"
although this figure also pledges his allegiance to this plan, being
appointed by "special dispensation" as God's servant to oversee the
workings of the whole.[154]

## 5. The middle of the second century CE and beyond

The teachings of Epictetus may, in fact, mark the culmination of the
Stoic–Cynic marriage debate. While the debate continues beyond

---

[149] Epictetus can also speak of God as the father and householder (οἰκοδεσπότης)
of human society, and the Cynic as his representive, e.g., *Diss.* 3.22.1–8.
[150] Epict. *Diss.* 3.22.77–82; see also 3.22.54, 96.
[151] See Deißner, *Das Idealbild.*
[152] Lucian *Demonax* 55.
[153] Cf. the description of "mild Cynicism" in Malherbe, "Self-Definition," 56–7.
[154] The phrase comes from R. D. Hicks, *Stoic and Epicurean,* Epochs of Philosophy (New York: Charles Scribner's Sons, 1920) 138. On the Stoic aspects of
Epictetus' Cynic see Karl Suso Frank, *Grundzüge der Geschichte des christlichen
Mönchtums,* Grundzüge 25 (Darmstadt: Wissenschaftliche Buchgesellschaft, 1979)
5–6; Malherbe, "Self-Definition," 50, 194 n. 27; and Margarethe Billerbeck, *Epiktet:
Vom Kynismus,* Philosophia Antiqua 34 (Leiden: E. J. Brill, 1978) 132.

the middle of the second century, our sources become increasingly scarce and there is little to suggest that these later authors took up the debate with the same fervor as the earlier ones. A possible exception is Aelius Herodianus, an Alexandrian born grammarian who served under the Stoic emperor Marcus Aurelius, and to whom the *Etymologicum Magnum* attributes the treatise *On Marriage and Life Together*. Unfortunately, the only remnant of this work is an etymology for the word "male."[155] Another possible exception is the philosopher Aurelianus Nicostratus (fl. middle second century?), a portion of whose treatise *On Marriage* is preserved by Stobaeus. All that survives, however, is a passage giving instruction on how to choose a wife and how to exercise prudence and self-control within marriage. To what degree it addressed other issues raised by the Stoic–Cynic debate is unclear.[156]

Aside from Herodianus and Nicostratus, we may point to three other authors from the middle to the late second century who provide information on the marriage debate. These are the rhetorician Hermogenes (fl. middle second century), the satirist Lucian of Samosata (ca. 120–85), and the sophist Maximus of Tyre (ca. 125– ca.185).[157] From Hermogenes we learn that the *thesis* "Should one marry?" (εἰ γαμητέον) continues to be used as an exercise in the rhetorical schools.[158] Lucian, in turn, makes brief allusion to Stoic and Cynic views on marriage in his anecdote on the exchange between Demonax and Epictetus, and in his parodies of Diogenes the Cynic.[159] And Maximus makes a similar allusion in reporting the philosophical heroism of Diogenes. According to Maximus,

---

[155] περὶ γάμου καὶ συμβιώσεως, *Etymologicum Magnum*, s.v. "ἄρσην" (cited below, p. 205).

[156] Stob. 4.536–9, 593–9 W.-H.

[157] On the influence of the marriage debate and the literature on household management on the neo-Pythagorean literature, probably also to be dated to this period, see Zeller, *Philosophie der Griechen* 3.2.158; Wilhelm, "Die Oeconomica," *Rh. Mus.* 70 (1915) 161–223, esp. 182–3; Alfons Städele, *Die Briefe des Pythagoras und der Pythagoreer*, Beiträge zur klassischen Philologie 115 (Meisenheim am Glan: Anton Hain, 1980) 166–9, 253–5, 267–8, 280, 321; Holger Thesleff (ed.), *The Pythagorean Texts of the Hellenistic Period*, Acta Academiae Aboensis, Humaniora 30/1 (Åbo, Finland: Åbo Akademi, 1965) 151–4; Armand Delatte, *Essai sur la politique pythagoricienne* (Liège/Paris: n.p., 1922; repr., Geneva: Slatkine, 1979) 163–8. On the dating of these documents, see Dassmann and Schöllgen, "Haus," 819–20; and the notes in Städele, *Briefe*. Also see the christianized Pythagorean collection, the *Sentences of Sextus* (second century?, Egypt?) 230b, 232, 235, 237.

[158] Hermogenes *Progymnasmata* 11.

[159] Lucian *Demonax* 55; *Vitarum auctio* 8–9; *Verae historiae* 2.18.

after Diogenes "stripped off all the encumbering circumstances (τὰς περιστάσεις πάσας) and liberated himself from fetters," he ranged the world as free as a bird, "not expending free time (ἀσχολούμενος) on the concerns of the city-state, not being strangled by the raising of children, not shut in by marriage."[160]

In the early third century, in his account of Augustus' speech to the married and unmarried men of Rome in the year 9 CE, the Roman historian Dio Cassius mentions several issues that are now familiar to us from the marriage discussions.[161] Again, at the end of that century or the beginning of the next, the author of *Ars rhetorica* informs us that the *thesis* "Should one marry?" is still one of the most commonly assigned rhetorical exercises in the *progymnasmata* curriculum.[162] We may see this first hand, moreover, in the writings of Libanius (fourth century) and Aphthonius (late fourth to early fifth century), although by the time we reach the *Progymnasmata* of the latter, it is really only the first few lines of his *thesis* εἰ γαμητέον that bear any resemblance to the earlier discussions.[163] Finally, again in the fourth century, the emperor Julian shows some awareness of certain elements of the marriage debate, as does the author of the *Amores* earlier in the century.[164]

## 6. First-century Judaism and early Christianity

Thus far we have traced the Stoic–Cynic marriage debate through Greek and Roman philosophical traditions. In this section we turn to Jewish and Christian sources, excluding 1 Corinthians. Our goal here is to demonstrate the extent to which this debate found a hearing in intellectual and cultural circles similar to those of Paul's own ministry. While most, if not all, of the Christian sources we will examine were written after Paul's day, the earlier ones nonetheless provide examples of how readily Stoic and Cynic views on marriage could be integrated into early Christian belief systems, while the later ones document the church's eventual disaffection with Stoic

---

[160] Maximus *Philosophumena* 36.5 Hobein. See also 32.9 H.
[161] Dio Cassius *Roman History* 56.1–10.
[162] [Dionysius of Halicarnassus] *Ars rhetorica* 2.1–2
[163] Libanius *Progymnasmata* 13.1 (*Opera* 8.550–61 Foerster); and Aphthonius *Progymnasmata* 13, trans. Ray Nadeau, "The Progymnasmata of Aphthonius," *Speech Monographs* 19 (1952) 264–85. On Libanius see Praechter, *Hierokles*, 143–7. On still other rhetoricians, see ibid., 143, 147–8.
[164] Julian *Oration* 6.185c-d; and [Lucian] *Amores* 19. For still other texts, see Praechter, *Hierokles*, 150.

views on marriage, a development that explains the later ascetic interpretation of 1 Corinthians 7. Regarding the Jewish sources, we will confine ourselves to three Hellenistic Jewish authors from the first century CE, Philo, Pseudo-Phocylides, and Josephus.[165]

## Philo of Alexandria

The Jewish philosopher Philo of Alexandria (fl. early first century CE) was an eclectic thinker who drew on several Greek philosophical traditions in the expression of his religious heritage. In his ethical theory, and particularly his political theory, Philo borrowed a considerable number of ideas from Stoicism.[166] His conception of the *kosmos* is very similar to that which the Stoic marriage discussions presume. He envisions the *kosmos* as consisting of city-states that are made up of households, the basis for which is marriage. The "economics" or "management" (οἰκονομία) of both household and city-state, Philo insists, begins with marriage, for without a wife a man is imperfect and homeless, but with a wife he has time for the affairs of his city-state while she attends to the management of the household.[167]

The influence of the Stoic marriage discussions on Philo's thinking may further be seen in his concern that the household provide the city-state with future generations of city dwellers. Philo claims that the violation of Mosaic regulations concerning legal, productive marriages undermines the affairs of households and cities alike, and he condemns pederasty and the exposure of newborns as practices that lead to the destruction of the cities.[168] "All true servants of God," he explains, "will fulfill the law of nature regarding the

---

[165] For Jewish sources before and after the first century CE see below, n. 188.

[166] Emil Schürer, *The History of the Jewish People in the Age of Jesus Christ (175 BC–AD 135)*, vol. 3.2, rev. and ed. Geza Vermes, Fergus Millar, and Martin Goodman (Edinburgh: T. and T. Clark, 1987) 887–8; Ray Barraclough, "Philo's Politics: Roman Rule and Hellenistic Judaism," *ANRW* 2.21.1 (1984) 493–7, 533–42; Max Pohlenz, "Philon von Alexandreia," *Nachrichten der Akademie der Wissenschaften zu Göttingen, philologisch-historische Klasse* 4 (1942) 461–78; Michel Spanneut, *Permanence du stoïcisme: De Zénon à Malraux* (Gembloux: J. Duculot, 1973) 119–23; Paul Wendland, "Philo und die kynisch-stoische Diatribe," *Beiträge zur Geschichte der griechischen Philosophie und Religion*, ed. Paul Wendland and Otto Kern (Berlin: Georg Reimer, 1895) 3–75.

[167] Philo *De Josepho* 29, 38–9 (on the latter see Goodenough, *The Politics of Philo*, 43–4, 48–50); *Quaest. et sol. in Gen.* 1.26; 4.165).

[168] Philo: *De specialibus legibus* 3.31; *De Abrahamo* 135–41; *De vita contemp.* 62; *De virtutibus* 131–2.

procreation of children,"[169] while persons involved in unfruitful marriages are "enemies of nature," overturning her statutes.[170] A recurring theme in Philo's writings, moreover, is his insistence that the goal of marriage is the procreation of legitimate children, not sexual pleasure.[171]

One also sees the influence of the Stoic marriage discussions in Philo's conception of the wise man. Philo tells us that the wise man is by definition well suited to civic affairs as well as household management.[172] The dissemination of philosophical virtue, according to Philo, results in better households and city-states because it produces men capable of managing these.[173] Indeed, Philo views the very practice of the duties of householder and citizen as "virtues."[174] Finally, in several of his writings Philo employs the Stoic categories of the "good man" and the "bad man." In interpreting Deuteronomy 28.6, "You shall be blessed in your coming in and you shall be blessed in your going out," Philo sees a reference to the good man (ὁ σπουδαῖος) being blessed as he fulfills his duties as statesman and householder. By contrast, in his treatise *On the Giants*, Philo speaks of the bad man (ὁ φαῦλος) as one who is without a home or city-state, and an exile.[175]

The Stoic conception of marriage as a primary responsibility for the man seeking to act in accord with the divine will has thus made significant impact on Philo's thought. But Philo, like Epictetus and certain other Stoics, also accommodates a number of Cynic ideas on marriage within his ethical theory. We observe this in his writings in two ways, in his personal code of ethics, and in his description of two groups of Jewish philosophers. Just as Epictetus attributed several Cynic views on marriage to an exemplary philosophical type,

---

[169] Philo *De praemiis et poenis* 108, νόμον φύσεως τὸν ἐπὶ παιδοποιίᾳ; cf. *De Decalogo* 119.
[170] Philo *De spec. leg.* 3.36, ἐχθροὶ τῆς φύσεως.
[171] E.g., Philo: *De virtu.* 207; *Quod deterius* 102, 171; *Quaest. et sol. in Gen.* 4.68, 154; *De Abr.* 248–9, 253; *De Jos.* 43; *De vita Mos.* 1.28
[172] Philo: *Quaest. et sol. in Gen.* 3.33; *De ebrietate* 91–2.
[173] Philo *De mutatione nominum* 149. See also *Hypothetica* 7.3, 14; and *De spec. leg.* 3.169–75, which reflect knowledge of the literature on household management. Wolfgang Schrage, "Zur Ethik der neutestamentlichen Haustafeln," *NTS* 21 (1974) 8 also sees the influence of this literature in *De Dec.* 165–7, but there is nothing in this passage that cannot be accounted for in terms of Philo's Jewish heritage. The same applies to Schrage's assessment of *4 Maccabees* 2.10–12 (ibid.).
[174] ἀρετῶν, Philo: *De fuga et inventione* 36; cf. Mus. *frag.* 3.42.28 L. (13.1 H.), cited above.
[175] Philo: *De praemiis* 113; *De gigantibus* 67; cf. *Quaest. et sol. in Gen.* 4.165; and *De spec. leg.* 3.1–3.

the Cynic, Philo too attributes these views to those whom he considers to be model philosophers, the Essenes and the Therapeutae. Whether these philosophers actually existed in the manner Philo supposes is a difficult question to answer.[176] It is enough for us, however, to know that Philo's description of them reflects knowledge of the Stoic–Cynic marriage debate, and that this knowledge had currency among his readership.

Philo describes the Essenes in two tractates, in the *Hypothetica* and in *Every Good Man is Free*, the second being a philosophical treatise very much in the Stoic and Cynic tradition in which the Essenes are brought in as an example.[177] According to Philo, the Essenes are philosophers[178] who pursue a communal lifestyle that is the "clearest proof of a perfected and abundantly happy life."[179] What makes this life possible, Philo explains, is freedom from the passions and from sensual desire, which he calls "the only true and real freedom."[180] Regarding marriage, a subject to which he devotes more than a fifth of the *Hypothetica*, Philo tells us that the Essenes "astutely perceive marriage as that which alone or for the most part is likely to undo their communal life."[181] This is because marriage forces a man to do things hostile to communal living by awakening in him the passions from which the Essenes seek to escape. A wife, Philo explains, is a selfish, jealous, and seductive creature, and when children arrive, a man is forced by the constraints of nature to care for them, too.[182] In the minds of the Essenes, marriage subjects a man to obligations that destroy his chances of attaining the true and only real freedom, causing him to pass into slavery.[183]

[176] See, e.g., Emil Schürer, *The History of the Jewish People in the Age of Jesus Christ (175 BC–AD 135)*, vol. 2, rev. and ed. Geza Vermes, Fergus Millar, and Matthew Black (Edinburgh: T. and T. Clark, 1979) 579–80, 593–7.
[177] Philo *Quod omnis probus* 62–3, 75–91; cf. 121–6 where "Diogenes the Cynic philosopher" is used as an example of the perfectly free man. On Stoic and Cynic influence in this text see Madeleine Petit (ed.), *"Quod omnis probus liber sit"*: *Introduction, texte, traduction et notes*, Les œuvres de Philon d'Alexandrie 28 (Paris: Éditions du Cerf, 1974) 39–42, 48–57, 68–78, 83–6, 110–14. See also Otto Hense, "Bio bei Philo," *Rh. Mus.*, n.s. 47 (1892) 219–40; Schürer, *History of the Jewish People*, 3.2.856; and Stanley Kent Stowers, *The Diatribe and Paul's Letter to the Romans*, SBLDS 57 (Chico, Calif.: Scholars, 1981) 69: "*Quod omnis probus liber sit* comes closer to being a typical diatribe than any of Philo's other works. Aside from a handful of allusions to the Pentateuch it could have been written by a Stoic."
[178] Philo *Quod omnis probus* 80–3, 88.
[179] Philo *Quod omnis probus* 91; cf. 84, and *Hypothetica* 11.1.
[180] Philo *Hypoth.* 11.3–4; *Quod omnis probus* 76–9, 88, 91.
[181] Philo *Hypoth.* 11.14.
[182] Philo *Hypoth.* 11.14, 16.
[183] Philo *Hypoth.* 11.17.

To be sure, this description of the Essenes' stance on marriage owes much to Jewish wisdom literature's negative assessment of women.[184] But Philo's reference to the responsibilities of married life, especially in the context of a discussion about philosophical freedom, points in another direction – to Cynic ideas from the Stoic–Cynic marriage debate. This complex of ideas is given fuller expression in Philo's description of yet another group of Jewish philosophers, the Therapeutae.[185]

Like the Essenes, the Therapeutae are philosophers who live the communal life in pursuit of perfect happiness.[186] They are "theoretically" oriented, Philo tells us, meaning that they consider the contemplative part of philosophy to be the "best and most godlike." As a consequence they devote their entire day to philosophical studies.[187] To accommodate this lifestyle they abandon all responsibilities related to marriage and the household, believing that concern for the necessities of life and managing property are at odds with philosophy since, among other things, they consume time, and conserving time is essential for the philosopher.[188] Beyond this, they also free themselves of their responsibilities to their city-states. Eschewing city life altogether they live in a loose philosophical community in the countryside as "citizens of heaven and the world."[189]

---

[184] See John Strugnell, "Flavius Josephus and the Essenes: *Antiquities* XVIII.18–22," *JBL* 77 (1958) 110; and, e.g., Qohelet 7.26–8; Sirach 47.14–19; *Test Reub* 5.3; 6.1, 3.

[185] Cf. Paul Wendland, "Die Therapeuten und die philonische Schrift vom beschaulichen Leben," *Jahrbücher für classische Philologie*, suppl. 22 (1896) 703–4: "[Philo] sees the Stoic ideal of the simple life in accord with nature actualized in the life-style of the Therapeutae... With this, his thoughts are moving completely in the sphere of the Stoic–Cynic diatribe." See also: ibid., 705; and "Philo und die kynisch-stoische Diatribe," 66–7.

[186] Philo *De vita contemp.* 2.11; 3.24; 11.90. As with the Essenes, Philo states several times that they are philosophers, e.g., 3.21, 22, 26, 28, 30.

[187] Philo *De vita contemp.* 8.67; 4.34.

[188] Philo *De vita contemp.* 2.13–18 (here χρόνος). As Wendland, "Die Therapeuten," 748–50, correctly points out, the need for "free time" for philosophy or academic study is also a theme elsewhere in Jewish literature. See Sirach 38.24, "the wisdom of the scribe comes about in opportunity for leisure" (σοφία γραμματέως ἐν εὐκαιρίᾳ σχολῆς); *m. Ketubot* 5.6; *m. Eduyot* 4.10; *t. Bekorot* 6.10–11; *b. Megillah* 27a; *b. Ketubot* 62; *b. Bar. Kidd.* 29b; and especially the rabbinic material on Rabbi Simeon ben Azzai, *t. Yebamot* 8.7; *b. Yebamot* 63b; *b. Sota* 4b. On the possibility of Stoic or Cynic influence on these texts see Henry A. Fischel: *Rabbinic Literature and Greco-Roman Philosophy*, Studia Post-Biblica 21 (Leiden: E. J. Brill, 1973), esp. 4–9, 90–7; "Studies in Cynicism and the Ancient Near East: The Transformation of a Chreia," *Religions in Antiquity: Essays in Memory of Erwin Ramsdell Goodenough*, ed. Jacob Neusner, Numen Suppl. 14 (Leiden: E. J. Brill, 1968) 372–411.

[189] Philo *De vita contemp.* 2.19; 3.22; 11.90.

In comparing these two, basically Cynic, positions on marriage, it is instructive to note that Philo presents the Therapeutae as the "contemplative" counterparts to the Essenes, who by contrast live the "active life."[190] Thus, while the exclusive devotion to philosophy and extreme cosmopolitanism of the Therapeutae bring them very close to the position on marriage we have seen in the *Cynic Epistles of Diogenes*, the "active" philosophy of the Essenes suggests a different Cynic orientation. As Philo explains, their philosophy encourages them in the practical matters of household management and politics (οἰκονομία, πολιτεία), and – although Philo is inconsistent on this point – they seem to live in city-states.[191] This would indicate that they held a Stoic view of the world similar to what Philo elsewhere attributes to the wise and good man, except for the fact that they forgo marriage. In turn, this places them close to those Stoics known to Cicero, who on the issue of marriage adopted a Cynic stance. Inasmuch as the Essenes manage their households without the benefit of a wife (a view also held by Josephus) they may even represent a position criticized by Antipater and Hierocles, since the latter speak against such households as being "incomplete."[192]

From our examination of Philo's writings thus far, it is evident that this author, like Epictetus, is able to accommodate several views on marriage from the Stoic–Cynic debate within his philosophical system. For this reason, however, like Seneca he also verges on inconsistency. Despite his pronounced Stoic leanings, some of Philo's beliefs pertaining to an individual's responsibilities to the city-state "tend to underline and enlarge upon the key ideas in 'De Vita Contemplativa'"[193] – i.e., his description of the Therapeutae.

With regard to cosmopolitan beliefs, Philo is largely Stoic.[194] But inherent in his cosmopolitanism is a sense of alienation that also reflects Platonic, Cynic, and Jewish mystical attitudes toward the

---

[190] Philo *De vita contemp.* 1.1, τῶν θεωρίαν ἀσπασαμένων versus τὸν πρακτικὸν βίον.

[191] Philo *Quod omnis probus* 72, 82–3; *Hypoth.* 11.1. Josephus *Jewish War* 2.124, 125 also says they live in city-states.

[192] Antip. *SVF* 3.254.27 (Stob. 4.507.9 W.-H.); Hierocles 52.20; 53.15 v.A. (Stob. 4.502.5–6; 4.503.12 W.-H.). On Josephus see below, next section. With regard to the Therapeutae, Philo says that the young men among them behave toward the older men and women "like genuine sons toward fathers and mothers" (*De vita contemp.* 9.72).

[193] Barraclough, "Philo's Politics," 544; cf. Wendland, "Die Therapeuten," 747–8. See also Goodenough, *The Politics of Philo*, 66–75.

[194] See, e.g., Barraclough, "Philo's Politics," 539.

*kosmos*, leading him ultimately to favor the contemplative life over the active one.[195] In the area of political and ethical theory, Erwin Goodenough points to what he calls a "warfare between statesman and philosopher in Philo's own life,"[196] for while Philo promotes marriage, household management, and political activities, "he alternates bewilderingly between this attitude toward the state and another one, the ascetic and individualistic attitude, which seems to have originated with the Cynics and to have run through much of Stoic and Sceptic teaching ..."[197]

Thus, Philo's positive stance toward marriage is qualified by the fact that his philosophical and religious allegiances are divided between a Stoic attitude that recognizes certain civic responsibilities to the *kosmos*, and an attitude which envisions an even higher calling to a contemplative, spiritual life.[198] It is this latter attitude that comes to expression in the famous opening lines to book three of his *Special Laws*, bringing to mind the Cynic position in the Stoic–Cynic debate. Here, in a sonorous, doleful lament Philo speaks nostalgically of a period in his life when he had "leisure time for philosophy" (φιλοσοφίᾳ σχολάζων) and contemplation of the *kosmos*, before he found himself violently plunged into "a great ocean of civil cares."[199]

---

[195] Ibid., 539–40; Wendland, "Die Therapeuten," 734; Ehrhardt, *Politische Metaphysik*, 204–5. At one point Philo even boasts that the Jewish people are the "contemplative race" (*Quaest. et sol. in Exod.* 2.42).

[196] Goodenough, *The Politics of Philo*, 83.

[197] Ibid., 69. As Goodenough further remarks: "The interesting thing is that Philo strongly upholds both solutions of this problem, insisting that the philosopher's concern with the true state, the world, cut him off from obligation or concern with society, and then insisting just as heartily that this contact with the world-state put the philosopher under special obligation to serve the human organization" (ibid.; see also 70–5).

[198] Cf. Barraclough, "Philo's Politics," 550: "Philo is concerned for a life of contemplation for the individual, stability for society and the *status quo* for the Jews in the Roman Empire. The contemplative life surpasses but does not contradict the political life" – perhaps, but they are in the very least mutually exclusive. See Goodenough, *The Politics of Philo*, 72 and n. 40; and the following discussion.

[199] Philo *De spec. leg.* 3.1–3. Cf. Philo's description of Moses commanding those in his charge to dedicate themselves to leisure "for the sole purpose of pursuing philosophy": σχολάζοντας ... μόνῳ τῷ φιλοσοφεῖν (*De vita Mosis* 2.211); ἑνὶ μόνῳ σχολάζοντας τῷ φιλοσοφεῖν (*De opificio mundi* 128) – both passages cited by Johann Jakob Wettstein, *Novum Testamentum Graecum* (Amsterdam: Dommerian, 1752; repr., Graz, Austria: Akademische Druck- und Verlagsanstalt, 1962) 2.126. Similarly, Philo *De praemiis* 122 speaks of the wise man devoting leisure time to discourses on wisdom and thereby achieving the blessed and happy life (ἐνσχολάσει τοῖς σοφίας θεωρήμασι, μακαρίας καὶ εὐδαίμονος ζωῆς ἐπιλαχών). Occasionally Philo, like his Therapeutae, even expresses an aversion toward the city-states: *De*

To some extent Philo attempts to account for these inconsistencies – this division of allegiance – by means of a temporal solution. The practical life of the householder and statesman, he says in his treatise *On Flight and Finding*, must come before the contemplative one, as a preparation and prelude to it. There is no justification, he says a few lines earlier in this treatise, for those – perhaps Cynics known to him in Alexandria – who go around filthy and destitute, having chosen a solitary life from the first.[200] By this measure he also castigates the early Greek philosophers Anaxagoras and Democritus for showing so little concern for their household affairs as they rushed off in pursuit of philosophy. The Therapeutae, by contrast, dispose of their goods thoughtfully, exercising good household management to the last.[201] Finally, Philo indicates that the Essenes and Therapeutae also fulfilled their civic responsibilities before taking up philosophical pursuits, for not only do the Therapeutae have households to dispose of, but members of both groups leave behind children of former marriages.[202] Even so, Philo's temporal solution does not solve all the problems. Not all Essenes have fulfilled the duty of procreation, and among the Therapeutae there are young unmarried men and women.[203] In fact, as we have seen, Philo himself admits to engaging in politics *after* pursuing the contemplative life, albeit against his will. The divisions in Philo's allegiances thus remain, and as Goodenough remarks, "his very inconsistency is a reflection of the spirit of the age."[204]

## Pseudo-Phocylides and Josephus

A contemporary of Philo and perhaps also from Alexandria,[205] the author known as Pseudo-Phocylides also gives us some indication of the influence the Stoic–Cynic marriage debates had on certain groups of Jews in the first century. In a collection of aphorisms,

---

*spec. leg.* 2.42–7; cf. *De Dec.* 2–13; *De ebr.* 99–103 (one also finds this in Musonius, *frag.* 11.84.10–11 L. [61.15–16 H.]: ... τῶν ἀστικῶν κακῶν, ἅπερ ἐμπόδιον τῷ φιλοσοφεῖν). On the political realities of Philo's day see Barraclough, "Philo's Politics," 417–86; Schürer, *The History of the Jewish People* 3.2.842–4.

200  Philo *De fuga* 36, 33.
201  Philo *De vita contemp.* 13–17. Cf. Philodemus' criticism of similar actions on the part of Cynics in his day, *On Household Management* coll. 12–13.
202  Philo *De vita contemp.* 13, 18; *Hypoth.* 11.13; cf. 11.3.
203  Philo *Hypoth.* 11.13 and *De vita contemp.* 8.67–8.
204  Goodenough, *The Politics of Philo*, 73.
205  P. W. van der Horst, *The Sentences of Pseudo-Phocylides*, (Leiden: E. J. Brill, 1978) 81–3.

which he has arranged in the form of a poem, this author includes a section that deals successively with three topics: the relations between husband and wife, between parents and children, and between a master and his slaves.[206] Not only does this reflect the general schema of the literature on household management, but as several scholars have noted, many of the aphorisms in the first group have close parallels in Stoic discussions on marriage.[207]

Finally, late in the first century CE, the Jewish historian Josephus shows some knowledge of the marriage debate. In his description of Jewish marriage laws, he attributes to Moses the Stoic dogma that procreation of legitimate children contributes to the welfare of the household and the city-state.[208] Similarly, in two other passages he upholds the Stoic position that the purpose of sexual relations is procreation not pleasure.[209] Beyond this, Josephus offers a picture of the Essenes which, consistent with Philo's, depicts them as supporting a modified Cynic position on marriage. According to Josephus, they are philosophers who have found marriage incompatible with their way of life and have established the sort of quasi-households that Antipater and Hierocles would have labeled "incomplete." In a passage that seems to parody the literature on household management, he explains that they live unmarried and provide each other with services, thereby eliminating the need for wives or slaves. As for children, the third subject treated by works on household management, Josephus tells us that they adopt the children of others and treat them as family, "thereby not abrogating the institution of marriage and the offspring that results from it."[210] In this last remark we see an Essene response to the Stoic concern for procreation. But not all Essenes, Josephus adds, were satisfied with this response, for some married, siding with the (Stoic) view that without marriage the race would die out. These, moreover, required their wives to undergo tests of fertility, and they never engaged in intercourse during the time of their wives' pregnancies – proof that they married for procreation, not lust.[211]

---

206 Pseudo-Phocylides *Sentences* 175–227.

207 E.g., van der Horst, *Sentences*, 225–44.

208 Josephus *Antiquities* 3.274.

209 Jos. *War* 2.161; *Against Apion* 2.199. On Josephus' awareness of the literature on household management, see *Against Apion* 2.201 and the discussions of this passage in Meeks, "Image of the Androgyne," 177 n. 67; and Wendland, "Die Therapeuten," 712.

210 Jos. *Ant.* 18.21; *War* 2.120–1.

211 Jos. *War* 2.160–1.

The New Testament

In comparison to the Jewish materials just examined, the influence exerted by the Stoic–Cynic marriage debate on Christian literature of the first and early second centuries appears to have been relatively meager. Even so, excluding for the moment 1 Corinthians 7, which we will examine in the next chapter, we can point to at least two texts from the New Testament that may demonstrate some awareness of this debate. The first is Matthew 19.10–12. Here the disciples of Jesus respond to his prohibition of divorce (19.3–9) with the surprising conclusion that it is "not beneficial to marry" (οὐ συμφέρει γαμῆσαι). What stands behind this conclusion may be a refusal on the disciples' part to become permanently involved in the responsibilities of a husband and householder in light of what they perceive to be a higher calling, the kingdom of heaven.[212] If this is accurate, then the disciples' position can be understood as a variation of the Cynic position that marriage was an impediment to the higher calling of philosophy. Carrying this interpretation a step further, we may also speculate on Matthew's purpose in juxtaposing this passage, which is from his special material ("M"), to Jesus' prohibition of divorce, which he received from Mark. It is possible that Matthew sought to bring a particularly Christian understanding of marriage – that it is permanent – to bear on the marriage debate, thereby condemning the sort of solution adopted by Philo's Essenes and Therapeutae, who simply abandoned their wives, families, and domestic responsibilities for the philosophical life. From Luke, moreover, we have evidence that such a solution may have had its advocates in early Christian circles, too.[213]

A second passage from the New Testament that merits our attention is Luke 10.38–42. Here Jesus is invited to the house of a woman named Martha. While Martha is distracted (περιεσπᾶτο) by her duties as hostess, her sister Mary sits attentively at Jesus' feet listening to his discourse. When Martha complains that Mary should also be helping, Jesus tells her that while she is concerned

---

[212] On the possible Stoic flavor of the term συμφέρει, see chap. 3 n. 374. The disciples' response is similarly construed by the followers of Basilides, an early second-century gnostic group. They claimed that Jesus' disciples took this position "on account of the circumstances arising from marriage (διὰ τὰ ἐκ τοῦ γάμου συμβαίνοντα)," "fearing the demands on their leisure time (ἀσχολία) associated with providing for the necessities of life" (Clem. Alex. *Strom.* bk. 3, chap. 1.1.4 [2.195.14–17 S.]).

[213] See Luke 18.28–30.

(μεριμνάω) about many things, Mary has chosen "the good portion" (τὴν ἀγαθὴν μερίδα). In all, I do not think it is unreasonable to see in this passage a reflection of the question so central to the marriage debate, whether involvement in domestic affairs distracted one from pursuing philosophy.[214] Although this question was usually posed with reference to men, Musonius Rufus, as we have noted, poses it with regard to women in his tractate, *That Women, Too, Should Pursue Philosophy*.[215] Such an interpretation of this passage is also suggested by Luke's use of the verbs "to be distracted" (περισπάομαι), and "to be concerned" (μεριμνάω), which parallel Stoic usage in the marriage debate.[216]

Besides these two passages, influence of the Stoic–Cynic marriage debate may be indicated by the presence in several early Christian writings of a form of moral exhortation known as the *Haustafel*, or household code.[217] Recent scholarship has concluded that these household codes, the aim of which was to order Christian life-styles on the model of a well-ordered household, derive their basic structure from the Hellenistic literature on household management.[218]

---

[214] Several scholars have compared the Lukan passage to Epictetus' discussion of marital responsibilities and the Cynic (*Diss.* 3.22.67–82). See, e.g., Archibald Robertson and Alfred Plummer, *A Critical and Exegetical Commentary on the First Epistle of St Paul to the Corinthians*, 2nd edn., ICC (Edinburgh: T. and T. Clark, 1914) 158; and Wolbert, *Ethische Argumentation*, 130–1; cf. Niederwimmer, *Askese und Mysterium*, 113 n. 162. See also Epict. *Diss.* 1.29.59.

[215] Musonius *frag.* 3.40.8–42.29 L. (9.17–13.3 H.). See also the *Cynic Ep. of Crates* 30, 32, 33; and D.L. 6.98 (regarding Crates' wife Hipparchia). Cf. 1 Tim. 2.11–15.

[216] See below, pp. 199–204. See also the discussion of this passage in Gerd Theissen: *Sociology of Early Palestinian Christianity* (Philadelphia: Fortress, 1977) 10–17; cf. 88, and *The Social Setting of Pauline Christianity: Essays on Corinth* (Philadelphia: Fortress, 1982) 39, 44–9. It is worth noting that starting with Origen the church fathers saw Martha and Mary as examples of the "active life" and the "contemplative life," respectively. On this see Ignace de la Potterie, "Le titre ΚΥΡΙΟΣ appliqué à Jésus dans l'Évangile de Luc," *Mélanges bibliques: En hommage au R. P. Béda Rigaux*, ed. Albert Descamps and André de Halleux (Gembloux: J. Duculot, 1970) 129 n. 2 (lit.).

[217] Aside from the texts usually named in this connection (Col. 3.18–4.1; Eph. 5.21–6.9; 1 Tim. 2.8–6.2; Titus 1.5–9; 2.2–10; 1 Pet. 2.18–3.7; *1 Clement* 1.3; 21.6–8; *Didache* 4.9–11; *Epistle of Barnabas* 19.5–7; Ignatius *Polycarp* 4.1–6.2; and Polycarp *Philippians* 4.2–6.1), the following should also be considered: Matt. 13.52 (cf. Sen. *Ep.* 64.7); Heb. 3.2–6; 1 John 2.12–14; and *perhaps* Rom. 13.1, 5.

[218] See Balch, *Let Wives Be Submissive*, 23–121; ibid., "Household Codes," 25–50; Klaus Thraede, "Zum historischen Hintergrund der 'Haustafel' des NT," *Jahrbuch für Antike und Christentum*, suppl. 8: *Pietas: Festschrift für Bernhard Kötting*, ed. Ernst Dassmann and K. Suso Frank (Münster: Aschendorff, 1980) 359–68; and the overviews in Witherington, *Women in the Earliest Churches*, 42–7; Fiorenza, *Bread Not Stone*, 72–4; Fiedler "Haustafel," esp. 1070–1; and David C. Verner, *The*

Given the interest that many Stoics took in this literature, indirect avenues of influence between Christian discussions of the well-ordered household and Stoic and Cynic discussions on marriage should not be ruled out. This is especially true for the extended household code in 1 Timothy 2.8–6.2, which stresses the importance of marriage and procreation and denounces certain persons who object to marriage,[219] perhaps some type of gnostics.[220]

### Second- and third-century Christian apologists[221]

After the period of the New Testament, as Christianity came more and more in contact with the greater Hellenistic culture, Stoic and Cynic arguments for and against marriage became increasingly appealing to leaders of the church. As several scholars have noted, four apologetic writings from the middle of the second century to the early third present a point of view that is prominent in many Stoic marriage discussions.[222] The passages in question, *Epistle to Diognetus* 5.4–6,[223] Athenagoras *Legatio* 33.1–2, Minucius Felix *Octavius* 31.5, and Justin Martyr *Apology* 1.27.1–3 and 29.1, all maintain that the sole purpose of marriage is the procreation of children. In addition, Justin, who admits familiarity with both Stoic and Cynic authors, and specifically with Musonius,[224] incorporates this viewpoint into his theology in a manner reminiscent of Matthew 19.10–12, claiming that Christians "would not marry in the first place except to raise children, or foregoing marriage we would live perfectly continent," for which he provides examples.[225] Regarding

---

*Household of God: The Social World of the Pastoral Epistles*, SBLDS 71 (Chio, Calif.: Scholars, 1983) 16–23, 84–91, cf. 91–111.

[219] 1 Tim. 5.14, βούλομαι οὖν νεωτέρας γαμεῖν, τεκνογονεῖν, οἰκοδεσποτεῖν, cf. 2.15; and 1 Tim. 4.3, κωλυόντων γαμεῖν – cf. Epict. *Diss.* 3.22.68, οὐδὲν κωλύσει καὶ γῆμαι αὐτὸν καὶ παιδοποιήσασθαι, re the Cynic in a city of wise men.

[220] See Martin Dibelius and Hans Conzelmann, *The Pastoral Epistles*, Hermeneia (Philadelphia: Fortress, 1972) 65–7. On the possibility that early gnostics were influenced by the Cynic marriage discussions, see below, nn. 243–4; cf. Jonas, *Gnostic Religion*, 145, commenting on Clement's report on Marcion in *Strom.* bk. 3, chap. 4.25 (2.207.6–25 S.): "Here the pollution by the flesh and its lust, so widespread a theme in this age, is not even mentioned ... it is the aspect of *reproduction* which disqualifies sexuality" (his emphasis).

[221] For this and the following sections, see Noonan, *Contraception*, 76–85.

[222] See Konrad Graf Preysing, "Ehezweck," 85–110; Stelzenberger, *Beziehungen*, 417–19; and Preisker, *Christentum und Ehe*, 179–80.

[223] The *Epistle to Diognetus* may be as late as the third century.

[224] Justin *Apol.* 2.3, 7–8; *Dialogue with Tryphon* 2.

[225] Justin *Apol.* 1.29.1 and 1.15.4–6.

Athenagoras, Preysing has argued that this author's use of the terms παιδοποιία ("child bearing") and παιδοποιεῖσθαι ("to bear children"), as well as the metaphor of a farmer sowing seed indicate the proximity of this text to Stoic discussions.[226] And finally, in the *Epistle to Diognetus* we sense the issue of cosmopolitanism, so prominent in the marriage debate: "[Christians] dwell in their own fatherlands, but as if sojourners in them; they share all things as citizens, and suffer all things as strangers. Every foreign country is their fatherland, and every fatherland is a foreign country. They marry as all men, they bear children, but they do not expose their offspring."[227]

### Clement of Alexandria

With Clement of Alexandria, at the end of the second century, we are in the presence of a church father who exhibits broad learning in Greek philosophical traditions. His ethical thought especially is influenced by Stoic ideas, in particular through the teachings of Philo and Musonius, and therefore it is not surprising that he also demonstrates currency with the marriage debate.[228] In book two, chapter twenty-three of his *Stromateis* ("Miscellanies"), for example, he gives a short synopsis of various Greek positions, including those of Plato, Democritus, Epicurus, the Stoics, and the Peripatetics.[229] Here he also identifies the basic question of the debate, "should one marry" (εἰ γαμητέον), and states that it was discussed with respect to the various circumstances of a man's life.

[226] Preysing, "Ehezweck," 97–100.
[227] *Letter to Diognetus* 5.5–6, trans. Kirsopp Lake, *The Apostolic Fathers*, vol. 2: *The Shepherd of Hermas, the Martyrdom of Polycarp, the Epistle to Diognetus*, LCL (Cambridge: Harvard University Press/London: William Heinemann, 1913) 359, 361.
[228] Regarding Stoic influence on Clement's view of marriage see Max Pohlenz, "Klemens von Alexandreia und sein hellenisches Christentum," *Nachrichten der Akademie der Wissenschaften zu Göttingen, philologisch-historische Klasse* 5.3 (1943) 144; and Broudéhoux, *Mariage et famille*, 115–37. See also Michel Spanneut, *Le stoïcisme des Pères de l'Eglise de Clément de Rome à Clément d'Alexandrie*, Patristica Sorbonensia 1 (Paris: Éditions de Seuil, 1957) 259–60; and Preisker, *Christentum und Ehe*, 200–211. Eusebius *Church History* 5.10.1–11.2 says that Clement's predecessor and teacher at the Christian catechetical school in Alexandria, Pantaeus, was a former Stoic. Concerning the influence of Philo on Clement's ethics of marriage, see Stelzenberger, *Beziehungen*, 419–21. On Clement's knowledge of Musonius see Wendland, *Quaestiones Musonianae*, 31–8, which he qualifies in his review of C. *Musonii Rufi reliquiae* ed. O. Hense, *Berliner philologische Wochenschrift* 26 (1906) 197–202; and Charles Pomeroy Parker, "Musonius in Clement," *Harvard Studies in Classical Philology* 12 (1901) 191–200.
[229] Clem. Alex. *Strom*. bk. 2, chap. 23.138.2–5 (2.189.12–20 S.).

Marriage itself he defines as "the legal union of a man and a woman for the procreation of legitimate children."[230] Beyond this Clement knows of the Stoic classification of marriage as an "indifferent" (ἀδιάφορον),[231] as well as their arguments that nature designed the human body for sexual union; that a household without a wife is "incomplete"; and that one must marry for the sake of one's homeland, the succession of children, and the wholeness of the *kosmos*.[232] Regarding this last idea he attributes to Plato the Stoic position that men who forgo marriage bring about a dearth of children and thereby destroy "both the cities and the *kosmos*, which is constituted by them."[233]

Clement not only knows of these various positions on marriage, however, he also adopts many of the Stoic arguments as his own. To some extent he regarded them as a welcome antidote against the dualistic ascetic groups of his day, such as the gnostics.[234] In the second book of his *Paedagogus*, for instance, he introduces chapter ten with a clear statement of the Stoic position that marital relations are to be undertaken entirely for the purpose of procreation.[235] This dogma, in turn, runs like a leitmotiv through book three of his *Stromateis*.[236] He even reads it into Paul's statements in 1 Corinthians 7.3–5, interpreting the duty owed one's spouse in verse 3 as procreation, and concluding that this is also the object of the verb "to withhold or defraud" in verse 5.[237]

[230] Clem. Alex. *Strom.* bk. 2, chap. 23.137.1, 3–4 (2.188.25–7; 189.1–8 S.). On Stoic influence here see Broudéhoux, *Mariage et famille*, 74; and the notes to the Greek text in the Stählin edition, 2.188–90.
    [231] Clem. Alex. *Strom.* bk. 2, chap. 23.138.5 (2.189.18–19 S.). On this see John R. Donahue, "Stoic Indifferents and Christian Indifference in Clement of Alexandria," *Traditio* 19 (1963) 438–46; and Broudéhoux, *Mariage et famille*, 34 n. 94. Cf. Clem. Alex. *Strom.* bk. 3, chap. 5.40.2; 41.4; 42.5 (2.214.11–13, 30–1; 215.20–1 S.).
    [232] Clem. Alex. *Strom.* bk. 2, chap. 23.139.3; 140.1 (2.190.2–5, 15–18 S.).
    [233] Clem. Alex. *Strom.* bk. 2, chap. 23.141.5 (2.191.10–15 S.), τάς τε πόλεις καὶ τὸν κόσμον τὸν ἐκ τούτων.
    [234] See, e.g., Gryson, *Les origines du célibat*, 7–13; and Oulton and Chadwick, *Alexandrian Christianity*, 22–39. For a time it was believed that Clement, in the tradition of the Stoics, wrote a tractate of his own on marriage; see Broudéhoux, *Mariage et famille*, 8–10.
    [235] Clem. Alex. *Paedagogus* bk. 2, chap. 10.83.1 (1.208.2–6 S.). On this see Broudéhoux, *Mariage et famille*, 77–9.
    [236] Clem. Alex. *Strom.* bk. 3, chap. 3.24.1; chap. 7.58.1–2; chap. 11.71.4; chap. 12.79.3; 81.4; 82.3; 89.2 (2.206.20–2; 222.27–223.1; 228.16–22; 231.23–5; 233.2–5, 21–5; 237.13–17 S.); cf. chap. 9.67.1 (2.226.19–25 S.). On this see Noonan, *Contraception*, 76–7. In *Strom.* bk. 2, chap. 18.93.1 (2.163.8–12 S.) Clement states that the man who does not want children ought not marry.
    [237] Clem. Alex. *Strom.* bk. 3, chap. 18.107.5 (2.246.5–9 S.); and chap. 15.96.2; 97.1 (2.240.14–18, 21–24 S.).

Another instance is book seven of the *Stromateis*, where Clement defines the true gnostic as one who necessarily takes on the responsibilities of marriage, having been trained in marriage, procreation, and the oversight of a household.[238] This, too, Clement is able to read back into his own Christian tradition, maintaining not only that *all* of Paul's letters contain *innumerable* rules "on marriages and on begetting children and on management of the household," but also that Jesus taught monogamy "for the sake of begetting children and oversight of the household."[239] Clement, however, stops short of basing his understanding of morality on the Stoic conception of the *kosmos*. While he is willing to admit that procreation assures the permanence of the world,[240] in an exegesis of Luke 14.26 he uses the connection Stoics saw between marriage, households, cities, and the *kosmos* to warn Christians *against* involvement with "the world" through marriage and procreation.[241] Here we detect a Christian form of the alienation from the cities and the *kosmos* that we saw in Philo's writings. In fact, it is in accord with this sense of alienation that Clement, like Philo, can also lend his support to several Cynic arguments against marriage, as we see in this exegesis of 1 Corinthians 7.8: "But if someone wants to be unencumbered (εὔζωνος), choosing not to raise children because of the time involved in raising children (διὰ τὴν ἐν παιδοποιίᾳ ἀσχολίαν), 'he should remain unmarried just as I do,' says the Apostle."[242]

Finally, we should point out that Cynic arguments are present in the views held by one of the heretical groups that Clement describes. As noted above, the followers of Basilides understood the

---

238 Clem. Alex. *Strom.* bk. 7, chap. 12.70.6–7 (3.51.1–10 S.), οὐ προηγουμένως ἀλλὰ ἀναγκαίως.

239 Clem. Alex. *Strom.* bk. 3, chap. 12.86.1 (2.253.20–3 S.); bk. 3, chap. 12.82.3 (2.233.21–5 S.). On the degree to which Clement was influenced by the literature on household management, see Broudéhoux, *Mariage et famille*, 139–69, 182–3.

240 Clem. Alex. *Paed.* bk. 2, chap. 10.83.1–2 (1.208.2–11 S.), τῆς τοῦ παντὸς διαμονῆς. See also bk. 2, chap. 10.96.1; 98.3 (1.215.1–5; 216.5–7 S.).

241 Clem. Alex. *Strom.* bk. 3, chap. 15.97.2–3 (2.240.24–241.2 S.): "But what [Christ] means is this: Do not let yourself be led astray by irrational impulses and have nothing to do with city customs (τοῖς πολιτικοῖς ἔθεσι). For a household consists of a family, and cities of households, as Paul also says of those who are absorbed in marriage that they aim to 'please the world' (κόσμῳ ἀρέσκειν [cf. 1 Cor. 7.33–4])," (trans. Chadwick in Oulton and Chadwick, *Alexandrian Christianity*, 86). On the idea of raising children for the city-state in Clement, see Broudéhoux, *Mariage et famille*, 80.

242 Clem. Alex. *Strom.* bk. 3, chap. 10.68.2 (2.226.34–227.2 S.). Cf. Walther Völker, *Der wahre Gnostiker nach Clemens Alexandrinus*, TU 57 (Berlin: Akademie/Leipzig: J. C. Hinrichs, 1952) 199–204.

"eunuchs" in Matthew 19.12 to be those who, in Cynic fashion, rejected marriage on account of its time-consuming responsibilities (ἀσχολία).[243] Another one of their considerations appears to have been that a man might be too poor to take on the responsibilities of raising children, an argument known to Musonius and rejected by him in his treatise *Whether All Children Born Should be Raised.*[244]

### Tertullian

In Clement's North African contemporary Tertullian we again find detailed knowledge of the marriage debate.[245] In contrast to Clement, however, this church father finds only the Cynic position useful. In his *Exhortation to Chastity*, Tertullian employs Cynic arguments to justify his own stance on the issue of "second marriages," or marriages contracted upon the death of a spouse. Marriage takes up all of one's time, he claims, but without a wife a man can give himself wholeheartedly to prayer, the study of Scripture, song, and the rebuking of demons, and put his full effort into such areas of Christian endeavor as martyrdom, persecution, and chastity.[246]

In Cynic fashion Tertullian also points to the burden of having children, which he considers the inevitable consequence of marriage. What wise man (*sapiens*), he asks, would voluntarily take on such responsibilities?[247] In addition, Tertullian criticizes the Stoic arguments that one should marry in order to secure help in managing a household and governing a family, and to lighten domestic worries (*curas domesticas*). These he writes off as mere excuses used by insincere or unstable Christians who wish to contract second marriages. If a man takes his Christian faith seriously, says Tertullian, he will take a "spiritual wife" for these tasks – an aged, pious widow.[248] Finally, Tertullian makes a mockery of the arguments that marriage insures against the temples being forsaken (used by

---

[243] Clem. Alex. *Strom.* bk. 3, chap. 1.1.4 (2.195.14–17 S.); see above, n. 212.
[244] Clem. Alex. *Strom.* bk. 3, chap. 1.2.4 (2.196.5–6 S.); Mus. *frag.* 15.98.17–27 L. (79.13 H. – only the very beginning of this passage appears in the Hense edn.). The gnostic practice of masturbation may also be a sign of Cynic influence; see the discussion of Cynicism above; and Robert M. Grant, *Early Christianity and Society: Seven Studies* (San Francisco: Harper and Row, 1977) 172 n. 9.
[245] See the discussion in Stelzenberger, *Beziehungen*, 423–6.
[246] Tertullian *De exhortatione castitatis* 10, 12.
[247] Tert. *De exhort. cast.* 12. Cf. *Acts of Thomas* 1.12 (early third century).
[248] *Uxorem spiritalem*, Tert. *De exhort. cast.* 12; *De monogamia* 16.

Antipater), and that it is necessary for the survival of the city-states, saying that a Christian's citizenship is a heavenly one.[249]

### Jerome and beyond

After Clement and Tertullian, the impact made by the Stoic–Cynic marriage debate on the writings of the church fathers is rather slight. The one exception is Jerome, at the end of the fourth century.[250] As we noted earlier, in his polemic against the heretical monk Jovinian he cites from writings on marriage by Theophrastus and Seneca, and by way of the latter is familiar with a couple of anecdotes about Epicurus and Cicero.[251] Aside from this, Jerome also knows several Cynic commonplaces on the disadvantages of marriage, such as the trials posed by a wife's pregnancy, the annoyance of crying babies, and the cares of household management.[252] The presentation of these in his tractate *Against Helvidius* even bears a tacit resemblance to Epictetus' enumeration in his discourse on Cynicism.[253] Not surprisingly, Jerome, like Tertullian, sides with the Cynics over the Stoics.

The general disinterest for the marriage debate among church fathers after the beginning of the third century, as well as their increasing dissatisfaction with the Stoic position in particular, may be accounted for, in part, by the interest the church took in the new ideals of virginity, continence, and sexual asceticism. These worked to de-emphasize the importance of marriage and cast a shadow of suspicion on arguments favoring the institution. Indeed, Ambrose, in his tractate *On Widows*, written around 337 CE, is moved to declare that the real goal of the Augustan marriage legislation was

---

[249] Tert. *De exhort. cast.* 12.

[250] See Stelzenberger, *Beziehungen*, 422–3, 426–38; Günther Christian Hansen, "Molestiae nuptiarum," *Wissenschaftliche Zeitschrift der Universität Rostock: Gesellschafts- und sprachwissenschaftliche Reihe* 2/12 (1963) 215–19; and Marrou, *History of Education*, 201 (on the use of the rhetorical *thesis* εἰ γαμητέον by the fathers). On John Chrysostom see Brown, *Body and Society*, 306–21. On Gregory Nazianzus (whom Jerome claimed as his teacher, *Adv. Jovin.* 1.13) and Gregory of Nyssa see the remarks in Ruether, "Misogynism and Virginal Feminism," 176–8.

[251] On Jerome's dispute with Jovinian see Brown, *Body and Society*, 359–61.

[252] Jerome *Letter* 22.2 (*To Eustochius*). In *Adv. Jovin.* 1.13, commenting on 1 Cor. 7.32–4, Jerome demurs, "This is not the place to describe the difficulties of marriage and to revel in rhetorical commonplaces (*in communibus locis rhetorico*)."

[253] Jerome *Contra Helvidium: De perpetua virginitate beatae Mariae* 22. Compare also Jerome's treatment of procreation in *Adv. Jovin.* 1.36 to the Cynics' disdain for raising citizens.

not to increase the population but to thwart chastity.[254] Some forty years later, Epiphanius would condemn the Elkesaites for the heresy of encouraging single people to marry;[255] and at that end of the century, Jerome would accuse his opponent Jovinian of praising marriage in order to denigrate virginity.[256] As Henri Crouzel elegantly framed the matter: "The insistence of the sages of the Portico on the need to people the earthly city met with less enthusiasm from the Fathers. The society which counted most for them was the Church, and her growth was facilitated more by the spiritual fecundity of virginity than by marriage."[257]

## 7. Conclusion

In this chapter I have outlined the central aspects of a debate on marriage that began in the Hellenistic period in Stoic and Cynic circles. I have also surveyed the extant texts that witness to this debate, a large number of which come from the first century CE and include several Jewish and Christian authors. The longevity of this debate, its wide dissemination, and its consistency through the centuries are an impressive indication that it addressed problems both basic and common to a wide range of people in the Hellenistic era.

By presenting these materials, however, I do not wish to suggest that the Stoic–Cynic marriage debate was the only forum for discussing marriage in the Hellenistic world, or even that it was the dominant one. Rather, I have selected these particular texts for analysis in the belief that they are representative of a discrete world view that also informs Paul's discussion of marriage in 1 Corinthians 7. For this reason as well I have resisted the temptation to

---

[254] Ambrose *De viduis* 14.84.

[255] Epiphanius *Haereses* 19.1.7. See the discussion of this passage in Gerard P. Luttikhuizen, *The Revelation of Elchasai* (Tübingen: J. C. B. Mohr, 1985) 119, 126, 202, 208.

[256] Jerome *Adv. Jovin.* 1.3.

[257] Henri Crouzel, "Marriage and Virginity: Has Christianity Devalued Marriage?" *The Way*, suppl. 10 (1970) 18. Cf. Noonan, *Contraception*, 84–5: "The evaluation of virginity cut across the valuation of procreation. Procreative purpose was valued as a rational control of marital intercourse ... The connection between procreation and an increase of population was not explored." See also Brown, *Body and Society*, 120–1, 138–9, 369; "The Notion of Virginity"; Eijk, "Marriage and Virginity"; the rambling but well-documented account in Robin Lane Fox, *Pagans and Christians* (New York: Alfred A. Knopf, 1987) 351–74; and Ford, *A Trilogy*, 230–3, who gives a table indicating the increased interest in virginity in the period from *1 Clement* to Jerome.

focus solely on elements in the debate that point to a material connection with Paul. While I have highlighted Greek words and phrases from each author that are "parallels" in this sense, and while I will use these parallels liberally in the next chapter to show Stoic and Cynic influence on Paul, my primary concern has been to delineate the philosophical and theological framework of each author's position so as to recover something of his world view.

What has emerged from this method of analysis is a uniform picture of marriage held by these authors that envisioned marriage as a set of responsibilities – responsibilities toward one's spouse, household, and community. Whether or not a person accepted these responsibilities, moreover, depended on his or her allegiance to a higher order or calling. Sometimes this was nature, sometimes the will of Zeus, sometimes the will of the Judeo–Christian God. It is on this basis that one decided whether marriage was morally incumbent, as well as desirable and beneficial, or whether, in light of obligations that took precedence over marriage, celibacy was preferable. Considerations such as a negative evaluation of human sexuality or sexual abstinence as a goal of celibacy played no part at all. How these insights into the Stoic–Cynic marriage debate and the world view that underlies it help us clarify Paul's views on marriage and celibacy is a matter I will explore in the next two chapters.

# 3

## STOIC AND CYNIC ELEMENTS IN
## 1 CORINTHIANS 7

A knowledge of Stoic and Cynic thinking on marriage is essential to
any proper understanding of Paul's statements on marriage and
celibacy in 1 Corinthians 7. This thesis, which we will shortly put to
the test, is neither new, as indicated in chapter one, nor unreasonable. The Stoic–Cynic marriage debate, as we saw in chapter two,
flourished among Paul's philosophical contemporaries, and Corinth
was a center of philosophical thought in the Hellenistic world,
situated, so to speak, at a crossroads to other philosophical centers.
With Rome to the northwest, Alexandria to the southeast, and
Athens at a distance of some fifty miles on its eastern flank, this
cosmopolitan port city was well positioned to catch the intellectual
breezes that circulated in the Roman Empire.[1] The prospect of Paul
finding an audience at Corinth attuned to Stoic and Cynic arguments about marriage was, therefore, quite good. As for the Apostle
himself, a growing number of investigations have demonstrated the
similarity between Paul's theology and ministry and that of Stoic
and Cynic moralists of his day,[2] and several scholars have argued

---

[1] According to Acts, several early leaders in the church at Corinth hailed from
Rome and Alexandria (Acts 18.2, 24; 19.1; cf. 1 Cor. 1.12; 3.4, 5, 6, 22; 4.6; 16.12),
and Paul came to Corinth via Athens, where he encountered Stoics and Epicureans
(Acts 17.18; 18.1).

[2] Especially important in this respect is Abraham J. Malherbe: *Paul and the
Popular Philosophers* (Minneapolis: Fortress, 1989), and *Paul and the Thessalonians*.
See also Theissen, *Social Setting*, 39–47; Grant, *Early Christianity and Society*, 68–75;
Howard Clark Kee, "Pauline Eschatology: Relationships with Apocalyptic and Stoic
Thought," *Glaube und Eschatologie: Festschrift für Werner Georg Kümmel zum 80.
Geburtstag*, ed. Erich Gräßer and Otto Merk (Tübingen: J. C. B. Mohr, 1985) 147–58;
Weiß, *Korintherbrief*, passim; Kurt Deißner, "Das Sendungsbewußtsein der Ur-
christenheit," *ZST* 7 (1929/30) 782–7; and cf. Karl Heinrich Rengstorf, "ἀποστέλλω,"
*TDNT* 1 (1964) 409–13. Paul's familiarity with Greek philosophical and rhetorical
traditions more generally is demonstrated in Hans Dieter Betz: *Der Apostel Paulus
und die sokratische Tradition: Eine exegetische Untersuchung zu seiner "Apologie" 2
Korinther 10–13*, BHT 45 (Tübingen: J. C. B. Mohr, 1972); and *Galatians*. Max

that passages throughout 1 Corinthians betray an awareness of Stoic–Cynic thought.[3]

Given the plausibility of Stoic and Cynic influence in 1 Corinthians 7, if not the likelihood of such influence, the present chapter will begin the interpretive process of reassessing Paul's views on marriage and celibacy in the context of Stoic and Cynic ideas. My approach will be to locate in 1 Corinthians 7 patterns of thought, argumentative structures, terminology, and phrasing that draw directly or indirectly on Stoic and Cynic traditions, and explain how they function in Paul's discussion with the Corinthians. While this will not constitute a sustained verse-by-verse commentary on the chapter, which is beyond the scope of this book, the intricacies of many of the passages examined will nonetheless be dealt with in full, and the chapter as a whole will be rendered accessible from a completely new perspective.

What my analysis will ultimately demonstrate is that Paul employed a number of Stoic and Cynic principles in addressing the various marital issues that had arisen at Corinth – issues that included whether a Christian could forgo sexual relations with his or her spouse, whether a Christian should divorce a non-Christian "outsider," and whether Christians should marry in times of severe economic or social uncertainty. My analysis will also make clear, however, that Paul did not wield these principles in a purely philosophical form. An important component of the investigation, consequently, will be an exploration of the way in which Paul reconciles Stoic and Cynic tenets with his own distinctive theological agenda, while at the same time melding them with other Judeo–Christian perspectives – specifically, sapiential and apocalyptic world views.

Because of the complexity of both 1 Corinthians 7 and our manner of approaching it, an overview of these findings, as well as a consideration of how they contribute to our understanding of Paul's view of marriage and celibacy, will be reserved for chapter four. In this way, chapter four will serve as a summary and conclusion to both the present chapter and the book as a whole.

Pohlenz, "Paulus und die Stoa," *ZNW* 42 (1949) 69–104, by contrast, questions the presence of direct Stoic influence in Paul; cf. Conzelmann, *1 Corinthians*, 10.

[3] E.g., 1 Cor. 3.22–3; 9.1–5; 11.14–15; 12.4–31. See Conzelmann, *1 Corinthians*, 80 n. 17, 152, 190, 211, 214.

## 1. A "Cynic" position for married Christians: 1 Corinthians 7.1-7

Our first indication that Stoic and Cynic ideas on marriage have had an impact on 1 Corinthians 7 appears in the opening words of the chapter. Scholars have long debated whether the words in 7.1b, "it is good for a man not to touch a woman," are Paul's own or, on the basis of 7.1a, "Now concerning what you wrote ...," a quotation from a letter he received from Corinth. John Hurd has argued persuasively for the latter option, pointing out that the statement in 7.1b contradicts what Paul says in favor of marital relations in 7.2–5, and that unless 7.1b is a quotation, Paul must be seen as having begun his discussion in 1 Corinthians 7 without any precise indication of his topic. Furthermore, Hurd and others have noted that Paul also appears to have begun his discussion in 1 Corinthians 8 with a quotation, namely, the words "all have knowledge" (8.1).[4]

Against this line of reasoning, several scholars maintain that 7.1b represents Paul's own words since the expression καλόν, "it is good," appears again in 7.8 and 7.26 (twice), and is thus "Pauline style" or "typically Pauline."[5] But this view is mistaken, for the expression in 7.1b is not the simple καλόν, "it is good," but καλὸν ἀνθρώπῳ, "it is good for a man," which occurs only here and in 7.26b. This second instance, moreover, provides additional evidence that in 7.1b we are dealing with a quotation of some sort. The Greek of 7.26 reads, νομίζω οὖν τοῦτο καλὸν ὑπάρχειν διὰ τὴν ἐνεστῶσαν ἀνάγκην, ὅτι καλὸν ἀνθρώπῳ τὸ οὕτως εἶναι, which usually understood to translate something like, "I think that this is good because of the present necessity, that it is good for a man to be thus." Accepting this manner of translation, several scholars have looked askance at Paul's wording of this verse because of the abruptness by which the second half is introduced, and because of

---

[4] Hurd, *The Origin of 1 Corinthians*, 120–3, 163; cf. 67. See also Helmut Merklein, "'Es ist gut für den Menschen, eine Frau nicht anzufassen': Paulus und die Sexualität nach 1 Kor 7," *Die Frau im Urchristentum*, ed. Gerhard Dautzenberg, et al., Quaestiones Disputatae 95 (Freiburg/Basel/Vienna: Herder, 1983) 230–1; Wolbert, *Ethische Argumentation*, 78; Yarbrough, *Not Like the Gentiles*, 93–6; and Schrage, "Zur Frontstellung," 215–16.

[5] So Conzelmann, *1 Corinthians*, 115 n. 10; and Niederwimmer, *Askese und Mysterium*, 81 n. 3. Sellin, "Hauptprobleme," 3002 n. 321 contends that if 7.1b were a quotation, Paul would have written ὅτι after verse 7.1a (as in 12.1; 16.1, 12), and there would be no δέ at the beginning of 7.2; but this is simply speculation. Regarding his argument that 7.1b agrees with what Paul says in 7.7, see our analysis of this verse below.

the apparent redundancy of the repeated καλόν, "this is good ... it is good." Weiß, for example, opines that the text as we now have it is "not pretty," and reckons with the possibility that the second half of the verse is an interpolation. Neuhäusler proposes that the second καλόν should be read as the comparative "better," on the basis of Semitic syntax, which has no proper comparative; and Allo describes the second half of the verse as a "pleonastic" explanation of the first.[6] Still other scholars see this awkward sentence as an example of Paul's clumsiness. Meyer calls it a "manifest confusion of expression" stemming from repetition on Paul's part during the process of dictation, and Bachmann queries, "Does Paul hesitate to say what there is to say?"[7] The two strangest explanations belong to Grosheide and Héring. Grosheide maintains that the τοῦτο ("this") in 7.26a refers to "the virgin state" (see 7.25), while Héring reasons that it refers back to 7.20, where Paul speaks of each Christian remaining in his or her calling.[8]

The extreme awkwardness that these scholars attribute to 7.26 vanishes, however, if we punctuate the verse to account for a quotation: "I think that this is good because of the present necessity, that 'it is good for a man' to be thus."[9] In this interpretation the first

[6] Weiß, *Korintherbrief*, 193, cf. Robertson and Plummer, *Critical and Exegetical Commentary*, 152; E. Neuhäusler, "Ruf Gottes und Stand des Christen: Bemerkungen zu 1 Kor 7," *BZ* n.s. 3 (1959) 57 n. 40; Allo, *Première épitre*, 177, cf. Thomas Charles Edwards, *A Commentary on the First Epistle to the Corinthians*, 2nd edn. (New York: A. C. Armstrong and Son, 1886) 190, and C. F. Georg Heinrici, *Der erste Brief an die Korinther*, MeyerK 5, 8th edn. (Göttingen: Vandenhoeck und Ruprecht, 1896) 237–9. In 1762 Mosheim, *Erklärung*, 311 also remarked that his contemporaries had difficulty with the syntax here.

[7] Meyer, *Critical and Exegetical Handbook*, 220; cf. Paul Wilhelm Schmiedel, *Die Briefe an die Thessalonicher und an die Korinther*, Hand-Commentar zum Neuen Testament 2/1 (Freiburg: J. C. B. Mohr, 1891) 104; and L. J. Rückert, *Der erste Brief Pauli an die Korinther*, Die Briefe Pauli an die Korinther 1 (Leipzig: K. F. Köhler, 1836) 200. Philipp Bachmann, *Der erste Brief des Paulus an die Korinther*, 4th edn., Kommentar zum Neuen Testament 7 (Leipzig: A. Deichert, 1936) 280.

[8] F. W. Grosheide, *Commentary on the First Epistle to the Corinthians*, NICNT (Grand Rapids, Mich.: William B. Eerdmans, 1955) 175 n. 6; Héring, *The First Epistle of Saint Paul*, 57.

[9] Or: "... present necessity: 'it is good for a man' to be thus." Cf. Hurd, *The Origin of 1 Corinthians*, 178–9, who also argues that 7.26 contained a quotation – because of the ὅτι, the repeated καλόν, and because καλόν appears in 7.1b, which he held to be a quotation. Joachim Jeremias, "Zur Gedankenführung in den paulinischen Briefen," *Abba: Studien zur neutestamentlichen Theologie und Zeitgeschichte* (Göttingen: Vandenhoeck und Ruprecht, 1966) 273 wanted to put both of the καλόν expressions in 7.26 in quotation marks.

καλόν may indeed be "Pauline style,"[10] while the second belongs to the expression καλὸν ἀνθρώπῳ, which Paul quotes as a catchword or "slogan." Since the sentence now reads in a logical manner, I would maintain that this is the most plausible interpretation of 7.26, and consequently we have every reason to believe that the expression in 7.1b, "it is good for a man not to touch a woman," also represents a quotation – especially in light of Hurd's compelling explanation of 7.1 and the mistaken nature of the argument to the contrary. Indeed, this approach clarifies two other aspects of 7.1b and 7.26b: it explains why in 7.1b Paul writes "it is good for a man not to ..." as opposed to the more natural "it is not good for a man to ..."; and it makes intelligible why Paul begins his discussion of virgins in 7.25 by stating what is good for a *man* (7.26b) – it is because in both cases the expression is a catchword.[11]

If we assume that 7.1b is a quotation, it is possible, as Hurd and others have suggested on the basis of 7.1a, that it derives from a letter Paul received from the Corinthians, although there is no way to prove this, as we do not have the letter. Even so, we may be able to speak even more precisely than this about its provenance. As we saw in chapter one of this study, the aversion to sexual intercourse expressed in 7.1b resists explanation in terms of a theology of sexual asceticism. It does, however, find an analogy in Cynic traditions that argue against both marriage and sexual relations generally, which we examined in chapter two. The reason given by these Cynics, moreover, is that sexual relations take up leisure time, or σχολή, which otherwise could be devoted to philosophical studies, progress toward virtue, and the attainment of well-being.[12] Paul employs a similar line of reasoning in 7.5 when he maintains that spouses may refuse one another if it is by mutual consent in order to "have leisure" for prayer. The term Paul chooses is σχολάζω, which he uses only here, although we have seen it and the noun σχολή

---

[10] Aside from 7.8, see 9.15, Gal. 4.18, and Rom. 14.21. But see below, pp. 208–10 for evidence that Paul's use of καλῶς and κρεῖσσον in 1 Cor. 7.37–8 is Stoic.

[11] In both verses, of course, ἄνθρωπος is generic ("man/human being"), as distinct from ἀνήρ ("man/husband/male human being").

[12] See, e.g., *Cynic Ep. of Diogenes* 44 (174.7–14 M.):

> But incessant liaisons with women – leave these alone altogether, as they require a lot of spare time (σχολή). For there is no spare time (σχολή) ... While intercourse with women brings enjoyment for many unphilosophical men, for whom, in turn, this practice is expensive, you will learn to work the trick from those who learned from Pan.

frequently in documents relating to the Stoic–Cynic marriage debate.[13]

In addition to these clues, the words "it is good for a man" (καλὸν ἀνθρώπῳ) may also have philosophical roots.[14] While I have been unable to find the exact expression outside of 1 Corinthians 7,[15] a close parallel is ἀγαθὸν ἀνθρώπῳ, found in Musonius Rufus. Given the connection that Stoics saw between the concepts καλόν and ἀγαθόν, moreover – their standard maxim for describing this connection being, "the morally beautiful (τὸ καλόν) alone is good (ἀγαθόν)"[16] – this is virtually the same thing.[17] From Musonius' use of the expression, furthermore, we can see that the activity of determining what is "good for a man" is not a chance idea, but was

[13] E.g., Antip. *SVF* 3.256.34 (Stob. 4.511.16 W.-H.); *Cynic Ep. of Diogenes* 44 (see previous note); Epict. *Diss.* 3.22.74; and Philo *De spec. leg.* 3.1–3. Wettstein, *Novum Testamentum Graecum*, 2.126 illustrates 1 Cor. 7.5 with Philo *De vita Mos.* 2.211 and *De op. mundi* 128 (cited chap. 2, n. 199). Similarly, Lodewijk Kasper Valckenaer, *Selecta e scholis Lud. Casp. Valckenarii in libros quosdam Novi Testamenti*, ed. Everwijn Wassenbergh (Amsterdam: Petri den Hengst et filii, 1817) 2.204–5, illustrates this passage with σχολάζειν τῇ φιλοσοφίᾳ ("to have leisure for philosophy"), *totum se tradere Philosophiae* ("to devote oneself completely to philosophy"), and *omnibus aliis relictis uni Philosophiae severa lege invigilare* ("all other things abandoned, to give strict attention to philosophy alone"), concluding that the extent to which 7.5 "belongs to precisely those types of sayings will also be easily perceived from Greek and Latin authors." As editor of one of the editions of Stobaeus, Valckenaer would have been familiar with Stoic discussions on marriage.

[14] We should note in passing that several French scholars have argued for a connection between the expression καλὸν ἀνθρώπῳ and Gen. 2.18 in the Septuagint version, where God observes, "It is not good that the man be alone" (οὐ καλὸν εἶναι τὸν ἄνθρωπον μόνον). Yet there a vast difference syntactically between Gen. 2.18 and 1 Cor. 7.1b, and the respective viewpoints of these passages are diametrically opposed: 1 Cor. 7.1b is a statement against sexual relations while Gen. 2.18 provides the rationale for marriage. To overcome these difficulties, these authors resort to theological dogmas that go well beyond Paul's discussion in 1 Cor. 7. See Héring, *The First Epistle of Saint Paul*, 49; Xavier Léon-Dufour, "Mariage et virginité selon saint Paul," *Christus* 11 (1964) 186–94, and "Mariage et continence selon S. Paul," *A la recontre de Dieu: Mémorial Albert Gelin*, ed. A. Barucq, et al., Bibliothèque de la Faculté Catholique Théologie de Lyon 8 (Le Puy: Xavier Mappus, 1961) 319, 323–7; Thaddée Matura, "Le célibat dans le NT d'après l'exégèse recente," *NRT* 97 (1975) 602; Jean Jacques von Allmen, *Pauline Teaching on Marriage*, Studies in Christian Faith and Practice 6 (London: Faith, 1963) 15–16; and Legrand, *Biblical Doctrine of Virginity*, 34, 35.

[15] *1 Clement* 51.3 is a comparative usage and derives from the gospel traditions – see 46.8 and, e.g., Mark 14.21.

[16] See, e.g., *SVF* 3.9.23–11.24. Philo *De posteritate Caini* 133 knows this as "the Stoic dogma" (τὸ στωικὸν ... δόγμα), and D.L. 7.100–1 links it with the Stoic tenet that only the wise man is "good and morally beautiful" (ἀγαθὸς καὶ καλός).

[17] Cf. Niederwimmer, *Askese und Mysterium*, 84, who observes that 7.1b speaks of what is good for a *human being*, not simply a Christian, and therefore contains nothing specifically Christian.

central to his understanding of the philosophical enterprise. Advising a Syrian king, Musonius states: "Do you imagine ... that it is more appropriate for anyone to study philosophy than for you, nor for any other reason than because you are a king? For the first duty of a king is to be able to protect and benefit his people (ἄνθρωποι), and a protector and benefactor must know what is good for a man (τί μὲν ἀγαθὸν ἀνθρώπῳ) and what is bad ..."[18]

Similar expressions also play an important role in the philosophies of other Stoics. Epictetus says that the task of his model philosopher, the Cynic, is one of searching out "what is friendly to men (τοῖς ἀνθρώποις φίλα) and what is hostile,"[19] and Dio tells us that while he was in exile people came to him asking about "good or evil" (ἀγαθὸν ἢ κακόν), and so he found it necessary to advise them "on what was fitting for men" (περὶ τῶν προσηκόντων τοῖς ἀνθρώποις).[20] Significantly, this last expression also appears in Musonius' tractate on marriage, where he uses it three times in an attempt to prove the Stoic position that one must marry. His argument is that the philosopher is a "teacher and guide to men of all things fitting for a man" (ἀνθρώπῳ προσηκόντων), including marriage (τὸ γαμεῖν).[21] A denial of this position, whether by Cynics or by Stoics who took a Cynic stance against marriage, might have sounded much like what Paul writes in 1 Corinthians 7.1b.[22]

The passage from Dio, finally, may be significant in another respect, for it depicts the philosopher holding forth on "what was fitting for men" in response to inquiries from his public. This, in turn, coincides with the circumstances of Paul's discussion, as implied by 7.1a, "Now concerning what you wrote ..." Indeed, discussions on marriage occasioned by such inquiries may have been common among Paul's philosophical contemporaries. In Plutarch's

---

[18] Mus. frag. 8.60.6–10 L. (32.7–13 H.), trans. Lutz, "Musonius Rufus," 61.
[19] Epict. Diss. 3.22.24. In 3.22.23 he says that the Cynic is sent by Zeus "to men, showing them concerning good things and bad" (πρὸς τοὺς ἀνθρώπους περὶ ἀγαθῶν καὶ κακῶν ὑποδείξων αὐτοῖς).
[20] Dio Chrys. Or. 13.12–13.
[21] Mus. frag. 14.92.6–9 L. (71.8–11 H.); and see 14.94.32 L. (75.20–1 H.), προσήκειν ἀνθρώπῳ (twice). See also frag. 4.46.8 L. (16.9–10 H.), τὴν ἀνθρώπῳ προσήκουσαν ἀρετήν, "the virtue appropriate for a man"; and Sen. Ep. 76.4, where Seneca explains that philosophical schools seek to ascertain "by what means a man is good" (in quo vir bonus).
[22] Note that Theon Progym. 125.15–20 S. (cited above, chap. 2, n. 107) explains that in making a case for having children one will maintain that marriage is "good" (καλός), while in refuting this thesis one will draw on the opposite arguments (ἐκ τῶν ἐναντίων).

*Amatorius*, for example, we learn of one that ostensibly took place when Plutarch and his friends were asked if it would be appropriate for a promising young gymnasium student to marry an influential widow in her thirties.[23] Similarly, Lucius begins Musonius' diatribe on marriage by having a young man ask the philosopher if marriage and life with a wife is an impediment to the philosopher; and Arrian, in recording Epictetus' description of the ideal Cynic, has an interlocutor ask Epictetus if the Cynic will undertake marriage as a preferred course of action.[24] Regarding Musonius and Epictetus, I am aware, of course, that stock figures who ask leading questions are a literary convention in diatribe-style writing. Even so, this consideration does not exclude the possibility that these inquisitive straight men actually reflect the real world of the Hellenistic moralist – a world, I am suggesting, that also peers through in 1 Corinthians 7.1.[25]

If, for these several reasons, we can understand 1 Corinthians 7.1b as representing a "Cynic" position, then 7.5 seems to represent a modification of that position, designed to meet the needs of married Christians. As we just saw, Paul allows for abstinence here *within marriage* so that Christians might spend time in prayer. It is only temporary abstinence that he authorizes, however, not a complete renunciation of marital intercourse, which would be the full Cynic position. For such abstinence to occur within marriage, moreover, Paul requires the mutual consent of husband and wife

---

[23] Plut. *Mor.* 748E–771E, esp. 750A. Martin, "Amatorius (Moralia 748E–771E)" 443 does well to remind us that the *Amatorius* "is a dramatic essay, not a historical document," although he adds, "To say this is not to deny that its setting and circumstances may include factual elements and that it reflects the conversation and behavior of Plutarch and his circles . . ."

[24] Mus. *frag.* 14.90.24–6 L. (70.11–13 H.) and see also 14.96.4–6, 7–8 L. (76.11–14, 16–17 H.); Epict. 3.22.67, 77. See also D.L. 6.3 where Antisthenes is asked by someone what sort of wife he should marry (told also of Bion, D.L. 4.48), and Theon *Progym.* 12.121.6–17 S.; cf. Juvenal *Sat.* 6. "O" 17 (between 6.365 and 6.366).

[25] On this see Rudolf Bultmann, *Der Stil der paulinischen Predigt und die kynisch-stoische Diatribe*, FRLANT 13 (Göttingen: Vandenhoeck und Ruprecht, 1910) 10–19, 64–74; and Stowers, *The Diatribe and Paul's Letter*, 53–8, 61. Stowers ventures that many of Epictetus' diatribes were "occasional responses addressed to specific problems, situations or individuals" (54). This tradition of requesting advice on marriage from moral leaders may have been institutionalized by the church near the end of the first century: Ignatius of Antioch *To Polycarp* 5.2 maintains that it is proper (πρέπει) for those contemplating marriage to seek out the "advice" of the bishop (γνώμη – cf. 1 Cor. 7.25) to insure that the resulting union is in accordance with the Lord rather than passionate desire (κατ' ἐπιθυμίαν). Cf. 1 Tim. 5.14; Epict 3.22.72; Ps-Clem. *Letter of Clement to James* 7.1; and *Homily* 3, chap. 68.1.

(σύμφωνος, 7.5), a provision he justifies using Stoic as well as Judeo–Christian moral reasoning. The Judeo–Christian component of his argument appears most prominently in verse 2. Here Paul holds that marital relations are necessary because permanent abstinence exposes a spouse to the danger of fornication (αἱ πορνεῖαι).²⁶ This theme is then repeated at the end of verse 5, where Paul states that a couple practicing abstinence must ultimately resume marital relations "so that Satan might not tempt you through your lack of control," and in verse 6, where he states that his counsel is based on "concession" (συγγνώμη) rather than command, meaning, evidently, concession to Satan and to human weakness.²⁷

Paul's argument in verses 3–4 and the beginning of verse 5, on the other hand, appears to draw on Stoic traditions. To begin with, I suspect that the rather heavy-handed conjunction ὁμοίως δὲ καί, "and likewise also," which Paul uses twice in 7.3–4 to stress the equality of roles between spouses, reflects a Stoic manner of comparison. In Arius' epitome of Stoic ethics, for example, this conjunction occurs fourteen times,²⁸ whereas in his account of Aristotelian ethics it appears only once.²⁹ A similar pattern is found in Diogenes Laertius.³⁰ Moreover, in Musonius' treatise *That Women, Too, Should Pursue Philosophy*, the phrase occurs, as in Paul, in two consecutive sentences, again stressing equality between men and women.³¹ Beyond this, the almost identical phrase, ὁμοίως τε καί, appears in Romans 1.27,³² a passage which owes a considerable

²⁶ On *porneia* as a concern for early Jews and Christians see, e.g., 1 Cor. 5.1; 6.13; Gal. 5.18; Niederwimmer, *Askese und Mysterium*, 67–8, 73; and Friedrich Hauck and Siegfried Schulz, "πόρνη," *TDNT* 6 (1968) 587–9. On marriage for the sake of avoiding *porneia*, see *Test. Levi*. 9.9–10 (cited Yarbrough, *Not Like the Gentiles*, 69). We should also not overlook that certain Stoics denounced extra-marital relations as well: see [Ocellus] *De univ. nat.* 44–5; Mus. *frag.* 12, *On Sexual Relations*; and Epict. *Diss.* 3.7.21; *Ench.* 33.8.
²⁷ Cf. 7.7. Brown, *Body and Society*, 55 paraphrases διὰ τὰς πορνείας in 7.2 as "'because of the temptation of immorality' that abstinence might bring."
²⁸ Arius in Stob. 2.67.19; 70.3, 4; 71.6; 78.4, 13; 82.18; 84.19; 86.8; 100.10; 103.12; 108.14; 109.12; 112.13 W.-H.
²⁹ Ibid., 2.138.17 W.-H.
³⁰ In the accounts of Plato and Aristotle (D.L. 3.1–109; 5.1–35) the term never occurs; in his account of Zeno (D.L. 7.1–160) it appears eight times: 7.43, 87, 97, 107 (ὁμοίως δ' ἔχει καί), 122, 126 (ὁμοίως τε καί), 147, 148.
³¹ Mus. *frag.* 3.38.30, 31 L. (9.5, 7 H.).
³² As the second part of a τε ... τε construction; otherwise we might have had ὁμοίως δὲ καί here as well.

debt to Stoic thought, the context again being gender issues.[33] Finally, the simpler ὁμοίως, "likewise," appears often in Musonius' discussion of whether boys and girls should receive the same education.[34] In 1 Corinthians 7 it occurs in verse 22, where Stoic influence is once again evident.[35] Other than the passages just cited, the word is not found in Paul's writings.

A further connection between 7.3-4 and Stoicism is the topic of these verses, namely, marital responsibilities, which as we saw in chapter two was at the very heart of the Stoic-Cynic marriage debate. In verse 3 Paul states that spouses must "render" (ἀποδίδωμι) to one another "that which is owed" (τὴν ὀφειλήν). This, quite plainly, is the language of obligation, as can also be seen from other New Testament texts and from the papyri.[36] But more specifically, it is the language of marital obligations, a fact made clear by marriage and divorce contracts from this period.[37]

With verse 4 Paul's consideration of marital responsibilities becomes more focused. Here he concentrates on the sexual obli-

---

[33] Rom 1.26-8: "For this reason, God gave them over to dishonorable passions (πάθη), for their females exchanged natural sexual usage (τὴν φυσικὴν χρῆσιν) for that which is contrary to nature (τὴν παρὰ φύσιν), and likewise also (ὁμοίως τε καί) the males, leaving natural sexual usage (τὴν φυσικὴν χρῆσιν) of females, were inflamed by their desire for one another, males committing unseemliness (τὴν ἀσχημοσύνην) with males ... God gave them over to a base mind, to do those things which are not fitting (τὰ μὴ καθήκοντα) ..." This is followed in verses 29-31 by a catalog of vices, a literary form also used by Stoics.

[34] Mus. frag. 4.44.8, 16-17 (δ' ὁμοίως καί); 46.9, 10, 15 L. (14.2, 13; 16.10, 13, 18 H.). It also serves to introduce the roles of husbands and wives in the household code in 1 Pet. 3.1, 7 (cf. 5.5), and those of the "sisters" and "brothers" in the household code in Ignatius Polycarp 5.1.

[35] See below.

[36] E.g., in Paul at Rom. 13.7; in the Gospels at Matt. 18.30, 34. In the papyri see, e.g., POxy II 278.17-19 (no. 286; 82 CE): "... so that they may secure us without liability or difficulty with regard to the aforementioned debt (ὀφειλήν), and repay it (ἀποδώσειν)." James Hope Moulton and George Milligan, The Vocabulary of the Greek Testament: Illustrated from the Papyri and Other Non-Literary Sources, pts. 1-8; (London: Hodder and Stoughton, 1915-29; repr., Grand Rapids, Mich.: William B. Eerdmans, 1980) 61 comment that the verb ἀποδίδωμι "is the appropriate one everywhere for the 'paying' of a debt, or 'restoring' of a due of any kind."

[37] Günter Häge, Ehegüterrechtliche Verhältnisse in den griechischen Papyri Ägyptens bis Diokletian, Graezistische Abhandlungen 3 (Cologne and Graz: Böhlau, 1968) 58; 76-7 n. 8; 78 n. 12; 115 and n. 49; 239 and n. 3; 240; 248-9; 278-80. John Chrysostom evidently felt that this language of obligation was too strong for speaking of marriage, for he substitutes "the honor being due" (ὀφειλομένην τιμήν) for Paul's "that which is owed" (PG 61.152). Likewise, both he, the New Testament mss. K and L, and most minuscules have "the kindness being due" (ὀφειλομένην εὔνοιαν, PG 51.216). See also Epictetus' claim that a husband must "render" (ἀποδιδόναι) various services to his wife and her relatives (Diss. 3.22.70).

gations that spouses have to one another, stating that neither the husband nor the wife has final say over his or her own body. Several scholars have attempted to understand this statement in light of Genesis 2.24, where marriage is described as an act by which husband and wife become "one flesh." Niederwimmer, for example, speaks of a deeper "mythological" understanding of marriage deriving from the Genesis passage, and points out that Paul uses Genesis 2.24 in 1 Corinthians 6.16 in his discussion of prostitutes.[38] Against this, however, Bruns has argued that no advocate of this theory can explain the precise logic that connects Genesis 2.24 to 1 Corinthians 7.4. To the contrary, he says, "If one wanted to derive justification for *potestas corporis* from Gen 2.24, the result would be either that both spouses have authority over the one body ..., or that both spouses have authority over their own bodies as well as that of the partner."[39] Although, as we shall see shortly, Bruns overstates his case – for 7.4 does describe the mutual, not the exclusive, authority that spouses exercise over each other's bodies – his overall objection is well taken, for Paul's reasoning carries no obvious allusion to the "one flesh" idea of Genesis 2.24.[40]

Other scholars have suggested a rabbinic origin for the idea expressed in 7.4,[41] and still others that it derives from Hellenistic wedding vows;[42] but there is insufficient evidence to sustain either of these suggestions.[43] Bruns himself has argued that 7.4 represents a

[38] Niederwimmer, *Askese und Mysterium*, 91–2; cf. Eph. 5.28–33. See also Doughty, "Heiligkeit und Freiheit," 174; and the studies by Greeven, Merk, and Maurer discussed in Bernhard Bruns, "'Die Frau hat über ihren Leib nicht die Verfügungsgewalt, sondern der Mann ...': Zur Herkunft und Bedeutung der Formulierung in 1 Kor 7,4," *MTZ* 33 (1982) 179–80.

[39] Bruns, "'Die Frau hat über ihren Leib'," 180.

[40] Cf. P. Richardson, "'I Say, Not the Lord': Personal Opinion, Apostolic Authority and the Development of Early Christian Halakah," *Tyndale Bulletin* 31 (1980) 79: "For some reason Paul does not rely at all upon, nor even allude to the Hebrew Scriptures in chapter 7. Even such an obvious reference as 'the two shall become one flesh' does not appear. Thus, one of the fundamental authorities he frequently uses is absent ..." (cf. p. 85).

[41] E.g., Rudolf Schnackenburg, "Die Ehe nach dem Neuen Testament," *Theologie der Ehe: Veröffentlichung des Ökumenischen Arbeitskreises evangelischer und katholischer Theologen*, ed. Gerhard Krems and Reinhard Mumm (Regensburg: Friedrich Pustet/Göttingen: Vandenhoeck und Ruprecht, 1969) 22; Ford, *Trilogy on Wisdom*, 65–6. Cf. Hermann L. Strack and Paul Billerbeck, *Kommentar zum Neuen Testament aus Talmud und Midrash* (Munich: C. H. Beck, 1956) 3.368–71. Against this see, e.g., Doughty, "Heiligkeit und Freiheit," 169.

[42] Mosheim, *Erklärung*, 278–9; Wolbert, *Ethische Argumentation*, 82, 93.

[43] Regarding the latter, Hans Julius Wolff, *Written and Unwritten Marriages in Hellenistic and Postclassical Roman Law*, Philological Monographs 9 (Haverford,

deep expression of Christian love, as seen in 1 Corinthians 13.5 and
Philippians 2.3–4.[44] He maintains that the specific formulation of
this love in terms of the marriage relation was occasioned by
gnostics in Corinth who promoted the idea that individuals had
complete power or freedom over their own bodies. According to
Bruns, 1 Corinthians 7.4 must be seen as a polemical statement, an
antithesis to a gnostic thesis that circulated in Corinth.[45] Bruns'
theory, however, is based on two doubtful premises. First, he
believes that 1 Corinthians 6.12–20 and 1 Corinthians 7 represent
libertine and ascetic manifestations of gnosticism, respectively – a
notion we rejected in chapter one; and second, he believes that the
verb ἐξουσιάζω ("to have power over something") in 7.4 is
"typical gnostic usage," on the basis of his conviction that Paul uses
the related ἔξεστιν ("it is lawful") in a gnostic manner in 1 Corinthians 6.12.[46] Yet, while ἐξουσιάζω and ἔξεστιν are etymo-
logically akin to one another, and while 6.12b contains a wordplay
based on this kinship, we have no indication that gnostics saw any
significant connection between these two terms. In fact, there is no
primary evidence that gnostics used either term. As Conzelmann
remarks: "The language [in 6.12] points to a previous history in
Stoicism. Only the Stoics and Cynics provide material for comparison."[47]

In the final analysis, the closest parallels to 1 Corinthians 7.4
must also be said to come from the Stoics, and indeed, from their
discussions on marriage.[48] As early as the second century BCE,
Antipater reasoned in his tractate *On Marriage* that unlike life's
other friendships and affections, which resemble "juxtaposed
mixings of beans," marriages were "complete fusions, as wine with
water." This was because husbands and wives "not only share a
partnership of property, and children ... and the soul, but these

Penn.: American Philological Association, 1939) 52 notes that the common rulership
clause (κοινῇ κυριεύειν) is absent in marriage law from the imperial period and later.
    [44] Bruns, "'Die Frau hat über ihren Leib'," 190, cf. 181, following Schrage, "Zur
Frontstellung," 230–1, cf. 229 n. 62. See also Heinrich Baltensweiler, *Die Ehe im
Neuen Testament: Exegetische Untersuchungen über Ehe, Ehelosigkeit und Ehescheidung*, ATANT 52 (Zurich/Stuttgart: Zwingli, 1967) 159.
    [45] Bruns, "'Die Frau hat über ihren Leib'," 182, 191.
    [46] Ibid., 183–9, 192–3.
    [47] Conzelmann, *1 Corinthians*, 108. Bruns, "'Die Frau hat über ihren Leib'," 183
even concedes that his proposed gnostic use of ἔξεστιν may have arisen under Stoic
influence.
    [48] This is emphasized especially by Weiß, *Korintherbrief*, 172 n. 2.

alone also share their bodies."⁴⁹ In his lecture *Is Marriage an Impediment to the Pursuit of Philosophy?* in the first century CE, Musonius asks, "To whom is everything thought to be common – bodies, souls, possessions – except a husband and wife?";⁵⁰ and elsewhere, in his lecture entitled *What is the Chief Aspect of Marriage?*, he states that married couples consider "everything common property and nothing one's own, not even the body itself."⁵¹ In the following century Hierocles echoed this sentiment, saying that the good husband and wife are those who "agree with one another" (συμφωνέω – cf. 7.5), having made "everything common, even as far as their bodies."⁵² The popularity of this Stoic tradition in Greece,

---

⁴⁹ Antip. *SVF* 3.255.12–18 (Stob. 4.508.11–17 W.-H.), οὐ γὰρ μόνον τῆς οὐσίας καὶ τῶν ... τέκνων καὶ τῆς ψυχῆς, ἀλλὰ καὶ τῶν σωμάτων οὗτοι μόνοι κοινωνοῦσι. For non-Stoic antecedents to this idea, see Xenophon *Oeconomicus* 10.3–5, where Ischomachus and his wife speak of themselves as sharing one another's bodies (τῶν σωμάτων κοινωνήσοντες ἀλλήλοις) and being a "partner of the body" (τοῦ σώματος ... κοινωνός). See also Isocrates *Nicocles* 40, which describes marriage as a "partnership of everything of life" (κοινωνία ... παντὸς τοῦ βίου), cited by Friedrich Zucker, "Socia unanimans," *Rh. Mus.*, n.s. 92 (1944) 210–11. By contrast, see Plato *Republic* 5.457C-466D, where the male and female guardians of a city are said to hold all things in common (κοινῇ πάντα) except their bodies. On the notion of marriage as a reciprocal relationship in the Hellenistic period see Vatin, *Recherches*, 33–4, 39–40, 54–6, 200–28; Eyben, "De latere Stoa," 352–3; Foucault, *Care of the Self*, 159–64, cf. 78–9; and Joseph Vogt, "Von der Gleichwertigkeit der Geschlechter in der bürgerlichen Gesellschaft," *Akademie der Wissenschaften und der Literatur, Abhandlungen der Geistes- und Sozialwissenschaftlichen Klasse* 2 (1960) 246–55. Cf. Veyne, "La famille," 48; and Broudéhoux, *Mariage et famille*, 17.
⁵⁰ Mus. *frag.*14.94.8–9 L. (74.7–8 H.), τίσι δὲ νενόμισται κοινὰ εἶναι πάντα, καὶ σώματα καὶ ψυχαὶ καὶ χρήματα, πλὴν ἀνδρὸς καὶ γυναικός; Cf. Dio Chrys. *Or.* 3.122: "His wife, moreover, he regards not merely as the partner (κοινωνός) of his bed and affections, but also as his helpmate in his counsel in action, and indeed in his whole life" (trans. Cohoon and Crosby, *Dio Chrysostom*, 1.159.)
⁵¹ Mus. *frag.* 13A.88.13–14 L. (67.9–68.1 H.), καὶ κοινὰ δὲ ἡγεῖσθαι πάντα καὶ μηδὲν ἴδιον, μηδ' αὐτὸ τὸ σῶμα.
⁵² Hierocles 54.19–22 v.A. (Stob. 4.505.12–16 W.-H.), συμφωνούντων μὲν ἀλλήλοις καὶ πάντα κοινὰ πεποιημένων μέχρι καὶ τῶν σωμάτων, to which he adds, giving a new emphasis to the traditions of Antipater and Musonius, "– nay, rather, even as far as their *spirits*" (μᾶλλον δὲ καὶ αὐτῶν τῶν ψυχῶν). See also Seneca *De ben.* 2.18.1–2: "Every obligation that involves two people makes an equal demand upon both ... it is true that a husband has certain duties, yet those of the wife are not less great. In the exchange of obligations each in turn renders to the other the service that he requires, and they desire that the same rule of action should apply to both, but this rule, as Hecaton says, is a difficult matter ... ," trans. John W. Basore (ed.), *Seneca: Moral Essays*, LCL (London: William Heinemann/New York: G. P. Putman's Sons, 1935) 3.85, 87.

moreover, is attested by its use in Plutarch,[53] and perhaps in an inscription from Mantinea, some forty miles southwest of Corinth.[54]

Against this comparison of 7.4 to Stoic materials, Bruns has argued that the Stoics (he cites only Musonius) insisted on the *mutual* ownership of bodies, whereas Paul speaks of the *exchange* of authority over one's body with a spouse.[55] But this assessment is only correct as far as an isolated reading of 7.4 goes. Bruns overlooks the notion of mutuality in Paul's larger argument, for as we have noted, Paul speaks in 7.5 of abstaining from sexual intercourse only "by mutual consent" (ἐκ συμφώνου). If we were to carry Bruns' reasoning to its logical conclusion, this demand for mutual consent would represent a limitation on the prerogatives that Paul has just accorded to spouses in 7.4, since a literal "exchange" of authority ought to mean that a spouse could unilaterally impose continence on his or her marriage partner by virtue of having exclusive rights over the other's body. But this is not only somewhat ludicrous, it also misreads Paul's argument. Paul, quite reasonably, imposes the requirement of mutual consent in 7.5 on the basis of his assertions in 7.3–4, not in contradiction to them. His demand, "Do not rob one another!" (μὴ ἀποστερεῖτε ἀλλήλους), which is the immediate justification for mutual consent in 7.5, arises directly out of his discussion of marital obligations in verses 3–4, and even reflects the language of marital obligation that he introduces in verse 3.[56] It is certainly not a qualification of his claim in 7.4.

[53] Plut. *Mor.* 142F-143A (*Coniu. praec.*): "As the mixings of liquids, according to what men of science say, extends throughout their entire content, so also in the case of married people there ought to be a mutual amalgamation of their bodies, property, friends, and relations," trans. Frank Cole Babbitt (ed.), *Plutarch's Moralia*, LCL (Cambridge: Harvard University Press/London: William Heinemann, 1962) 2.325. See also 138E-F, 140E-F; and *Mor.* 769F (*Amatorius*); and cf. *Mor.* 156D (*Septem sapientium convivium*). Regarding Stoic influence on these passages see Helge Almquist, *Plutarch und das Neue Testament: Ein Beitrag zum Corpus Hellenisticum Novi Testamenti*, Acta Seminarii Neotestamentici Upsaliensis 15 (Uppsala: Appelberg, 1946) 96–7; Long, *Hellenistic Philosophy*, 159–60; and Voelke, *Les rapports*, 150.

[54] Wilhelm Dittenberger, *Sylloge Inscriptionum Graecarum*, 3rd edn. (Leipzig: S. Hirzel, 1917; repr., Hildesheim: Georg Olms, 1982) 2.783.30–4. The inscription dates from the late first century BCE and speaks of a wife being "commingled" (συγκερασθεῖσα) with her husband in marriage, "for lives were yoked with lives and souls with bodies" (ἐζεύγνυντο γὰρ βίοι βίοις καὶ σώμασιν ψυχαί). On Stoic usage of the term συγκεράννυμι see Conzelmann, *1 Corinthians*, 214 and n. 34 (regarding 1 Cor. 12.24, "God combined the body," ὁ θεὸς συνεκέρασεν τὸ σῶμα).

[55] Bruns, "'Die Frau hat über ihren Leib'," 181.

[56] Noted by Weiß, *Korintherbrief*, 173; and Wolbert, *Ethische Argumentation*, 81. See Exod. 21.10 LXX: "... he will not deprive (ἀποστερήσει) her of her necessities,

In reality, then, Paul's assertion that "the wife does not rule over her own body, but the husband does . . ." implies no "exchange" of rights between partners. Rather, it means that the wife *alone* does not rule over her own body, but the husband does *also*, and vice versa for the husband, just as we find in Stoic documents. From a syntactical standpoint, moreover, this is not at all surprising, since Paul uses the very same manner of elliptical expression later in the chapter, in verses 32–4: "The unmarried man concerns himself with the things of the Lord . . . the married man concerns himself with the things of the world . . . and he is divided." Here again Paul seems to have set up two mutually exclusive categories. Yet, as several scholars have pointed out, since Paul is speaking about a Christian man in both cases, he most certainly means that the unmarried man concerns himself with the things of the Lord *alone*, while the married man *also* concerns himself with the things of the world. Otherwise it would be impossible to explain why the latter is "divided."[57] Thus, despite Bruns' objection, 1 Corinthians 7.4 is most likely a Stoic argument that Paul has enlisted for his own purposes.

At this point let us briefly summarize our findings. The logic of 1 Corinthians 7.1–6 appears to be something like this: In 7.1b Paul quotes a Cynic view on sexual relations, "it is good for a man not to touch a woman." This represents a Corinthian position, and may come from their letter to Paul. Given the many parallels with Stoic

and clothing, and sexual relations." For the use of στερέομαι in marriage contracts see Häge, *Ehegüterrechtliche Verhältnisse*, 73–4, 79–80, although he notes (163–4) that the term does not occur in the CE. Regarding the possible influence of Exod. 21.10 LXX on Jewish and non-Jewish marriage contracts in Egypt, see Jacob J. Rabinowitz, *Jewish Law: Its Influence on the Development of Legal Institutions* (New York: Block Publishing Co., 1956) 45–7, 56–60, 65–6. Cf. Sirach 28.15; and [Arist.] *Oeconomicus* 3.2:

> Wherefore a man of sound mind ought not to forget what honours are proper to his parents or what fittingly belong to his wife and children; so that rendering to each and all their own, he may obey the law of men and of gods. For the deprivation we feel most of all is that of the special honour which is our due . . . Now to a wife nothing is of more value, nothing more rightfully her own, than honoured and faithful partnership with her husband . . .

[Trans. Hugh Trendennick and G. Cyril Armstrong (eds.), *Aristotle*, vol. 18: *Metaphysics: Books X-XIV, Oeconomica, and Magna Moralia*, LCL (Cambridge: Harvard University Press/London: William Heinemann, 1935) 409.]

[57] So Niederwimmer, *Askese und Mysterium*, 113; Barrett, *Commentary on the First Epistle*, 179; cf. Clem. Alex: *Strom.* bk. 3, chap. 12.88.2–3 (2.236.28–237.4 S.); *Paed.* bk. 2, chap. 10.109.4 (1.223.1–9 S.). As is often noted, Johann Albrecht Bengel, *Gnomon of the New Testament* (Philadelphia: Perkinpine and Higgins, 1864; repr., 1888) 2.199 styled Paul's elliptical manner of expression in 7.4 an "elegant paradox."

authors in 7.1–5, it was evidently held by members of the congregation with an interest in Stoic philosophy, as Stoics sometimes held Cynic views on marriage. In 7.2–6 Paul qualifies this view with Stoic assertions on the mutuality of the marriage relationship and with Judeo–Christian concerns about extra-marital sexual relations. The result, in 7.5, is a modified Cynic position for married Christians that condones limited degrees of abstinence within marriage.

With this, however, our understanding of these verses is still incomplete, for there is a final aspect of 7.5 that requires our attention. In this verse Paul allows for sexual abstinence within marriage so that spouses might have leisure for prayer. This is a rather strange notion. The rationale behind it seems to be either that sex is time-consuming or "distracting,"[58] which would be a Cynic view, or that it rendered one ritually impure, and hence religiously unfit for prayer.[59] It may be that these two possibilities overlap, as Niederwimmer suggests, since ritual purification itself is time-consuming.[60] In any event, the notion that sex is in tension specifically with prayer, and that these two activities must be cordoned off into distinct spaces of time is not Stoic. Rather, our closest parallel comes from the *Testament of Naphtali*, a pseudepigraphical work

[58] So Heinrici, *Das erste Sendschreiben*, 190–1, noting that there is no mention of ritual uncleanness here, and citing Plut. *Vit.* 69C (*Numa*), which speaks of a worshipper's need for σχολή. See also Wettstein, *Novum Testamentum Graecum*, 2.126, and Valckenaer, *Selecta e scholis*, 2.204–5, cited above, n. 13. For Jewish materials see Steven D. Fraade, "Ascetical Aspects of Ancient Judaism," *Jewish Spirituality: From the Bible through the Middle Ages*, ed. Arthur Green, World Spirituality: An Encyclopedic History of the Religious Quest (New York, Crossroad, 1986) 13.274–5. M. Ketubot 5.6 speaks of "seasons [for marital duty] spoken of in the Law," with reference to Exod. 21.10 (see above, n. 56). Philo *De Dec.* 96–101 says that the Sabbath was set aside that one might have time to philosophize and have leisure (σχολάζω) to contemplate nature, while *Jubilees* 50.8 forbids sexual intercourse on the Sabbath. Clem. *Paed.* bk. 2, chap. 10.96.2 (1.215.6–11 S.) says that Christians should not use time during the day for intercourse, but for praying, reading, or doing good.

[59] On ritual purity and sexual continence see especially Richard E. Oster, Jr., "Use, Misuse and Neglect of Archaeological Evidence in Some Modern Works on 1 Corinthians (1 Cor 7,1–5; 8,10; 11,2–16; 12,14–26)" *ZNW* 83 (1992) 60–4, although he too quickly dismisses the possibility of Stoic–Cynic influence. See also Lohse, *Askese und Mönchtum*, 25–41 (with lit.); Schrage, "Zur Frontstellung," 222–3; Exod. 19.15; Lev. 15.16–18; 1 Sam. 21.4–6; Jos. *Against Apion* 2.198, 203; and Plut. *Mor.* 655D (*Quaestionum convivalium*), cf. 712C.

[60] Niederwimmer, *Askese und Mysterium*, 93 n. 54. In any case, there is no mention here of the idea that sex is *morally* defiling. There is also no evidence for Brown's contention that 7.5 points to "protracted bouts of abstinence, like those with which contemporary Jewish prophets prepared themselves to receive their visions" (Brown, *Body and Society*, 55). The issue here is continence for prayer, not visions.

dated to the period 100 BCE–100 CE. One of the main purposes of this work is to instruct its readers to discern the order of God's commandments in the end time. Consequently, it depicts the patriarch Naphtali telling his sons that God has made them to exist in a world of "order" (τάξις), and that they must do nothing "out of its proper time" (ἔξω καιροῦ αὐτοῦ).[61] After some ramification, this theology is summed up near the end of the *Testament* with the following words:

> For the commandments of the Law (αἱ ἐντολαὶ τοῦ νόμου) are double, and they are fulfilled with a regular method. For there is a time for intercourse with his wife (καιρὸς γὰρ συνουσίας γυναικὸς αὐτοῦ) and a time of continence for his prayer (καιρὸς ἐγκρατείας εἰς προσευχὴν αὐτοῦ). And there are two commandments; and if they should not be in their order they produce sin. It is also thus for the other commandments. Be, therefore, wise in God, and discerning, knowing the order of his commands and the ordinance of everything, so that the Lord will love you.[62]

Here we see the dichotomy between sex and prayer put forth as the paradigmatic example of how a follower of God must be careful to discern the structure of God's will in the "last times."[63] The somewhat clumsy expressions "*his* wife" and "*his* prayer" in Naphtali's admonitions to his sons seems to indicate, moreover, that it had a previous history outside of this text and is being quoted here as a well-established dogma.[64] The verbal similarities between *Testament of Naphtali* 8.8 and 1 Corinthians 7.5 are also noteworthy. Whereas Paul permits continence within marriage "for a set time" (πρὸς καιρόν), the former speaks of a "time" (καιρός) for intercourse with one's wife and a "time" (καιρός) for continence. Furthermore, Paul is concerned that if the Corinthians overstep this set time, they will be tempted to sin due to their "lack of continence"

---

61  *Test. Naph.* 2.9–10; cf. 3.1–5 and 7.1. On the idea of apocalyptic "times" see also Luke 21.24; 1 Thess. 5.1; and cf. Dan. 2.21.

62  *Test. Naph.* 8.7–10.

63  *Test. Naph.* 8.1.

64  Jürgen Becker, *Untersuchungen zur Entstehungsgeschichte der Testamente der Zwölf Patriarchen* (Leiden: E. J. Brill, 1970) 214–18, 228 has argued that the underlying sources of *Test. Naph.* chaps. 2, 3, and 8 are in the style of "synagogue sermons." Given a Semitic original for this text, one could also perhaps read the disconcerting αὐτοῦ as referring to either God ("He has a time for . . .") or, as 8.7 might suggest, the Law ("it has [specifies] a time for . . ."), but in both cases we would expect a dative rather than the genitive.

A *"Cynic" position for married Christians* 125

(ἀκρασία), while the *Testament of Naphtali* holds that overstepping either the "time of sexual intercourse" or the "time of continence" (ἐγκράτεια)[65] will also result in sin. Finally, both the *Testament of Naphtali* and Paul speak of their respective teachings in the context of "commandments." The former maintains that this teaching on intercourse and prayer *is* a commandment (ἐντολή) for the last times, while Paul, by contrast, states that his ruling in 7.5 is not based on a commandment (οὐ κατ' ἐπιταγήν) but on "concession" (κατὰ συγγνώμην).[66]

For several reasons, therefore, it would appear that 1 Corinthians 7.5 and *Testament of Naphtali* 8.7–10 draw on a common tradition. This, in turn, provides us with our first clue as to the motivation for continence among the Corinthians. Evidently, like many other Christians in the first century, the Corinthians lived in fervent expectation of the Second Coming.[67] Adhering to some form of the tradition now preserved in the *Testament of Naphtali*, they held that prayer in the period before the eschaton was particularly important,[68] even to the extent that the more profane activity of sexual intercourse needed to be curtailed, since the latter, for whatever reason, inhibited prayer.

If this is correct, then Paul's argument in 1 Corinthians 7.1–6 must be understood as combining elements of Stoic philosophy with both the Judeo–Christian concern about *porneia* and apocalyptic ideas. Yet how is this possible? The link between these various spheres of thought has come about, I would suggest, through the medium of Jewish wisdom literature, for not only is the avoidance of *porneia* an important theme in this literature, but in the Hellenistic period Jewish wisdom feeds into both popular philosophy[69] and apocalyptic texts.[70] In fact, the *Testaments of the Twelve Patriarchs*,

65 Cf. Paul's use of ἐγκρατεύομαι in 1 Cor. 7.9.
66 In 7.25 Paul will give advice on the basis of apocalyptic "necessity" (ἀνάγκη), rather than a command of the Lord (ἐπιταγὴ κυρίου).
67 See 1 Cor. 1.7; 15.51–2; and the discussion of 7.25–31 below.
68 On the importance of prayer in apocalyptic times see Phil. 4.5b-6; Luke 21.34–6; and 1 Pet. 4.7. In Philippians and Luke prayer is contrasted with "worrying" (μεριμνάω) and with the cares or "worries" (μέριμναι) of life, which will be Paul's topic in 1 Cor. 7.32–4.
69 As seen, e.g., in Sirach, Philo, and the *Sentences of Pseudo-Phocylides*.
70 See, e.g., Jonathan Z. Smith, "Wisdom and Apocalyptic," *Map is Not Territory: Studies in the History of Religions*, Studies in Judaism in Late Antiquity 23 (Leiden: E. J. Brill, 1979) 67–87. The mixing of popular philosophy with wisdom and apocalyptic traditions is also attested in the synoptics; see, e.g., John S. Kloppenborg, *The Formation of Q: Trajectories in Ancient Wisdom Collections*, Studies in Antiquity and Christianity (Philadelphia: Fortress, 1987) passim; Burton L. Mack, *A*

of which the *Testament of Naphtali* is a part, is a case in point for precisely this type of syncretism: on the one hand, it stands somewhere between Jewish wisdom and apocalyptic traditions, and takes a very pronounced position against *porneia,*[71] and on the other hand, some scholars detect the influence of Stoicism in the *Testaments.*[72]

Paul concludes his argument in 7.1–6 with a statement that may again combine wisdom and Stoic thinking. He says in verse 7: "I want all men to be as I myself also am; but each has his own

*Myth of Innocence: Mark and Christian Origins* (Philadelphia: Fortress, 1988) 57–62, 67–9, 73–4, 325–31; Theissen: *Sociology of Early Palestinian Christianity,* 8–16; and *Social Setting,* 27, 39, 44–9, 50, 58. On Theissen, see Richard A. Horsley, *Sociology and the Jesus Movement* (New York: Crossroad, 1989) 46–7, 116–19.

[71] See, e.g., Howard Clark Kee, "Testaments of the Twelve Patriarchs," *The Old Testament Pseudepigrapha,* ed. James H. Charlesworth (Garden City, N.Y.: Doubleday, 1985) 1.779–80.

[72] See ibid.: 779; 782 n. 1c; 783 n. 4b; "The Ethical Dimensions of the Testaments of the XII as a Clue to Provenance," *NTS* 24 (1978) 269; and Harm W. Hollander, *Joseph as an Ethical Model in the Testaments of the Twelve Patriarchs* (Leiden: E. J. Brill, 1981) 95, 103–4 n. 56 (with lit. and criticism of Kee). Indeed, one possible instance of Stoic influence occurs in *Test. Naph.* 2.1–10, where our author first introduces his doctrine of divine order and appropriate times. Here he employs the image of the human body, a metaphor of divine order often found in Stoic authors (see, e.g., Conzelmann, *1 Corinthians,* 211 and n. 8). Paul also uses this metaphor in 1 Cor. 12.12–26: compare *Test. Naph.* 2.8a, "For God made all [parts of the body – see 2.8b] good, in the correct order," with 1 Cor. 12.18, "God set the members, each one of them in the body as he wanted"; and *Test. Naph.* 2.10a, "For if you should tell the eye to hear, it cannot," with 1 Cor. 12.17a, "If all the body is an eye, where is the hearing?" *Test. Naph.* 8.7–10 may itself have originated as an esoteric interpretation of another wisdom tradition, namely Qoh. 3.1–8. There we are told that "there is a proper time (καιρός / ʿēt) for every activity under heaven," and provided with several examples. In *Test. Naph.* 8.7–10 these "proper times" have been given apocalyptic significance, enabling those who are "wise in God and discerning" (8.10) to participate in God's ordering of the last times, thereby keeping themselves from sin (8.9). If Stoic-minded Corinthians had been familiar with both the *Naphtali* tradition and its underlying text from Qohelet, they may have been persuaded that these traditions spoke directly to their consternations about marriage. This is because the verse immediately before Qoh 3.1–8 promises wisdom to "the good man" (τῷ ἀνθρώπῳ τῷ ἀγαθῷ), whereas the sinner, whom *Test. Naph.* 8.9 identifies as the person acting contrary to God's ordering of the times, is given "distraction," or περισπασμόν (2.26, cf. 3.10), which in the Stoic–Cynic marriage debate was the antithesis of "leisure" (σχολή). For a philosophical counterpart to this doctrine of appropriate times, see Plut. *Mor.* 653B–655D (*Quaest. convival.*), which is a treatise entitled "On the Proper Time for Sexual Intercourse" (περὶ καιροῦ συνουσίας – cf. *Test. Naph.* 8.8), and the adage that D.L. 4.42 attributes to Arcesilaus (ca. 315–240 BCE): "But this very thing belongs especially to philosophy, to know the proper time of each thing" (τὸ τὸν καιρὸν ἑκάστων ἐπίστασθαι). Cf. also Clem. Alex. *Strom.* bk. 3, chap. 12.81.5 and chap. 14.94.3 (2.233.5–6; 239.16–18 S.), who refers to a proper time for begetting children (ὁ τῆς παιδοποιίας καιρός), and declares that Adam's sin was desiring the gift of marriage before the proper time.

*charisma* from God, one in this way, one in that way." In interpreting this statement, a few scholars have taken the position that
Paul intends to depict both marriage and continence as a *charisma*,
or "gift of grace" (χάρισμα).[73] Most, however, reject this theory,
arguing that Paul speaks only of continence as a gift. Niederwimmer, an advocate of the latter position, even ridicules the former
position as no more than "an adventurous misunderstanding,"
adding, "*Marriage for Paul is not grace, rather, a sign for the dearth
of grace*, namely for the dearth of the charisma of ἐγκράτεια
[continence] ... As for the other gifts of grace, through which the
married are compensated, it is self-evident that marriage (!) is not
intended."[74] Yet such an extreme characterization of 7.7 finds little
support in the preceding verses. If I have interpreted 7.1–6 accurately, we see Paul in these verses attempting to put a damper on the
inclinations of married Christians who endorse a Cynic position
against marriage, arguing that only a limited degree of abstinence is
possible within marriage. Since divorce for Christians is also out of
the question (7.10–11), it would run counter to his purpose for Paul
to conclude his discussion in verses 1–6 by implying that marriage
brands one with a "stigma of the necessity of sex."[75] Unless we are
to understand Paul as risking taunting his readers by announcing
that some are excluded from the *charisma* of continence, but will be
compensated with some other, unspecified gift, it makes better sense
to read verse 7 as an effort by Paul to reconcile these Corinthians to

---

[73] E.g., Cartlidge, "Competing Theologies of Asceticism," 47; Allo, *Première
épitre*, 159; and Tischleder, *Wesen und Stellung*, 14 n. 33 (citing others).

[74] Niederwimmer, *Askese und Mysterium*, 96 n. 70 (emphasis and over-punctu-
ation his); cf. Weiß, *Korintherbrief*, 176; Lietzmann, *An die Korinther*, 30; and
Conzelmann, *1 Corinthians*, 118.

Niederwimmer is followed by Brown, *Body and Society*, 56–7, who concludes that
for Paul and the Corinthians "marriage, like household slavery, was a 'calling'
devoid of glamor." Brown (ibid.) also refers to the gift in 7.7 as the "prophetic gift of
continence" and the "apostolic gift of celibacy," which, he explains, "was too
precious a thing to extend to the Church as a whole." Rather, he says, "Paul tended
to solve the issue of the precise position of celibacy in the Christian church by
sweeping it into the high trajectory of his own apostolic calling." This baroque
elaboration on Niederwimmer derives from a very superficial reading of the text. Paul
never refers to the gift in 7.7 as a "calling," nor is it possible to show that he
considered it an "apostolic" or "prophetic" gift. To the contrary, we have no reason
to think that the "virgins" in 7.25ff., among whom Paul promotes celibacy, are either
apostolic or prophetic, and in 9.5 Paul speaks of marriage, not celibacy, as an
apostolic right, noting that the "other apostles and the brothers of the Lord and
Cephas" were married.

[75] So Niederwimmer, *Askese und Mysterium*, 96.

their fate rather than goad them regarding their presumed short-comings.[76]

Aside from this, the preceding verses indicate that the contrast Paul draws in 7.7 is not one between incontinent married Christians, on the one side, and continent unmarried Christians, on the other, but between those married Christians who are able to forgo sexual relations and those who are not. This is clearly his concern in 7.4–6, at least. Most probably, therefore, Paul's mention of the *charismata* is a reminder to those spouses who are advocating abstinence that all Christians, including their own husbands and wives, are not endowed with the same gifts.[77] What we see in 1 Corinthians 7.7, in other words, is both Paul's deference to the celibate tendencies of these spouses, and his insistence that their demands are overbearing.

It is from this perspective that we should also interpret the beginning of verse 7, where Paul says, "I want all men to be as I myself also am, *but* ..." (θέλω δὲ πάντας ... ἀλλὰ ...). Since Paul lived in a celibate state himself (1 Cor. 7.8; 9.5), these words probably function in a "diplomatic" manner, enabling Paul to identify with the Corinthians and advise them.[78] A similar manner of persuasion may be found elsewhere in Paul, namely, in 1 Corinthians 14. In an attempt to quell the Corinthians' enthusiasm for speaking in tongues (chapters 12–14), Paul expresses both his empathy and his reservations by stating in 14.5, "I want you all to speak in tongues – *but rather* that you might prophesy" (θέλω δὲ πάντας ... μᾶλλον δὲ ...), and in 14.18–19, "I thank God I speak in tongues more than all of you, *but* ..."[79] It is surely more than coincidence that the topic here, as in 7.7, is *charismata*.[80]

With this understanding of 7.7, let us return to our initial concern for evidence of Stoicism and Jewish wisdom in this verse. On what

[76] Cf. Cartlidge, "1 Corinthians 7 as a Foundation," 224; and Schrage, "Zur Frontstellung," 233–4.

[77] This is a point that Paul will have occasion to make again, more elaborately, in 1 Cor. 12.

[78] So Witherington, *Women in the Earliest Churches*, 29–30; see also Baumert, *Ehelosigkeit und Ehe*, 55–6.

[79] On the rhetorical intent of 1 Cor. 14.5, 18–19 see Gerd Theissen, *Psychological Aspects of Pauline Theology* (Philadelphia: Fortress, 1987) 292–4; and Meeks, *First Urban Christians*, 121.

[80] Bartchy, *ΜΑΛΛΟΝ ΧΡΗΣΑΙ*, 149–50 has also noted this similarity between 7.7a and 1 Cor. 14.5. Niederwimmer has been persuaded completely by Paul's rhetorical strategy – see *Askese und Mysterium*, 95 ("The contrast between wish and reality determines the text. V. 7a sounds like a deep sigh, and v. 7b like a consolation for – [Paul] himself and for the others...") and 94 n. 61 ("That which Paul actually wishes is [according to verse 7] clearly celibacy ...").

basis, after all, can Paul or the Corinthians maintain that continence is a gift from God? Even though this notion is all but lacking for the first century, it does have a parallel of sorts in Wisdom of Solomon 8.20–1, where, in his zeal to possess Lady Wisdom, king Solomon fashions a plan:

> As a child I was naturally clever, and was possessed of a good soul – or, rather, being good, I entered into an undefiled body. But knowing that I would not otherwise be in possession (ἔσομαι ἐγκρατής)[81] unless God should give (ἐὰν μὴ ὁ θεὸς δῷ) – and this was discretion, to know whose gift it is (τίνος ἡ χάρις) – I appealed to the Lord . . .[82]

While modern translators are in agreement that the "possession" of which Solomon speaks is the possession of Lady Wisdom, and that wisdom is also what he desires that God give him,[83] the Greek of this verse nonetheless borders on ambiguity. For Paul or for a Corinthian devoted to celibacy, Solomon's words could easily be construed to mean that the gift (χάρις) which God gives is continence (ἐγκράτεια), which is the idea we find in 1 Corinthians 7.7b.

As for the inspiration that may have led to this particular interpretation of Wisdom 8.20–1, we have already seen from 1 Corinthians 7.1–5 that a negative, "Cynic" position on sexual relations seems to have been current among the Corinthians, probably mediated via Stoic thought. In addition, Paul's empathetic wish in 7.7a, that all could be like him, suggests that his celibate lifestyle served as a model for the Corinthians, readily imitated by some. In 1 Corinthians 9.1–5, moreover, in justifying his lifestyle more generally, Paul's words closely resemble a passage from Epictetus. Paul declares, "Am I not free (οὐκ εἰμὶ ἐλεύθερος)? Am I not an apostle? Have I not seen Jesus our Lord? . . . Do I not have a right to

---

[81] The future expresses the direct discourse of the thought.

[82] Cited in this connection by a number of scholars, e.g., Kümmel in Lietzmann, *An die Korinther*, 176; Chadwick, "'All Things to All Men'," 265 n. 3; and Weiß, *Korintherbrief*, 176 n. 1. Weiß also cites *Aristeas* 248 and 327 (177 n. 1 – the latter inverted as "237" in his text), but these refer to discretion in the behavior of children and self-control in matters of health (both times σωφροσύνη), not sexual continence. Other passages which scholars sometimes cite include *1 Clement* 35.2 and 38.1–2, but these are dependent on Paul – see William A. Heth, "Unmarried 'For the Sake of the Kingdom' (Matthew 19.12) in the Early Church," *Grace Theological Journal* 8 (1987) 74. See also Clem. Alex. *Strom.* bk. 3, chap. 1.4.3; chap. 7.57.2 (2.197.10–11; 222.18–19 S.).

[83] E.g., David Winston, *The Wisdom of Solomon: A New Translation with Introduction and Commentary*, AB 43 (Garden City, N.Y.: Doubleday, 1979) 199.

travel with a Christian sister as a wife, as do the rest of the apostles and the brothers of the Lord and Cephas?" This we may compare with claims that Epictetus puts in the mouth of his ideal philosopher, the Cynic: "Look at me! ... no wife, no children ... And what do I lack? Am I not without pain? Am I not without fear? Am I not free (οὒκ εἰμι ἐλεύθερος)?"[84] In light of this similarity, and given the Stoic influences identified in 1 Corinthians 7.1–5, it is quite possible that the Corinthians saw in Paul and elsewhere in their society a Stoic model of celibacy that they sought to imitate. This, in turn, may have led them to claim a "gift" of continence on the basis of Wisdom 8.20–1, a gift which Paul, before them, may have claimed. As with the preceding six verses, therefore, 1 Corinthians 7.7 may also represent a combination of ideas from Stoic philosophers and Jewish sages.

## 2. Marriage out of passion: 1 Corinthians 7.8–9

Our next indication of Stoic and Cynic influence in 1 Corinthians 7 comes in 7.9. In 7.8 Paul advises those who have been previously married and are now single[85] to remain single. Verse 9 then adds an exception: if they cannot control themselves (ἐγκρατεύομαι) they should marry, "for it is better to marry than to burn" (κρεῖττον γάρ ἐστιν γαμῆσαι ἢ πυροῦσθαι). Although this justification for marriage is similar to what we find in 7.2, 5–6, the emphasis is not the same. There it is the prevention of a sin, *porneia*, that makes marital relations necessary. Here it is the force of one's sex drive, which Paul, along with his Stoic, Cynic, and Jewish contemporaries, seems to have considered a natural or God-given aspect of human existence.[86]

Inasmuch as this difference in emphasis is significant, we need to look beyond the Judeo–Christian concern for *porneia* if we are to locate statements that approximate the rationale of 7.9. These are found in the marriage discussions of several Stoics, including [Ocellus], Musonius, and Hierocles, where nature is depicted as promoting marriage by equipping human beings with strong sexual

---

[84] Epict. *Diss.* 3.22.47–8. On the resemblance of these two passages see Conzelmann, *1 Corinthians*, 152 and n. 7; and Theissen, *Social Setting*, 39, 44.

[85] This is how I understand οἱ ἄγαμοι "the unmarried" (see 7.11, 34).

[86] For Paul, along with 1 Cor. 7.3–5, 7, see Rom. 1.26–7. For Stoics and Jews, see next note.

urges.[87] An even closer parallel is provided by Epictetus in his discussion of marriage for the Cynic. In the midst of offering several reasons why the Cynic cannot marry, Epictetus is interrupted by an objection: the renowned Cynic Crates married. Yes, replies Epictetus scornfully, but this was a special case. Not only was his wife Hipparchia fully his equal, being "another Crates," but this marriage was necessitated "out of passionate love" (ἐξ ἔρωτος).[88] Finally, we may point out that Paul's image in 1 Corinthians 7.9 of passionate love as something burning is also found in Jewish wisdom literature,[89] in the writings of moralists such as Seneca, Plutarch, and Philo,[90] and in an epigram in the *Greek Anthology* in which Crates speaks of the difficulty of quenching the "flame" (φλόξ) of passion.[91] In Paul, moreover, it reappears in the Stoic-sounding Romans 1.27.[92]

### 3. Marriage as slavery to an outside influence: 1 Corinthians 7.10–24

The unholiness of a non-Christian spouse as grounds for divorce (7.10–15a)

From his discussion of remarriage for formerly married Christians in 7.8–9, Paul moves to the related topic of divorce and remarriage for Christians presently married in 7.10–11, a practice which he

---

[87] See [Ocellus] *De univ. nat.* 44; Mus. *frag.* 14.92.9–17 L. (71.11–72.3 H.); and Hierocles 52.28–53.8 v.A. (Stob. 4.502.15–503.5 W.-H.). Cf. *Test. Reub.* 2.2–8, which maintains that the "spirit of procreation and intercourse" was given to human beings at creation "that there be in them every work of man."

[88] Epict. *Diss.* 3.22.76. See also 4.1.147, cited below, p. 209. The *Cynic* position in the time of the Empire, by contrast, was that sexual desire necessitated sex, not marriage; Crates was the exception.

[89] See Prov. 6.27–8; Sirach 9.8b; 23.17; *Test. Jos.* 2.2.

[90] Sen. *De ben.* 4.14.1; *De mat.* in Jer. *Adv. Jovin.* 1.49; Plut. *Mor.* 138F (*Coniu. praec.*), 752D, 753A, 759B-C, 765B-C (cf. 762D and 764B-D) (all *Amator.*), and in Stob. 4.468.21–469.3 W.-H.; Philo *De Dec.* 122; *De spec. leg.* 3.10.

[91] *Grk. Anth.* 9.497.

[92] To be sure, it also occurs in erotic and satirical authors, but since these would surely have scoffed at the suggestion that the flame of sexual passion is properly extinguished in marriage, the source of 7.9b is best postulated among those writings just cited. It is also quite possible that the clause, "it is better to marry than to burn," is a maxim that Paul is quoting. This is suggested by two things: it makes use of the traditional Attic spelling of "better" (κρεῖττον), rather than the koine spelling (κρεῖσσον), which Paul prefers elsewhere (1 Cor. 7.39; 11.17; Phil. 1.23); and the rhetorical flourish at the end, provided by the assonance between "to marry" and "to burn" (γαμῆσαι ἢ πυροῦσθαι), is also indicative of a maxim.

forbids. Here he bases his position on Jesus' prohibition of divorce, the implications of which, according to Paul, bear on the separation of spouses as well. In 7.12–24 Paul turns to yet another related topic, the question of divorce among Christians who have non-Christian spouses. For some reason Jesus' words do not apply in this situation, as they did in 7.10–11. Perhaps this is because their validity was seen as resting on the equality of rights that they accorded marriage partners, an equality that vanished if a non-Christian husband or wife felt no compunction to abide by Jesus' injunction. In any case, Paul is thus obliged to give his own ruling in this matter (see verse 12a) and supply appropriate justifications. For our purposes this is especially fortunate since the particular justifications Paul gives allow us to postulate why the Corinthians objected to living with non-Christian spouses. And here, again, we find Stoic and Cynic influence.

In 7.12–15a Paul begins his treatment of this question by considering two scenarios, both of which he presents in the form of an "if ... then" proposition. In the first, verses 12–13, he states that if a non-Christian spouse agrees (συνευδοκέω) to continue living with the Christian, then the Christian must not divorce him or her. His justification for this ruling follows in verse 14. In the second scenario, which comes in verse 15a, Paul considers the other possibility. He states that if the non-Christian leaves, then the Christian must simply abide by that decision. In contrast to the first, no justification follows this second ruling; rather, it concludes with the abrupt and definitive sounding "if he leaves, let him leave" (εἰ ... χωρίζεται, χωριζέσθω). Evidently, Paul felt no need to justify the actions of a non-Christian, and, as the tone of his conclusion seems to indicate, he saw divorce or abandonment on the part of the non-Christian as a *fait accompli* over which the Christian had no control anyway. Paul's initial justification for demanding that a Christian not divorce a non-Christian is thus contained in 7.14. Here he maintains, "For the unbelieving husband has been made holy by the wife, and the unbelieving wife has been made holy by the brother," adding further, "Otherwise (ἐπεὶ ἄρα) your children are unclean, but as it is (νῦν δέ) they are holy."

In reconstructing the issues that Paul addresses in 7.12–24, it seems reasonable to assume from this verse that the Corinthians have objected to living with unbelievers based on a conviction that the latter were unclean, and that through an association as close as marriage, which, as Paul insists, must include sexual relations

(7.3–5),[93] an unbeliever would render them unclean as well. In this way, Paul's statement that the Christian spouse has made the non-Christian "holy" may be seen as a refutation of this conviction. Not only does the non-Christian not pollute the Christian, Paul says, but the reverse is true: Christians "decontaminate" a non-Christian, overcoming his or her uncleanness with their holiness.

The rest of verse 14 is Paul's substantiation of this ambitious claim. His logic, as scholars generally agree, depends on the assumption that the Corinthians considered their children to be "holy," regardless of how they viewed their spouses.[94] Why they held this position, we do not know,[95] but it seems to make the best sense of Paul's otherwise unsupported assertion, "but as it is, they are holy." On the basis of this assumption, Paul designs an argument that both establishes his own position and shows that the Corinthians' position leads to an untenable conclusion. If, he says in essence, the Corinthians are right in holding that the close associations with an

---

[93] In contrast to the explicitness of 7.3–5, and perhaps out of deference to his audience, Paul speaks in verses 12–13 of unbelievers agreeing to "live with" (οἰκεῖν μετά) their Christian spouses. In a section of his *Marriage Precepts* that is flavored with Stoic imagery, Plutarch makes a similar distinction between συμβιοῦν, which he considers the full union of a husband and wife, and συνοικεῖν, which he calls a lesser union (*Mor.* 142F).

[94] E.g., Bachmann, *Der erste Brief*, 270; Lietzmann, *An die Korinther*, 31; Joseph Blinzler, "Zur Auslegung von I. Kor. 7,14," *Aus der Welt und Umwelt des Neuen Testaments: Gesammelte Aufsätze 1*, Stuttgarter Biblische Beiträge (Stuttgart: Katholisches Bibelwerk, 1969) 180–2; Wolbert, *Ethische Argumentation*, 102–3.

[95] Scholars generally reject the suggestion that the children's holiness stems from Jewish proselyte baptism, our knowledge of which comes from late rabbinic sources in any case. See Gerhard Delling, "Nun aber sind sie heilig," *Studien zum Neuen Testament und zum hellenistischen Judentum: Gesammelte Aufsätze 1950–1968*, ed. Ferdinand Hahn et al. (Göttingen: Vandenhoeck und Ruprecht, 1970) 264–6; and Blinzler, "Zur Auslegung," 166. For those supporting this interpretation see Lietzmann, *An die Korinther*, 31; Herbert Braun, "Exegetische Randglossen zum 1. Korintherbrief," *Gesammelte Studien zum Neuen Testament und seiner Umwelt*, 2nd edn. (Tübingen: J. C. B. Mohr, 1967) 192. If, however, it was the Corinthians' opinion that a spouse was indeed more vulnerable than the children because of the intimacy of conjugal relations, then an argument from child baptism would be even more superfluous. See next note.

Christian baptism must also be excluded as the source of their holiness, not only because it makes nonsense of Paul's argument, but also because it is irrelevant. If the children were holy by virtue of being baptized, then Paul could not prove from their holiness what he wants to prove, namely, that a Christian makes his or her unbelieving partner holy; and if the conceded point in Paul's argument was that baptism secured the holiness of the children, it is difficult to see why this whole matter surfaced in the first place, for the believing spouse was also baptized and therefore should be in no more danger of pollution than the children. On this see Blinzler, "Zur Auslegung," 167–9, 183; Weiß, *Korintherbrief*, 182; and Kümmel in Lietzmann, *An die Korinther*, 177. If, however, it was the Corinthians' opinion that a spouse was indeed more vulnerable than the children because of the intimacy of conjugal relations, then an argument from child baptism would be even more superfluous. See next note.

unbeliever demanded by marriage render them unclean, then their children, who are the product of one of marriage's closest associations, would also be unclean.[96] But since their children are not only not unclean, but instead holy, then the Corinthians' fear that the uncleanness of an unbelieving spouse is something that pollutes is unfounded – indeed, the reverse must be true: through marriage and sexual relations the holiness of the Christian spreads contagiously; the non-Christian spouse "has been made holy" by the believing wife or husband.

If this is an accurate interpretation of Paul's first argument in 7.12–24, then two aspects of 7.14 warrant our attention. First, we should note that Paul designates the children of a Christian parent as "holy" (ἅγιος), and says of the unbelieving spouse that he or she "has been made holy" (ἡγίασται). By this Paul cannot mean that either the children or the spouse has been saved, for neither has acquired this holiness through faith, which is elsewhere Paul's prerequisite for salvation. With the children, holiness has apparently been imparted "genetically" at birth, while the spouse, whom Paul continues to call an "unbeliever" (verse 15a), has received it through contact with the Christian.[97] Furthermore, in verse 16, Paul speaks of the spouse's salvation as still a future possibility. This means that the concept of holiness in 7.14 must signify an acceptability or usefulness to God quite apart from salvation.[98] This is perhaps not as strange as it first appears, for in 1 Thessalonians 5.23 Paul prays that God will make the Thessalonians "thoroughly holy" (ἁγιάσαι ... ὁλοτελεῖς). Since the Thessalonians are already Christians, this, too, must refer to something other than salvation.

The second aspect of 7.14 that warrants our attention is that Paul does not make a clear distinction in this verse between the physical

---

[96] Delling: "Nun aber sind sie heilig," 267–9; "Zur Exegese von I. Kor. 7,14," *Studien zum Neuen Testament und zum hellenistischen Judentum: Gesammelte Aufsätze 1950–1968*, ed. Ferdinand Hahn et al. (Göttingen: Vandenhoeck und Ruprecht, 1970) 283; and "Lexikalisches zu τέκνον: Ein Nachtrag zur Exegese von I. Kor. 7,14" in ibid., 270–80 holds that Paul is speaking of grown children. But if Paul's point of reference was simply the children's familial association with their unbelieving parents, not their physical origin from their parents' sexual union, his argument would be extremely vulnerable. In this case the Corinthians could reply, Yes, but the analogy with children is inappropriate, for while a child may remain holy in his or her interaction with a non-Christian parent, this interaction is not nearly as close as that between a husband and wife (which Delling, "Nun aber sind sie heilig," 268 also admits).

[97] On other, less likely possibilities see Meyer, *Critical and Exegetical Handbook*, 204–5; and Delling, "Nun aber sind sie heilig," 257–61.

[98] The NEB translation renders this as the unbelieving spouse "belongs to God."

and the moral spheres of human interaction. Instead of speaking of "cleanness" as the opposite of "uncleanness," or of "unholiness" as the opposite of "holiness," he mixes these categories, claiming that the children involved are not "unclean" but rather "holy." In a similar fashion, he also talks of holiness as something that can be transferred between spouses and from parents to children. What this implies is that the concerns of the Corinthians which Paul addresses in 7.12–24 have to do with the fear of *moral* pollution via *physical* association with non-Christians. In our attempt to determine why the Corinthians have objected to living with non-Christian spouses, it will be useful for us to examine two other texts from the Corinthian correspondence in which these same concerns appear.

The first of these is 1 Corinthians 5–6. From 1 Corinthians 5.9–13 we learn that Paul had written a previous letter to the Corinthians on the subject of associating with non-Christians, which the Corinthians have misunderstood. Paul says:

> I wrote to you in the letter not to mix together with sexually immoral persons – not at all meaning with the sexually immoral of this world, or with greedy persons and robbers, or idolaters. Otherwise (ἐπεὶ ... ἄρα), you would need to go out of the world. But as it is (νῦν δέ), I wrote to you not to mix together if someone calling himself a brother should be a sexually immoral person, or a greedy person, or an idolater, ... With such a person do not eat together. For what business is it of mine to judge outsiders? ...

Given their misunderstanding of this earlier letter, it takes little imagination to see how some Corinthians could have inferred from Paul's earlier instructions that marriages between Christians and non-Christians were dangerous. This would explain why, after addressing the problem of relations with non-Christians in a general way in chapters five and six, Paul found it necessary to return to this matter in 7.12ff. Indeed, Paul even uses the same argument *ad absurdum* in 7.14 that he uses in chapter five, as can be seen from the expressions "otherwise" (ἐπεὶ ... ἄρα) and "but as it is" (νῦν δέ) in 5.10–11.

Beyond this, 1 Corinthians 5.9–13 appears to reflect the same fear of moral defilement through physical association that we find in 7.14. Thus verse 9 speaks of "mixing together" (συναναμίγνυσθαι) with immoral persons, while verse 11 forbids both mixing and "eating together" (συνεσθίειν) with Christians who act immorally.

Several verses later, in chapter six, Paul continues this quasi-physical language of pollution. In 6.11 he maintains that Christians have been "washed" of immoral behavior (ἀπολούω); and in 6.15–16 he contends, on the basis of Genesis 2.24, that Christians who "join themselves" (κολλάομαι) to prostitutes become "one flesh" with them, stating in 6.18 that this is a sin against the body.[99] These last verses also show us that Paul's concern, as in 7.12–15a, has to do with associations of a sexual nature with non-Christians.[100] In fact, 6.15–18 is practically a mirror image of 7.14, for Paul rules here that an illicit relationship with a non-Christian pollutes the Christian, whereas in 7.14 he rules that marriage with a Christian sanctifies the non-Christian. Finally, the rather surprising claim of 7.14–16, that the unbelieving spouse is "made holy" by the Christian, but not thereby saved, may be clarified by what Paul says in 6.1–11. In these verses he distinguishes between Christians, whom he calls the "holy ones" (ἅγιοι), and "unbelievers" (ἄπιστοι), whom he identifies as the "unjust" (ἄδικοι), by maintaining that Christians have both been made holy *and justified*. Presumably, it is this act of justification (through faith) that the unbelieving spouses in 7.12–16 lack.[101]

The second text which may add to our understanding of 1 Corinthians 7.12–15a is the mysterious 2 Corinthians 6.14–7.1. While scholars still have many questions regarding the function of these six verses in their present context, they generally agree that these verses form a cohesive unit in their own right, with no obvious connection, at least, to what precedes or what follows. This raises the possibility that they are either a set piece that Paul is quoting, a misplaced text, or an interpolation.[102] After an apparent break in the flow of thought at the end of 2 Corinthians 6.13, this section begins with an

---

[99] Meeks, *First Urban Christians*, 153 comments that in 1 Cor. 5–6 Paul "takes as self-evident that pure/impure can be a metaphor for moral/immoral."

[100] While Paul generalizes his discussion in 5.9–13 so as to include a variety of evil doers, his primary concern is with the sexually immoral (πόρνοι).

[101] We should also note that in 1 Cor. 6 and elsewhere Paul specifies the agent of a Christian's holiness as Christ (1 Cor. 1.2), or his name (1 Cor. 6.11), or the Holy Spirit (1 Cor. 6.11, Rom. 15.16), whereas in 1 Cor. 7.14 it is the Christian spouse. H. D. Betz (written communication, February 13, 1991) has suggested to me that Paul's notion of holiness in 1 Cor. 7.14 reflects his theology of the goodness of the created order, citing Paul's ruling on food in Rom. 14.20: "All things are clean (πάντα μὲν καθαρά), but they are wrong for the one who eats causing moral offense."

[102] See the discussions in M. E. Thrall, "The Problem of II Cor. vi. 14–vii. 1 in Some Recent Discussion," *NTS* 24 (1977/78) 138–48, and J. Murphy-O'Connor, "Philo and 2 Cor 6.14–7.1," *RB* 95 (1988) 62–9.

imperative in verse 14a, followed by a series of rhetorical questions in verses 14b–16a:

> Do not be incompatibly yoked (ἑτεροζυγέω) to unbelievers (ἄπιστοι). For what communion is there with justice and lawlessness? – or what partnership (κοινωνία) with light towards darkness? What agreement (συμφώνησις) of Christ is there with Beliar? – or what share for a believer (πίστος) with an unbeliever (ἄπιστος)? What agreement does the temple of God have with idols?

Verse 16b then leads into a collection of citations from the Old Testament (verses 6.16c–18), and the section is brought to a close in 7.1 with another imperative: "Let us cleanse ourselves from every defilement of flesh and spirit, making holiness perfect in fear of God."[103]

As with the problem of the passage's function, scholars have also failed to reach a consensus regarding its authorship or provenance. While some hold to a Pauline origin, others have suggested that it is non-Pauline or anti-Pauline, noting that it contains vocabulary that does not appear elsewhere in Paul's letters, and that its imagery and theology are more at home among Christians seeking to live by the Torah, or in documents from Qumran, than with Paul.[104] Yet whether 2 Corinthians 6.14–7.1 comes from Paul's hand or another's, or whether it stems from circles associated with Qumran or those around Antioch or Corinth, we can be fairly confident, by virtue of its inclusion in 2 Corinthians, that it was an important text for the Corinthian church – assuming, that is, that it is not a late interpolation. If this is accurate, it is possible that the Corinthians had invoked the authority of this text in support of their position against marriages to unbelievers. And, in fact, it is not hard to see how they might have done this.

To begin with, not only is the subject in 2 Corinthians 6.14–7.1 once again the danger of associating with unbelievers, but as in 1 Corinthians 7.12–14, the image used is one of defilement through

---

[103] For a detailed analysis of the structure of this passage see Hans Dieter Betz, "2 Cor 6:14–7:1: An Anti-Pauline Fragment?" *JBL* 92 (1973) 89–99.

[104] See the discussions in Betz, "An Anti-Pauline Fragment?," 99–108; Thrall, "The Problem of II Cor. vi. 14–vii. 1," 133–8, 148 n. 1; Murphy-O'Connor, "Philo and 2 Cor 6:14–7:1," 56–62; and Victor Paul Furnish, *II Corinthians*, AB 32A (Garden City, N.Y.: Doubleday, 1984) 371–8, 382–3.

physical contact with them.[105] 2 Corinthians 6.17, for example, presents a paraphrase of Isaiah 52.11 that reads, "Come out from among them and separate yourselves ... and do not touch (ἅπτομαι) an unclean thing"; and as we just saw, 2 Corinthians 7.1 speaks of cleansing both "body and spirit" (σαρκὸς καὶ πνεύματος) of defilement as a way of "perfecting holiness," thereby contrasting uncleanness with holiness, as does 1 Corinthians 7.14.[106] Beyond this, the opening exhortation in 2 Corinthians 6.14 against becoming "incompatibly" or "strangely" yoked (ἑτεροζυγέω) with non-Christians could easily have been pressed into service by the Corinthians as a prohibition of mixed marriages, especially since "yoke-partner" (σύζυγος) was a common term for wife, and marriage could be described as a process by which a man is "yoked" (ζεύγνυμι) to a woman.[107]

Finally, there are several smaller similarities between 2 Corinthians 6.14–7.1 and 1 Corinthians 7 that could indicate a connection. Thus, 2 Corinthians 6.14–16 derides the possibility of communion or partnership between Christians and non-Christians, as well any "agreement," συμφώνησις, between Christ and Beliar, while 1 Corinthians 7.12–13 stipulates that marriage to an unbeliever *depends* on his or her agreement to live with them.[108] In 1 Corinthians 7.5, furthermore, Paul also speaks of the necessity of agreement between spouses, this time using the cognate substantive σύμφωνον. Nowhere else in Paul's correspondence do we find either talk of agreement between believers and unbelievers, or words from the συμφων-stem. Again, the occurrence of "Beliar" as the name for Satan in 2 Corinthians 6.15 may clarify the background of Paul's

---

[105] Cf. Betz's summary of the theology of this passage: "The purpose of the Christian life is to achieve the state of holiness and thus to become acceptable to God in the final judgement ... Because of this goal, any contact with people outside of the covenant must be eliminated" ("An Anti-Pauline Fragment?," 108; cf. 104).

[106] Both Delling, "Nun aber sind sie heilig," 261–2, and Braun, "Exegetische Randglossen," 194 argue for the affinity of these two passages.

[107] Also suggested by Jerome *Adv. Jovin.* 1.10; Hurd, *The Origin of 1 Corinthians*, 237; and Thrall, "The Problem of II Cor. vi. 14–vii. 1," 134–5, cf. 147–8. In this manner, 2 Cor. 6.14ff., like 1 Cor. 6.15–18, is a mirror image of 1 Cor. 7.14, for as Thrall notes, "in I Corinthians [vii.14] the unbeliever is sanctified by a mixed marriage: in II Cor. vi.14–vii.1 the Christian is polluted by it" (ibid., 135). It should be further noted that Lev. 19.19, which may be the source of the word ἑτεροζυγέω in 2 Cor. 6.14, speaks of "different yokes" of cattle (ἑτερόζυγος) in the context of *mating and breeding* them.

[108] 2 Cor. 16a prohibits an agreement (συγκατάθεσις) between the temple of God and idols. This image of the church as God's temple occurs again in 1 Cor. 3.16–17 (cf. 1 Cor. 6.19).

caution in 1 Corinthians 7.5 against Satan leading Christians into sexual misconduct. The name Beliar, which is not particularly common,[109] appears in both the *Code of Damascus* and the *Testament of Reuben* in descriptions of Satan in his role as one who provokes people to commit *porneia*.[110] Paul's warning in 1 Corinthians 7.5 may thus reflect an understanding of Satan implied in the name Beliar in 2 Corinthians 6.15.[111] That this description of Satan should appear in the *Testament of Reuben*, moreover, further enhances the attractiveness of this suggestion – for two reasons: first, because *Testament of Reuben* 4.1 speaks of God as giving Reuben's sons each a wife, for which the author uses the word "yoke-partner" (σύζυγος); and second, because *Testament of Reuben* 3.5 uses the same euphemism for sexual intercourse as 1 Corinthians 7.1, stating that the patriarch Judah never "touched" (ἅπτομαι) his wife Bilhah after her rape by Reuben. Elsewhere in Paul this word occurs only in the Isaiah paraphrase in 2 Corinthians 6.17.

Our investigation of 1 Corinthians 7.12–15a, and particularly Paul's assertion in 7.14 regarding the holiness of non-Christian spouses, has now led us to examine two other passages, 1 Corinthians 5–6 and 2 Corinthians 6.14–7.1. These passages indicate that the Corinthians held a general aversion to establishing formal relations or even associating with non-Christians, out of concern that such contact was polluting. In this context, the problem Paul addresses in 1 Corinthians 7.12–24 may be understood as a particular instance of this general aversion. Hence, our initial hypothesis, based on our interpretation of 7.14, appears to be confirmed, and we may conclude with a fair amount of confidence that the Corinthians objected to living with non-Christian spouses out of fear that physical association with unbelievers polluted them, thereby threatening their relationship with God.

Having thus defined the basic issues behind 1 Corinthians 7.12–15a, we may now attempt to set this passage in a larger social and ideological context. To some extent the Corinthians' concerns are readily comprehensible against the backdrop of the religious

[109] Ten authors altogether; see Theodore J. Lewis, "Belial," *Anchor Bible Dictionary* 1 (1992) 655–6.
[110] *CD* 4.15–17; *Test. Reub.* 4.8, 10; 6.3. Cf. *Test. Sim.* 5.3; *Mart. Isa.* 2.4–5; and *Lives of the Prophets* 17.2.
[111] According to Schrage, *Die konkreten Einzelgebote*, 220, 1 Cor. 7.5 is the only place in Paul "where, in a paraenetic-ethical context, Satan is expressly referred to as part of a warning." See also 1 Cor. 5.5, where Paul rules that the man guilty of the sexual offense described in 5.1 be handed over to Satan.

syncretism that characterized much of the Hellenistic period. It finds
a broad analogy, for example, in the Hellenistic Jewish polemic
against intermarriage with Gentiles,[112] or the Roman polemic
against "foreign cults," which claimed that new religions destroyed
marriages and households by converting the wives of Roman citizens.[113] The Corinthian perspective is that of the converts, however,
not the proponents of an established religion, and so the tensions
evident in 1 Corinthians 7.12–15a find a more fruitful analogy
among the Stoics and the Stoic writings of Philo, and in the wisdom
tradition of Ben Sira, which itself bears several marks of Stoicism.[114]

In Ben Sira the "convert" is the wise man, and hence an aversion
to outsiders expresses itself in the form of warnings against close
association with persons not pursuing wisdom and righteousness.
"Grudge every minute spent among fools, but linger among the
thoughtful," says the author in 27.12 (NEB). In 9.14–16 Ben Sira
advises that the righteous be one's dinner partners (cf. 1 Corinthians
5.11); and in Sirach 13, in a caution against associating with rich and
greedy men, we find several rhetorical questions that bear a palpable
resemblance to 2 Corinthians 6.14–16:

> Will a clay pot have fellowship (κοινωνέω) with an iron
> kettle? (13.2) . . .
>
> Will a wolf have fellowship with a lamb? – so also a sinner
> with a pious man. What peace does a hyena have with a
> dog? – and what peace does a rich man have with a poor
> man?                                                    (13.17–18)

Ben Sira's objection to these associations stems from his concern
that the righteous wise man will be adversely influenced by the
unrighteous fool. Sirach 12.13–14, for example, warns against
attaching oneself to a sinner and thereby becoming involved with[115]
his sins. As with the Corinthians, Ben Sira also employs the
metaphor of defilement. In 13.1 he admonishes, "Whoever touches
(ὁ ἁπτόμενος) pitch will be defiled, and whoever associates (ὁ

---

[112] See, e.g., Gerhard Delling, "Ehehindernisse," *RAC* 4 (1959) 681–2.
[113] See, e.g., Balch, *Let Wives Be Submissive*, 65–76. Cf. the concern expressed in
Wisdom 14.22–7 that idol worship undermines marriages.
[114] See Raymond Pautrel, "Ben Sira et le stoïcisme," *RSR* 51 (1963) 535–49; and
Martin Hengel, *Judaism and Hellenism: Studies in their Encounter in Palestine during
the Early Hellenistic Period* (Philadelphia: Fortress, 1974) 1.83–8, 147–53, 157–62.
[115] Lit., "kneaded together with," συμφύρω – cf. 1 Cor. 5.6–8 where Paul uses the
image of leaven and bread dough. See also Gal. 5.9 and Mark 8.15 par.

κοινωνῶν) with a proud man will become like him" (RSV); and in 22.13 he advises, "Do not talk much with a foolish man, and do not visit an unintelligent man ... and you will not be soiled when he shakes himself off."[116] In fact, according to Ben Sira, the very search for wisdom requires a certain purity. Recounting his own experiences in the concluding chapter of his work, he says: "I directed my soul to [Wisdom], and through purification (ἐν καθα- ρισμῷ) I found her."[117]

In the same way as the general concern at Corinth for associating with outsiders surfaces in Paul's discussion of marriage in 1 Cor- inthians 7.12–15a, Ben Sira also treats marriage as a particular instance of this broader problem. In Sirach 25.16–24 he details the disastrous consequences of a wise man having to associate with an evil wife; and in 26.7 he exclaims that an evil wife is a "rolling ox-yoke" (βοοζύγιον σαλευόμενον). The image here is that of two oxen being mismatched under the same yoke, causing it to bob painfully up and down, which is reminiscent of the "incompatible yoking" of 2 Corinthians 6.14. That this image had some currency in wisdom literature as a metaphor for marriage is also indicated by Sirach 25.8, which reads "Happy is he who lives with an intelligent wife; and he who does not plow with ox and ass together."[118]

Finally, as with the Corinthians, Ben Sira sees divorce as a solution to these impossible partnerships. Thus, while Sirach 7.26 admonishes, "Do you have a wife after your own soul? – do not divorce her,"[119] Sirach 25.25–6 hands down the verdict for less fortunate marriages: "Do not give water an outlet; nor an evil wife brashness. If she does not go according to your directions, cut her off from your flesh."[120] Here a textual variant is worth our atten- tion. In some Greek manuscripts verse 25 advises against giving an

---

[116] Cf. Wisdom 4.10–14, and 2.16, where the ungodly say of the righteous man: "We are considered by him as something base, and he avoids our ways as unclean."

[117] Sirach 51.20 (RSV). Cf. Wis. 8.20 (cited above, p. 129), where the author sees an "undefiled body," σῶμα ἀμίαντον (received at birth), as prerequisite to Solomon's search for wisdom. See also Wis. 1.3–5; 7.27.

[118] Although the second clause appears only in the Heb. and Syr., not in the Grk., it is undoubtedly original since Ben Sira promises us ten happy thoughts (25.7), and without this clause he would have only nine. Patrick W. Skehan and Alexander A. Di Lella, *The Wisdom of Ben Sira*, AB 39 (New York: Double Day, 1987) 340 hold that the reference in the second clause is to a man with two contentious co-wives. This is possible but not necessary.

[119] This is the LXX; the Heb. reads: "Do you have a wife? – do not hate her." On the Stoic–Cynic background of this verse see below, pp. 159–64, and 189.

[120] The Hebrew adds here "take and divorce her." See also Prov. 18.22a (LXX), and the "one flesh" idea of Gen. 2.24.

evil wife "power" (ἐξουσία) as opposed to "brashness" (παρρησία). This is similar to the advice given in Sirach 33.20 (Eng. 33.19): "In your lifetime do not give power over yourself (ἐξουσία ἐπὶ σέ) to son or wife, brother or friend." In 47.19, in turn, after recounting the extraordinary wisdom and success of King Solomon, Ben Sira fingers the cause of his downfall: "You laid your loins beside women and were overpowered through your body (ἐνεξουσιάσθης ἐν τῷ σώματί σου)." In all three of these passages the wording approaches the expression Paul uses in 1 Corinthians 7.4, where he asserts, evidently in response to misgivings on the part of the Corinthians, that spouses do not have exclusive power (οὐκ ἐξουσιάζει) over their own bodies. From this the possibility emerges that the Corinthians who were married to unbelievers objected to the idea of "coming under their power" physically.[121]

As informative as these comparisons with Sirach might be, even closer parallels are to be found in Stoic authors and in the Stoic writings of Philo. Just as some Cynics nourished a strong disdain for non-philosophers, as noted in chapter two, there is evidence that some Stoics also shunned these "laymen," although others, like Epictetus, discouraged such an attitude.[122] But even Epictetus objected to becoming too intimate with outsiders.[123] In one lecture he speaks in terms reminiscent of Paul's assertion in 1 Corinthians 5.10, that Christians would have to "leave the world" to avoid unbelievers,[124] and elsewhere he explains that it is "for this reason that the philosophers advise us to leave even our own countries."[125] This last citation, moreover, belongs to an entire lecture on the dangers of social relations, which begins by addressing the issue of eating with outsiders,[126] and describes their influence as something defiling. "We ought to enter cautiously into such social intercourse with laymen," Epictetus warns, "remembering that it is impossible

---

[121] With Solomon, it should be noted, the reference is also to "outsiders," since the women who overpower him are *foreign* wives (see Sirach 47.20 and 1 Kgs. 11.1–8).

[122] E.g., Epict. *Diss.* 2.12.1–4.

[123] E.g., Epict. *Diss.* 4.2.1.

[124] Epict. *Diss.* 1.12.18–19: "For look you, can we escape from men? And how is it possible? . . . What alternative remains, then, or what method can we find for living with them?" (trans. Oldfather, *Epictetus*, 1.93, 95).

[125] Epict. *Diss.* 3.16.11, trans. Oldfather, *Epictetus*, 2.107, 109.

[126] Aside from 1 Cor. 5.11, Paul addresses the question of eating with outsiders in 10.23–30.

for the man who brushes up against the person who is covered with soot to keep from getting some soot on himself."[127]

In Philo this philosophical apprehension toward outsiders as a source of pollution is seen at the beginning of his treatise *That Every Good Man is Free*. After introducing this most Stoic of themes with a Pythagorean maxim that the philosopher "should not walk the well-traveled ways," Philo explains that the wise have "opened up a new pathway, in which the outside world can never tread ... and have brought to light the ideal forms which none of the unclean may touch."[128] Later in the treatise Philo presents the Essenes, whom he describes as separating themselves from evil persons, as these would be detrimental to their souls, "like a disease brought by a pestilential atmosphere."[129]

In Philo's treatise *On the Sacrifices of Abel and Cain*, we again meet with the language of defilement and disease, although in this text Philo combines Stoic and Jewish traditions in a manner that may clarify the background of Paul's contention that unbelievers are sanctified by a believing spouse. In considering the statement in Numbers 3.12–13 that the Levites are a "ransom" for Israel's firstborn, Philo first interprets these verses in terms of the soul's desire for freedom. But, he continues, it may be that Moses meant to illustrate another truth "and one that we could ill spare, namely that every wise man is a ransom for the fool." This is because, as he says further on, the wise are like "physicians who fight against the infirmities of the sick."[130] Here, quite plainly, Philo has identified the Levite with the Stoic wise man in the latter's role as physician to the human soul.[131] Following this, Philo gives a similar interpretation of the Levitical cities of refuge, which, according to Leviticus 25.32, are "ransomed forever." After again considering these words

---

[127] Epict. *Diss.* 3.16.1–6, trans. Oldfather, *Epictetus*, 2.105, 107. See also *Diss.* 1.27.1–6; and Malherbe, *Paul and the Thessalonians*, 36–52, who cites texts describing the fragile condition of new converts to philosophy.
[128] Philo *Quod omnis probus* 3–4, trans. F. H. Colson (ed.), *Philo*, LCL (Cambridge: Harvard University Press/London: William Heinemann, 1929) 9.11, 13. This understanding of "unclean" compares well with Epictetus' statement in *Diss.* 4.11.5–8 that the philosopher must cleanse out all "impurity of the soul," defining this impurity as "bad beliefs" (δόγματα πονηρά). See also *Diss.* 3.22.19, where he says that the Cynic's governing principle must be "pure" (καθαρόν).
[129] Philo *Quod omnis probus* 76, trans. Colson, *Philo*, 9.55.
[130] Philo *De sacr. Abelis et Caini* 118–20, 121–4, trans. F. H. Colson and G. H. Whitaker (eds.), *Philo*, LCL (London: William Heinemann/New York: G. P. Putnam's Sons, 1929) 2.181, 183, 185.
[131] On the wise man as physician see Malherbe, *Paul and the Thessalonians*, 23 n. 71.

as a metaphor for the soul's journey toward perfection, he proposes that the Levites are good men (σπουδαῖος) who purify bad men (φαῦλος) by virtue of their holiness.[132] From these texts we can see that Philo's understanding of the redemption of outsiders by insiders is, in part, based on Stoic social theory, even though he chooses to express this redemption largely in the language of his own Judaism. In light of this example, it is not impossible that Paul's claim in 1 Corinthians 7.14, that unclean, non-Christian spouses are "made holy" by their Christian spouses, may also rely on Stoic notions of social interaction, this time expressed in terms of Paul's Judeo–Christian faith.

Pursuing the Stoic background of 1 Corinthians 7.12–15a from still another perspective, we may note that a principal source of the Stoics' attitude toward outsiders was their concept of friendship. For the Stoics, friendship was a "partnership,"[133] and strictly an insider affair, based on the sharing of a common lifestyle. As Arius Didymus puts it, "They admit friendship among the wise alone, since only among these is there oneness of mind regarding the things pertaining to one's manner of life."[134] From Arius we also learn, however, that Stoics limited friendship to the wise because they held that friendship required trust or "faithfulness" (πίστις), which only wise men possess.[135] The dogma that trust is essential to friendship

---

[132] Philo. *De sacr. Abelis et Caini* 128. Cf. Wis. 6.24, "A multitude of wise men is the salvation of the world" (RSV).

[133] κοινωνία, Arius in Stob. 2.74.3–5 W.-H. (*SVF* 3.27.3–4); cf. D.L. 7.124. This passage from Arius also defines a common belief about one's manner of life as an "agreement," or συμφωνία. This is perhaps another indication of the philosophical provenance of 2 Cor. 6.14–7.1, as both terms appear in 6.14–15. See also Stob. 2.94.1–4; 2.106.13–15 W.-H.

[134] Arius in Stob. 2.108.15–18 W.-H. Cf. D.L. 7.124, who reports that Stoics held that friendship existed "only among the good, on account of their likeness." As this last reference indicates, the Stoic ideal of friendship was, to some degree, a variation on the fairly widespread notion that a friend must be a person "like oneself," or "another self." Hence, in Epictetus, when a young man asks whether the Cynic, if he falls ill, can convalesce in another's home, Epictetus understands this as a question about friendship and replies, "But where will you find me a Cynic's friend? For such a person must be another Cynic. . ." (Epict. *Diss.* 3.22.62–5, trans. Oldfather, *Epictetus*, 2.153). For a discussion of this topos and Paul's use of it in Gal. 4.12, see Betz, *Galatians*, 221–3. See also Balch, "Stoic Debates," 437, who cites Arist. *N.E.* 1170b 6–7 and *E.E.* 1245a 30 (cf. *N.E.* 1170b 5–19). For Paul's use of philosophical notions of friendship in 2 Corinthians see Peter Marshall, *Enmity in Corinth: Social Conventions in Paul's Relations with the Corinthians*, WUNT 2/23 (Tübingen: J. C. B. Mohr, 1987) 1–34, 130–258.

[135] Arius in Stob. 2.108.18–25 W.-H.: "For true friendship, and not that which is falsely called, is impossible without trust (πίστις) and steadfastness. But among the

and a distinctive mark of the wise man is found in Epictetus as well. In his lecture *On Friendship*, for instance, he states that the governing principle of the bad man is "not trustworthy" (οὐκ ἔστι πιστόν),[136] and elsewhere he refers to those not living philosophical lives as "untrustworthy" (ἄπιστος).[137] On the other hand, he sees conversion to philosophy as a movement from being ἄπιστος to πιστός,[138] and he several times refers to the philosopher as πιστός, and at least once calls him ὁ πιστός.[139] These characterizations of friendship and the wise man are particularly suggestive, I would argue, since the terms πιστός and ἄπιστος also appear in 1 Corinthians 7.12–15a (as well as 1 Corinthians 6.6 and 2 Corinthians 6.14–15), and since both authors, like Paul, use this word group to distinguish between insiders and outsiders.[140]

One might object to this comparison, however, on grounds that Paul would have understood these terms very differently than the Stoics. That is, given his concept of salvation, Paul would have defined πιστός and ἄπιστος as "belief or trust in Christ" and "unbelief or lack of trust in Christ," rather than as "trusting/ trustworthy" and "untrusting/untrustworthy." Yet this objection carries little weight when we consider that Paul uses πιστός to refer to faith in the Divinity only once in his letters. This is Galatians 3.9, in a description of Abraham based on Genesis 15.6, and the reference here is to faith in God, not Christ. Elsewhere Paul uses the term to denote the trustworthiness of God,[141] and his own or Timothy's trustworthiness as servants of God.[142] We also have slight warrant for assuming that the Corinthians themselves held this supposedly "normative" Pauline understanding of πιστός. Indeed, since Paul uses ἄπιστος only in the Corinthian correspondence,[143] it is quite possible that this pair of terms hails from Corinth and had a special significance for the church there. In light of these considerations, I suggest that the notions of "trustworthy," "trusting," and "trust in Christ or God," all of which are encompassed by the πιστός word

bad, who are untrustworthy (ἄπιστοι) ... they say there is no friendship." Cf. 2.112.9–15 W.-H (*SVF* 3.147.9–13).
[136] Epict. *Diss.* 2.22.25
[137] Ibid., 1.3.7; 1.29.21; 2.4.11; cf. *SVF* 2.41.16–17.
[138] Epict. *Diss.* 4.9.17.
[139] Ibid., 1.4.18, 20; 2.14.13; 2.22.26–7, 29–30; 3.20.5; 4.1.133; 4.13.17–24; and 3.23.18.
[140] In 1 Cor. 14.23–4 it is even coupled with "outsider," ἰδιώτης.
[141] 1 Cor. 1.9; 10.13; 2 Cor. 1.18; 1 Thess. 5.24; cf. 2 Thess. 3.3.
[142] All in 1 Corinthians: 4.2; 4.17; 7.25.
[143] 1 Cor. 6.6; 7.12, 13, 14, 15; 10.27; 14.22, 23, 24; 2 Cor. 4.4; 6.14, 15.

group, were not as distinct in the minds of the Corinthians as they might have been for the Stoics or Paul. The Corinthians, in other words, may have used πιστός and ἄπιστος in both Stoic and Christian senses in distinguishing themselves from non-Christians, and 1 Corinthians 7.12–15a may be a reflection of this usage.

Finally, in considering the potential for Stoic influence on this passage, we may point out that, as with the Corinthians (and Ben Sira), the Stoics' aversion to outsiders is also seen in their understanding of marriage. An important piece of evidence in this regard comes from a non-Stoic (in fact, anti-Stoic) source. In his treatise entitled *On Common Conceptions, Against the Stoics*, Plutarch complains that Stoics are inconsistent, for while they label outsiders as unreliable (ἄπιστοι),[144] they nevertheless entrust (πιστεύωσιν) some with money and allow others to marry their daughters.[145] From this report we can see that Stoics experienced uncertainties in their relations with outsiders not unlike those which plagued the Corinthians, including uncertainties in the realm of "mixed" marriages.

From the Stoics themselves, moreover, it becomes clear why marriage with outsiders would surface as an issue, for along with their belief that a "partnership" could exist only among the wise, they held that marriage was life's closest partnership. As we noted above, Antipater, Musonius, and Hierocles all describe marriage as life's only partnership in which all things are shared, including the partners' souls and bodies, and Musonius states that no other partnership is "more necessary or affectionate."[146] Antipater, in turn, demands that there be a singleness of purpose in marriage, and insists that a man's wife be "another like himself."[147] [Ocellus] asserts that a man should marry a woman who is sympathetic in spirit and most like himself, or he will have division and disagreement instead of unity of purpose and agreement (συμφωνία).[148] Dio Chrysostom maintains that the welfare of the household depends on

---

144 As well as "unjust" (ἄδικοι) – cf. 1 Cor. 6.1, 9.
145 Plutarch *Mor.* 1062E–F (*De commun. not.*), trans. Harold Cherniss (ed.), *Plutarch's Moralia*, LCL (Cambridge: Harvard University Press/London: William Heinemann, 1976) 13.2.689.
146 Mus. *frag.* 14.94.2–3 L. (73.18–74.1 H.).
147 οἷον ἑαυτὸν ἕτερον, Antip. *SVF* 3.255.18–21 and 3.256.31 (Stob. 4.508.17–21 and 4.511.13 W.-H.). Cf. *SVF* 3.256.24–5 (Stob. 4.511.4–6 W.-H.), where Antipater speaks of a married man "having become two in place of one" (δύο γεγονὼς ἀνθ' ἑνός).
148 [Ocellus] *De univ. nat.* 48–9. Cf. 1 Cor. 7.5; 2 Cor. 6.14–15.

the like-mindedness of its master and mistress;[149] and Hierocles defines the beauty of a household as the "yoking" (ζεῦγος) of a man and a woman who agree (συμφωνέω) with one another.[150]

Again, as we saw above, Epictetus justifies Crates' marriage to Hipparchia on the basis that this woman was "another Crates," and he even concedes that in an ideal society *any* Cynic could marry, since all relationships resulting from marriage would be with other Cynics.[151] Likewise, Musonius requires that spouses be matched to one another with respect to discretion, righteousness, and virtue,[152] and then lets fly a series of rhetorical questions whose similarity to 2 Corinthians 6.14–16 rivals that of the verses we cited from Sirach 13:

> For what sort of marriage without concord is good? – what sort of partnership (κοινωνία) beneficial? How could persons be like-minded with one another when they are evil? – or, how could a good person be like-minded with an evil one? No more than a straight piece of wood might fit with a twisted one, or both being twisted, fit with one another.[153]

Not surprisingly, these high expectations for marriage also raised the question among Stoics as to what happens when philosophers find themselves involved in unions that fall short of the ideal. Like the Corinthians, who looked to Paul for counsel on divorce, Musonius, too, considers this option. In a passage that describes marriage as a "yoke" (ζεῦγος), Musonius explains that when the partnership of marriage lacks a common goal, and a spouse refuses to "pull together with his or her yoke-partner" (ὁμόζυγος), the couple often separates completely.[154] From 1 Corinthians 7.12–15a

---

[149] Dio Chrys. *Or.* 38.15, which continues, "What else is the good marriage, other than a husband's oneness of mind with his wife? And what else is the bad marriage, other than the discord of these two?"

[150] Hierocles 54.19–22 v.A. (Stob. 4.505.12–16 W.-H.). Cf. 1 Cor. 7.5; 2 Cor. 6.14–15.

[151] Epict. *Diss.* 3.22.68, 76; cf. *Cynic Ep. of Crates* 33.

[152] Mus. *frag.* 13B.90.12–13 L. (69.13–16 H.).

[153] Mus. *frag.* 13B.90.13–17 L. (69.16–70.3 H.). On the image of the straight and twisted sticks, see D.L. 7.127.

[154] Mus. *frag.* 13A.88.15, 24–9 L. (68.2, 13–19 H.). On Musonius' use of ὁμό-ζυγος ("one of like-yoke") cf. 2 Cor. 6.14, ἑτερο-ζυγέω ("to yoke differently"). Note also that an inscription from Mantinea which may reflect Stoic thought speaks of lives "yoked with lives and souls with bodies" (Dittenberger, *Sylloge*, 2.783.32–3, cited above, n. 54).

we see that the Corinthians were asking Paul if they could do just that.[155]

Thus far our investigation of 1 Corinthians 7.12–24 has shown that the dynamics as well as the rhetoric of the Corinthian situation are remarkably close to what we find in the Stoics and in two Jewish authors influenced by Stoicism, namely, Ben Sira and Philo. With this, however, our information on the issues behind this passage is not exhausted, for 7.14, which served as the starting point for our investigation, represents only the first justification that Paul gives for his ruling on mixed marriages. A second comes in 7.15b–24.

## Marriage to an unbeliever as a form of slavery (7.15b–24)

With 7.15b Paul begins a new thought, stating that Christians have not been "enslaved" (δουλόομαι) by their marriages with un-believers.[156] The difficulty here is in determining what exactly Paul is denying: in what way could someone be "enslaved" to his or her spouse?[157] Several scholars, emphasizing the "bondage" aspect of slavery, interpret οὐ δεδούλωται to mean "not bound like a slave," or simply "not bound."[158] Thus, Roberts maintains that οὐ δεδούλωται means "not under slavery or bondage in the sense of being required to prevent separation," saying that the phrase draws on the verb "to leave" (χωρίζεσθαι) in 7.15a. Baltensweiler sees the "bond" in question as deriving from the notion in Genesis 2.24 that spouses become "one flesh," an idea, as we have seen, which

---

[155] Cf. *De vita contemp.* 2.13–18, where Philo maintains that the Therapeutae have abandoned their non-philosophical wives and families in pursuit of the contemplative life.

[156] Paul's words in 7.15b, δεδούλωται ... ἐν τοῖς τοιούτοις, should probably be read as "enslaved ... in such matters" rather than "to such ones," since the Christian and the non-Christian are always spoken of in the singular in this passage, although either translation is possible.

[157] W. M. L. DeWette, *Kurze Erklärung der Briefe an die Corinther*, 3rd edn., ed. Hermann Messner, Kurzgefasstes exegetisches Handbuch zum Neuen Testament 2/2 (Leipzig: S. Hirzel, 1855) 64, lists conjectures going back to the church fathers.

[158] E.g., Lietzmann, *An die Korinther*, 31; Baltensweiler, *Die Ehe*, 193; Wolbert, *Ethische Argumentation*, 104; Conzelmann, *1 Corinthians*, 119 (cf. 123 n. 42); and the RSV. A more literal interpretation is pursued by Boaz Cohen, *Jewish and Roman Law: A Comparative Study* (New York: Jewish Theological Seminary of America, 1966) 1.394 n. 83, who suggests Paul means that "partners to such a marriage are not like slaves, whose marriage according to the Roman view, was permanent unless it was broken up by the master." But this conjures up the image of both the Christian and the unbeliever as slaves under a common master, whereas Paul considers the possibility of slavery only for the Christian, and gives no emphasis at all to the idea of a slave master.

surfaces in 1 Corinthians 6.15–17. And Niederwimmer, confessing that the sense of οὐ δεδούλωται is unclear, suggests three possibilities: "not bound" to the non-Christian spouse, "not bound" to the marriage agreement, and "not bound" by Jesus' prohibition of divorce, which Paul cites in 7.10–11.[159] The difficulty with all these conjectures is that in moving from "enslaved," to "slavishly bound," to simply "bound," these scholars move beyond the semantic range of δουλόω. Indeed, if Paul had meant "bound," one would have expected the more natural δέδεται, as in 7.27 and 7.39.[160]

Against this, however, we should note that an older generation of scholars had argued that 7.39 actually justified the translation of οὐ δεδούλωται as "not bound," for after stating that a wife is "bound" (δέδεται) to her husband as long as her husband is alive, Paul goes on to say that when the husband dies the woman is "free" (ἐλευθέρα) to marry whom she will. Since being "bound" functions here as the opposite of being "free," these scholars surmised that "bound" and "enslaved" were practically equivalents of one another.[161] Yet the logic of this argument is not sound, for a relation in Greek between "bound" (δέομαι) and "free" (ἐλεύθερος) in no way guarantees a corresponding relation between "bound" (δέομαι) and "enslaved" (δουλόομαι). This argument also does not give enough attention to the influence of legal terminology on the wording of 7.39, for not only is a woman's status of being "free to marry whom she chooses" a standard part of ancient divorce documents,[162] but the legalese of 7.39 is well illustrated by the fuller

[159] R. L. Roberts, Jr., "The Meaning of *Chorizo* and *Douloo* in I Corinthians 7.10–17," *Restoration Quarterly* 80 (1965) 184; Baltensweiler, *Die Ehe*, 195 n. 127; Niederwimmer, *Askese und Mysterium*, 104 n. 118.

[160] So also Heinrici, *Der erste Brief*, 225; and Wolbert, *Ethische Argumentation*, 105. Even Roberts feels compelled to clarify matters in this regard ("The Meaning of *Chorizo*," 182).

[161] A. Tholuck, *Exposition, Doctrinal and Philological, of Christ's Sermon on the Mount According to the Gospel of Matthew*, 2nd edn., The Biblical Cabinet 6 (Edinburgh: Thomas Clark, 1843) 1.341–2; followed by DeWette, *Kurze Erklärung*, 64; cf. Heinrich Greeven, "Ehe nach dem Neuen Testament," *Theologie der Ehe: Veröffentlichung des Ökumenischen Arbeitskreises evangelischer und katholischer Theologen*, ed. Gerhard Krems and Reinhard Mumm (Regensburg: Friedrich Pustet/ Göttingen: Vandenhoeck und Ruprecht, 1969) 76.

[162] See P. W. Pestman, *Marriage and Matrimonial Property in Ancient Egypt: A Contribution to Establishing the Legal Position of Women*, Papyrologica Lugduno-Batava 9 (Leiden: E. J. Brill, 1961) 73–4, cf. 181; and Ludwig Blau, *Die jüdische Ehescheidung und der jüdische Scheidebrief* (Strassburg: Karl J. Trübner, 1912) 2.18–28, cf. 28–42, esp. 39 and nn. 3–4.

wording of Romans 7.2–3: "the married woman is *bound by law* (δέδεται νόμῳ) to her living husband . . . but if her husband should die she is *free from the law* (ἐλευθέρα ἐστὶν ἀπὸ τοῦ νόμου) . . ."[163] Therefore, while it is true that "bound" and "free" can function as counterparts, this pertains to legal parlance, and we have no evidence that δουλόω ever functions to describe the legal relation between spouses. Indeed, this would be especially surprising in the instance under consideration, since 7.15b has reference to both sexes – "the sister or the brother" – not simply to the wife, as in 7.39. Thus, while a wife could be legally "bound" to her husband, as opposed to being "free to marry" someone else of her own choosing, the idea that a husband could be legally "bound" to his wife in this way, let alone "enslaved" to her, must be ruled out as an interpretation of 7.15b.

The primary mistake inherent in all these attempts to explain the meaning of δεδούλωται is the assumption that the function of 7.15b is to explain Paul's ruling in 7.15a, "if the unbeliever leaves, let him leave." Between verses 15a and 15b, however, there is no connecting particle, and as I have suggested above, verse 15a seems to require no explanation. Beyond this, since the topic of slavery comes up again in 7.21–3, there is sufficient reason to believe that 7.15b introduces what follows rather than concludes what precedes.[164]

If we now turn from the possible legal connotations of δεδούλωται and cast an eye in the direction of the philosophers, we find that the notion of marriage as a form of slavery plays a significant role in texts connected with the Stoic–Cynic marriage debate. In his description of the Essenes in the *Hypothetica*, for example, Philo tells us that these philosophers nurture within their celibate community the "true and only real freedom." As a consequence they shun marriage, believing that when a man marries he becomes "a slave in place of a freeman."[165] Philo also recognizes that marriage is a form

---

[163] Several early mss. even read "bound *by law*" in 1 Cor. 7.39, supplying νόμῳ from Rom. 7.2–3; cf. Johannes B. Bauer, "Was las Tertullian 1 Kor 7 39?" *ZNW* 77 (1986) 284–7.

[164] See Conzelmann, *1 Corinthians*, 125 n. 4; DeWette, *Kurze Erklärung*, 66.

[165] ἀντ᾽ ἐλευθέρου δοῦλος, Philo *Hypoth.* 11.3, 17. Philo is somewhat inconsistent on his view of the Essenes' freedom, perhaps because of the influence of Jewish wisdom literature. Elsewhere he says that the Essenes' philosophy of life establishes a freedom that *cannot* be enslaved (ἡ ἀδούλωτος ἐλευθερία, *Quod omnis probus* 88), which is in line with the Stoic doctrine of philosophical freedom. It may be a similar inconsistency on the part of the Corinthians that Paul is questioning when he introduces this Stoic doctrine of freedom in 7.17–24, contrasting it with being "slaves of [doctrines of] men" (7.23); see below.

of slavery for the wife, although this is something he actively endorses. Somewhat earlier in the *Hypothetica*, in a passage indebted to the literature on household management, he maintains that in proper marriages women "serve" (δουλεύειν) their husbands.[166] Similarly, Musonius, in rejecting the idea that wives who pursue philosophy will abandon their housework, praises the philosophical wife as one who does work which some consider a "slave's task" (δουλικά);[167] and in a Latin work on household management incorrectly attributed to Aristotle, the author claims that a wife will submit (*obsequor*) to her husband's wishes more conscientiously than if she had been purchased (*emptio*), adding that she has, in fact, been purchased inasmuch as her husband has given her a part in his life and the procreation of his children.[168] On a different note, Antipater rails against bachelors who refuse to marry because they see the entrance of a wife into their household as equivalent to a foreign garrison occupying a city. Antipater says they hold this opinion because they themselves are incapable of ruling (ἄρχειν), being, rather, "slaves of passion" (ἡδονῆς δοῦλοι) and susceptible to capture by a woman's beauty or her dowry.[169] In a similar fashion, Hierocles contends that those who marry for the wrong reasons bring a "tyrant instead of a wife" into their homes.[170]

From the wider philosophical milieu of the Hellenistic period we also have several aphorisms connecting marriage with slavery. Stobaeus preserves a line from Euripides which holds that a wife's possessions "enslave the husband, and he is no longer free," and one from Anaxandrides, a poet of the Middle Comedy, to the effect that a poor man who marries becomes a slave (δοῦλος) to his wife, whether she is rich or poor.[171] Stobaeus also has three other lines from Euripides which may be relevant: "For the chaste wife is nothing but a man's slave";[172] "Yoked in wedlock, he is no longer

---

[166] Philo *Hypoth.* 7.3 (see above, chap. 2, n. 173).
[167] Mus. *frag.* 3.42.8 L. (12.1–2 H.).
[168] [Arist.] *Oecon.* 3.1.
[169] Antip. *SVF* 3.255.36–256.4 (Stob. 4.509.18–510.1 W.-H.)
[170] τύραννον ἀντὶ γυναικός, Hierocles 55.11 v.A. (Stob. 4.506.19–20 W.-H.).
[171] Stob. 4.532.15 (δουλοῖ τὸν ἄνδρα, κοὐκέτ' ἔστ' ἐλεύθερος); and 4.513.7–11 W.-H. Cf. Pseudo-Phocylides *Sentences* 200, and [Plutarch] *Mor.* 13F (*De liberis educandis*).
[172] πᾶσα γὰρ δούλη πέφυκεν ἀνδρὸς ἡ σώφρων γυνή, Stob. 4.494.10 W.-H., from his *Oedipus*. On this image cf. Dionysius of Halicarnassus *Ancient Orators* 1.1.

free";[173] and "A great tyranny for a man are children and wife."[174] The popularity of these last sayings is indicated by the fact that Stobaeus records the first one twice, and it is known to Clement of Alexandria;[175] the second one Stobaeus again records twice, attributing it elsewhere to the tragedian Hippothoon;[176] and the second and third sayings also appear in the extremely popular *Sentences* of Menander.[177] From the *Sentences*, furthermore, we have another maxim on this theme: "Having married, know that you are a slave for life."[178] That sayings of this nature may have circulated among the Corinthians or otherwise had an influence on Paul's writing of 1 Corinthians 7 is made plausible, moreover, by Paul's citation of a proverb in 1 Corinthians 15.33 which is elsewhere attributed to Menander.[179]

In the context of the argumentative structure of 1 Corinthians 7 and its reliance on Stoic and Cynic traditions, furthermore, there are several ways in which this philosophical characterization of marriage as slavery could have functioned. First, this characterization of marriage, which is pronounced invalid by Paul, seems to be part of a Corinthian argument. As such it could well have served to undergird the Corinthians' perspective that marriage to an outsider was an avenue by which unwanted, foreign influences imposed themselves on a believer's life. This, for example, is the image that Philo has in mind in reporting that marriage ruins the idyllic community of the Essenes, and it is part and parcel of Antipater and Hierocles' description of marriage as tyranny or the hostile takeover of a city-state.[180] Second, the political metaphor for slavery used by

---

[173] ζευχθεὶς γάμοισιν οὐκέτ' ἔστ' ἐλεύθερος, Stob. 4.496.11 W.-H., from his *Antigone*.
[174] μεγάλη τυραννὶς ἀνδρὶ τέκνα καὶ γυνή, Stob. 4.494.4 W.-H., from his *Oedipus*.
[175] Also at Stob. 4.529.8–10 W.-H.; Clem. Alex. *Strom.* bk. 4, chap. 8.63.3 (2.277.10 S.).
[176] Stob. 4.519.5–6 W.-H.
[177] Menander *Sententiae* 282, 506 Jaekel.
[178] δοῦλος εἶναι διὰ βίου, Menander *Sent.* 529 J. Cf. Achilles Tatius 1.8.9.
[179] Menander *frag.* 187 Körte. On the Hellenistic background of the verses just before this one (i.e., 1 Cor. 15.29–32), see Malherbe, *Paul and the Popular Philosophers*, 78–9.
[180] In *Quod omnis probus* 45 Philo makes an explicit connection between the enslavement of a city-state by a tyrant and the slavery of an individual. We are also reminded here that 2 Cor. 6.14 speaks of being "incongruously yoked" with unbelievers, and that the image of a yoke can represent slavery as well as marriage (see, e.g., the line from Euripides just cited; see also Gal. 5.1; Acts 15.10; Sirach 28.19–20; 30.35 [Eng. 33.26]; 40.1).

Antipater and Hierocles reminds us that Stoics often spoke of the antithesis of slavery, personal freedom, in terms of kingship or rule. Thus, according to Diogenes Laertius, the Stoics held that "not only are the wise free, but also kings," and Philo explains that "the wise man alone is both free and rules."[181] Since the Corinthians, too, seem to have thought of themselves as kings in this philosophical sense,[182] their understanding of marriage to an unbeliever as a form of slavery may have intensified their negative appraisal of such unions inasmuch as these threatened the Corinthians' presumed royal status. That this would be a reasonable conclusion to draw within the framework of Stoic thought can be seen from Epictetus, who repeatedly maintains that marriage to a non-Cynic robs the Cynic of his kingdom.[183]

A third and final way in which the philosophical characterization of marriage as slavery could make sense in the context of 1 Corinthians 7 is suggested by the close connection that Stoics saw between freedom and "power" (ἐξουσία). Diogenes Laertius, for example, reports as a Stoic doctrine that freedom is the "power of independent action" (ἐξουσία αὐτοπραγίας),[184] and Dio Chrysostom concludes a discussion of slavery by stating, "And so, necessarily, the discerning are free, and they have the power (ἐξεῖναι αὐτοῖς) to do as they want."[185] Philo, in turn, defines the free person as one who has power (ἐξουσία) "to do everything and live as he wishes," saying that the one to whom these things are "allowed" (ἔξεστιν) would be free;[186] while Epictetus holds that wishing for something that is in someone else's power (ἐξουσία) is to act as a slave (δουλεύειν).[187] As I proposed above, on the basis of Paul's use of the verb "to have power" (ἐξουσιάζω) in 7.4, the

---

[181] D.L. 7.122, οὐ μόνον δὲ ἐλευθέρους εἶναι τοὺς σοφούς, ἀλλὰ καὶ βασιλέας, and Philo *De post. Caini* 138 (*SVF* 3.89.7–9), ὁ σοφὸς μόνος ἐλεύθερός τε καὶ ἄρχων.

[182] See Paul's rebuff in 1 Cor. 4.8: "Already you are filled! Already you have become rich! Without us you have become kings (ἐβασιλεύσατε)! And would that you did reign (ἐβασιλεύσατε), so that we might rule as kings with you (συμβασιλεύσωμεν)!" On Stoic influence here see Conzelmann, *1 Corinthians*, 87, and *SVF* 3.158.34–159.37.

[183] Epict. *Diss.* 3.22.72, 75, 79–81.

[184] D.L. 7.121. A version of this was known to Origen (*SVF* 3.147.7–9).

[185] Dio Chrys. *Or.* 14.16 (*SVF* 3.87.2–3).

[186] Philo *Quod omnis probus* 59 (*SVF* 3.88.34–6). Cf. 1 Cor. 6.12 and 10.23: πάντα (μοι) ἔξεστιν.

[187] Epict. *Diss.* 4.7.10 and *Ench.* 14.2. See also Antipater *SVF* 3.255.35 (Stob. 4.509.16 W.-H.), who complains that bachelors who refuse to marry think they have been given the right (ἐξουσία) to engage in illicit sex.

Corinthians he addresses in 7.12ff. may have objected to physically coming under the power of an unbelieving spouse during sexual intercourse. If this is true, then part of their argument for viewing marriage to an unbeliever as slavery may have rested on Stoic teachings such as these, which equated power with freedom, and the loss of power with slavery.[188]

Proceeding to the next few verses of our passage, we find still further evidence that Paul's argument here derives from a philosophical context. In 7.15c Paul introduces the idea of the Christian "call," and asserts that Christians with non-Christian spouses have been called by God "in peace" (ἐν εἰρήνῃ). Although a few scholars have attempted to interpret this in the sense of God calling the Corinthians *to* peace,[189] Paul's reference is most certainly to a state of peace in which God found the Corinthians when he originally extended his call.[190] What Paul means by "peace," on the other hand, is not altogether clear, but it is likely that he is speaking of the

---

[188] Paul's use of the term ἐξουσία supports this suggestion. It occurs seven times in 1 Corinthians in this sense of personal power (1 Cor. 7.37; 8.9; 9.4, 5, 6, 12, 18), in one instance manifestly drawing on a Stoic topos on freedom – i.e., 1 Cor. 9.4 (on this see above, n. 84, and cf. p. 86; on 7.37 see below, pp. 207–9). The word also occurs in 11.10 (a husband's authority as a restriction on his wife's freedom) and 15.24 (of "cosmic powers"). In 1 Cor. 6.12, furthermore, Paul suggests ironically that one may be "overpowered" (ἐξουσιάζομαι) by the improper use of his or her personal power. In his other letters, seven times altogether, the word denotes either God's power, Paul's authority as a church administrator, or civil authority; but never personal power (2 Cor. 10.8; 13.10; Rom. 9.21; 13.1–3; cf. 2 Thess. 3.9 [freedom not to work]).

In this light, it is also tempting to consider the possibility of a connection between Paul's use of the verb "to deprive" (ἀποστερέω) in 7.5 and the Stoic view that slavery was the "privation" (στέρησις) of independent action (D.L. 7.122), in contrast to freedom, which was the "power" of independent action. With his word choice in 7.4–5, Paul may be inferring that persons who are reluctant to maintain sexual relations within marriage are actually depriving their spouses of freedom/power through their demand for what they mistakenly (verse 4) view as their own freedom/power.

[189] E.g., Joachim Jeremias, "Die missionarische Aufgabe in der Mischehe (1. Kor 7,16)," *Abba: Studien zur neutestamentlichen Theologie und Zeitgeschichte* (Göttingen: Vandenhoeck und Ruprecht, 1966) 297 n. 13 says ἐν εἰρήνῃ may be read as εἰς εἰρήνην, citing the evidence of the Greek church fathers; Cohen, *Jewish and Roman Law*, 1.394 n. 83 thinks 7.15b is modelled on Judg. 21.13 ("and he called them to peace," καὶ ἐκάλεσαν αὐτοὺς εἰς εἰρήνην); and Gustav Billroth, *A Commentary on the Epistles of Paul to the Corinthians* (Edinburgh: Thomas Clark, 1837) 1.188 suggests that ἐν εἰρήνῃ = εἰρηνικῶς ("peacefully").

[190] See C. K. Barrett, *A Commentary on the First Epistle to the Corinthians*, HNTC (New York/Evanston: Harper and Row, 1968) 168–70; Neuhäusler, "Ruf Gottes," 45 n. 6; and Baltensweiler, *Die Ehe*, 192, who sees, correctly, that 7.15b is analogous to 7.18b, ἐν ἀκροβυστίᾳ κέκληταί τις; ("has someone been called *in the state* of uncircumcision?").

peace between a husband and wife, for he uses this term regularly in his letters to refer to harmony between individuals.[191]

Significantly, Paul proposes this "peace" rather than "freedom" as the alternative to slavery. Since the Corinthians evidently saw their marriages to unbelievers as a form of slavery, they would naturally think of freedom, the solution to their problem, in terms of divorce or separation from their spouses. Paul's first inclination, therefore, is to promote marital peace, not emancipation. Inevitably, however, Paul must find a way to support his claim in verse 15b that the Corinthians are not enslaved. He does this in 7.17–24 with a Christian reworking of the philosophical *topos* that freedom and slavery have nothing to do with one's outward circumstances of life. But before Paul advances his argument in this direction, he pauses to interject another sort of challenge to the Corinthians' desire to be freed from their non-Christian spouses. In 7.16 he follows the assertion that Christians have been "called in peace" with an explanation in the form of two rhetorical questions: "For (γάρ) what do you know (τί οἶδας), wife, if you will save (σώσεις) your husband? Or what do you know, husband, if you will save your wife?" Although the syntax of these questions is not transparent, scholars have concluded that they express either a genuine uncertainty or a mild optimism regarding the conversion of the unbelieving spouse. It is unlikely, in other words, that Paul is suggesting to his readers that they will *not* convert their spouses.[192] If this is correct, then the force of these questions is to point out to the Corinthians that far from being unholy, unclean outsiders, their

---

[191] 1 Cor. 14.33; 2 Cor. 13.11; Rom. 14.17–19 (which speaks of "serving," δουλεύων, Christ in peace); 1 Thess. 5.13. Elsewhere in early Christianity peace is spoken of as something belonging to a household. In Matt. 10.13//Luke 10.5–6 Jesus' disciples are described as bringing peace to households through their salutation, and Matt. 10.34–6//Luke 12.49–53 contrasts peace with the division of households. A form of this last saying is also found in *Gos. Thom.* 16, and a third saying of Jesus on household peace at *Gos. Thom.* 48. Stoics and Cynics may also have spoken of peace in this manner. Lucian *Demonax* 9, for example, recalls that the Cynic Demonax "was concerned both with reconciling brothers who were quarrelling, and with arbitrating peace for wives with their husbands" (καὶ γυναιξὶ πρὸς τοὺς γεγαμηκότας εἰρήνην πρυτανεύειν). This, in turn, resembles Epictetus' claim that the Cynic "oversees" humanity, determining "who is treating his wife well, who badly; who quarrels; what household is stable, what not" (Epict. *Diss.* 3.22.72); and it compares favorably to the concern for harmony between spouses that we find among the Stoics generally (see above, pp. 146–7).

[192] See Jeremias, "Die missionarische Aufgabe," 296–7; and Sakae Kubo, "I Corinthians vii. 16: Optimistic or Pessimistic?" *NTS* 24 (1977/78) 539–44, esp. 542, 544.

non-Christian husbands and wives, with whom they were called in marital peace, are actually prime candidates for conversion.[193] Divorce, therefore, Paul is saying, must be seen as an uncalculated and overhasty course of action from this perspective as well.

The effectiveness of this supplementary argument lies, in large part, in its philosophical pedigree, for in all likelihood 7.16 has roots in a Stoic or Cynic tradition. This is suggested by two things. First, the form of this verse is the direct address of the Stoic–Cynic diatribe. From its beginning in verse 12, Paul has handled the question of mixed marriages in the third person singular or the second person plural. In verse 16, however, we find the second person singular, which is most satisfactorily explained as a shift to diatribe style. This conclusion is supported not only by the fact that the closest parallels to the syntax of Paul's questions, τί (γὰρ) οἶδας ... εἰ, come from Epictetus,[194] but also by Paul's generous use of the diatribe style in the rest of 1 Corinthians 7.[195]

Our second reason for identifying the source of 7.16 as Stoic or Cynic is based on its similarity to an apocryphal saying preserved by Stobaeus, in which the issue is again one of "knowing" whether one will "save" one's spouse: "Plato, being asked, 'May I pursue philosophy if I marry?' said, 'Not knowing (οὐκ εἰδώς) that you will even save (σώζειν) your own self, will you assist in saving (συνδιασώσεις) a wife upon your shoulders?'"[196] Although neither the date nor the provenance of this saying can be determined with

---

[193] Just as Christians render their non-Christian spouses holy, Paul is saying, they may also convert them. Cf. 1 Pet. 3.1–6 where the author suggests that wives might convert their unbelieving husbands.

[194] Epict. *Diss.* 2.20.28–31; 2.22.31 (twice); and 2.25.2 (cited in Jeremias, "Die missionarische Aufgabe," 294–6), which are of the form πόθεν οἶδας εἰ (or εἴση ἄν), "whence do you know (will you know) if ... ?" All other examples scholars have cited are of the form τίς οἶδεν εἰ, "who knows if ... " These include: 2 Sam. 12.22; Esth. 4.14; Jonah 3.9; Joel 2.14; *Joseph and Aseneth* 11.12 (cited in Jeremias, "Die missionarische Aufgabe," 292–4); Qoh. 2.19; 3.21 (cited in Kubo, "I Corinthians vii. 16: Optimistic or Pessimistic?," 541–2); Tobit 13.8 (τίς γινώσκει εἰ, cited in Baumert, *Ehelosigkeit und Ehe*, 85 n. 171); Achilles Tatius 7.6.2; Apuleius *Metamorphoses* 1.15.4; 6.1.2; 6.5.4; and 10.26.2 (cited in Burchard, "Joseph and Aseneth," 2.219 n. *i* 2).

[195] Verses 18, 21, and 27 – see below. Paul also uses diatribe style elsewhere in 1 Corinthians, e.g., at 15.35–6. On the history of research into Paul's use of the diatribe style see Stowers: *The Diatribe and Paul's Letter*, 7–78; "The Diatribe," *Greco-Roman Literature and the New Testament: Selected Forms and Genres*, ed. David E. Aune, SBLSBS 21 (Atlanta: Scholars, 1988) 51–83; and Thomas Schmeller, *Paulus und die "Diatribe": Eine vergleichende Stilinterpretation*, NTAbh, n.s. 19 (Münster: Aschendorffsche Verlagsbuchhandlung, 1987).

[196] [Plato] in Stob. 4.520.9–12 W.-H., cited Delling, *Paulus' Stellung*, 81 n. 159.

certainty, its resemblance to 1 Corinthians 7.16 is, in my opinion, too striking to be dismissed as coincidence. Furthermore, while the speaker is said to be Plato, the question he is asked as well as his reply mirror the concerns of the Stoic–Cynic marriage debate. To assume that this saying had some currency in Stoic or Cynic circles in the first century, and to see it or a related saying as the inspiration for 1 Corinthians 7.16 is, therefore, not at all unreasonable.[197] There is, of course, an obvious difference between this saying and 7.16. In the one, "Plato" stresses the difficulty of saving a future spouse, in the other, Paul seeks to persuade the Corinthians that the salvation of their present spouses is still an open question. In light of this, it is possible that some version of the "Platonic" saying was known to the Corinthians and perhaps used by them as an argument for leaving an "unclean" spouse. Paul, by contrast, makes use of this saying by emphasizing the Corinthians' ignorance of God's ultimate intentions for their spouses. In all, Paul seems to have chosen the better argument, for while the "Platonic" saying works well as a warning against initiating marriage, Paul's version is a compelling argument for staying married, which is the issue here.

Following this supplementary argument in 7.16, Paul returns to his initial contention in verse 15b that Christians who are married to non-Christians are not "enslaved." He does this by using the almost casual transition phrase "In any event ... ," or "Only ..." (εἰ μή), and by elaborating on the idea of the Christian call, which he introduced in verse 15c.[198] In this way 7.17–24 serves as the continuation and conclusion of the argument begun in 7.15b-c.[199] It is not, as scholars often contend, a conclusion to the first half of chapter seven or the theological centerpiece of the entire chapter.[200]

In addressing the themes of slavery and the Christian call in

[197] While Stoics and Cynics were more apt to quote a saying from Socrates and use him as their model, they also, on occasion, cited Plato, e.g., *Cynic Ep. of Diogenes* 44 (174.9–10 M.); Epict. *Diss.* 1.28.4; 2.17.6; 2.18.20; 2.22.36; 4.1.172.

[198] So also Meyer, *Critical and Exegetical Handbook*, 209–10. It should be noted that 7.17b repeats the perfect κέκληκεν ("has called") of 7.15c; by contrast, verses 20 and 24 run parallel to each other, using the aorist of καλέω.

[199] So also Neuhäusler, "Ruf Gottes," 45 n. 4; Bartchy, *ΜΑΛΛΟΝ ΧΡΗΣΑΙ*, 133; and Yarbrough, *Not Like the Gentiles*, 112. Niederwimmer, *Askese und Mysterium*, 105 and n. 123, followed by William F. Orr and James Arthur Walther, *I Corinthians: A New Translation*, AB 32 (Garden City, N.Y.: Doubleday, 1976) 216, erroneously suggests that 7.17–24 is a digression on peace (verse 15c).

[200] See, e.g., Weiß, *Korintherbrief*, 183; Hurd, *The Origin of 1 Corinthians*, 89, 178; and Baumert, *Ehelosigkeit und Ehe*, 19, 99–160 (esp. 158). Ironically, Heinrici, *Der erste Brief*, 249 notes that several commentaries in his day saw 7.17–24 as an interpolation or a misplaced text.

7.17–24, Paul utilizes as his framework his teaching on the equality in Christ of Jews and Greeks, slaves and free, punctuating it at the beginning and end (verses 17, 24)[201] with the admonition that Christians remain in the condition in which they were called. This teaching also appears in Galatians 3.28, where a third pair, male and female, is used.[202] But whereas in Galatians Paul focuses on the pair Jew–Greek, using the other two pairs simply as examples,[203] here his real subject is the pair slave–free, while the pair circumcised–uncircumcised represents the example.[204] 1 Corinthians 7.17–24 also shows itself to be different from Galatians 3.28 in that it emphasizes the Christian's indifference to the external conditions of life, not the equality of those "in Christ."

The point Paul wishes to drive home in verses 17–24 is twofold: first, that no Christian can be enslaved by the circumstances of his or her life, by virtue of God's "call" to become a Christian; and second, that undue concern for changing the circumstances of one's life disregards the efficacy of God's call, and thereby represents a form of slavery in itself. In this way, the pair circumcised–uncircumcised (7.18–19) functions here to illustrate the general principle that outward circumstances are of no consequence to the Christian, and therefore a Christian should not seek to make a change in one way or the other. With the pair slave–free (7.21–2) Paul then goes a step beyond this, declaring that God's call actually *reverses* the circumstances of one's life, for the Christian slave is now the Lord's *freed*man, while those who were free before their call are now Christ's slaves. With this declaration, the refrain of verses 17 and 24 that Christians should remain in the circumstances of life in which they were called now takes on new meaning. The longing to "better" one's station in life becomes, in effect, a denial of the significance of

---

[201] On the meaning of 7.20, see below.

[202] On the absence of this pair in 1 Cor. 7.17–24 see Betz, *Galatians*, 200 (regarding 1 Cor. 12.13).

[203] Cf. Gal. 5.6 and 6.15 where only the pair circumcised–uncircumcised appears.

[204] It is fairly common for Paul to join his real subject with examples in this way, thereby establishing a larger context for his argument. In 1 Cor. 12.4–6, for instance, he contrasts the variety of Christian "gifts," "services," and "workings" to the oneness of the Spirit, the Lord, and God, respectively, but from verses 7–11 it becomes clear that his interest lies only with the *gifts* of the *Spirit* (see Conzelmann, *1 Corinthians*, 208). Likewise, in 12.8–10 he enumerates several gifts of the Spirit (cf. 12.28–30; 13.1–3), but as we soon learn from chapter 14, it is only the gifts of prophecy and speaking in tongues that really concern him. It is in this context, incidentally, that Paul also reproduces the paradigm Jew–Greek, slave–free (12.13), both pairs now serving as examples.

the change that God has already brought about.[205] This, in turn, makes one a "slave of men" (verse 23), by which Paul must be referring to a spiritual bondage to doctrines or ideologies "of men" (cf. 3.1–4), since the Christian slave of verses 21–2 cannot "become" (γίγνομαι) a slave of men in the physical sense, as he already is one.[206]

With regard to the issue of mixed marriages at Corinth, Paul's implied conclusion in all of this is that Christians married to non-Christians are not enslaved – his initial claim in 7.15b. These Christians are in fact no more enslaved to their spouses than other Christians are slaves to earthly masters, something which Paul has shown to be a matter of indifference. Any attempt by these Christians to shake off their supposed yoke of slavery by divorcing a non-Christian spouse must be viewed as a rejection of God's grace and at the same time the subjection of themselves to true slavery – that of the spirit.[207]

As it stands, with 7.17–24 Paul has fashioned a highly Stoicized version of his teaching on God's transforming grace, both in form and in content. In terms of form, these verses move with the distinctive rhythms of the Stoic–Cynic diatribe style of instruction.[208] The rhetorical pattern that Paul employs here has the following elements. A statement of fact in the form of a rhetorical question[209] is made about someone, often in the direct address of the second person singular. Next comes an imperative, the purpose of which is to deny the importance of this fact for future action.

---

[205] Cf. Bartchy, *ΜΑΛΛΟΝ ΧΡΗΣΑΙ*, 140.

[206] Cf. 1 Cor. 6.20.

[207] Cf. Juncker, *Ethik*, 2.161–2, who sees 7.17–24 as clear evidence that some Corinthians felt they had to break off marital relations in order to be holy, equal, and free.

[208] Noted by several scholars, e.g., Weiß, *Korintherbrief*, 184–5; Conzelmann, *1 Corinthians*, 5, 126; and Bultmann, *Der Stil der paulinischen Predigt*, 69.

[209] Edgar J. Goodspeed, *Problems of New Testament Translation* (Chicago: University of Chicago Press, 1945) 155–6 argues against translating the statement of fact as a rhetorical question on the basis of PTeb 421, θέλις αὐτὸ πωλῆσαι πώλησον, θέλις αὐτὸ ἀφεῖναι τῇ θυγατρί σου ἄφες, which he translates, "If you wish to sell it sell it; if you wish to give it to your daughter, give it to her." F. Blass and A. Debrunner, *A Greek Grammar of the New Testament and Other Early Christian Literature*, trans. and rev. Robert W. Funk (Chicago Press/London: University of Chicago, 1961) 262 (§494), in turn, remark that while the statement of fact corresponds to a protasis, it is unnecessary to translate it as a question. But none of these scholars takes into account the Latin and Hebrew examples from Seneca and Sirach (see below), the syntax of which calls for a question mark. Goodspeed's citation of the papyri does, however, show the kinship of the diatribe style to everyday speech patterns.

Lastly, an explanation that the original statement of fact is a matter
of indifference is sometimes added.
    In 7.17–24 this rhetorical pattern appears three times. In 7.18 we
get two statements of fact and two imperatives: "Someone was
called having been circumcised? – let him not remove the circumcision!²¹⁰ Someone has been called in an uncircumcised state? – let
him not be circumcised!" Verse 19 then gives a combined explanation: "Circumcision is nothing and uncircumcision is nothing;
rather, keeping the commandments of God." In verse 21 we get the
third statement of fact and the third imperative, this time followed
by a qualification, the meaning of which is still disputed among
scholars: "You were called as a slave? – don't let it concern you! But
if indeed you can become free, rather use [it] (μᾶλλον χρῆσαι)."²¹¹
Verse 22 then supplies an explanation: "For the slave who is called
in the Lord is the Lord's freedman; likewise, the one called as a
freeman is Christ's slave."²¹² From verses 21–2 we see that Paul's
interest in using this particular diatribe form has even prevented him
from finishing the paradigm Jew–Greek, slave–free, since he cannot
very well add to verse 21a, "You were called as a freeman? – don't
let it concern you!" or " – don't become a slave!," for the imperative
would not represent a reasonable course of action.²¹³All the same,
verse 22 proffers the explanation for this missing statement and
imperative, just as if they were there, although the intervening
remark (verse 21b) tends to obscure this inconsistency. As we shall
see below, Paul retains this mention of the freeman in verse 22 in
order to introduce into his discussion a Christian version of the
Stoic paradox on freedom.

    ²¹⁰ For the history of this intriguing medical procedure see Emil Schürer, *The
History of the Jewish People in the Age of Jesus Christ (175 BC–AD 135)*, rev. Geza
Vermes and Fergus Millar (Edinburgh: T. and T. Clark, 1973) 1.149 n. 28.
    ²¹¹ On the force of the last clause in 7.21 see Baumert, *Ehelosigkeit und Ehe*,
114–56; Bartchy, *MAΛΛON XPHΣAI*; and Margaret E. Thrall, *Greek Particles in
the New Testament: Linguistic and Exegetical Studies*, NTTS 3 (Grand Rapids,
Mich.: William B. Eerdmans, 1962) 78–82. The use of a set rhetorical form in this
verse opens up the possibility, of course, that the imperative here does not represent
Paul's own command. In this way, the qualification, which is clearly an addition to
the set form, may be Paul's attempt to avoid a misunderstanding, carrying the
meaning that slaves, while they should not regard their disenfranchised state as an
indication of their worth before God, should also not forgo the opportunity to work
toward their emancipation. See now, Will Deming, "A Diatribe Pattern in 1 Cor. 7:
21–22: A New Perspective on Paul's Directions to Slaves" *NovT* (forthcoming).
    ²¹² On ὁμοίως, "likewise," in this verse as an indication of Stoic influence, see
above, pp. 116–17.
    ²¹³ Noted by Meyer, *Critical and Exegetical Handbook*, 218; Weiß, *Korintherbrief*,
187; and Neuhäusler, "Ruf Gottes," 47; cf. Bartchy, *MAΛΛON XPHΣAI*, 157.

Parallels to this pattern of rhetoric can be found in several Hellenistic authors. The one most often cited is that by the Cynic Teles, from his treatise *On Self-Sufficiency*, and it is noteworthy that Teles employs the same elliptical expression, "use [it]," that we find in 1 Corinthians 7.21b:

> Therefore one should not try to change circumstances, but rather to prepare oneself for them as they are, just as sailors do ... And as for you, < regard > your present situation, use it (χρῶ). You have grown old? – do not seek the things of a young man! Again, you have become weak? – do not seek to carry and submit your neck to the loads of a strong man! ... Again, you have become destitute? – do not seek the rich man's way of life ...! Therefore, as I say, I do not see how circumstances themselves have anything troublesome, not old age or poverty or lack of citizenship.[214]

Our next examples come from an epigram attributed to Posidippus and from its alter ego attributed to Metrodorus.[215] Here we see some variation in the basic pattern inasmuch as the future tense, not an imperative, follows the statement of fact. Posidippus writes, "You have a marriage? – you will not be without cares! You don't marry? – you live being even more alone! ... Youth is foolish; grey hair, again, is feeble."[216] To this Metrodorus mocks back, "You have a marriage? – your house will be the most excellent! You don't marry? – you live being even more at ease! ... Youth is strong; grey hair, again, is pious."[217]

---

[214] Teles *frag.* 2.10.65–80 O'Neil, trans. Edward N. O'Neil (ed.), *Teles (The Cynic Teacher)*, SBLTT 11/SBLGRS 3 (Missoula, Mont.: Scholars, 1977) 11, punctuation modified slightly.

[215] The date and authorship of both epigrams is uncertain. See Pierre Waltz and Guy Soury, *Anthologie grecque, première partie: Anthologie Palatine* (Paris: Société d'édition «Les belles lettres», 1974) 3.183; and A. S. F. Gow and D. L. Page (eds.), *The Greek Anthology: Hellenistic Epigrams*, vol. 2: *Commentary and Indexes* (Cambridge: Cambridge University Press, 1965) 502, although the suggestion of Gow and Page that these poems are post-Hellenistic does not take into account the parallels presented here.

[216] Posidippus in Stob. 5.842.6–9 W.-H., and *Grk. Anth.* 9.359. T. B. L. Webster, *Hellenistic Poetry and Art* (London: Methuen, 1964) 56 n. 3 compares Posidippus' sentiment to that found in Theophrastus *On Marrying*. Johannes Geffcken, *Kynika und Verwandtes* (Heidelberg: Carl Winter, 1909) 10 called this epigram a "poetic diatribe"; and Wolfgang Speyer, *Naucellius und sein Kreis* (Munich: C. H. Beck, 1959) 96 n. 4 termed it "popular-philosophical discourse." On the use of diatribe in epigrams see Geffcken, *Kynika*, 6–13.

[217] *Grk. Anth.* 9.360.

Another sort of variation occurs in Sirach 7.22–6, which includes this diatribe form in a collection of proverbs. Instead of stressing the indifference of a certain condition through the imperative, the author uses it simply to give advice, following it with another such imperative rather than an explanation:

> You have cattle?[218] – tend them! And if they are profitable to you, let them stay with you. You have children [i.e., sons]? – discipline them! And make them obedient from their youth. You have daughters? – be on guard for their chastity! And do not show yourself to be too lenient with them ... You have a wife? – do not despise her![219] And do not trust yourself to a woman you hate.[220]

In the first century Philo, Seneca, and Plutarch also use this particular diatribe pattern. In his treatise *On Joseph*, where Philo has a tendency to present Joseph as a Stoic wise man, he describes this patriarch's rise to power in Egypt as a matter of philosophical necessity. Since life is full of disturbance and confusion (ταραχὴ καὶ ἀταξία), Philo explains, the statesman must come on the scene to give teachings as to the truth of things. Among these teachings are eight examples of our diatribe form:

> This is another's? – don't desire it!
> This is yours? – use it, not misusing it!
> You have abundance? – share! For the beauty of riches is
>     not in purses, but in aiding those in need.
> You have little? – don't begrudge the rich! For no one
>     would show compassion to a slanderous pauper.
> You're famous and have received honors? – don't brag!
> Your fortunes are lowly? – nonetheless, don't let your
>     spirits fall!
> All advances for you as you planned? – beware of change!

218 Here and in the following lines the expression used is "noun + *lĕkā*" (LXX, noun + σοί ἐστιν), as Hebrew has no verb "to have."
219 LXX: "You have a wife after your soul? – do not divorce her!" (γυνὴ σοί ἐστιν κατὰ ψυχήν; μὴ ἐκβάλῃς αὐτήν). On the difference between the Heb. and the Grk., see Rudolf Smend, *Die Weisheit des Jesus Sirach* (Berlin: Georg Reimer, 1906) 70–1; and Warren C. Trenchard, *Ben Sira's View of Women: A Literary Analysis*, Brown Judaic Studies 38 (Chico, Calif.: Scholars, 1982) 28.
220 Alexander A. Di Lella, *The Hebrew Text of Sirach* (The Hague: Mouton, 1966) 58 describes the pattern here as "a vigorous and concise bit of Hebrew poetry"; Juncker, *Ethik*, 2.204 compares Sirach 7.18–28 to a household code. See also Trenchard, *Ben Sira's View*, 27–8. On Stoic influence in Sirach, see above, n. 114. Ben Sira was, of course, an eager *collector* of philosophical maxims.

> You stumble often? – hope for success! For when things
> turn among men, they tend toward their opposites.[221]

Here again, in the sixth example, we find the elliptical mode of
expression that occurs in 1 Corinthians 7.21b.

In his tractate *On Tranquility of the Mind*, Seneca admonishes a
person to pursue virtue, regardless of outward circumstances, giving
us the following examples:

> Is he not permitted to be a soldier? – let him seek public
> office! Must he live in a private station? – let him help his
> countrymen by his silent support! Is it dangerous even to
> enter the forum? – in private houses, at the public specta-
> cles, at feasts let him show himself a good comrade, a
> faithful friend, a temperate feaster! Has he lost the duties of
> a citizen? – let him exercise those of a man! The very reason
> for our magnanimity in not shutting ourselves up within the
> walls of one city, in going forth into intercourse with the
> whole earth and in claiming the world as our country, was
> that we might have a wider field for our virtue. Is the
> tribunal closed to you, and are you barred from the rostrum
> and the hustings? – look how many broad stretching coun-
> tries lie open behind you, how many peoples! Never can
> you be blocked from any part so large that a still larger will
> not be left open to you.[222]

In Plutarch an instance of this diatribe configuration occurs in his
work *On Borrowing*. As part of an argument against borrowing, he
cites an adage showing the futility of the practice: "You have
means? – don't borrow! ... You are without means? – don't borrow!"[223] Although Plutarch is no Stoic, a Stoic origin for this saying
is suggested not only by its rhetorical structure, but also by Plutarch's explanation of it, which employs quotations from Cato and

---

[221] Philo *De Jos.* 143–4, cited by Henry St. John Thackeray, *The Relation of St. Paul to Contemporary Jewish Thought* (London: Macmillan, 1900) 239, who also cites Philo *Quod omnis probus* 48, where we find a ninth example of sorts, on the theme of slavery: "You're a slave? – you have no share in speech (λόγος)!" This maxim was also known to the Stoic emperor Marcus Aurelius (11.30). The use of the diatribe style in Philo's OT exegesis is noted by Wendland, "Philo und die kynisch-stoische Diatribe," 62–3; and Stowers, *The Diatribe and Paul's Letter*, 69, 93.
[222] Sen. *De tranquillitate animi* 4.3–4, trans. Basore, *Seneca: Moral Essays*, 2.229, punctuation modified slightly.
[223] Plut. *Mor.* 829F (*De vitando aere alieno*), cited by Almquist, *Plutarch*, 97, who also cites *Mor.* 1103D (*Non posse suaviter*), which is a variation on this pattern.

Crates, as well as anecdotes about Musonius, Cleanthes, and Zeno.[224]

Finally, from the second century, Epictetus supplies us with still other examples of this rhetorical form:

> Never say about anything, "I lost it," but rather, "I gave [it] back." Your little child died? – it was given back! Your wife died? – she was given back![225]

> Remember that you must conduct yourself as in a banquet. Has something been passed around down to you? – reach out your hand and politely take some! It goes on by? – don't hold [it] back! It hasn't come yet? – don't set your desire on [it] at a distance, but stay put until it is down by you! Thus toward children, thus toward a wife, thus toward public office, thus toward wealth, and some day you will be worthy of the banquet of the gods.[226]

Just as the form of 7.17–24 borrows from Stoic–Cynic discourse, so does its content. This is seen most clearly in verses 22–3, which reflect the Stoic paradox that the wise and good man is always free although he be a slave, while the bad man is forever a slave even if he is a king.[227] The Stoics held this doctrine because they believed that moral choice, not outward circumstances of life, defined freedom. To be free was to pursue virtue; to be a slave was to become entangled in human misconceptions about life, analogous to Paul's idea of becoming "slaves of men."[228] This philosophical understanding of freedom and slavery is widely attested in the Stoicism of the Empire. We find it in Arius, Philo, Seneca, Dio Chrysostom, and Epictetus.[229]

---

[224] Plut. *Mor.* 829F, 830B-D.

[225] Epict. *Ench.* 11.

[226] Epict. *Ench.* 15. Johannes Weiß, *Beiträge zur Paulinischen Rhetorik* (Göttingen: Vandenhoeck und Ruprecht, 1897) 23 cites Epict. *Diss.* 1.12.22, but the pattern is too different to be considered a parallel. The same holds for James 5.13–14.

[227] Noted by several scholars, including Weiß, *Korintherbrief*, 187; Bultmann, *Der Stil der paulinischen Predigt*, 82; Betz, *Galatians*, 195; and F. Stanley Jones, *"Freiheit" in den Briefen des Apostels Paulus: Eine historische, exegetische und religionsgeschichtliche Studie*, Göttinger Theologische Arbeiten 34 (Göttingen: Vandenhoeck und Ruprecht, 1987) 27–37.

[228] For discussions of the Stoic notion of freedom see, e.g., Greeven, *Das Hauptproblem*, 28–33; and Pohlenz, *Freedom in Greek Life*, 113–15. See also *SVF* 3.85.21–89.24.

[229] E.g., Arius in Stob. 2.101.14–20 W.-H.; Philo *Quod omnis probus*; Dio Chrys. *Or.* 14 and 15; Epict. *Diss.* 4.1. For Seneca see Griffin, *Seneca*, 260. Curiously it is not

One reason that Paul may have considered the Stoic doctrine of freedom particularly apropos to the Corinthian situation is that it distinguished between slavery of the body and the "true" slavery of the mind.[230] Earlier in this section, with reference to 7.15b and 7.4, I suggested that the Corinthians saw their marriages to non-Christians as a form of slavery because of the control (ἐξουσία) that a non-Christian spouse exercised over the Christian's body. If this is correct, Paul's insistence here on a Stoic definition of slavery and freedom has the effect of denying that such conjugal control over a Christian's body has any relevance for the issues of true slavery and freedom.

Quite justifiably, several scholars have cautioned against drawing too close an analogy between 1 Corinthians 7.22–3 and Stoic thought. The Stoics, they point out, held that freedom is achieved through the individual's own efforts to live according to nature and virtue, while for Paul freedom comes to the individual only through God's help, manifested in Christ. Thus, even though Epictetus can picture the philosopher responding to a tyrant with the words, "Zeus has set me free!,"[231] it is Zeus as sustainer of the cosmos that Epictetus has in mind, whose *logos* provides all persons with the means to make themselves free, not Zeus as personal redeemer. Yet this fundamental difference in theological orientation does not, as these scholars freely admit, diminish the likelihood that the Stoic paradox of freedom has left its mark on our passage.[232]

---

found in Musonius, but this may be an indication of how incomplete our records are of his teachings.

[230] Philo even lauds this as the "greatest dogma" (τὸ δογματικώτατον), declaring that the wise man is free "even if he should have a thousand masters of the body" (κἂν μυρίους τοῦ σώματος ἔχῃ δεσπότας, *De post. Caini* 138). See also Philo *Quod omnis probus* 17–19; Sen. *De ben.* 3.20.1–2; Dio Chrys. *Or.* 15.29; and Epict. *Diss.* 1.19.9; 3.22.38–44.

[231] Epict. *Diss.* 1.19.9, cited in Weiß, *Korintherbrief*, 190. Cf. Epict. *Diss.* 3.24.67–8; 4.1.111–14, and Oldfather's note on this last passage (*Epictetus*, 2.282 n. 1).

[232] See Weiß, *Korintherbrief*, 189–90; Kümmel in Lietzmann, *An die Korinther*, 177; Conzelmann, *1 Corinthians* 127–8. Adolf Bonhöffer, *Epiktet und das Neue Testament*, Religionsgeschichtliche Versuche und Vorarbeiten 10 (Gießen: Alfred Töpelmann, 1911) 170–2 – followed by J. N. Sevenster, *Paul and Seneca*, NovTSup 4 (Leiden: E. J. Brill, 1961) 189–90, and Neuhäusler, "Ruf Gottes," 44 – maintains that Paul's demand in 7.21 that one remain a slave is un-Stoic, but this interpretation of 7.21, as we noted above, is disputed.

Along these same lines, another difference between 7.22–3 and Stoic thinking on which some scholars have insisted may represent only dissimilarity rather than incompatibility. Thus Conzelmann, *1 Corinthians*, 128 maintains that Paul's "dialectic of freedom in servitude" in verse 22 is "alien" to Stoic thought. While this is true, a Stoic like Seneca can nonetheless give his full assent to the Epicurean saying, "If

A second possibility for seeing the influence of Stoic thought on the content of 1 Corinthians 7.17–24 is Paul's statement in 7.20 that every Christian should remain "in the call (κλῆσις) to which he was called."[233] This admonition is peculiar in two ways. First, it is out of step with the rest of the section, for in verses 17, 18, 21, and 24 Paul insists that Christians should remain in the *circumstances* in which they were called, whereas here it is the call itself that is at issue; and second, it does not, at least initially, seem to make much sense for Paul in this context to admonish Christians to remain in their Christian call, or, in effect, to "remain Christians." Given these difficulties, scholars have generally opted for understanding κλῆσις as "state," "condition," or "status." This yields the translation, "... in the state in which he was called,"[234] and brings 7.20 back into line with the other verses in this section. These meanings for the word κλῆσις are not found elsewhere in early Christian literature, however, nor are they clearly attested anywhere in ancient Greek literature.[235] Furthermore, the overall context of 7.17–24, if not verse 20 itself, strongly favors the meaning "Christian call."

In his commentary on 1 Corinthians, Weiß proposed that the difficulty with 7.20 had come about because the Christian sense of the word κλῆσις had been flavored by Stoic popular philosophy. As proof for his theory he cited Epictetus *Discourses* 1.29.33–49 and 2.1.39.[236] In the first passage, Epictetus states that the philosopher often acts "as a witness called by God" when faced with demanding

---

you would enjoy real freedom, you must be the slave of philosophy" (*philosophiae servias oportet*), adding that "the very service (*servire*) of philosophy is freedom (*libertas*)" (*Ep.* 8.7, trans. Richard M. Gummere [ed.], *Seneca: Ad Lucilium, epistulae morales*, LCL [London: William Heinemann/New York: G. P. Putnam's Sons, 1930] 1.41). From this perspective Barrett's assessment of the matter is more exacting: "the paradoxical theme that it is in service that perfect freedom is found is for Paul focused not upon an impersonal and pantheistic *logos*, but upon the personal and historical Redeemer, Jesus Christ" (*Commentary on the First Epistle*, 173). Even here, however, we should note that Paul can speak of Christians as slaves "to righteousness" (Rom. 6.18; cf. 6.17, 20, "slaves of sin").

[233] Or *by which* he was called (ῇ); see the next note.

[234] In this case the relative pronoun ῇ is seen as the equivalent of ἐν ῇ, which, given the syntax of the sentence, poses no particular problem. See Walter Bauer, *A Greek-English Lexicon of the New Testament and Other Early Christian Literature*, 2nd edn., rev. F. Wilbur Gingrich and Frederick W. Danker (Chicago: University of Chicago Press, 1979) 584 (s.v. "ὅς, ῇ, ὅ, 6").

[235] See, e.g., Karl Ludwig Schmidt, "καλέω," *TDNT* 3 (1965) 491–2 n. 1; Neuhäusler, "Ruf Gottes," 43–4; and Bauer, *Greek-English Lexicon*, 436 (s.v. "κλῆσις, 2").

[236] Weiß, *Korintherbrief*, 187.

situations;[237] and in the second passage Epictetus addresses the philosopher as one "who has trusted in him (πεποιθότως) who called you to these things," referring to the various trials that a philosopher must face, such as being enchained, tortured, exiled, or put to death. From these two passages Weiß concluded that Epictetus understood God's call in the sense of a philosopher receiving a "mission" (*vocatio*, die Mission) from God, and therefore it approximated the philosopher's "occupation" or "profession" (Beruf).[238] Proposing, further, that the relative pronoun in 7.20 should be translated in a "modal" sense,[239] Weiß maintained that Stoic influence on this verse could justify understanding it as an admonition to Christians to remain in the "form of the call" in which they were called.

In the end, Weiß's proposal clarifies nothing, however, for even the meaning "occupation" and a modal interpretation of ᾗ will not allow us to translate κλῆσις as "form of call."[240] Beyond this, Epictetus' understanding of the words καλέω and κλῆσις is considerably more distant from Paul's than Weiß assumed. For Epictetus, the philosopher is called by God *as a philosopher* to meet a particularly challenging or trying "situation" (περίστασις).[241] With Paul, by contrast, God's call *initiates* a person's conversion to Christianity; it is not an occasional commission that comes to one who is already a Christian.[242]

Having said this, it is nonetheless still possible that Stoic usage lies behind the apparent difficulty in 7.20. A third passage from Epictetus, not considered by Weiß, points in this direction. This is *Enchiridion* 7, where Epictetus introduces the metaphor of a sea voyage. When a ship puts in, he explains, the passengers are allowed

---

[237] ὡς μάρτυς ὑπὸ θεοῦ κεκλημένος, Epict. *Diss.* 1.29.46. At 1.29.49 Epictetus speaks of the philosopher's "call which God has called," τὴν κλῆσιν ἣν κέκληκεν – cf. 1 Cor. 7.20.

[238] Weiß, *Korintherbrief,* 187.

[239] Ibid., on the basis of 7.17, "each *as* (ὡς) God has called"; but this modal reading of the pronoun is not supported by 7.24, where we find, "each *in which* (ἐν ᾧ) he was called."

[240] Weiß's further suggestion (*Korintherbrief,* 187) that poverty, lack of education, and low social status are themselves the κλῆσις referred to in 1 Cor. 1.26, speaks for itself. (Here Paul's statement, "consider your call," is shorthand for "consider how the event of your call took place." This shorthand does not work for 7.20, however.)

[241] The word Epictetus uses at 1.29.33, 34.

[242] See Bonhöffer, *Epiktet und das Neue Testament,* 37–9, 207–8; Juncker, *Ethik,* 2.163–6; and Schmidt, "καλέω," 493. A possible exception may be Paul's own call to be an apostle, but this also seems to have coincided with his "conversion" (Gal. 1.15), and it has nothing to do with the sense of "call" in 1 Cor. 7.15c, 17–24.

a brief shore leave. They may wander in search of fresh water or shellfish, but they must always be mindful of their ship. Turning about frequently, "for fear lest the captain should call (καλέω)," they must be prepared at any moment to drop what they are doing and heed his summons. Applying this metaphor to the philosophical life, Epictetus continues: "So it is also in life: If there be given you, instead of a little bulb and a small shell-fish, a little wife and child, there will be no objection to that; only, if the Captain [i.e., God] calls (καλέω), give up all these things and run to the ship, without even turning around to look back."[243]

Here we see that the philosopher's call sometimes requires him to abandon his, presumably non-philosophical, wife and children. This raises the possibility that it is the Corinthians, rather than Paul, who had understood the notion of "call" in a Stoic sense, and that, having felt themselves thus called to respond to some unusual and trying situation, they proceeded to use a Stoic tradition like the one in *Enchiridion* 7 to justify abandoning their non-Christian spouses. Although Paul does not mention any urgent situation here, a few verses later (7.26–31) we learn that the Corinthians stood face to face with a "present necessity" that promised "hardship in the flesh" to all those who were married. Given that we have already identified apocalyptic concerns behind the celibacy in 7.5, this may have been the crisis that touched off, or at least fueled, the Corinthians' desire to be done with their non-Christian spouses.[244]

A principal advantage of this hypothesis is that it makes good sense of Paul's admonition in 7.20, that a Christian must "remain in the call in which he was called." What Paul is saying here, according to this interpretation, is that those Corinthians who are married to unbelievers must stay in their original Christian call.[245] They are not to follow an "additional" call or commission,[246] occasioned by a crisis, which, after the manner of the Stoics, would require them to leave their unbelieving spouses. This understanding of 7.20 also explains why Paul affords so much space (verses 15c, 17–24) to the notion of God's call in discussing the meaning of God's grace for mixed marriages. In Galatians, by contrast, he uses the concept of

---

[243] Trans. Oldfather, *Epictetus*, 2.489, 491.

[244] Cf. Luke 18.29, which speaks of Jesus' disciples leaving their wives for the sake of the kingdom of God (cf. Luke 14.26).

[245] This also clarifies the otherwise unexpected admonition to "remain beside God" (μενέτω παρὰ θεῷ) in 7.24, which some mss. simply omit, and which Weiß, *Korintherbrief*, 191 labeled as "hardly to be interpreted with certainty."

[246] Cf. the idea of "another gospel" in Gal. 1.6–9.

"faith" to clarify the doctrine of grace. Here, however, he employs the terms καλέω and κλῆσις ten times in these few verses, as compared to twice in the rest of 1 Corinthians,[247] and sixteen more times in all his other letters.[248]

A last instance of Stoic influence on 7.17–24 is perhaps to be found in verse 19, where Paul states: "Circumcision is nothing and 'uncircumcision' is nothing – rather, keeping the commandments of God" (τήρησις ἐντολῶν θεοῦ). Like 7.20, the final clause in this verse appears to diverge from the overall theme of 7.17–24. Instead of encouraging Christians to remain in the condition in which they were called, it exhorts them to keep God's commandments. Consequently, just what Paul means by these "commandments" has become a matter of scholarly debate. Several scholars have seen them as the equivalent of "faith working through love," or "a new creation," on the basis of Galatians 5.6 and 6.15, where the paradigm circumcised–uncircumcised also occurs.[249] The problem with this suggestion is that it clearly derives from the context of Galatians and the issues under discussion in the Galatian churches. In 1

---

[247] Namely, 1 Cor. 1.9 and 1.26. This does not count 10.27 (καλέω in the sense of being invited to dinner) or 15.9 (in the sense of being called by a title). He also uses the cognate adj. "called" (κλητός) at 1.1, 2, 24. Regarding the misunderstanding of "call" among the Corinthians, it is noteworthy that only in 1 Cor. 1.26 and 7.20 does Paul use the term κλῆσις to speak of an individual's call (as opposed to God's calling of the individual), and only here does he speak of it with reference to the outward circumstances of the individual's life. (κλῆσις also occurs at Rom. 11.29 and Phil. 3.14; and 2 Thess. 1.11.)

Noteworthy, too, is the number of times that words of the καλ- and κλη- group occur in 1 Cor. 1.1–9 in combination with notions that play an important part in 7.12–15a: the church at Corinth is comprised of those who are "made holy" (ἁγιάζω) and "called holy" (κλητοὶ ἅγιοι); and God is "faithful" (πιστός), through whom the Corinthians were "called" (καλέω) into partnership (κοινωνία) with Christ – all of which is in addition to Paul's use of κλητός, ἐπικαλέω, and ἐκκλησία elsewhere in these verses. This may indicate that the notion of being called was central to the Corinthian self-identity. Rom. 1.1–7 also has several words from the καλ- and κλη- group, but Romans may be styled after 1 Corinthians here, as are other parts of Romans.

[248] Half of which are in Romans (cf. end of previous note): Rom. 8.30 (twice); 9.11, 24, 25 (twice), 26; 11.29. The others occur in Gal. 1.6, 15; 5.8, 13; Phil. 3.14; 1 Thess. 2.12; 4.7; 5.24 (also 2 Thess. 1.11; 2.14). This does not count Rom. 4.17 (καλέω in the sense of call into being) or 9.7 (in the sense of designate). It does, however, count Rom. 9.25 and 26, where Paul interprets Hosea 2.1, 25 to mean "call," even though the LXX meaning of καλέω is clearly "name." Paul also uses the adj. κλητός at Rom. 1.1, 6, 7; 8.28.

[249] So, e.g., Lietzmann, *An die Korinther*, 32; Wolbert, *Ethische Argumentation*, 118; and Gottlob Schrenk, "ἐντέλλομαι, ἐντολή," *TDNT* 2 (1964) 552, who notes gratuitously that this is "wholly in line with the meaning of the καινὴ ἐντολή [new commandment] according to the Johannine view."

Corinthians 7.17–24, however, we would expect Paul to draw his conclusions about "what is important" from matters at hand in Corinth. As an alternative, Baltensweiler suggests that the "commandments of God" in verse 19b should be understood as "the will of God, which equally encompasses both Jews and pagans," taking this meaning from 1 Corinthians 7.18–19a.[250] But even this interpretation coincides more with Paul's thesis in Galatians (and Romans) than with anything in our passage.

In a very different vein, Sanders has suggested that the "commandments of God" refer to the Torah. Yet, observing further that circumcision is one of the commandments of the Law, and that the first part of verse 19 proclaims "circumcision is nothing," Sanders comes to the awkward conclusion that 7.19 is "one of the most amazing sentences that [Paul] ever wrote."[251] If anything, therefore, Sanders' analysis would seem to rule out the idea that 7.19b is a reference to the Torah – a notion that is equally questionable from the perspective of Paul's theology. Finally, Neuhäusler has proposed that the last clause in 7.19 be understood as the vestige of a pre-Pauline baptismal ceremony in which converts were exhorted to remain in their new calling by "keeping the commandments of God."[252] While this is certainly plausible, given that 7.17–24 is ultimately based on a baptismal liturgy,[253] it cannot be the whole answer, for Paul has reworked the baptismal traditions in these verses to such a degree that we would hardly expect the intrusion of a superfluous vestige into his argument.

To my mind, the most satisfying solution to the problem of 7.19b comes from Stoic materials found in Epictetus. In his entry on ἐντολή in the *Theological Dictionary of the New Testament*, Schrenk explains that the Stoics had an aversion to this word because they associated it with a "primitive form of morality."[254] While this characterization is in the main true, it requires some qualification, for in Epictetus we have five passages in which the term ἐντολαί signifies the very essence of Stoicism. Thus, in book one of his *Discourses*, when an interlocutor asks Epictetus for direction (ἔντει-

[250] Baltensweiler, *Die Ehe*, 151.
[251] E. P. Sanders, *Paul, the Law and the Jewish People* (Philadelphia: Fortress, 1983) 103.
[252] Neuhäusler, "Ruf Gottes," 46 and nn. 11–12.
[253] Cf., e.g., 1 Cor. 12.13 and Gal. 3.27–8; and see also Matt. 28.19–20, where Jesus instructs his disciples to baptize all peoples, teaching them "to keep all that I commanded you" (τηρεῖν πάντα ὅσα ἐνετειλάμην ὑμῖν).
[254] Schrenk, "ἐντέλλομαι," 547.

λαί μοι), he replies, "What directions shall I give you (τί σοι ἐντείλωμαι)? Has not Zeus given you directions (ἐντέταλται)?" And in book three, when Epictetus considers how he will justify his life before Zeus, he envisions himself demanding of the Deity, "Have I in any respect transgressed Thy commands (ἐντολαί)?"[255]

In all these five passages, moreover, Epictetus mentions themes integral to Paul's discussion of the Christian call in 7.17–24, including true freedom, faithfulness, the jurisdiction one has over one's own body, and the concept of power (ἐξουσία). For example, in book four, in a passage that presents a dialogue between the philosopher and a tyrant, the latter threatens, "Am I not master of your body (σῶμα)? ... Am I not master of exile or bonds?" To this Epictetus vaunts back, "... no one has authority (ἐξουσία) over me. I have been set free (ἠλευθέρωμαι) by God, I know His commands (ἐντολαί), no one has power any longer to make a slave of me ... I yield up to you all these things and my whole paltry body (σωμάτιον) itself, whenever you will."[256] Finally, again in book three, Epictetus maintains that God's commandments are all-sufficient, serving as the philosopher's refuge even in the adverse circumstances to which he may, in the Stoic sense, be called. Thus even in the face of poverty, sickness, loss of status, or exile, Epictetus can hold his ground, asking rhetorically, "am I any longer to take thought as to where I am, or with whom, or what men say about me? Am I not wholly intent upon God, and His commands (ἐντολαί) and ordinances?"[257]

Given the similarities in theme and vocabulary between 1 Corinthians 7.17–24 and these passages from Epictetus, and given the dearth of convincing alternative hypotheses, I suggest that when Paul speaks in 7.19b of "keeping the commandments of God," he is

[255] Epict. *Diss.* 1.25.3 and 3.5.8 (trans. Oldfather, *Epictetus*, 1.157 and 2.43). The first quote continues: "– But if you keep (τηρῶν) these, are you in need of some others? – But hasn't he commanded (ἐντέταλαι) these ...?" (1.25.6). The other three passages are: Epict. *Diss.* 3.24.113–14; 4.3.9–10, 12; and 4.7.16–18. Note that at 1.25.4 and 4.3.12 Epictetus refers to Zeus' commandments as "ordinances," διατάγματα (see also *Diss.* 4.4.32). Likewise, in 7.17 Paul uses the related verb διατάσσομαι, "I ordain." Elsewhere in Paul this verb occurs only in 1 Cor. 9.14 (regarding orders for evangelists – cf. Epict. *Diss.* 3.22.2–4), 11.34 and 16.1 (regarding order within the church), and once outside of 1 Cor., in Gal. 3.19 (of God's ordaining the Jewish Law).
[256] Epict. *Diss.* 4.7.16–18, trans. Oldfather, *Epictetus*, 2.367; cited in Conzelmann, *1 Corinthians*, 128 n. 34 (regarding 7.23), and 110 n. 11 (re 6.12). See also Epict. *Diss.* 1.25.2, 4, 5; 3.5.7; 4.3.9, 10.
[257] Epict. *Diss.* 3.24.113–14, trans. Oldfather, *Epictetus*, 2.221. On the resemblance between this passage and 1 Cor. 4.9–13, see Conzelmann, *1 Corinthians*, 88 and n. 36.

using a Judeo–Christian expression that has Stoic implications.[258] Since, for Epictetus, observing what God has commanded is the equivalent of "being a philosopher," Paul would be using the expression in a general sense to mean "being a Christian." Commensurate with our understanding of 7.20, this meaning would forbid Christians from taking on any additional "calls" that might nullify their original call, since, according to Epictetus, one must hold to God's commandments even in adverse circumstances.[259]

Taking this line of interpretation one step further, I suspect that in addition to this general meaning of "keeping the commandments of God," Paul also has a more immediate point of reference in mind. The only commandment he claims to have in 7.1–24, or in the entire chapter for that matter, is Jesus' prohibition of divorce in 7.10–11. As we observed earlier, the whole discussion of mixed marriages in verses 12–24 is occasioned precisely by the recognition that this prohibition does not apply to Christians with non-Christian spouses. It is possible, then, that through his discussion of freedom

[258] Another passage that should be considered is Philo's Stoic sounding *Legum allegoria* 1.93–5 (*SVF* 3.139.35–140.6 [partial]), where he distinguishes between three categories: injunction, prohibition, and "commandment with exhortation" (ἐντολὴ καὶ παραίνεσις). The first, he says, is designed for the person who acts correctly (κατορθόω), the second for the bad man (ὁ φαῦλος), and the third category (he mentions only "exhortation") is "for the neutral man (ὁ μέσος), he who is neither bad nor good (φαῦλος/σπουδαῖος)." This neutral man Philo depicts as an "infant" (νήπιον), saying that he is "just now learning." Elsewhere, in a discussion of philosophical freedom, Philo again employs this image of an infant, saying that the souls of persons unfamiliar with either philosophical freedom or slavery are naked "like those of mere infants" (τῶν ... νηπίων). They must, according to Philo, "be tended and nursed by instilling first, in place of milk (γάλα), the soft food of instruction given in the school subjects, later, the harder, stronger meat, which philosophy produces. Reared by these to manhood and robustness, they will reach the happy consummation which Zeno, or rather an oracle higher than Zeno, bids us seek, a life led agreeably to nature" (*Quod omnis probus* 160, trans. Colson, *Philo*, 9.101). In 1 Cor. 3.1–2 Paul describes the Corinthians with precisely this image: "And I myself, brothers, was not able to speak to you as spiritual persons but as fleshly, as infants (νήπιοι) in Christ. I gave you milk (γάλα) to drink, not solid food, for you were not yet able" (cf. 13.11). For the popularity of this simile among the Stoics, see Johannes Behm, "βρῶμα, βρῶσις," *TDNT* 1 (1964) 643 n. 7.

[259] Cf. Epict. *Diss.* 3.24.98–9, where the philosopher is described as remaining steadfast in his station as householder. Indeed, it is possible that the Corinthians had given an apocalyptic bent not only to the Stoic concept of "call," but also to their concept of "commandment," in which case they may have held that a special interpretation of "the commandments" was necessary in the end times, as in the *Testament of Naphtali*. See above, pp. 123–6, and cf. the notion of an interim law at Qumran – e.g., E. P. Sanders, *Paul and Palestinian Judaism: A Comparison of Patterns of Religion* (Philadelphia: Fortress, 1977) 270–1. On "keeping the commandments" in the context of wisdom and apocalyptic literature, see, e.g., Sirach 1.26 and Rev. 12.17.

and the Christian call, and through his use of the Stoic notion of commandments, Paul is inferring that Jesus' commandment indeed has a counterpart in the more encompassing "commandments" of Christian existence.[260] This, in fact, makes good sense in light of 7.17, where Paul describes how Christians married to non-Christians should live, employing the phrase, "as the Lord apportioned to each one." Since the only action of "apportioning" by Jesus in the chapter is, again, his prohibition of divorce in verses 10–11, it lies close at hand that Paul is suggesting to the Corinthians that the transforming grace of God's call governs mixed marriages in the same way as Jesus' prohibition of divorce governs Christian marriages. If this is true, 7.18–24 would then represent Paul's attempt to show the veracity of this suggestion, forming an appropriate conclusion to his treatment of mixed marriages.

### 4. Paul's argument against marriage by reason of adverse circumstances: 1 Corinthians 7.25–8

With the phrase "Now concerning virgins ..." in 7.25 Paul introduces a new topic into the chapter. Until now he has addressed questions relevant to married people – whether they can separate, whether they can divorce, whether they can remarry; in 7.25ff. he will take up the question of whether virgins should marry.[261] The first four verses of this new section contain several Stoic elements, some of which are already familiar to us from our examination of 7.1–24. In 7.26 Paul speaks of what is "good for a man" (καλὸν ἀνθρώπῳ), an expression he uses in 7.1, and for which we have analogies in Stoic authors. In contrast to 7.1, however, where Paul follows this phrase with a Cynic-like judgement on marriage, here he states explicitly that he is giving his own advice (γνώμη) as one who has been shown mercy by the Lord to be πιστός, or "trustworthy" (verse 25). As we saw from 7.12–15a, this notion of being πιστός was important to the Corinthians and appears to draw

---

[260] Cf. Matt. 5.17–19, 31–2, where Jesus' interdiction of divorce is set in a discussion of "the commandments" (αἱ ἐντολαί); and 1 Cor. 14.37, where Paul speaks of a "commandment of the Lord" (κυρίου ἐντολή).

[261] The introduction of this new topic is signalled by the parallelism between 7.1 and 7.25–6: "Now concerning what you wrote / it is good for a man / but because of ..." vs. "Now concerning virgins / because of / it is good for a man ..." (περὶ δὲ ὧν ἐγράψατε / καλὸν ἀνθρώπῳ / διὰ δέ vs. περὶ δὲ τῶν παρθένων / διά / καλὸν ἀνθρώπῳ). If 7.25ff. was simply a continuation of 7.1–24 we might have expected something like "To the virgins I say ..." (τοῖς δὲ παρθένοις λέγω), after the model of 7.8, 10, 12.

on the Stoic ideal of the trustworthy wise man. Paul will express this same thought in 7.40 in a manner more specifically Christian when he claims support for his advice (γνώμη) from God's Spirit, verse 40 forming a ring-composition, or *inclusio*, with verse 25.

The advice that Paul gives in verses 25–6 is that virgins should remain unmarried in light of the "present necessity." Justification for this position is then offered in verse 27, in diatribe style: "You are bound to a wife? – don't seek release! You are released from a wife? – don't seek a wife!" The syntactical pattern of this verse is the same as that in verses 18 and 21, and in the several examples that we cited from Stoic and Cynic authors. Its subject matter, in turn – the indifference of both marriage and the single life – is especially close to the examples from Posidippus, Metrodorus, and Sirach 7.26 (LXX), giving the impression that Paul is dependent on a tradition here, rather than just a rhetorical style as in verses 18 and 21.[262] This impression is reinforced, moreover, by the realization that Paul is actually interested in only the second half of verse 27, which deals with being single and getting married. The first half deals with being married and "loosing" oneself from the relationship, which was Paul's topic in 7.1–24. To some extent, as well, verse 27a repeats the Lord's command in verses 10–11, whereas Paul has stated in verse 25 that he has no command of the Lord relevant to his present discussion.[263]

A link in verse 27 specifically with the issues of the Stoic–Cynic marriage debate can be seen in Paul's emphasis on the obligations imposed by married life. This comes through in the expressions

---

[262] Oddly, only the text from Posidippus has been cited as a parallel to 7.27, and only by Johannes Leipoldt, *Griechische Philosophie und frühchristliche Askese* (Berlin: Akademie, 1961) 35 n. 1. Still another version of the maxim in 7.27 is found in Clem. Alex. *Strom.* bk. 3, chap. 15.97.4 (2.241.3–4 S.), in the form of a saying of Jesus: "Again the Lord says, 'He who is married should not divorce, and he who is not married should not marry'" (ὁ γήμας μὴ ἐκβαλλέτω καὶ ὁ μὴ γαμήσας μὴ γαμείτω). Alfred Resch, *Agrapha: Aussercanonische Schriftfragmente*, TU, n.s. 15/3–4 (Leipzig: J. C. Hinrichs, 1906) 182–3 (agraphon 145) points to the similarities between this passage and 1 Cor. 7.11 and 7.32–6 (not 7.27 for some reason), and suggests that it comes from the *Gospel of the Egyptians*, an apocryphal work that Clement cites in *Strom.* bk. 3, chap. 15.92–3 (2.238.23–8 S.). Its more immediate context, however, is the Cynic argument against marriage in bk. 3, chap. 15.97.3 (2.240.27–241.2 S., cited above, p. 103 n. 241), and given Clement's inclination to link it with Jesus rather than Paul, it is possible that a version of this maxim may have had an existence in philosophical circles independent of 1 Cor. 7.27.

[263] If this seeming repetition of 7.10–11 were an integral part of his argument in 7.25ff., then Paul would also be risking the implication that Jesus' prohibition of divorce was valid only in light of the "necessity" mentioned in 7.26 (noted by Doughty, "Heiligkeit und Freiheit," 204).

"bound to a wife," "seek release," and "released from a wife." While being "bound" (δέομαι) to a husband, as we have seen from 7.39 and Romans 7.2, is a common manner of expressing a woman's relation to her husband, it is not the usual expression for describing a man's relation to his wife. The terms "release" (λύσις) and "released" (λύομαι), on the other hand, are rarely, if ever, used to describe divorce.[264] All three of these terms, however, function well in describing obligations between individuals as being either in force or terminated.[265] Thus here, as in 1 Corinthians 7.3–5, Paul appears to have adopted the Stoic–Cynic perspective of seeing marital obligations as the primary issue in considering questions of marriage.[266]

With verse 28a Paul completes the diatribe form begun in verse 27 in an unusual manner. As we know from our investigation of 7.18–19, 21–2, this diatribe pattern is composed of a statement and an exhortation, sometimes followed by an explanation as to why the statement is a matter of indifference, as the exhortation indeed claims it is. In verse 28a, however, Paul claims that the second exhortation, "don't seek a wife!," is *itself* a matter of some indifference, for if a single person marries, he or she nonetheless does not sin. Paul then finishes out the verse by explaining to the Corinthians that those who marry will have "tribulation in the flesh," and he would spare them this by encouraging them not to marry.

Taken as a whole, what Paul has written in 7.25–8 is the Stoic argument against marriage, with an important modification. As we saw in chapter two, Stoics who objected to marriage maintained that "circumstance" (περίστασις) often prevented one from

---

[264] Hilgenfeld, *Die Glossolalie*, 135 notes that Euseb. *C.H.* 5.18.2 blames the Montanists for "dissolutions of marriages" (λύσεις γάμων). Otherwise, only the related verb ἀπολύω can mean "to divorce."

[265] On λύσις and λύω see Moulton and Milligan, *Vocabulary of the Greek Testament*, 382, 384.

[266] 1 Cor. 7.29, 32–5, like 7.3–5, also speak of marital obligations. As an alternative to this interpretation, several scholars have suggested that Paul is speaking of engagements and breaking engagements in verse 27: Johann Christian Konrad von Hofmann, *Die heilige Schrift neuen Testaments: Zusammenhängend untersucht* (Nördlingen: C. H. Beck, 1864) 2.2.164; Weiß, *Korintherbrief*, 194–5 (who suggests "spiritual engagement"); J. K. Elliott, "Paul's Teaching on Marriage in I Corinthians: Some Problems Considered," *NTS* 19 (1972/73) 220–3; and Baumert, *Ehelosigkeit und Ehe*, 420–5. But there is no evidence that the vocabulary in 7.27 refers to engagement, about which little is known for this period in Greece anyway; see Fee, *The First Epistle*, 331–2. Elliott, who carries this suggestion over into 7.29, mistakenly claims that "if [Paul] were thinking of those already married, ἔχοντες γυναῖκας ["those having wives"] would be a strange way of referring to husbands" ("Paul's Teaching on Marriage," 222). But "having a wife" is normal Greek usage for "being married" – see, e.g., 7.12–13.

embracing the responsibilities of married life. Cicero was familiar with this Stoic adaptation of the "Cynic" position against marriage, and we find it in Hierocles and Epictetus as well. This is also what we find here in Paul. The adverse circumstances at issue in Corinth are designated in verse 26 as "the present necessity," and Paul makes it very clear that this is the basis on which he is advising these virgins not to become "bound" by the obligations of marriage: "I think, therefore, that this is good *because of the present necessity* (διὰ τὴν ἐνεστῶσαν ἀνάγκην): 'it is good for a man' to be thus."

The most illuminating cipher for 7.25–8 is not Cicero, Hierocles, or Epictetus, however, but the writings of Cicero's contemporary, Arius Didymus. In his treatment of Stoic ethical theory, Arius explains that the Stoics classified marriage as an "indifferent matter." This meant that although marriage was morally neutral, it was sometimes an advantage for the individual to marry, and sometimes a disadvantage, depending on the prevailing circumstances of the individual's life. For one to marry under normal circumstances was, therefore, "fitting," but marriage under adverse circumstances was an error or "sin," ἁμάρτημα.[267] In 7.25–8 Paul's words reveal a knowledge of this Stoic line of reasoning point for point. His use of the diatribe pattern in verse 27 serves to define both marriage and the single life as matters of indifference; in verse 28b he points out that marriage in the present situation is disadvantageous for the Christian, bringing "tribulation in the flesh" to those who marry; while in verse 28a he consciously departs from Stoic opinion, maintaining that even under these circumstances the person who marries "did not sin" (οὐχ ἥμαρτες/ἥμαρτεν).[268] This last move would seem to be clear evidence that Paul's Corinthian audience included some who had so thoroughly combined their Christian faith with Stoic doctrine that Paul was obliged to distinguish between Christian and Stoic terminology regarding such basic ideas as sin.

Paul's reason for contradicting the Stoic view of sin in verse 28a is obvious. For the Stoics, the concept of sin encompassed improper or "unfitting" conduct in both the moral and the practical spheres

---

[267] Arius in Stob. 2.86.1–16 W.-H., see above, pp. 73–4. See also [Ocellus] *De univ. nat.* 48, who says that people who marry for the wrong reasons, such as wealth and social standing, "err" (ἁμαρτάνω). Cf. *Test. Naph.* 8.7–10 (cited above, p. 124), who maintains that things done out of their proper time (including conjugal relations) constitute sin.

[268] Gnomic aorist, probably in sympathy with the gnomic character of verse 27. Note the second person sing. of the diatribe.

of life (although Stoics themselves would not have made such a distinction). Even actions in matters they considered morally neutral could be "sinful" if they were not done in accord with rational thinking and utilitarian motives. For Paul, however, "sin" has reference only to moral conduct. Something like marriage, therefore, which both he and the Stoics considered morally neutral, cannot in and of itself be sinful for Paul, even if it produces hardships. Interestingly enough, almost a century and a half after Paul writes, we again find evidence that the Stoic notion of sin has influenced Christian thinking on marriage. As part of his interpretation of the apocryphal saying of Jesus, "Eat every plant, but do not eat the plant that has the bitterness," Clement of Alexandria writes:

> Therefore, a man ought not to think that marriage on rational principles (κατὰ λόγον) is a sin (ἁμάρτημα), supposing that he does not look on the bringing up of children as being bitter...; but if a man regards the rearing of children as bitter because it distracts him (μεταπερισπῶσα) from the things of God on account of the time it takes up (διὰ τὰς χρειώδεις ἀσχολίας), he may yet desire to marry because he does not take easily to a bachelor's life.[269]

### 5. Apocalyptic "circumstances": 1 Corinthians 7.29–31

As we just saw, the argument that Paul uses in 7.25–8 insists that "circumstances" of life can prevent one from marrying. For Stoics these circumstances could include such things as a person's financial misfortune, the acceptance of an important military assignment, the advancement of scholarship, or the general chaotic state of society. For Paul they are supplied by the apocalyptic situation in which he envisioned his church in Corinth. As a consequence, intertwined with and immediately following his Stoic-like argument in verses 25–8, Paul employs an appreciable amount of apocalyptic material – that is, language and themes which early Jews and Christians associated with the end of the world. In verse 26 Paul says that his advice is based on the present "necessity" (ἀνάγκη), and in verse 28 he tells those who plan to marry that they will have "tribulation" (θλῖψις).

---

[269] Clem. Alex. *Strom.* bk. 3, chap. 9.67.1 (2.226.19–24 S.), trans. Chadwick in Oulton and Chadwick, *Alexandrian Christianity*, 71. Cf. Col 3.19. Ironically, Meyer, *Critical and Exegetical Handbook*, 191 excluded a Stoic interpretation for 1 Cor. 7 on the basis of Paul's use of "sin" here and in verse 36 (on which, see below).

Both these terms occur with some frequency in apocalyptic literature as part of a specialized vocabulary describing the distress of the
last days.[270] In verse 29a Paul then elaborates ("I say this,
brothers") with the apocalyptic theme that the "time" has been
"drawn together" (καιρός/συστέλλομαι), and he concludes this
section in verse 31b by using the apocalyptic rationale, "for the form
of this world is passing away."

Between verses 29a and 31b, moreover, as part of his elaboration
of the "tribulation" in verse 28, Paul introduces several lines of
apocalyptic material describing how one must conduct oneself in the
last days: "Henceforth, such that[271] even those having wives should
be as not (ὡς μή) having, and those weeping as not weeping, and
those rejoicing as not rejoicing, and those buying as not taking
possession, and those using the world as not using it fully." Parallels
to these verses may be found in both Jewish and Christian apocalyptic literature, and it is even possible that Paul is citing from an
apocalyptic source here. The themes of buying, rejoicing, and mour-

---

[270] E.g., Zeph. 1.15; Luke 21.23. See Schrage, "Die Stellung zur Welt," 131 n. 12;
Heinrich Schlier, "θλίβω, θλῖψις," *TDNT* 3 (1965) 144–6; and L. Legrand, "Saint
Paul et célibat," *Sacerdoce et Célibat: Études historiques et théologiques*, ed. Joseph
Coppens, Bibliotheca Ephemeridum Theologicarum Lovaniensium 28 (Gembloux:
Duculot/Louvain: Peeters, 1971) 320–1.

John G. Gager, Jr., "Functional Diversity in Paul's Use of End-Time Language,"
*JBL* 89 (1970) 330–3 has argued against an apocalyptic meaning for the terms ἀνάγκη
and θλῖψις in 7.26–8, noting that Paul never uses ἀνάγκη in connection with the End
elsewhere, including 2 Cor. 6.4 and 1 Thess. 3.7, where it occurs together with θλῖψις
(on this, see also Malherbe, *Paul and the Thessalonians*, 46–8). Yet with 1 Cor. 7.26–8,
not only are the following verses 29–31 apocalyptic (see below), as Gager himself
recognizes ("Functional Diversity," 332), but Gager also overlooks the possibility
that 7.26 is *present* apocalyptic language, for he assumes that his translation of
ἐνεστῶσα ἀνάγκη as "present difficulty" (as opposed to "impending disaster," RSV),
rules out an apocalyptic interpretation (on this, see below). Beyond this, Gager never
provides a cogent non-apocalyptic alternative for these terms. On the one hand, he
states that "Paul clearly presents [marriage] as a kind of θλῖψις" (ibid., 331), which is
not supported by the text. And on the other hand, he says that Paul uses ἀνάγκη in an
"ambiguous manner" (meaning that it is *nonetheless* apocalyptic?), and compares
Paul's usage to *Hypoth.* 11.17, where Philo gives the Essene position that a husband is
either bound by the love charms of his wife or cares for his children out of the
"necessity of nature" (ἀνάγκη φύσεως). From this he concludes, quite erroneously,
"As in Paul, the married man or woman is lured away from his primary (religious)
concern by the seductive ploys of the mate. Both Philo and Paul use the term ἀνάγκη
to describe the marital situation . . ." (ibid., 331). But neither does Philo speak of both
"the married man or woman," nor does Paul speak of "seductive ploys of the mate,"
nor can Gager show from Philo's use of ἀνάγκη how Paul uses the term to describe
the marital situation, since 1 Cor. 7.26 speaks of ἀνάγκη as a reality for both the
married and the unmarried alike.

[271] Translating τὸ λοιπὸν ἵνα, see below.

ning, for example, occur in Ezekiel's vision of the end time: "The time has come! Behold the day! The one buying should not rejoice; the one selling should not mourn ..."[272] Two passages from the Gospel of Luke, in turn, picture the eschaton as taking by surprise those who have become entrenched in the activities of buying, selling, and marrying. In Luke 14.15–24 the invited guests are shut out from the eschatological banquet because they insist on attending to their recent purchases of a field or oxen, or looking after a recently acquired wife; and in Luke 17.26–37 Jesus tells his disciples that the Son of Man will come suddenly upon the world, destroying those who are distracted with marriages, buying, selling, eating, drinking, planting, and building. In a similar fashion, passages from the *Apocalypse of Elijah* and *Sibylline Oracles* 2 maintain that the eschaton will bring an end to buying, selling, and marrying.[273]

Along with these particular motifs, the distinctive "as not" (ὡς μή) phrases of 7.29b–31a find an analogy in two further apocalyptic texts. The first is Isaiah 24.2 (LXX), which depicts, through a series of ὡς-phrases, the radical social and economic disorientation brought on by the coming of the Lord: "And the people will be as (ὡς) the priest, and the slave as the lord, and the maid servant as the mistress. He who sells will be as he who buys, and he who lends as he who borrows, and he who owes as the one to whom he owes."[274] The second text comes from 4 Ezra 15–16, a third-century Christian addition to 4 Ezra 1–14. Originally in Greek, but now preserved only in Latin, this text represents by far our closest parallel to 1 Corinthians 7.29b–31a:

> Hear my words, O my people; prepare for battle, and in the midst of the calamities be like strangers on the earth. Let him that sells be like (*quasi*) one who will flee; let him that buys be like one who will lose; let him that does business be like one who will not make a profit; and let him that builds a house be like one who will not live in it; let him that sows be like one who will not reap; so also him that prunes the vines, like one who will not gather the grapes; them that marry, like those who will have no chil-

272 Ezek. 7.12 LXX: ἥκει ὁ καιρός, ἰδοὺ ἡ ἡμέρα· ὁ κτώμενος μὴ χαιρέτω, καὶ ὁ πωλῶν μὴ θρηνείτω.
273 *Apoc. Elijah* 2.31; *Sib. Or.* 2.327–9.
274 Cited as a parallel by Heinrici, *Das erste Sendschreiben*, 207 n. 1.

dren; and them that do not marry, like those who are widowed.[275]

Because of the striking similarities between these verses from 4 Ezra 15–16 and 1 Corinthians 7.29b–31a, some scholars have questioned whether this late Christian text is not, in fact, dependent on the latter.[276] While this possibility must remain open, it should be noted that Schrage, who was the first to subject these texts to a detailed comparison, has offered several good reasons for assuming that both of them draw independently on a common source.[277]

Quite apart from 4 Ezra 16.40–4 and Schrage's considerations, however, other aspects of 1 Corinthians 7.29b–31a seem to indicate that Paul is not simply enlisting various apocalyptic motifs in support of his argument here, but is citing from a specific apocalyptic tradition or source. First, there is the syntax that begins verse 29b. The Greek reads τὸ λοιπὸν ἵνα, which is unusual because the conjunction ἵνα normally takes first position in its clause. While there are other instances in Paul of ἵνα standing in other than first position, none are nearly as harsh as this one. Bauer, consequently, included 7.29b in his discussion of this syntactical formation only with reservation,[278] and Lietzmann declared that the preceding τὸ λοιπόν "stands lost between two sentences."[279] This difficult syntax is clarified, however, if we assume that ἵνα is the beginning of a quotation. In this case it would stand first in its clause, and the words τὸ λοιπόν, "henceforth," could be understood as a transitional phrase provided by Paul to introduce this quotation.[280]

A second reason for taking these verses as a quotation is that they contain several things which scholars consider untypical of Paul,

---

[275] 4 Ezra (2 Esdras) 16.40–4 RSV (Vulgate, 16.40–5).

[276] For an analysis of the formal similarities between the two texts see Schrage, "Die Stellung zur Welt," 147–9.

[277] Ibid., 139–49.

[278] Bauer, *Greek-English Lexicon*, 378 (s.v. "ἵνα IV").

[279] Lietzmann, *An die Korinther*, 34.

[280] Another possibility, less likely in my mind, is to take the entire group τὸ λοιπὸν ἵνα as the beginning of a quotation and assume that this odd syntax made better sense in the context from which Paul is citing. Scholars have also pointed out that the words in verse 29a, "I say this, brothers" (τοῦτο δέ φημι, ἀδελφοί), reappear in 15.50, where Paul may again be quoting an apocalyptic tradition. See Weiß, *Korintherbrief*, 197; Schrage, "Die Stellung zur Welt," 138–9; Siegfried Schulz, "Evangelium und Welt," *Neues Testament und christliche Existenz: Festschrift für Herbert Braun zum 70. Geburtstag am 4. Mai 1973*, ed. Hans Dieter Betz and Luise Schottroff (Tübingen: J. C. B. Mohr, 1973) 486–7; and Ulrich B. Müller, *Prophetie und Predigt im Neuen Testament: Formgeschichtliche Untersuchungen zur urchristlichen Prophetie*, SNT 10 (Gütersloh: Gerd Mohn, 1975) 132–6, 158–9.

and therefore not his creation. Braun, for instance, has observed that the "Stoic-like" indifference toward weeping and rejoicing expressed in 7.30 is difficult to reconcile with such passages as 1 Corinthians 16.17, Romans 12.15, or Philippians 3.18, where Paul speaks highly of and encourages such emotions.[281] Schrage has noted that in 7.29b–30a Paul writes atypically of the painful end of the old age with no mention of the glory and salvation of the new.[282] Finally, in terms of word usage, the coupling in 7.31a of the verb χράομαι ("to use") with an accusative object (τὸν κόσμον, "the world") is not only singular for Paul, but very rare elsewhere in Greek literature.[283]

Having now documented Paul's use of apocalyptic materials in verses 25–31, and possibly even an apocalyptic source in verses 29b–31a, let us consider the function of these materials in his larger discussion. In what way, in other words, do they supply the "circumstances" of the Stoic argument against marriage? Some scholars believe that Paul's emphasis in these verses is on the brevity of time before Christ's imminent return. His argument in that case would be that "time is running out" for such ongoing human activities as marriage: if the world will soon end, what is the purpose of procreation?, or, as one study put it, "why undertake the responsibilities and involvements of family life if the transformation of all things is at hand?"[284] Another possibility is that Paul is discouraging marri-

[281] Herbert Braun, "Die Indifferenz gegenüber der Welt bei Paulus und bei Epiktet," *Gesammelte Studien zum Neuen Testament und seiner Umwelt*, 2nd edn. (Tübingen: J. C. B. Mohr, 1967) 166–7. Rom. 12.15, e.g., admonishes, "Rejoice with those rejoicing; weep with those weeping" (χαίρειν μετὰ χαιρόντων, κλαίειν μετὰ κλαιόντων). To the three passages cited by Braun we may add Rom. 9.1–2; 1 Cor. 13.6; 2 Cor. 2.4, 6–7; 7.7–10; and Phil. 1.18, 19; 4.4, 10.

[282] Schrage, "Die Stellung zur Welt," 138–9, cf. 126–30; and Braun, "Die Indifferenz gegenüber der Welt," 162, 165. In 7.29b we also miss the man–woman/husband–wife parallelism that Paul carefully maintains in the earlier part of the chapter and continues in 7.32–4. This is true as well for 7.27, which I have also suggested is a citation, although Paul's addition of 7.28 makes this less obvious. That Paul speaks only of men in 7.29b is especially noticeable since his topic, ultimately, is virgins (7.25).

Some scholars have also maintained that the admonitions in 7.30–31a (concerning weeping, rejoicing, buying, and using) are not particularly relevant to Paul's discussion of the marriage of virgins. I will argue below, however, that they are. See Rex, "Das ethische Problem," 89; Schrage, "Die Stellung zur Welt," 138; Schulz, "Evangelium und Welt," 486–7; and Wimbush, *Worldly Ascetic*, 28.

[283] See Schulz, "Evangelium und Welt," 486–7; Wimbush, *Worldly Ascetic*, 28 n. 22; and Blass and Debrunner, *Greek Grammar*, 84 (§152.4). Elsewhere Paul uses χράομαι (properly) with the dative: 1 Cor. 9.12, 15; 2 Cor. 1.17; 3.12.

[284] Leander E. Keck and Victor Paul Furnish, *The Letters of Paul*, Interpreting Biblical Texts (Nashville: Abingdon, 1984) 85. See also Gager, "Functional Diver-

age in anticipation of the new, heavenly existence that awaits God's chosen after the End, an existence in which they would be "as angels," no longer marrying.[285]

Yet given that 7.25–31 speaks only of the decline of the old age and not the in-breaking of the new, and points to the "necessity" and "tribulation" of that time, it does not appear that Paul's objective is to emphasize either the imminence of the End or any heavenly existence that might follow it. Rather, his focus here is on the hardships that were expected to beset the world in the period *before* the End.[286] It is these hardships, according to Paul, not the anticipation of a future millennium,[287] that require consideration as "special circumstances," since they make married life difficult by undermining the social and economic context within which marriages take place and thrive. According to his elaboration of the expression "tribulation in the flesh," under these conditions human emotion is stifled (verse 30a), activities essential to establishing a household and providing for a family can be performed only with reservation (verses 30b–31a), and a man must "have" his wife "as if not having" (verse 29b). This last claim is especially revealing, moreover, because it reflects the situation presupposed in 7.2–5. There, husbands and wives are instructed to "have" each other (verse 2), which for Paul includes conjugal rights (verses 3–4); but due to apocalyptic expectations, couples are nonetheless allowed to break off sexual relations to engage in prayer (verse 5). This compromise, as we have called it, between the "Cynic" position of verse 1b and the Stoic understanding of marriage in verses 3–4, is there-

sity," 332; Wimbush, *Worldly Ascetic*, 32, 50, 84; and Franz Laub, *Eschatologische Verkündigung und Lebensgestaltung nach Paulus: Eine Untersuchung zum Wirken des Apostels beim Aufbau der Gemeinde in Thessalonike*, BU 10 (Regensburg: Friedrich Pustet, 1973) 174–8.

[285] See L. Legrand, "The Prophetical Meaning of Celibacy – I," *Scripture* 12 (1960) 97–105, esp. 104–5, who combines these two views; and Nagel, *Motivierung der Askese*, 20–34, who draws a parallel between Paul and the Montanists, among others. On the tenuous nature of such parallels see Frederick Charles Klawiter, "The New Prophecy in Early Christianity: The Origin, Nature, and Development of Montanism, AD 165–220" (Ph.D. diss., University of Chicago, 1975) 14–15, 17, 31–3, 96–9, 130–193; and Christine Trevett, "Apocalypse, Ignatius, Montanism: Seeking the Seeds," *VC* 43 (1989) 321–2. See also our discussion of "realized eschatology" in chapter 1.

[286] Seen by several scholars: Doughty, "Heiligkeit und Freiheit," 204; Schmithals, *Gnosticism in Corinth*, 235 nn. 158–9; Merklein, "'Es ist gut für den Menschen'," 248–51; Hierzenberger, *Weltbewertung bei Paulus*, 32 n. 1 (somewhat reluctantly); and Baumert, *Ehelosigkeit und Ehe*, 17, 209; cf. Yarbrough, *Not Like the Gentiles*, 104.

[287] Nor, we might add, an eschatological reward for a life of sexual abstinence.

fore also a matter of "having" a spouse "as if not having," by reason of apocalyptic circumstances.[288] In the context of Paul's attempt in 7.25ff. to dissuade virgins from marriage, this underscoring of the implications of the end time for the sexual side of marriage serves to counter the (possibly Stoic) argument in 7.9, that one should marry for the purpose of securing licit sexual gratification.

Paul's emphasis on the exigencies of the last days to the exclusion of other apocalyptic themes is also evident in the two statements that bracket the apocalyptic material in 7.29b–31a, namely, ὁ καιρὸς συνεσταλμέμος ἐστίν in verse 29a, and παράγει γὰρ τὸ σχῆμα τοῦ κόσμου τούτου in verse 31b. The first is usually translated "the time is short" or "shortened,"[289] and is seen as expressing Paul's conviction that Christ's coming was imminent. This translation does not do justice to the meaning of the verb συστέλλω, however, which carries the sense of "drawing together," "gathering in," "compressing," or "contracting."[290] From these definitions it is clear that συστέλλω can describe something as "short" or "shortened" only in the sense that it is made more compact, not in the sense that it is "*cut* short" or made smaller by subtraction.[291] Outside of 1 Corinthians 7.29a, moreover, it is never used with reference to time,[292] and thus it seems unlikely that Paul would resort to this particular verb if his meaning were simply that time were "short," a notion he could have expressed in several other, more common ways.

A more appropriate translation of ὁ καιρὸς συνεσταλμένος ἐστίν, therefore, is "the time is compressed," or "the time is con-

---

[288] There is thus no reason to hold that 7.29b contradicts or stands in tension with 7.2–5, as several scholars have suggested: Fee, *The First Epistle*, 340; Elliott, "Paul's Teaching on Marriage," 222; cf. Schrage, "Die Stellung zur Welt," 151; and Niederwimmer, *Askese und Mysterium*, 110–11.

[289] By analogy with such passages as Mark 13.20: "And if the Lord did not shorten the days (ἐκολόβωσεν κύριος τὰς ἡμέρας), no flesh would be saved." On this theme in apocalyptic literature see Baumgarten, *Paulus und die Apokalyptik*, 222 nn. 139–40.

[290] On the meaning of this word and its translation here see Karl Heinrich Rengstorf, "στέλλω," *TDNT* 7 (1971) 596–7; and Bauer, *Greek-English Lexicon*, 795 (s.v. "συστέλλω").

[291] Beyond this, the notion that the time has been shortened, which would have been very important information for a religious group expecting the eschaton (1 Cor. 1.7–8; 15.23–8, 51–8), plays no part elsewhere in 1 Corinthians.

[292] Noted by Baumgarten, *Paulus und die Apokalyptik*, 222 n. 133; and Günter Klein, "Apokalyptische Naherwartung bei Paulus," *Neues Testament und christliche Existenz: Festschrift für Herbert Braun zum 70. Geburtstag am 4. Mai 1973*, ed. Hans Dieter Betz and Luise Schottroff (Tübingen: J. C. B. Mohr, 1973) 259.

tracted." Further, since the word καιρός does not denote just a period of time, but a "proper" or "correct" time for something,[293] I would argue that verse 29a is best understood as "time is at a premium," or "opportunity is tight."[294] This interpretation coincides well with what follows in verses 29b–31a, where those who are married, weeping, rejoicing, or acquiring goods are told that they must live "as if not" being or doing these things. It also crosses paths, once more, with our understanding of 7.5. As our examination of this verse indicated, the language of Paul's ruling that spouses must allow for periods of sexual activity as well as prayer reflects the Corinthians' familiarity with (and deference to) an apocalyptic tradition which insisted that God had specified "proper times" (καιροί) for various activities. The idea was that the normal routine of one's life had to be changed in the last days. Since there was no longer sufficient opportunity for everything, one needed to live according to a special routine or "order" whereby certain activities alternated with one another. Thus, there was a "time" for sexual intercourse and a corresponding "time" for prayer. If my understanding of συστέλλω and καιρός in verse 29 is accurate, then Paul is making reference to this apocalyptic tradition of "proper times" again here. In the words of this verse: "let those having wives be as not having them," since opportunity for such things "has been compressed."

The second statement that underscores Paul's narrow focus on the hardships of the end time is verse 31b, "for the form of this world is passing away." This apocalyptic announcement has several parallels in early Christian literature. In the synoptic gospels, Mark 13.31 par. proclaims that "heaven and earth will pass away" (ὁ οὐρανὸς καὶ ἡ γῆ παρελεύσονται); and a tradition from "Q" (Matthew 5.18 and Luke 16.17) compares the passing away (παρέρχομαι) of heaven and earth to the passing away of the Law. The eucharistic blessing in *Didache* 10.6 includes the request, "let this world pass away" (παρελθέτω ὁ κόσμος οὗτος); while 1 John 2.17 declares that "the world is passing away (ὁ κόσμος παράγεται), along with its allurement," and 2 Peter 3.10 describes the coming of the Lord as a day "in which the heavens will pass away (παρελεύ-

---

[293] See, e.g., Gerhard Delling, "καιρός," *TDNT* 3 (1965) 458–62.
[294] Cf. Gal. 6.10; Heb. 11.15; and Baumert, *Ehelosigkeit und Ehe*, 208–11, 432–9. See also the sentiment in *Cynic Ep. of Diogenes* 44: "For there is no spare time (σχολή) – not only for the poor man to beg, according to Plato, but for the one hastening on the shortcut to well-being" (174.9–10 M.).

σονται) ... the elements will burn and dissolve, and the earth and the works in it will be exposed." In contrast to all of these parallels, however, Paul speaks in 1 Corinthians 7.31b not of this world as passing away, but "the *form* of this world." To some extent, this notion may also be present in 2 Peter, since it speaks of "the earth *and the works in it*" (καὶ τά ἐν αὐτῇ ἔργα).[295] Yet the thing that sets Paul apart even from this passage is that he speaks *only* of the "form," or σχῆμα, of this world as passing away.

While scholars have proposed a wide range of definitions for the word σχῆμα,[296] it seems best to take its meaning from the admonitions in the preceding verses, since 7.31b both provides the rationale for 7.29b–31a,[297] and appears to summarize and conclude this section of Paul's argument.[298] These admonitions, as we have seen, demand a remoteness from marriage, from emotional involvement, and from the acquisition of goods and "use" of the world. From this vantage point the expression "form of this world" would describe the world's social and economic "infrastructure" – that is, the social and economic context that makes these activities possible. Because the upheavals of the last days disrupt this infrastructure, Paul is saying, Christians living in that time must hold themselves aloof from all that depends on it, including these otherwise normal and innocuous human activities. Thus, by speaking of the "form of this world" as passing away, which we should probably understand as an intentional modification of a standard apocalyptic topos, Paul once again places the emphasis on the hardships of the end time. Even though he uses the word κόσμος here ("cosmos, world"), the more "cosmological" events of the eschaton – the Second Coming, the destruction of the earth and the creation of a new one – all recede into the background.[299]

A final aspect of 7.25–31 that indicates Paul's intention of using these apocalyptic hardships as the "circumstances" of his argument against marriage is the fact that he has cast this passage in the

---

[295] 1 John 2.16, in turn, prefaces his apocalyptic announcement with a description of what is "in the world": "the lust of the flesh, and the lust of the eyes, and the pride of life"; cf. 2.15.

[296] Chronicled in Hierzenberger, *Weltbewertung bei Paulus*, 61–3.

[297] "*For* (γάρ) the form of this world is passing away."

[298] Thus 7.32a makes a new start: "But (δέ) I want you to be without care ..."

[299] See Becker, "Erwägungen zur apokalyptischen Tradition," 600; and Baumgarten, *Paulus und die Apokalyptik*, 223–4. The "world" (κόσμος) in verse 31 is thus not the stage of super-human forces and events, but the arena of mundane affairs – as in the verses immediately following (verses 32–4).

present tense. His reference point in verse 26 is the "*present* (ἐνεστῶσα) necessity";³⁰⁰ he maintains in verse 29 that the time "*is* (ἐστίν) constricted"; and he concludes this section in verse 31 with the statement that the form of this world "*is* passing away" (παράγει).³⁰¹ To be sure, this language is uncharacteristic of apocalyptic texts, which usually speak of future events. It would be wrong, however, to assume that the present tense has no place in apocalyptic thought. Not only have several scholars identified a present aspect to the apocalyptic ideas in Paul's theology,³⁰² but there exist other texts that speak of apocalyptic events as occurring in the present. These are 1 John 2.17 (cited above),³⁰³ 1 Peter 4.17,³⁰⁴ and 4 Ezra 4.26.³⁰⁵

What Paul is suggesting by this use of the present is that the "necessity" of verse 26, which is evidently some immediate economic or political crisis so apparent to the Corinthians that it

³⁰⁰ Scholars generally agree that a future meaning for εςνεστῶσα is highly unlikely. See the discussions in Allo, *Première épitre*, 178; Delling, *Paulus' Stellung*, 77; Schrage, "Die Stellung zur Welt," 131 and n. 13 (with lit.); and Baumert, *Ehelosigkeit und Ehe*, 171–2. Elsewhere in his letters (Rom. 8.38; 1 Cor. 3.22; and Gal. 1.4) Paul consistently uses this verb to refer to present time; and our closest parallel to 1 Cor. 7.26, namely the variant reading at 3 Macc. 1.16, describes a prayer for help in the "present necessity": βοηθεῖν τῇ ἐνεστώσῃ ἀνάγκῃ. (Likewise, the preferred reading for 3 Macc. 1.16 is τοῖς ἐνεστῶσιν, "in the present situation.")

³⁰¹ In addition, Schrage, "Die Stellung zur Welt," 148 notes that the admonitions in 7.29b-31a use the present participle whereas the parallel passage in 4 Ezra 16.40–4 is cast entirely in the future tense.

³⁰² E.g., Weiß, *Korintherbrief*, 201; Braun, "Die Indifferenz gegenüber der Welt," 161; Schrage, "Die Stellung zur Welt," 148; and Rudolf Bultmann, "Ist die Apokalyptik die Mutter der christlichen Theologie? Eine Auseinandersetzung mit Ernst Käsemann," *Exegetica: Aufsätze zur Erforschung des Neuen Testaments*, ed. Erich Dinkler (Tübingen: J. C. B. Mohr, 1967) 476–7. Cf. Countryman, *Dirt, Greed, and Sex*, 212: "For Paul, the value of celibacy was directly related to the chaotic and troubling times which had *already* begun and would lead shortly to the end of this world and the inbreaking of the reign of God" (my emphasis).

³⁰³ On the apocalyptic character of this passage see 1 John 2.18–29 and the commentary in Raymond E. Brown, *The Epistles of John*, AB 30 (Garden City, N.Y.: Doubleday, 1982) 313–14.

³⁰⁴ "It is the time to begin the judgement from the house of God" ([ὁ] καιρὸς τοῦ κρίμα ἀπὸ τοῦ οἴκου τοῦ θεοῦ); cf. 4.7, "The end of all things has drawn near" (πάντων δὲ τὸ τέλος ἤγγικεν).

³⁰⁵ "The world rapidly hastens to pass away" (*festinans festinat saeculum pertransire*), cited by Weiß, *Korintherbrief*, 201. This text dates from ca. the late first century CE, now preserved in a Latin translation from Greek, which is probably a translation from Hebrew. See also 4 Ezra 5.55, "a creation just now growing old and passing the strength of its youth" (*iam senescentis creaturae et fortitudinem iuventutis praeterientis*); 14.10, "the times are close to growing old" (*tempora adpropinquant senescere*); and the discussion of these passages in Michael Edward Stone, *Fourth Ezra*, Hermeneia (Minneapolis: Augsburg Fortress, 1990) 93–4, 420–1.

requires no further explanation, may represent but a foretaste of the apocalyptic tumult to come. He makes this connection, moreover, because the Stoic argument he is using depends on there being circumstances that presently stand in the way of marriage; speculation about future circumstances would not have met this need. By pointing out this possible link between an actual crisis at Corinth and the future hardships of the last days – a link the Corinthians themselves, in all probability, also assumed[306] – Paul can credibly argue that the current situation may not blow over, but matters could get worse: those who marry will have tribulation in the flesh, while those who have wives must "henceforth" be as not having them (verses 28–9).[307]

That Paul or the Corinthians could so easily integrate apocalyptic and Stoic ideas might, at first, seem surprising. Upon closer inspection, however, it is apparent that in placing the emphasis on the tumult of the end time, Paul is tapping into a tradition of visions and expectations of ominous events that must have seemed tailor-made for the purpose. These events included war, earthquakes, and famines,[308] all of which promised to destroy the social and economic fabric of society, thereby making the responsibilities of married life difficult or impossible to fulfill. In the midst of this calamity – as the "form of this world" passed away – a man or a woman would have little opportunity to look after the needs of a spouse, raise children, or bother with establishing and managing a household.[309]

---

[306] See above, p. 125. Note that Mark 13.8 speaks of famines, earthquakes, and war as the *beginning* of the end time suffering.

[307] On the translation of τὸ λοιπόν ("henceforth, from now on") see Conzelmann, *1 Corinthians*, 130 n. 3 (lit.). The future tense of Paul's statement that those who marry "will have" (ἕξουσιν) tribulation has its immediate reference, of course, in the possibility of future marriages; it also points toward the development and duration of an apocalyptic crisis (but not its beginning).

[308] E.g., Mark 13.8. See also Schürer, *The History of the Jewish People*, 2.514–15 (lit.); and Strack-Billerbeck, *Kommentar*, 4.2.977–81, 986.

[309] It should be noted that the "tribulation" (θλῖψις) of which Paul speaks in 7.28 is not the general apocalyptic hardship, but this hardship as experienced specifically by those who marry. See Weiß, *History of Primitive Christianity*, 581; Niederwimmer, *Askese und Mysterium*, 107 n. 137; cf. 109; Schrage, "Die Stellung zur Welt," 131; and Wolbert, *Ethische Argumentation*, 198–9; cf. 120.
Apocalyptic texts also predicted a disintegration of moral standards, which worked toward the destruction of the household. See Wilhelm Bousset, *Die Religion des Judentums im späthellenistischen Zeitalter*, 3rd edn., ed. Hugo Gressmann, HNT 21 (Tübingen: J. C. B. Mohr, 1926) 250–1, who cites *1 Enoch* 99.5; 100.1f.; *Jub.* 23.59; *4 Ezra* 5.9; 6.24; and *2 Baruch* 70.6. See also Mark 13.12 par., and Matt. 10.34–6. On the a-familial ethos of the eschatological "kingdom of God," see Elisabeth Schüssler

As a result, apocalyptic texts, like Paul, also warn of the disastrous effects that the last days will have on marriage and take a stand against the initiation of new marriages. The prophet Joel, in preparing the Israelites for the Day of the Lord, thus commands the cessation of all weddings: "Assemble the people, sanctify the congregation (ἁγιάσατε ἐκκλησίαν) ... let the bridegroom leave his chamber and the bride her room."[310] The Book of Revelation reports that the destruction of "Babylon" will bring an end to the joyful sounds of its inhabitants, including "the voice of the bridegroom and bride";[311] and 4 Ezra 15–16, the text with so many similarities to 1 Corinthians 7.29b–31a, predicts disaster both for those planning marriage and for those already married: "Virgins shall mourn because they have no bridegrooms; women shall mourn because they have no husbands ... Their bridegrooms shall be killed in war, and their husbands shall perish of famine."[312] In *2 Baruch* the admonition against marriage is coupled with a warning against having children: "And you, bridegrooms, do not enter, and do not let the brides adorn themselves. And you, wives, do not pray to bear children, for the barren will rejoice more. And those who have no children will be glad, and those who have children will be sad."[313] The hardships of childbearing in the last days is also a motif in the synoptic tradition, coming to expression in Jesus' pronouncement of woes and blessings on people. In Mark 13.17 par. Jesus tells his disciples, "Woe to those who are pregnant and to those nursing in these days"; and in Luke 23.29 Jesus predicts that the inhabitants of Jerusalem will soon be telling their daughters, "Blessed are the sterile and the wombs that never conceived and breasts that never nursed," a saying also preserved in the *Gospel of Thomas* 79.[314]

---

Fiorenza, *In Memory of Her: A Feminist Theological Reconstruction of Christian Origins* (New York: Crossroad, 1983) 145–51; and Kevin J. Coyle, "Empire and Eschaton: The Early Church and the Question of Domestic Relationships," *Église et Théologie* 12 (1981) 35–94.

310  Joel 2.16 LXX; cf. 1.8.

311  Rev. 18.21–3 (echoing Jer. 16.1–9).

312  4 Ezra (2 Esdras) 16.33–4 RSV; cf. Zech. 12.12–14.

313  *2 Baruch* 10.13–14, trans. A. F. J. Klijn, "2 (Syriac Apocalypse of) Baruch," *The Old Testament Pseudepigrapha*, ed. James H. Charlesworth (Garden City, N.Y.: Doubleday, 1985) 2.624; a Jewish apocalypse from the end of the first or beginning of the second century CE.

314  See also Luke 11.27–8; *Sib. Or.* 2.190–3; and cf. *Acts of Paul and Thecla* 3.5 (a beatitude formed from 1 Cor. 7.29b). Thackeray, *Relation of St. Paul*, 106, and Friedrich Guntermann, *Die Eschatologie des Hl. Paulus*, NTAbh 13/4–5 (Münster: Aschendorffsche Verlagsbuchhandlung, 1932) 89–90 also point to texts that predict complications and horrors associated with childbirth in the last times: 4 Ezra 5.8

From the perspective of first-century Christians living in the Greek world and familiar with both Stoic and apocalyptic thought, the integration of these two traditions in 7.25–31 is, therefore, perhaps not so remarkable. What gives one pause for reflection, however, is the extent to which this integration has taken place in our passage. To begin with, even the phraseology here is sometimes not clearly either Stoic or apocalyptic. As we have seen, Paul introduces the apocalyptic material in 7.29b–31a with the words, τοῦτο δέ φημι, ἀδελφοί, ὁ καιρὸς συνεσταλμένος ἐστίν· τὸ λοιπόν . . ., "This I say, brothers, the time is constricted; henceforth, . . ." As Bonhöffer has pointed out, however, the expression τοῦτό φημι occurs frequently in Epictetus' *Discourses* as a means of introducing an opinion or clarification.[315] Paul's statement about the "time," on the other hand, finds its closest parallel in Dio Chrysostom's words, "It is already time, henceforth . . ." (καιρὸς ἤδη τὸ λοιπόν), spoken to an angry mob intent on plundering his estate.[316] And verse 31a, "let those using the world be as not fully using [it]" (οἱ χρώμενοι τὸν κόσμον ὡς μὴ καταχρώμενοι), comes very close to the philosophical banter Philo assigns to his ideal statesman: "This is yours? – use [it], not misusing [it]!" (χρῶ μὴ παραχρώμενος).[317] In fact, Philo's words are approximately those of 7.31a set to the rhythm of the diatribe pattern that we examined in connection with 7.18, 21, and 27.[318]

(menstruating women giving birth to monsters); 6.21 (premature births); *1 Enoch* 99.5 (sinful women practicing abortion, and exposing and devouring newborns). Baumert, *Ehelosigkeit und Ehe*, 192, on the other hand, claims that apocalyptic traditions about pregnancy, childbirth, and nursing are irrelevant since Paul does not mention these matters here. But the issues of pregnancy and reproduction do appear to stand behind 7.3–5, 14, and 34, and as I shall argue in the conclusion (chapter 4), Paul purposefully avoids explicit mention of childbearing in 1 Cor. 7.

[315] Bonhöffer, *Epiktet und das Neue Testament*, 199. τοῦτό φημι also occurs at 1 Cor. 15.50, and φημί by itself occurs at 10.15, 19. Outside of these four instances in 1 Corinthians, the first person form does not appear in the NT.

[316] Dio Chrys. *Or*. 46.13, cited by Wettstein, *Novum Testamentum Graecum*, 2.129.

[317] Philo *De Jos*. 144, cited by Wettstein, *Novum Testamentum Graecum*, 2.129.

[318] See above, pp. 159–64, 174–5. As noted there, this same passage is cited by Thackeray, *The Relation of St. Paul*, 239 in connection with 7.18, 21.

Aside from these examples, our nearest parallel to Paul's expression "the form of this world" (τὸ σχῆμα τοῦ κόσμου τούτου) comes from Philostratus' *Life of Apollonius of Tyana* 8.7.7, where Apollonius asks, "And what is the form of this world?" (καὶ τί τὸ σχῆμα τοῦ κόσμου τοῦδε;). According to Philostratus, this is a direct quote from Apollonius' *Apologia pro vita*, which the latter had planned to give before the Emperor Domitian (81–96 CE). Whether we may trust Philostratus on this point, however, is uncertain. Apollonius, incidently, is said to have been a close associate of Musonius – see *Life of Apollonius* 4.46; and Lutz, "Musonius Rufus," 3 and n. 1. Finally, Romano Penna, "San Paolo (1 Cor 7,29b–31a) e Diogene il

But the one "Stoic" or "near-Stoic" feature of 7.25–31 with which scholars have been most fascinated is the expression "as not" (ὡς μή), which serves as a leitmotiv for the apocalyptic injunctions in verses 29b–31a. In the admonitions to those having wives to be "as not" having wives, to those weeping or rejoicing to be "as not" weeping or rejoicing, and to those making purchases and using the world to be "as not" owning or fully using, scholars have seen a resemblance to the Stoic ideal of mental and spiritual calmness, or ἀταραξία.[319] Weiß, for example, maintained that Stoic ἀταραξία "shines through here." Edwards writes, "If we can imagine St. Paul putting together an ethical theory after the manner of a Greek philosopher, we have the pith of it in [verse 30]"; and Legrand concurs: "the text of verses 29–31 could have been signed by an Epictetus or a Seneca."[320] Again, Conzelmann states, "This appears at first sight to be the passage most strongly subject to Stoic influence in all of the Pauline epistles"; and Bornkamm says, "In themselves these words could be described as a classic paraphrase of the Cynic and Stoic ideal of severance from all earthly ties and detachment from all that fortune and circumstances may bring, whether good or evil."[321] Finally, Chadwick gives this assessment of the passage: "[Paul's] demand for continence is set within the eschatological framework of Christian thought, fused with Stoic–Cynic ideas about the soul's detachment and ἀταραξία."[322]

This almost unanimous agreement among scholars seems to be warranted, moreover, by the several passages from Seneca and Epictetus (among others) that these scholars cite. Thus Seneca, in

Cinico," *Biblica* 58 (1977) 237–45 sees a parallel between 7.29b–31a and D.L. 6.29, where Diogenes the Cynic is described as praising "those who were intending to marry and did not marry" as well as "those who were intending to raise children and did not raise children" (τοὺς μέλλοντας γαμεῖν καὶ μὴ γαμεῖν ... καὶ τοὺς μέλλοντας παιδοτροφεῖν καὶ μὴ παιδοτροφεῖν). But this is a distant parallel and seems to me to be only a coincidence.

[319] The seminal study here is Braun, "Die Indifferenz gegenüber der Welt"; see also the authors cited in the following notes, and Schrage, "Die Stellung zur Welt," 132–4, who surveys the literature and lists relevant passages from Epictetus.

[320] Weiß, *Korintherbrief*, 199, citing from Epictetus, Teles, and Philo (198 n. 2; 200 nn. 1 and 3); Edwards, *Commentary on the First Epistle*, 194; Legrand, "Saint Paul et célibat," 322.

[321] Conzelmann, *1 Corinthians*, 133; Bornkamm, *Paul*, 206. Cf. Niederwimmer, *Askese und Mysterium*, 110 n. 50, who says that, separated from the framing of verses 29a and 31b, verses 29b–31a would be thoroughly Stoic; and Darrell J. Doughty, "The Presence and Future of Salvation in Corinth," *ZNW* 66 (1975) 72 n. 50, who speaks of "Stoic language" bracketed between apocalyptic assertions.

[322] Chadwick, "'All Things to All Men'," 268, cf. 267.

one of his *Moral Epistles*, says of possessions, "Let us use these things (*utamur illis*) . . . and let us use them sparingly (*utamur parce*), as if (*tamquam*) they were given for safe-keeping and will be withdrawn . . . If anyone has put his trust in goods that are most fleeting, he is soon bereft of them, and, to avoid being bereft, he suffers distress (*adfligitur*)."³²³ In another *Epistle* he states that the wise man can be self-sufficient and still marry and raise children, "Yet all the good will be limited to his own being." To illustrate this he recounts the philosophical triumphs of Stilbo in the wake of Megara's sacking by Demetrius I of Macedonia: "For Stilbo, after his country was captured and his children and his wife lost, as he emerged from the general desolation alone and yet happy, spoke as follows to Demetrius . . ., 'I have all my goods with me!'"³²⁴ In a similar fashion, Epictetus maintains that the end of philosophy should be for each person to pass his life to himself, "free from pain, fear, and perturbation (ἀταράχως), at the same time maintaining with his associates both the natural and the acquired relationships, those namely of son, father, brother, citizen, husband, wife, . . ."³²⁵ Elsewhere, after praising the man who does not value his person beyond its God-given worth, Epictetus advises:

> Now if someone should also take this same attitude toward his property and his children and his wife, as this man takes toward his body, and under some frenzy and desperation simply be so disposed that he would in no way act so as to have these things or not have them (τὸ ἔχειν ταῦτα ἢ μὴ ἔχειν) . . . what sort of tyrant or body guards or swords of theirs would still be frightening to him?³²⁶

A last example is Epictetus' description of Socrates as "having a wife and children, but as belonging to another."³²⁷ "Later on," he says, referring to Socrates' trial before the Athenian people, "he didn't behave as having children or as having a wife, did he?"³²⁸

³²³ Sen. *Ep*. 74.18, trans. Gummere, *Seneca*, 2.125. Cf. Epict. *Ench*. 11.
³²⁴ Sen. *Ep*. 9.17–18, trans. Gummere, *Seneca*, 1.53. In 9.19 Seneca adds: "This saying of Stilbo makes common ground with Stoicism; the Stoic also can carry his goods unimpaired through cities that have been burned to ashes; for he is self-sufficient" (trans. Gummere, *Seneca*, 1.55).
³²⁵ Epict. *Diss*. 2.14.8, trans. Oldfather, *Epictetus*, 1.309 (who inadvertently omits "husband" from his trans.); cf. *Diss*. 3.24.58–60.
³²⁶ Epict. *Diss*. 4.7.5.
³²⁷ Epict. *Diss*. 4.1.159, γυναῖκα καὶ παιδία ἔχοντα, ἀλλὰ ὡς ἀλλότρια.
³²⁸ Epict. *Diss*. 4.1.162, trans. Oldfather, *Epictetus*, 2.301, μή τι ὡς τέκνα ἔχων ἀναστρέφεται, μή τι ὡς γυναῖκα; See also *Ench*. 11, where Epictetus says of things

Despite the impressive weight of this evidence, however, many scholars, including most of those just cited, hold that 1 Corinthians 7.29b-31a ultimately cannot be understood in terms of Stoic thought.[329] Schrage, followed by Schulz, has taken this position, pointing to Paul's dependence on an apocalyptic source for these verses, which, as we have seen, is a genuine possibility. Reasoning that this dependence in itself is sufficient to exclude any Stoic influence, he concludes that any resemblance to authors such as Epictetus is purely coincidental.[330] Approaching the matter on a philosophical and theological plane, Schrage also argues that the apocalyptic motivation behind 7.29b-31a is entirely incompatible with Stoicism. The admonitions here to live "as not," according to Schrage, are inspired by Paul's belief that the end of the world was at hand: since the things of this life would shortly be no more, the Christian should avoid becoming overly involved with them. Such an expectation of the world's imminent and definitive demise, says Schrage, would be incomprehensible to an Epictetus, since Stoic eschatology saw the world as constantly in transition, subject to a steady cycle of conflagration and renewal that knew no meaningful beginning or definitive end.[331]

In reply to Schrage, we may first question the exclusiveness he imputes to both apocalyptic and Stoic ideologies. On the one hand, his readiness to understand apocalyptic thought as completely separate from other modes of thought stands in need of correction.[332] As the research of others has shown, apocalypticism is far from a clearly circumscribed entity, sealed off from "outside"

given by God: "care for it as belonging to another, as travellers care for the inn" (ὡς ἀλλοτρίου αὐτοῦ ἐπιμελοῦ, ὡς τοῦ πανδοχείου οἱ παριόντες).

[329] Those who do not rule out Stoic influence include Weiß, *Korintherbrief*, 199 (who changes his position in *History of Primitive Christianity*, 583 n. 62); Braun, "Die Indifferenz gegenüber der Welt," esp. 343–4; and Chadwick, "'All Things to All Men'," 267–8. See also Doughty, "Presence and Future of Salvation," 72 n. 50; and cf. Niederwimmer, *Askese und Mysterium*, 110 n. 149.

[330] Schrage, "Die Stellung zur Welt," 136, 137–8; Schulz, "Evangelium und Welt," 487 (although he discounts Schrage's argument from 4 Ezra 16.40–4).

[331] Schrage, "Die Stellung zur Welt," 135–8, 153, following Braun, "Die Indifferenz gegenüber der Welt," 162, 164. Weiß, *History of Primitive Christianity*, 583 n. 62, and Deißner, "Das Sendungsbewußtsein der Urchristenheit," 788–90 also point to the differences between Pauline and Stoic eschatology. For a general comparison of these two eschatologies see Kee, "Pauline Eschatology," 137–40, 144–7, 151–5.

[332] Cf. Conzelmann, *1 Corinthians*, 133 n. 26; and Balch, "Stoic Debates," 429–30: "Schrage argues in too rationalistic a manner about social influences, whether these are from Jewish apocalyptic or from Stoic ethics." Ironically, Countryman, *Dirt, Greed, and Sex*, 213 n. 21 takes Balch to task for focusing too narrowly on Stoic influence and ignoring the eschatological content of Paul's argument.

influences.[333] Indeed, Schrage himself cautions against such abso-
lutes in the syncretistic world of late Hellenism;[334] and his own
research in other quarters has led him to the conclusion that certain
topoi (in fact, *peristasis*-catalogs) were shared by apocalyptic and
Stoic authors.[335]

On the other hand, Schrage's observations on the apocalyptic
motivation for the admonitions in 7.29b–31a – given that they are
correct – hardly constitute sufficient grounds for ruling out Stoic
influence on these verses. Paul was, after all, Christian, not Stoic,
and the same holds true for his church at Corinth. We should
expect, therefore, that any Stoic ideas in 1 Corinthians will bear a
certain amount of Christian coloring. Just how much coloring is
admissible before we decide that a passage is not, or no longer,
Stoic, seems to me to be something of an open question: Do
non-Stoic motivations for the Stoic ideal of mental and spiritual
calmness necessarily render this ideal un-Stoic? Certainly scholars
would be wary of applying this litmus test to, say, the Stoic elements
in Philo.[336]

But apart from this caveat, I would maintain that Schrage has
simply misread the apocalyptic motivation behind 7.29b–31a.
According to him, Paul's concern here is with the imminence of the
world's destruction. As I have argued above, however, Paul's
immediate, if not sole, point of emphasis in these verses pertains not
to the imminence of the End, but to the social and economic
upheaval that was to precede the End.[337] Insofar as my reading of

333 See esp. Hans Dieter Betz, "On the Problem of the Religio-Historical Understanding of Apocalypticism," *Journal for Theology and Church* 6 (1969) 134–56, esp.
155: "... Jewish and, subsequently, Christian apocalypticism as well ... must be seen
and presented as peculiar expressions within the entire development of Hellenistic
syncretism." Cf. Meeks, "Social Functions of Apocalyptic Language," 703.

334 Schrage, "Die Stellung zur Welt," 125.

335 Wolfgang Schrage, "Leid, Kreuz und Eschaton: Die Peristasenkataloge als
Merkmale paulinischer theologia crucis und Eschatologie," *EvT* 34 (1974) 143–7
(with extensive lit.) shows that catalogs of trials and sufferings occur in both
Stoic–Cynic diatribes and Jewish apocalyptic lists of woes; cf. 165–6, 171–2, 174. See
also Conzelmann's remark on the *peristasis*-catalog in 1 Cor. 4.9–13: "The Stoic
picture of the philosopher's struggle as a spectacle for the world is taken over by Paul
into his world-picture ... and reshaped in terms of his eschatology" (*1 Corinthians*,
88).

336 See Conzelmann's remark on 1 Cor. 7.29b–31a: "Even the eschatological
grounding is not in itself an objection... Paul could simply have changed the world
picture, and yet have taken over in his attitude toward the world the aloofness of the
Stoics" (*1 Corinthians*, 133).

337 Schrage sees a sense of imminence in two places: in the word καιρός (v. 29a),
which he translates as "the time yet remaining before the Parousia," ("Die Stellung

this passage is correct, not only is the incongruence that Schrage sees between apocalyptic and Stoic eschatology a moot point, as it plays no part here, but further, the apocalyptic rationale for Paul's argument in 7.29b-31a finds a very close analogy in Epictetus' discourse *On Cynicism*, and, significantly, in the section of this discourse which deals with marriage. Here Epictetus explains that the Cynic will forgo marriage given the present "order of things,"[338] by which he refers not to the static transience of the world, but to the chaotic state of society in his day, which he likens to a "battle-field."[339]

Yet, these considerations aside, the main objection that scholars have raised against understanding 7.29b-31a as an expression of Stoic calmness is their claim that Paul could not espouse this ideal since it would contradict basic tenets of his theology. As Conzelmann explains, "The non-Stoic character of the relationship to the world [in 7.29b-31a] emerges only in the wider context. Paul's advice is not to withdraw into the safe and unrestricted realms of the inner life, but to maintain freedom in the midst of involvement."[340] By contrast, according to Schulz, Epictetus "demands ἀταραξία fundamentally, [and] excludes compassion and engaging oneself for the concrete needs of one's fellow human beings."[341] Likewise, Schrage points out that any notion of "non-engagement" with the world would be limited in Paul's theology by the value he places on love. For Paul, compassion is something positive, whereas it is negative for the Stoics.[342] By the same token, Schrage contends, the θλῖψις, or "pressure from outside" (as he translates it), that Paul

---

zur Welt," 131–2), and in the μή of the ὡς μή admonitions, which he translates as "(already) no (longer)" (ibid., 148). Both of these are blatant over-interpretations of Paul's words.

[338] Epict. *Diss.* 3.22.69, "the order of things being such as it is" (τοιαύτης δ' οὔσης καταστάσεως); 3.22.76, "in this order of things" (ἐν ταύτῃ τῇ καταστάσει). Cf. Paul's use of σχῆμα ("form" of this world) in 7.29b.

[339] Epict. *Diss.* 3.22.69. Cf. Yarbrough, *Not Like the Gentiles*, 105: "Even Paul's eschatological argument has analogy in Epictetus' discourse on the Ideal Cynic in that the Cynic does not marry because the present order is 'like a battlefield'"; and Gager, "Functional Diversity," 332: "As with Paul, the motivation for celibacy [in Epictetus] is the desire to devote oneself without distraction to a religious obligation, and justification for this is rooted in unusual, external, and presumably not permanent [?] circumstances." Note also that Plutarch claimed Cicero, early in his career, temporarily took up the contemplative life (τὸν σχολαστὴν καὶ θεωρητικὸν βίον), due to the turmoil of the political situation (*Vit.* 862A [*Cicero*]).

[340] Conzelmann, *1 Corinthians*, 133.

[341] Schulz, "Evangelium und Welt," 487–8.

[342] Schrage, "Die Stellung zur Welt," 134; cf. 138; *Die konkreten Einzelgebote*, 23 n. 42; and, "Zur Frontstellung," 223–4; 231 n. 68.

speaks of in verse 28 would be inconceivable for Epictetus, who held that "what pressures and plagues people is not things and people, but the person himself with wrong δόγματα [beliefs]."[343]

Although the above arguments are widely accepted,[344] they are in need of qualification on two grounds: first, because they exaggerate the difference between Paul's theological principles and the Stoic ideal of ἀταραξία; and second, because they overlook the function of 7.29b–31a in Paul's discussion. While it is true that the Stoics sought to live free from inner disturbance (ταραχή) and "passion" (πάθος), this rarely led them to the conclusion that they must withdraw from the world. Indeed, as we saw in chapter two, the central issue of the Stoic–Cynic marriage debate was whether one should engage oneself on behalf of human society. Should one establish a household? raise and educate children? participate in politics? safeguard the ancestral altar? make one's house a rampart for the city-state? – in short, should one pursue the active life over the contemplative life? These were some of the questions that occupied major Stoic teachers throughout the Hellenistic period, and mostly they elicited affirmative answers.[345]

Regarding the matter of attending to the needs of others, Antipater, Musonius, and Hierocles all agree that a man must provide for his family, sharing both his possessions and his body with his wife; and Epictetus claims that his ideal Cynic will make the entire world his family, and "in this way care for them all."[346] Some "pressure from outside" – what Hierocles called the "concerns" (μέριμναι) of day-to-day living[347] – was thus seen by these Stoics as inevitable. In fact, on these grounds, Antipater encouraged taking

---

[343] Schrage, "Die Stellung zur Welt," 135. These statements from Conzelmann, Schulz, and Schrage, it should be noted, are all directly dependent on Braun, "Die Indifferenz gegenüber der Welt," 166.

[344] See also Kümmel in Lietzmann, *An die Korinther*, 178; Hierzenberger, *Weltbewertung bei Paulus*, 43, 50; and in the older literature, Heinrici, *Das erste Sendschreiben*, 218–20; Bonhöffer, *Epiktet und das Neue Testament*, 35–6; and Allo, *Première épitre*, 180. Héring's objection to Stoic influence on 7.29b–31a on the grounds that "the Stoic forbade emotion," confuses emotion with πάθος (passion or emotional suffering detrimental to one's well-being). As we have seen, Epictetus does not forbid the emotion love (ἔρως); and Arius, on the other hand, lists "rejoicing" (χαίρειν), which Paul uses in 7.30, as a "correct" Stoic action (κατορθώματα, Stob. 2.96.20–1 W.-H.).

[345] See also the discussion of Stoic retirement into oneself in the midst of activities in Festugière, *Personal Religion*, 58–64; and the literature on *oikeiosis*, the Stoic notion of social affinity and dependency, cited in chap. 2, n. 15.

[346] Epict. *Diss.* 3.22.81, οὕτως πάντων κήδεται; see also 3.22.72–3, 77, 83.

[347] Hierocles 53.30–54.1 v.A. (Stob. 4.504.7–9 W.-H.)

on the additional responsibilities of married life, reasoning that a wife could keep her husband "undistracted" (ἀπερίσπαστος) from some of these concerns.[348] While Epictetus, to the contrary, argued that his Cynic would avoid marriage in order to remain "undistracted," it was only so the latter could take on yet greater responsibilities and concerns.[349] In either case it is difficult to overlook that Hierocles, Antipater, and Epictetus are using the same terminology to discuss this dilemma as Paul uses in 7.32–5.[350] The divide between Paul and the Stoics on the concept of ἀταραξία is, therefore, not nearly as great as scholars have portrayed it.

On the other hand, it would appear that it is not even necessary for us to reconcile the Stoic-like ἀταραξία of 7.29b–31a with Paul's overall theology, given the function of these verses in Paul's argument. As I suggested above, Paul is using the apocalyptic material in these verses to define the "circumstances" of his (Stoic) argument against marriage. In effect, this material constitutes the "facts" of an argument from expediency, and as such it requires no theological justification. To put the matter another way, the admonitions here to live "as not" are not Paul's, but represent the authoritative voice of apocalyptic tradition describing what life in the last days, in fact, demands. Indeed, in light of Paul's efforts in 7.3–5 to limit sexual abstinence among spouses, it would be very odd if the admonition to have a wife "as not having" was his own. Rather, introduced with the explanatory phrase, "this I say, brothers," verses 29b–31a serve as so many examples of the "tribulation" that, according to Paul, *necessarily* awaits those who marry in the "present necessity."[351]

As part of an argument against marriage based on expediency, verses 29b–31a thus function as a warning that marriage in the last times will *as a matter of fact* be unfulfilling. Just as some Stoics held that circumstances caused them to act uncharacteristically as Cynics, a certain amount of uncharacteristic, Stoic-like detachment toward the things of married life is now required of Christians, according to Paul. Christians will act, but "as not," and husbands will have wives, but "as not," for Christian marriage in its ideal

---

[348] Antip. *SVF* 3.257.3–4 (Stob. 4.511.20–512.1 W.-H.).

[349] Epict. *Diss.* 3.22.69.

[350] See the next section.

[351] On the various functions of apocalyptic material in ethical discourse see Gager, "Functional Diversity"; Meeks: "Social Functions of Apocalyptic Language"; *First Urban Christians*, 174–9; and John S. Kloppenborg, "Symbolic Eschatology and the Apocalypticism of Q," *HTR* 80 (1987) 287–306.

form will cease to exist, and for this reason, Paul is saying, it is "good for a man" not to get involved.

In sum, I would contend that there is no need to interpret 7.29b–31a in a manner that makes it compatible with Paul's ethic of Christian compassion, and thus no objection to our seeing these verses as an expression of Stoic calmness and detachment. This is not to deny, however, that 7.29b–31a also owes a considerable debt to its apocalyptic heritage. In the final analysis we must reckon with a high degree of integration between Stoic and apocalyptic materials here, which is one more indication that Paul's audience in Corinth stands intellectually and spiritually between Judeo–Christian and Stoic traditions. It may also imply that these verses stem from some form of "Stoic-apocalyptic" thought whose source was in Corinth.

### 6. The commitments of married life and finding time for the Lord: 1 Corinthians 7.32–5

Paul's debt in 1 Corinthians 7 to Stoic and Cynic thinking on marriage has been most apparent to scholars in 7.32–5, where he compares the allegiances of married Christians with those of unmarried Christians. The unmarried, he explains, are committed to pleasing the Lord, and consequently concern themselves with "the things of the Lord," while the married are committed to pleasing their spouses, and hence concern themselves with "the things of the world." As we noted earlier, Paul must mean that married Christians are committed *both* to their spouses *and* to the Lord, since they are, in fact, Christians, and since this is the only way to account for his assertion in verse 34a that they are "divided."[352] From Paul's emphasis on marital obligations in verses 27 and 28b, and his mention of buying and possessing and "using the world" in 7.30–1, we may further surmise that his expression "the things of the world" has reference to the day-to-day responsibilities of a householder and his wife.[353] It is a preoccupation with these things, he contends, that

---

[352] See above, p. 122.

[353] Cf. Juncker, *Ethik*, 2.185–6, who would include pregnancy, child rearing, and household management. Weiß, *Korintherbrief*, 201, followed by Niederwimmer, *Askese und Mysterium*, 111, posits a connection between verse 28b, Paul's desire to spare the Corinthians "tribulation in the flesh," and his statement in verse 32, "I want you to be without care."

divides Christians and stands in the way of their devotion to Christ "without distraction."[354]

Regarding the "unmarried woman and the virgin" in verse 34, moreover, Paul appears to have an additional message, saying that these women concern themselves for the things of the Lord so they might be "holy both in body and in spirit" (ἁγία καὶ τῷ σώματι καὶ τῷ πνεύματι). As our investigation of 7.3–5 and 7.12–24 has indicated, part of the controversy over marriage in Corinth involved a person's control or "authority" over his or her own body. While Paul insists on the Stoic ideal of mutual control of bodies within marriage (verse 4), some of the Corinthians seem to have objected to this on the grounds that it inhibited prayer (see verse 5), or that this sort of an arrangement with an unbeliever prevented them from achieving the ideals of "holiness" and freedom (see verses 14, 15b). With this mention of holiness in verse 34, therefore, Paul is evidently bringing the issue of controlling one's body into play once again. In contrast

---

[354] See Baumert, *Ehelosigkeit und Ehe*, 260–2, who correctly emphasizes that marriage brings involvement with the world, and it is this involvement, not marriage itself or the spouse, that "divides" a Christian. Thus Paul's words do not imply a direct tension between allegiance to the Lord and allegiance to one's spouse. The tension, rather, is between one's concern for "things of the world" and "things of the Lord" (cf. Weiß, *Korintherbrief*, 202). Niederwimmer's contention, on the basis of 7.29b (perhaps following Braun, "Die Indifferenz gegenüber der Welt," 160), that a wife is a "thing of this world" (*res huius mundi*), and his assessment of 7.32–4 as meaning that the married person is "not completely a Christian" but only a "'half' Christian" is simply an attempt to sensationalize Paul (*Askese und Mysterium*, 113 and n. 164; 114; cf. 123). The same holds true for Brown, *Body and Society*, 56, who says that the "married lacked the supreme quality of the undivided heart," which, for Paul, was a "crushing disqualification." Both authors contradict what Paul himself says on grace and the circumstances of one's life in 7.17–24, as well as what he says in 7.36–40 (see below).

We should also resist the temptation to interpret the division of the married man (and presumably the married woman) in psychological terms. Marriage for Paul is not "anxiety producing," as Wimbush, *Worldly Ascetic*, 64 claims; nor is Balch, "Stoic Debates," 435 justified in making a distinction between the "distractions" spoken of by Stoics and Paul's "anxiety." As Legrand points out, commentators too often "think spontaneously of a heart divided in its affections in the modern romantic sense of the term." It is rather, he continues, that "the wife 'pleased' her husband by giving him the children he wanted... and by conducting the household efficiently... For the husband, it was a matter of securing for his wife wealth, comfort and social consideration" (*Biblical Doctrine of Virginity*, 94, 95–6). Likewise, Moulton and Milligan, *Vocabulary of the Greek Testament*, 26 say of the word ἀμέριμνος, "It will be seen that the NT meaning alone is attested from the vernacular documents. Its tone in them suggests that 'anxiety' rather exaggerates the word. So in Mt 28.14 we might paraphrase '... so that you need not trouble'; and in I Cor 7.32 the verb that follows clearly does not suggest *anxious* care" (their emphasis). See also Rudolf Bultmann, "μεριμνάω," *TDNT* 4 (1967) 591, who says that μεριμνάω expresses an "intentness on something," or a "striving after something."

to married women, who must share their physical existence with another, unmarried women and virgins, he argues, can be "dedicated to Christ" (so the NEB) with all their resources, both spiritual and physical.[355] That Paul says this of single women but not single men suggests, furthermore, that the women in Corinth were concerned particularly about the burden of bearing and raising children.

Clearly, the logic of 7.32–5 runs parallel to the "Cynic" position on marriage, for as we saw in chapter two, Cynics as well as Stoics who held a Cynic position both opposed marriage inasmuch as attending to the needs of a marriage relationship compromised their commitment to philosophy. It is not simply the logic of this passage, however, that exhibits similarities with the Stoic–Cynic marriage debate, but also Paul's choice of words here. The most obvious case is ἀπερισπάστως, "without distraction," an adverb which appears at the end of 7.35. In chosing the adverbial form of this word, Paul has selected an exceptionally rare word indeed. Outside of Stoic authors and the Stoic-minded Clement of Alexandria, it occurs only four times in Greek literature before the third century – twice in Polybius and twice in the papyri.[356] Among the Stoics it appears once in Epictetus, in a discussion of contemplative philosophy, and

---

[355] So also Bachmann, *Der erste Brief*, 287. Neither chastity, virginity, nor abstinence is the goal here; see Heinrici, *Der erste Brief*, 244; Juncker, *Ethik*, 2.183–91; Tischleder, *Wesen und Stellung*, 95–7. The expression "holy in body," in turn, probably stems from the Corinthians; see Barrett, *Commentary on the First Epistle*, 181:

> The unmarried woman's special aim is presumably therefore to be holy not only in spirit but in body; she wishes to sanctify her body by abstinence from sexual relations. But this is not consistent with Paul's teaching in general, for he believes that all Christians, married or unmarried, must be holy in body . . . Moreover, in the present chapter he has told married men and women that through their marriage they *sanctify* their unbelieving partners, and that the children born of these marriages are *holy*. We must conclude therefore that in *that she may be holy both in body and in spirit* we have words quoted from the Corinthian ascetical party. Paul approves the sentiment, though he would not himself confine it to the unmarried. [his emphasis]

Characteristically, Niederwimmer, *Askese und Mysterium*, 115 insists that "holy in body" represents the ideal of unviolated continence, and that this is "evidently the view of the apostle."

[356] Polybius 2.20.10; 4.18.6; on the papyri see Ceslas Spicq, *Notes de lexicographie néo-testamentaire*, Orbis Biblicus et Orientalis 22/1 (Fribourg: Éditions Universitaires/Göttingen: Vandenhoeck und Ruprecht, 1978) 1.123 and n. 2. Bonhöffer, *Epiktet und das Neue Testament*, 108, 135 calls ἀπερισπάστως "a Hellenistic word particularly beloved of the Stoics."

once in Marcus Aurelius;[357] and in Clement's *Stromateis* it appears three times. Since none of the occurrences in Clement relate directly to 1 Corinthians 7.35, moreover, Clement's propensity for this word points to his interest in Stoic philosophy rather than a reliance on Paul.[358] Also significant is the fact that the adjectival form, ἀπερί-σπαστος, occurs in both Antipater's and Epictetus' discussions of marriage. The former claims that a man must marry in order to remain "undistracted,"[359] while the latter teaches that the Cynic must avoid marriage so as to be "undistracted," giving himself "wholly to the service of God" (ὅλον πρὸς τῇ διακονίᾳ τοῦ θεοῦ).[360] As many scholars have observed, this last phrase is materially very close to Paul's expression, "undistracted devotion to the Lord" (εὐπάρεδρον τῷ κυρίῳ ἀπερισπάστως).[361] Finally, Epictetus, Hiero-

[357] Epict. *Diss.* 1.29.58–9; Marcus Aurelius 3.6. It is also found as a variant reading for ἀπεριστάτως ("without special circumstances") in Arius' account of Stoic ethics (v.l. at Stob. 2.86.16 W.-H.).

[358] Clem. Alex. *Strom.* bk. 3, chap. 6.53.3 (2.220.20–4 S.), where Clement denies the gnostic claim that marriage is evil, saying that some of the apostles travelled with wives, devoting themselves "undistractedly" to preaching; *Strom.* bk. 4, chap. 25.157.2 (2.318.5–7 S.), where he states that faith joins a Christian "inseparably" to Christ; and *Strom.* bk. 7, chap. 3.13.3 (3.10.23–6 S.), where, drawing on Plato *Rep.* 613B, Clement explains that the true gnostic brings himself and his followers into a passionless state εἰς ἀπάθειαν through "uninterrupted" communion with the Lord.

[359] Antip. *SVF* 3.256.33–257.10 (Stob. 4.511.15–512.7 W.-H.). Noted by Bon-höffer, *Epiktet und das Neue Testament*, 108 (cf. Balch, "Stoic Debates," 432). Cf. Clement's interpretation of 1 Cor. 7.29b, where he says that Paul intended marriage to be "free from passion" (ἀπροσπαθής) as well as "undistracted" from love for the Lord (*Strom.* bk. 7, chap. 11.64.2 [3.46.6–8 S.]). For other instances of Clement's use of the adjective in a philosophical context see *Strom.* bk. 2, chap. 2.9.3 (2.117.19–20 S.), where, in Stoic fashion, Clement explains that knowledge relies on an "unwavering power of decision" (ἀπερίσπαστος προαίρεσις); and *Strom.* bk. 6, chap. 10.82.4 (2.473.7–8 S.), where he speaks of the gnostic's "continual" use of Greek philosophy.

[360] Epict. *Diss.* 3.22.69. The adjective also occurs in Sirach 41.1 and Wisdom 16.11, but nowhere else in the Bible. In the Apostolic Fathers, Ignatius' use of the adjective at *Ephesians* 20.2, in his demand that the Ephesians obey the bishop and presbytery "with an undistracted mind" (ἀπερισπάστῳ διανοίᾳ), may reflect the Stoic tradition found in Epict. *Diss.* 2.21.22, where Epictetus maintains that to study philosophy one must bring one's mind (διάνοια) undistracted to the class (ἀπερί-σπαστον . . . εἰς τὴν σχολήν). Regarding the issue at Corinth of physical autonomy versus the debt of conjugal relations owed to one's spouse, it is interesting to note that the adjective can also mean "without liability"; see POxy II 278.17–19 (no. 286; 82 CE): ". . . so that they may secure us without liability (ἀπερισπάστους) or difficulty with regard to the aforementioned debt (ὀφειλήν), and repay it (ἀποδώ-σειν)" also cited above, n. 36, re Paul's use of τὴν ὀφειλὴν ἀποδιδότω in 1 Cor. 7.3.

[361] Cf. *Sent. of Sextus* 230a, "Marriage He gives you to decline, so that you may live as a companion to God (ὡς πάρεδρος θεῷ)." This may be dependent on 1 Cor. 7.35, or both passages may be drawing on a common tradition.

cles, and Clement use several other words cognate with ἀπερι-σπάστως when discussing marriage. Epictetus speaks of a wife and children as something by which a man might "be distracted" (περι-σπᾶσθαι), and calls the activities of married life "distraction" and "busyness" (περισπασμόν/ἀσχολία).[362] Similarly, Hierocles refers to the "distractions" (περισπασμοί) of a householder's life in the city-state, although he says these are abated by a wife;[363] and Clement describes marriage as "distracting" someone from the things of God (μεταπερισπῶσα τῶν θείων) because of the busyness (ἀσχολία) involved .[364]

Along with chosing what may be considered a specialized term in Stoic philosophy, however, Paul has given ἀπερισπάστως a place of particular emphasis in his argument by putting it at the very end of verse 35, far removed from any verb. The emphatic positioning of this adverb is, in fact, so extreme that Paul has written a sentence that is almost incomprehensible on the basis of normal Greek usage. This was apparent in the fourth century to the great translator and exegete St. Jerome. Expressing dissatisfaction at his own Latin translation of 7.35, he exclaims, "The Latin words do not convey the meaning of the Greek. What words shall we use to render πρὸς τὸ εὔσχημον καὶ εὐπρόσεδρον [*sic*] τῷ κυρίῳ ἀπερισπάστως?"[365] We know also that Jerome's contemporary John Chrysostom solved the problem by simply removing the offending adverb from his text; and according to Jerome, Latin translators regularly omitted the entire clause.[366]

In recent times C. K. Barrett has repeated Jerome's judgement. Giving his own paraphrase of verse 35, Barrett confesses, "close translation is scarcely possible."[367] Other commentators have elected to clarify Paul's difficult syntax by rewriting it in Greek, or by suggesting the presence of an understood verb "to be." Lietz-mann, for example, proposes ἵνα καλοὶ πάρεδροι τοῦ κυρίου

[362] Epict. *Diss.* 4.1.159; 3.22.72.
[363] Hierocles 53.31–54.1 v.A. (Stob. 4.504.9 W.-H.), cited by Balch, "Stoic Debates," 435.
[364] Clem. Alex. *Strom.* bk. 3, chap. 9.67.1 (2.226.22–3 S., cited above, p. 177). See also *De vita contemp.* 1.1, where Philo describes the Therapeutae as "single-mindedly devoted to philosophical theory" (οἱ θεωρίαν ἀσπασάμενοι).
[365] Jerome *Adv. Jovin.* 1.13, trans. Fremantle in Schaff and Wace (eds.), *Select Library*, 357. In his exegesis of 1 Cor. 7, this is the only part of the text that Jerome deems necessary to cite in Greek.
[366] John Chrysostom *Homily 20 on 1 Corinthians* (*PG* 61.159); Jerome *Adv. Jovin.* 1.13.
[367] Barrett, *Commentary on the First Epistle*, 182.

ἀπερισπάστως γένησθε as the equivalent of Paul's τὸ ... εὐπάρε-δρον τῷ κυρίῳ ἀπερισπάστως;[368] and Billroth suggests that Paul has "added ἀπερισπάστως as if εἶναι had been employed,"[369] a notion that seems to have inspired the reading εἶναι ἀπερισπάστους in the second-century manuscript 𝔓[15].[370]

The best explanation for Paul's syntax in 7.35 is given (somewhat cryptically) by Blass and Debrunner, who propose that the adverb ἀπερισπάστως modifies the verbal aspect of εὐπάρεδρον, "devo-tion," a noun formed from the verb (εὐ)παρεδρεύω, "to sit beside."[371] In Latin this noun would be classified as a *gerundium*, and its modification by an adverb would be a fairly common syntax. For Greek, however, this construction is extremely rare.[372] On the basis of these observations, it appears that in selecting the rare adverb ἀπερισπάστως, and in placing it in a position of unusual emphasis, Paul has not only employed something of a Stoic watchword, but has used it in a rather dramatic way as the capstone of his discussion in 7.32–5.

Aside from ἀπερισπάστως, several other words in 7.32–5 may indicate a connection between this passage and either Stoic thought or the general philosophical milieu of the Stoic–Cynic marriage debate. One of these is the verb ἀρέσκω, "to please," which Paul uses three times in verses 32–4 in the sense of "pleasing the Lord" and "pleasing one's spouse." This word also occurs in Antipater and Epictetus, the latter claiming that a philosopher must be able to maintain his marital relation with spiritual composure (ἀταράχως) and at the same time "please God"; the former stating that the entire "goal and purpose" of a wife's existence is to "please her husband."[373]

---

[368] Lietzmann, *An die Korinther*, 35.
[369] Billroth, *A Commentary on the Epistles of Paul,* 1.202.
[370] Forming an *inclusio* with 7.32, ἀμερίμνους εἶναι. See also next note.
[371] Blass and Debrunner, *Greek Grammar*, 63 (§117.1). Cf. Rückert and Wahl, who paraphrase 7.35 as τὸ ... (εὐ)παρεδρεύειν τῷ κυρίῳ ἀπερισπάστως (Rückert, *Der erste Brief*, 208; Christian Abraham Wahl, *Clavis Novi Testamenti Philologica*, 3rd edn. [Leipzig: Joh. Ambros. Barth, 1834] 210, s.v. "εὐπάρεδρος").

[372] The one other example in the NT that I am aware of is 1 Tim. 4.3, "... for reception with thanksgiving" (εἰς μετάλημψιν μετὰ εὐχαριστίας), where "with thanksgiving" modifies the verbal aspect of "reception."

[373] Epict. *Diss.* 2.14.8, 12; Antip. *SVF* 3.255.22–3 (Stob. 4.509.1–2 W.-H.). The word also has a place in Pythagorean discourse on marriage. In *Melissa to Cleareta* (late first-early second century CE) the author says that a wife must hold it as an unwritten law to please her husband by fulfilling his wishes (3.2.19–22 T.); and Stobaeus records this anecdote about Theano: "Being asked what would be fitting for a wife (τί πρέπον εἴη γυναικί), Theano said, 'Pleasing her own husband (τὸ τῷ ἰδίῳ

In 7.35 Paul assures the Corinthians that his advice not to marry is for their "benefit," πρὸς ... τὸ σύμφορον. Although a common term in deliberative rhetoric, σύμφορον and the cognate verb συμφέρω, "to benefit," were also popular among the Stoics.[374] Thus [Ocellus] speaks of the importance of forming marriages with the "benefit of the community" in mind (πρὸς τὸ συμφέρον τῷ κοινῷ).[375] Musonius describes the lawgivers' encouragement of procreation as "good and beneficial" (καλὸν καὶ συμφέρον).[376] And Hierocles champions marriage as something both "beneficial" (σύμφορον) and profitable.[377] Paul, of course, has taken the opposite, "Cynic" view, arguing that avoiding marriage is beneficial.[378]

Again, in 7.32–4 Paul uses words from the μέριμνα- stem five times in an elaborate play-on-words, or *paronomasia*, with the verb μερίζομαι, "to be divided" (verse 34a). These are the adjective ἀμέριμνος, usually translated "without care" (verse 32), and the verb μεριμνάω, "to care, be concerned about something" (verses 32, 33, 34 [twice]). While words from this stem are common in early Christian literature, especially in the synoptic gospels, they also occur in documents relating to the philosophical discussion of marriage. Hierocles uses the noun μέριμνα in speaking of the "cares" of the busy householder;[379] and it occurs in a popular line

ἀρέσκειν ἀνδρί)"' (Stob. 4.587.8–10 W.-H.). Beyond this, while Musonius does not use this particular word, the concept of spouses pleasing one another plays an important role in his understanding of marriage; see Mus. *frag.* 3.40.25–8 and 42.5–9 L. (11.1–5 and 11.20–12.2 H.), *frag.* 13A.88.17–29 L. (68.6–7 H.), and *frag.* 14.94.2–19. (73.17–75.5 H.).

374 See Konrad Weiss, "φέρω," *TDNT* 9 (1974) 72–3; and Margaret M. Mitchell, *Paul and the Rhetoric of Reconciliation: An Exegetical Investigation of the Language and Composition of 1 Corinthians* (Louisville, Ky.: Westminster/John Knox, 1991) 33–4. Arius in Stob. 2.100.15–23 W.-H. says the Stoics considered συμφέρον another term for "virtue," ἀρετή. In Paul, words from the συμφερ- root occur only in the Corinthian correspondence, and mostly in 1 Cor. (1 Cor. 6.12; 7.35; 10.23, 33; 12.7; 2 Cor. 8.10; 12.1). In Matt. 19.10, in light of Jesus' ruling on divorce, the disciples conclude, "it is not beneficial to marry" (οὐ συμφέρει γαμῆσαι); see our analysis of this passage, above, p. 98.

375 [Ocell.] *De univ. nat.* 48.

376 Mus. *frag.* 15.96.25 L. (15A.78.4–5 H.). Theon *Progym.* 125.15 S. uses the same phrase. Cf. n. 378.

377 Hierocles 53.20, 25 v.A. (Stob. 4.503.18, 504.1 W.-H.). Cf. 54.14 v.A. (Stob. 4.505.4 W.-H.), "most profitable," λυσιτελέσατος.

378 Note that Theon *Progym.* 125.15–20 S. (cited above, chap. 2, n. 107) explains that in making a case for having children one will demonstrate, among other things, that marriage is "beneficial" (συμφέρον), while in refuting this *thesis* one will draw on the *opposite* arguments (ἐκ τῶν ἐναντίων).

379 Hierocles 53.30 v.A. (Stob. 4.504.7 W.-H.), cited by Balch, "Stoic Debates," 431, correcting Rudolf Bultmann, "μεριμνάω," 590, who states that the

from one of Menander's plays advising the character Parmenon that marriage "brings many cares to one's life" (μερίμνας τῷ βίῳ πολλὰς φέρει).[380] The adjective ἀμέριμνος, in turn, appears both in the epigram by Posidippus that we cited above,[381] and in a maxim attributed to Menander: "Do not say that a wife has a life free from care" (βίος ἀμέριμνος [ἢν γυναικὶ μὴ λαλῇς).[382] Especially interesting in this respect is Luke 10.38–42, which I suggested in chapter two also shows influence of the Stoic–Cynic marriage debate.[383] Here, in Luke's description of Martha's "concern" for the duties of a householder, we find not only the verb form μεριμνάω, together with the verb περισπάομαι, "to be distracted," which is cognate with Paul's ἀπερισπάστως, but also a description of Mary sitting at Jesus' feet, listening to his words (παρακαθεσθεῖσα πρὸς τοὺς πόδας τοῦ κυρίου ἤκουεν τὸν λόγον αὐτοῦ), in which some scholars see a dramatization of Paul's notion of "undistracted devotion to the Lord" (εὐπάρεδρον τῷ κυρίῳ ἀπερισπάστως).[384]

Finally, Paul's use of *paronomasia* in 7.32–4 may itself point to Stoic influence. It is well known that Stoics often used etymologies or even simple assonance between words (i.e., false etymologies) to uncover the religious, moral, and metaphysical truths that they

---

word "is not found in the Stoa." Plutarch's remark (*Mor.* 830A [*De vit. aere ali.*]) that freedom from care (ἡ ἀμεριμνία) is the benefit of poverty may also be inspired by its Stoic context (829F, 830B-D). See also *Cynic Ep. of Anacharsis* 3 (40.6 M.), which admonishes the tyrant Hipparchus to turn from his drunkenness to a life concerned with the proper things, βίος μεριμνητικός.

[380] Menander *frag.* 575 Körte (in Stob. 4.517.12–14 W.-H.), cited Wettstein, *Novum Testamentum Graecum*, 2.129.

[381] Posidippus in *Grk. Anth.* 9.359, "You have a marriage? – you will not be without cares (οὐκ ἀμέριμνος)!" (see p. 161); cited in this connection by Weiß, *Korintherbrief*, 201 n. 6.

[382] Menander *Sent.* Pap. 14.17 Jaekel.

[383] See above, pp. 98–100.

[384] E.g., Weiß, *Korintherbrief*, 205; Robertson and Plummer, *Critical and Exegetical Commentary*, 158; Niederwimmer, *Askese und Mysterium*, 113 n. 162; and Wolbert, *Ethische Argumentation*, 200–1 n. 76. Félix Puzo, "Marta y María: Nota exegética a Lc 10,38–42 y 1 Cor. 7,29–35," *Estudios Eclesiásticos* 34 (1960) 856 has noted, furthermore, that Jesus' statement in Luke 10.42, that Mary has chosen "the good portion (μερίς)," uses a word cognate with Paul's "to be divided" (μερίζομαι), which is integral to the *paronomasia* in 1 Cor. 7.34. Likewise, Jutta Brutscheck, *Die Maria-Marta-Erzählung: Eine redaktionskritische Untersuchung zu Lk 10, 38–42*, Bonner Biblische Beiträge 64 (Frankfurt/Bonn: Peter Hanstein, 1986) 147 points out that Jesus reprimands Martha in Luke 10.41 not because she is concerned with worldly things, but because these concerns distract her from Jesus' teaching: she, like the married man of 1 Cor. 7.33–4, is "divided." It is also possible that Paul's use of μεριμνάω, etc. has an apocalyptic bent; see above, n. 68.

believed were hidden in words.[385] With regard specifically to the
marriage discussions, furthermore, we know that Antipater was
familiar with the derivation of "bachelor" (ἤθεος) from "godlike"
(ἰσόθεος),[386] while Aelius Herodianus saw a connection between
"male" (ἄρσην) and the verbs "to give drink" (ἄρδω) and "to
water" (ἔρδω), reasoning that the male "waters" the female and her
offspring.[387] With his use of assonance in verses 32–4 Paul is
employing this same method to draw a connection between the ideas
of "cares" (μεριμνα-) and "being divided" (μερίζομαι). The "truth"
he intends to reveal through this word play is that Christians with
too many worldly cares are divided in their allegiance to Christ.[388]

### 7. Good and better, sin and blessedness: 1 Corinthians 7.36–40

In the last verses of chapter seven Paul addresses the men who are
evidently the prospective husbands of "the virgins" (verses 25ff.),[389]
and he advises widows concerning remarriage. To the men, Paul
says in verses 36–8:

---

[385] See Heymann Steinthal, *Geschichte der Sprachwissenschaft bei den Griechen
und Römern mit besonderer Rücksicht auf die Logik*, 2nd edn. (Berlin: Ferd.
Dümmler, 1890) 1331–2; and Karl Barwick, *Probleme der stoischen Sprachlehre und
Rhetorik*, Abhandlungen der sächsischen Akademie der Wissenschaften zu Leipzig:
Philologisch-historische Klasse 49/3 (Berlin: Akademie, 1957) 60. On Stoic interest in
etymology generally, see Barwick, *Probleme*, 29–33, 58–69, 70–9; and Ilona Opelt,
"Etymologie," *RAC* 6 (1966) 802–4. Bultmann, *Der Stil der paulinischen Predigt*, 76
suggests that the *paronomasia* here has come into Paul's writing via the Stoic–Cynic
diatribe.
[386] Antip. *SVF* 3.255.35–256.2 (Stob. 4.509.15–19 W.-H.). This etymology was
also known to Gavius Bassus (fl. mid first century BCE), who, in addition, is said to
have derived "bachelors" (*caelibes*) from "gods" (*caelites*), noting that both groups
live carefree (Quintilian 1.6.36). Richard Reitzenstein, "Etymologika," *PW* 6.1,
half-vol. 11 (1907) 809 sees Stoic influence in this last etymology, due to its use of
word compounds.
[387] From his *On Marriage and Life Together*, cited in *Etymologicum Magnum*, s.v.
"ἄρσην."
[388] For this same theme elsewhere in early Christianity see Mark 4.19 par.; Matt.
6.25–34; Luke 21.34–6; and Bultmann, "μεριμνάω," 590–3. In Paul the adjective
ἀμέριμνος occurs only here; the verb μερίζω only in the Corinthian correspondence,
two of those occurrences being here and 1 Cor. 7.17 (the others are 1 Cor. 1.13 and 2
Cor. 10.13); and the verb μεριμνάω, which appears four times here, appears elsewhere only at 1 Cor. 12.25; Phil. 2.20; 4.6. The noun μέριμνα is found in Paul only at
2 Cor. 11.28.
[389] The exact relationship between these men and their virgins remains a matter of
controversy among scholars; see above, chap. 1, n. 131.

If someone thinks he is acting unseemly (ἀσχημονεῖν) toward his virgin, if he should be over the limit (ὑπέρ-ακμος) and it must be thus (καὶ οὕτως ὀφείλει γίνεσθαι), he should do what he wants (ὃ θέλει ποιείτω), he does not sin (οὐχ ἁμαρτάνει), they should marry. But he who stands firm in his heart, not having necessity (μὴ ἔχων ἀνάγκην), but has power (ἐξουσία) over his own will, and has decided this in his own heart, to keep his own virgin, he will do well (καλῶς ποιήσει). So both he who marries his own virgin does well (καλῶς ποιεῖ), and he who does not marry will do better (κρεῖσσον ποιήσει).

Then to the widows, Paul says in verses 39–40 that a woman, in his opinion, is "more blessed" (μακαριωτέρα) if she remains a widow, although she is free to marry whom she wants, as long as the man is a Christian ("only in the Lord").

Depending on how we interpret this difficult section, we may identify several elements that could indicate Stoic influence. As in 7.28, it appears that Paul again finds it necessary to distinguish between Stoic and Christian notions of sin, reassuring the men that even in adverse circumstances (verse 26) one commits no *moral* error in marrying his virgin. Further, if we understand ἀσχημονεῖν ("to act unseemly"), ὑπέρακμος ("over the limit"), and οὕτως ὀφείλει γίνεσθαι ("it must be thus") in a sexual sense, then we have the same rationale for marriage as we saw in 7.9, and for which we have a parallel in Epictetus.[390] Epictetus, as we remember, justifies Crates' marriage to Hipparchia on account of Crates' "passionate love" for her (ἐξ ἔρωτος).[391] Perhaps also relevant here is a short epigram in the *Greek Anthology* in which Crates confesses that when neither hunger nor time can quell love's "flame" (φλόξ, cf. 7.9), one's remaining remedy is the "noose" (βρόχος).[392] In verse 35 it is precisely this "noose" (βρόχος) that Paul denies applying to the Corinthians' necks in advising the virgins not to marry. This is the only occurrence of βρόχος in the New Testament.

Again, Paul's use of ἀσχημονεῖν, "to act unseemly," may in itself point in the direction of Stoic and Cynic philosophy, for as Bon-höffer has noted, this served as one of the Stoics' "favorite expres-

---

[390] Alternately, ὑπέρακμος could be interpreted as referring to the virgin being "over marriageable age." On the difficulties in translating this word, see Bauer, *Greek-English Lexion*, 839 (s.v. "ὑπέρακμος").

[391] Epict. *Diss.* 3.22.76.

[392] *Grk. Anth.* 9.479, θεραπεία σοι τὸ λοιπὸν ἠρτήσθω βρόχος.

sions."[393] This word and its cognates occur several times in the *Cynic Epistles*, Musonius, Dio Chrysostom, and Epictetus,[394] while Paul, in good Stoic fashion, speaks of male homosexuality as ἡ ἀσχημοσύνη, "shamefulness," in Romans 1.27.[395] In 1 Corinthians 7.35–6, moreover, as part of the transition from his topic in verses 32–5 to that in verses 36–8, Paul contrasts ἀσχημονεῖν with τὸ εὔσχημον, "that which is seemly." This same antithesis between what is seemly and what is unseemly or shameful is also found in the *Cynic Epistles of Crates* and in Epictetus;[396] and it recurs in 1 Corinthians 12.23–4, in a metaphor depicting the church as a human body, which, in all likelihood, Paul has taken over from Stoic philosophy.[397] As for τὸ εὔσχημον, Arius reports that the Stoics saw "seemly living" (τὸ εὐσχημόνως ζῆν) as a source of well-being,[398] and they sometimes referred to "correct actions" (τὰ κατορθώματα) as "seemly actions" (εὐσχημονήματα).[399] Finally, in Paul's stipulation that widows remarry "only in the Lord," we are reminded of the concerns he addresses in 7.12–24 regarding Christians living with non-Christian spouses, which, as we saw, have counterparts among the Stoics.[400]

Beyond these points, Paul's manner of expression throughout 7.36–40 appears to draw on language and concepts that the Stoics used to describe the wise and good man. We may illustrate this through a comparison with a passage from Philo's treatise *That Every Good Man is Free*, where he presents three syllogistic proofs in support of his thesis:

> He who does everything with discernment does everything well (εὖ ποιεῖ πάντα). He who does everything well, does everything correctly. He who does everything correctly also acts without sin (ἀναμαρτήτως) ... such that he will have power to do everything and live as he wants (ὥστ᾽ ἐξουσίαν σχήσει πάντα δρᾶν καὶ ζῆν ὡς βούλεται). To whom these

---

[393] Bonhöffer, *Epiktet und das Neue Testament*, 135; cf. 109 and n. 1.
[394] E.g., Epict. *Diss.* 3.22.2, 8, 15, 52. In 3.22.15 (cited in this connection by Heinrici, *Das erste Sendschreiben*, 213 n. 1), Epictetus maintains that unless the Cynic puts his sexual life in order, he will disgrace himself (ἀσχημονέω) before his public.
[395] Cf. Mus. *frag.* 12.86.3, 8–10 L. (64.4–7 H.).
[396] *Cynic Ep. of Crates* 10 (62.4–5 M.); Epict. *Diss.* 2.5.23; cf. 4.9.5, 8–9.
[397] See Conzelmann, *1 Corinthians*, 211 and n. 8 (lit.).
[398] Arius in Stob. 2.80.10–11, ἐν ᾧπέρ ἐστιν τὸ εὐδαιμόνως [sc. ζῆν].
[399] Arius in Stob. 2.97.5–9 W.-H.
[400] In line with this, Thrall, "The Problem of II Cor. vi. 14–vii. 1," 134–5, 147–8 suggests a correspondence between 1 Cor. 7.39 and 2 Cor. 6.14a.

things are allowed (ἔξεστιν), he would be free ... Again,
the man whom it is not possible to compel or impede (μήτ᾽
ἀναγκάσαι μήτε κωλῦσαι), this one would not be a slave
(δοῦλος). It is not possible to compel or impede the good
man. Therefore the good man is not a slave ... Again, if he
is compelled (ἀναγκάζεται), it is clear that he does something unwillingly. But...⁴⁰¹ actions are either correct
actions (κατορθώματα) from virtue, or sins (ἁμαρτήματα)
from vice, or middle things and indifferents (μέσα καὶ ἀδιά-
φορα). Those from virtue, he is not forced but does will-
ingly... Those from vice – from these he flees, nor does he
do them in his dreams. Neither [is he forced to do] indifferent things, naturally, toward which his mind is in equi-
librium ... Wherefore it is clear that he does nothing
unwillingly, nor is he compelled. But if he were a slave he
would be compelled; and hence the good man will be
free.⁴⁰²

From this passage we can see that just as Philo describes the wise
man as doing all things well (εὖ ποιεῖ πάντα),⁴⁰³ having power
(ἐξουσία) to act,⁴⁰⁴ and not being compelled (ἀναγκάζομαι)⁴⁰⁵ in
any way, not even with regard to "indifferent" things, so Paul
describes the man who does not marry as doing well (καλῶς
ποιέω),⁴⁰⁶ having power (ἐξουσία) over his own will, and having no
necessity (ἀνάγκη) to marry – an act, as we saw earlier, that Stoics
considered to be an "indifferent."⁴⁰⁷ Likewise, just as Philo presents
his wise man as acting without sin (ἀναμαρτήτως)⁴⁰⁸ and at the

---

⁴⁰¹ The text is unclear at this point.

⁴⁰² Philo *Quod omnis probus* 59–61.

⁴⁰³ See also Arius in Stob. 2.66.14–67.2 W.-H. (*SVF* 3.148.37–149.1); *SVF* 1.53.14; and D.L. 7.125.

⁴⁰⁴ See also D.L. 7.121 (cited above, p. 153), where freedom is defined by the Stoics as "power of independent action" (ἐξουσία αὐτοπραγίας).

⁴⁰⁵ See also Philo *Quod omnis probus* 30, 61; Arius in Stob. 2.99.19–20 W.-H. (*SVF* 1.53.3 and 3.150.10–11); and Cicero *De fin.* 3.26 (*SVF* 3.153.17).

⁴⁰⁶ Paul's use of καλῶς instead of εὖ is in line with the general tendency among New Testament authors to favor the former over the latter, and in this case may have been further prompted by the catchword in 7.1, 26 "it is good for a man" (καλὸν ἀνθρώπῳ). According to Arius, Stoics considered τὸ καλῶς ζῆν to be the equivalent of τὸ εὖ ζῆν (Stob. 2.78.1–2 W.-H.). Interestingly, Mark 7.37 says that Jesus was praised as one who "has done all things well" (καλῶς πάντα πεποίηκεν).

⁴⁰⁷ The presence of both Stoic and apocalyptic (7.26) meanings of ἀνάγκη in 1 Cor. 7 is still further evidence that the Corinthians have blended these two realms of thought.

⁴⁰⁸ See also Arius in Stob. 2.99.7–8; 2.109.7; 2.112.20 (*SVF* 1.52.29–30; 3.163.12; 3.147.16–17); Epict. *Diss.* 4.8.6; and D.L. 7.122.

same time living as he wants (ζῆν ὡς βούλεται), so Paul tells the man who marries that he should do what he wants (ὃ θέλει ποιείτω),[409] he does not sin (οὐχ ἁμαρτάνει), but rather, like the man who remains single, he does well (καλῶς ποιέω).[410] On the other hand, we may assume from what Paul says in verse 36 that the man who marries, unlike the man who remains single, does "have necessity." This, however, would also have been possible to reconcile with the Stoic understanding of the wise man, for, according to Epictetus, passionate love was a "special circumstance" (περίστασις) that could compel a Cynic even as great as Crates to marry.[411] As Epictetus explains elsewhere, "one would consider even more worthy of pardon the man who is compelled by passion (τὸν ὑπ' ἔρωτος ἀναγκαζόμενον) to do something contrary to what seems proper – seeing the better thing but being powerless to pursue it – for he is held back by something forceful, and in some sense divine."[412]

Regarding the widows in 7.39–40, Paul's statement that a woman "is free to marry whom she wants (ἐλευθέρα ἐστὶν ᾧ θέλει γαμηθῆναι) ultimately derives, as we have seen, from the legal formulae of divorce documents.[413] Even so, Paul may have selected this particular turn of phrase because, once again, it resembles the Stoic claim that the wise man is free, since, as Philo says, "he has the power to do everything ... as he wants" (ἐξουσίαν σχήσει πάντα δρᾶν ... ὡς βούλεται). Similarly, there is a possibility that Paul's judgement of a widow who remains single as "more blessed" (μακαριωτέρα) reflects the Stoic dogma that the good and wise man is

---

[409] Even closer to Paul than Philo's phrase is one from Dio Chrys. *Or.* 14.16 (*SVF* 3.87.2–3): "it is allowed to [the discerning] to do as they want" (ἐξεῖναι αὐτοῖς ποιεῖν ὡς ἐθέλουσι).

[410] Stoics also spoke of not sinning as the counterpart of doing well: Arius in Stob. 2.99.7–12; 2.102.20–103.1 (*SVF* 1.52.29–32; 3.149.16–22); 2.106.6–11; and *SVF* 2.41.24–5.

[411] Epict. *Diss.* 3.22.76, just cited regarding 7.36. See also *Cynic Ep. of Crates* 35 (88.4–5, 12 M.), where Crates is depicted as advising his friend Aper not to flee necessity (ἀνάγκη), which includes living with a body (ἀνάγκη μὲν γὰρ ζῆν μετὰ σώματος).

[412] Epict. *Diss.* 4.1.147. The divine origin of passionate love to some extent explains the contradiction between what Epictetus says concerning Crates and his statement in *Diss.* 3.13.10–11 that the teachings of the philosophers (ὁ λόγος ὁ τῶν φιλοσόφων) give one peace even from eros. Not surprisingly, there is some discussion among Stoics as to whether the wise man will fall in love. See *SVF* 3.164.1–15; 3.180.13–181.30; Epict. *Diss.* 2.21.7; D.L. 7.113; and Sen. *Ep.* 116.5; 123.15; cf. D.L. 10.117–20 (Epicurus).

[413] See above, n. 162.

"blessed" (μακάριος).[414] This term is also found in popular maxims about marriage. A line from Menander reads, "... and a thing which they call blessed, I take no wife";[415] and one from Euripides runs: "Blessed is he, whoever marries and obtains a good wife; and he who does not marry."[416]

In all, with verses 36–40 Paul appears to be ending his discussion on marriage with an effort to reconcile himself to his Stoic-minded audience. Whatever they decide on the question of marriage, Paul is suggesting, they will be acting as wise men and women, even if their decisions should contradict his own best judgement (see verses 25–6). Yet, in giving his congregation this latitude, Paul makes his own preference clear enough. Although the man who marries "does well," he says, the one who does not marry "will do *better*,"[417] and the widow who forgoes a second marriage is "*more* blessed."[418] He then underscores this position with the closing remark, "– and I, for my part, think that I have the Spirit of God."[419]

[414] See Arius in Stob. 2.100.3–5 (*SVF* 1.53.9 and 3.150.16); Cicero *De fin.* 3.31 (*SVF* 1.92.20); Philo *De praemiis* 122 (cited above, chap. 2, n. 199); and *SVF* 3.154.3; 3.188.15; 3.190.11–20.

[415] Menander *frag.* 3 K. (from *Brothers*, bk. 2), χὢ μακάριόν φα < σιν >, γυναῖκ' οὐ λαμβάνω.

[416] Euripides in Stob. 4.525.16–526.1 W.-H., μακάριος, ὅστις εὐτυχεῖ γάμον λαβὼν ἐσθλῆς γυναικός· εὐτυχεῖ δ' ὁ μὴ λαβών. See also Eur. *Orestes* 602–4 (Stob. 4.528.1–4 W.-H.). The term μακάριος is seldom in Paul. Outside of the comparative in 1 Cor. 7.40, it occurs in Rom. 4.7, 8, and 14.22, the first two instances being quotations from Ps 32.1–2, and the third inspired by the situation in Corinth (cf. 1 Cor. 8.7–13; 10.27–11.1). There is a possibility that in 7.40 the term also has apocalyptic overtones. See Luke 23.29, "Blessed (μακάριαι) are the sterile and the wombs that never conceived and breasts that never nursed"; and the discussion of the eschatological aspects of this word in Friedrich Hauck, "μακάριος, D.1," *TDNT* 4 (1967) 367–9.

[417] Cf. Epictetus' description of the man compelled by love as one who sees "the better thing" (τὸ ἄμεινον), but is unable to do it (*Diss.* 4.1.147, just cited).

[418] This use of the comparative may have been occasioned, in part, by a maxim such as the one just cited from Euripides, which pronounces both the unmarried and the married "blessed." See also *Cynic Ep. of Crates* 35 (88.4–6, 15–17 M.), where Crates says that the one who recognizes necessity (ἀνάγκη) and does it is "the blessed man" (ὁ μακάριος ἀνήρ).

[419] Or, "– and I also think that I have the Spirit of God," which, as noted above, is a Christian counterpart to Paul's Stoic-like claim of trustworthiness in 7.25. The very popular translation of 7.40b as "and I think *that I also* have the Spirit of God" (see, e.g., Weiß, *Korintherbrief*, 210; Lietzmann, *An die Korinther*, 36, 37; Barrett, *Commentary on the First Epistle*, 186; and the Eng. trans. JB, NEB, REB, and NRSV) is grammatically impossible: κἀγώ, which is the nominative, goes with the verb δοκῶ; it cannot be construed with ἔχειν, as if it were the subject of the infinitive clause. This point is also noted by Robertson and Plummer, *Critical and Exegetical Commentary*, 161, but ignored, it would seem, by everyone else, in favor of the idea that Paul is battling "pneumatics" or spiritualistic gnostics in 1 Cor. 7, a theory we dismissed in chapter one.

# 4

## A NON-ASCETIC INTERPRETATION
## OF PAUL

Our investigation has now come full circle. It began, in chapter one, with an evaluation of recent scholarly attempts to define the theological motivation for celibacy in 1 Corinthians 7. As we saw, the vast majority of scholars today attribute to Paul and the Corinthians an ascetic way of thinking, although there is little agreement as to its provenance, and the arguments leading to this conclusion do not hold up well under critical scrutiny. Next, in chapter two, we examined a number of discussions on marriage and celibacy from the Hellenistic world that collectively constituted a debate between Stoic and Cynic moralists. Outlining the various positions represented in these discussions, we charted their historical development from pre-Hellenistic Greece, through their popularization in first-century Greece and Rome, to their limited acceptance by several church fathers in the second century, and their ultimate neglect by Christian theologians in subsequent centuries. Finally, in chapter three, we examined Paul's statements in 1 Corinthians 7 in light of these discussions, highlighting several parallels, both in argumentation and in manner of expression.

It is these latest findings that will occupy us in the present chapter. Rather than rehearse them in a typical summary fashion, however, I would like to explore their implications in a way that will clarify three important aspects of 1 Corinthians 7: (a) the identity of Paul's audience, (b) Paul's own understanding of marriage and celibacy, and (c) his place in the history of Christian asceticism. Briefly stated, I will argue that the theology of Paul's audience in 1 Corinthians 7 represents a syncretistic form of thinking that united popularized Stoic philosophy with apocalyptic and sapiential traditions. From this I will show that Paul's discussion in 1 Corinthians 7 is considerably more subtle and complex than scholars have hitherto perceived, and I will pursue my contention that Paul is far removed from any understanding of marriage based on the practice of sexual asceticism. Finally, challenging the place customarily assigned to Paul in the history of Christian asceticism, I will argue that Paul should be placed before and outside of this history, not within it as one of its founding fathers.

## 1. Paul's audience in 1 Corinthians 7

We must admit from the start that we have no direct information on the recipients of 1 Corinthians 7. What we have is indirect information in the form of Paul's statements to them. If we assume, however, that Paul accurately assessed the disposition of his readership and formulated his position accordingly – something we would expect from any successful administrator in the ancient world moderately acquainted with the basics of public discourse and rhetoric – we may nevertheless be able to reach some tentative conclusions as to who these Corinthians were.

Since our investigations in chapter three reveal that much of 1 Corinthians 7 bears a Stoic imprint, this would indicate that Paul's audience both understood and was receptive to Stoic ideas. They appear, for example, to be familiar with Stoic objections to close association with outsiders, as well as the correlate, that friendship is a partnership based on agreement of lifestyles (7.12–14). They also seem to acknowledge Stoic notions of true slavery and true freedom, which Paul has couched for them in diatribe style (18–19, 21–2; cf. 7.16, 27–8); and they may have been familiar with the Stoic ideal of mental and emotional detachment (7.29b–31a).

Beyond this, the Corinthians seem to have had a considerable appreciation for arguments current in the Stoic–Cynic marriage debate. The statement at the very beginning of 1 Corinthians 7, that sexual intercourse is not good for a man, which finds analogies in certain Cynic authors, was evidently part of the Corinthian argument against marriage, and may have come from their letter to Paul mentioned in 7.1a. The Corinthians also understand the argument used by some Stoics that forbade marriage in adverse circumstances due to the need for leisure time (7.5, 25–35). In Stoic fashion they questioned whether marriage in such situations was a sin (7.28, 36); and they appear to accept the Stoic claims that spouses have mutual ownership of each other's bodies (7.4), and that marriage is sometimes necessitated by the circumstance of passionate love (7.9, 36).

Not only does 1 Corinthians 7 suggest a knowledge of Stoic thought on the part of its recipients, however, it also suggests an appreciation for specialized Stoic vocabulary and phraseology. The expressions καλὸν ἀνθρώπῳ (7.1, 26), ὁμοίως δὲ καί (7.3–4), and the verb σχολάζω (7.5), all point in this direction, as do ἀμέριμνος and μεριμνάω (7.32–4), ἀρέσκω (7.33–4), σύμφορον, ἀπερισπάστως (7.35), the pair εὔσχημον/ἀσχημονέω (7.35–6), and the several expressions descriptive of the wise man in 7.36–40: ὃ θέλει ποιείτω, οὐχ ἁμαρτάνει, μὴ ἔχων ἀνάγκην, ἐξουσίαν ἔχει, καλῶς ποιέω, ἐλευθέρα ἐστὶν ᾧ θέλει γαμηθῆναι, μακαριωτέρα. As we have seen, it is even possible that the terms πιστός, ἄπιστος (7.12–15, 25), καλέω, κλῆσις (7.15–24), and the phrases τήρησις ἐντολῶν θεοῦ (7.19), τοῦτο δέ φημι, ὁ καιρὸς συνεσταλμένος ἐστίν, τὸ λοιπόν (7.29), and χρώμενοι ... ὡς μὴ καταχρώμενοι (7.31) also reflect a greater or lesser degree of Stoic flavoring in Paul's speech for the benefit of his audience.

To conclude that the Corinthians were Stoics, however, is too facile, for according to Paul, they identified themselves primarily as followers of Christ. This suggests a syncretistic or popularized form of Stoicism at Corinth, something that may also be indicated by the number of similarities between Paul's statements in 1 Corinthians 7 and popular maxims from the general philosophical milieu of the Hellenistic world – maxims attributed to Menander, Euripides, Plato, and Crates. Still another important aspect of this chapter is Paul's concern in 7.2, 5–6 for extra-marital sex, or *porneia*, which he combines with the Stoic notion of marital duty (7.3–5), and follows with the idea that continence is a gift from God (7.7). This, in turn, points to a Stoicism informed by Jewish wisdom traditions similar to what we find in Sirach and Philo. Lastly, we must account for the apocalyptic elements in 1 Corinthians 7, which we find in 7.5 (combined with Stoic concerns for marital duty and Judeo–Christian concerns for *porneia*) and in 7.26–31, where Paul employs "Stoic-like" apocalyptic materials as the "circumstances" of an essentially Stoic argument against marriage. Given that our closest parallel to 7.5 comes from the *Testament of Naphtali*, a Stoicism not unlike that which we have in the *Testaments of the Twelve Patriarchs*, which also draws on wisdom and apocalyptic ideas, suggests itself.

In sum, Paul's language and argumentation in 1 Corinthians 7 imply that the Corinthians to whom this chapter was addressed included Christians whose faith embodied a considerable degree of integration between Stoic and Judeo–Christian belief systems. If this conclusion is correct, it holds important implications both for

New Testament scholarship and for Classical studies. Regarding the latter, we may now add a new source to our limited store of information on late Stoicism. It is a source, moreover, with several attractive characteristics. It can be dated and geographically fixed with precision to the middle of the first century CE in Corinth. Being part of a Christian document, it represents an example of Stoic morality as adapted for use in a non-Stoic system of thought, thereby further documenting the popularization of Stoicism in the period of the Empire. And thirdly, it provides us with direct access to an actual controversy on marriage, thus distinguishing itself from the many theoretical treatments and descriptions of marriage discussions that we examined in chapter two. 1 Corinthians 7, it would appear, is our one surviving example of what was evidently a widespread, but otherwise strictly oral undertaking in the Hellenistic world.

As for New Testament scholarship, our conclusions about the identity of the recipients of 1 Corinthians 7 provide new options for understanding the Corinthian correspondence as a whole. By linking one of the interest groups at Corinth to Stoic tendencies within Christianity, our work here may enable scholars to clarify other sections of 1 and 2 Corinthians from this perspective. Research along these lines has the potential of dislodging time-honored theories of gnostic and enthusiastic influence at Corinth, as we have done in part in chapter one, thereby clearing the way for a new assessment of the dynamics of the Corinthian church and its historical development. Beyond this, our demonstration of Paul's own facility and willingness to work with Stoic systems of thought in 1 Corinthians 7 provides us with a valuable perspective on the cultural, rhetorical, and sociological aspects of his westward mission into Macedonia, Achaia, and Rome.

## 2. Paul's understanding of marriage and celibacy

### Preliminary considerations

Before we attempt to define Paul's position on marriage and celibacy, there are several initial matters we must address. From our identification of Paul's audience in 1 Corinthians 7 it is evident that this chapter cannot be read as a general statement on marriage and celibacy, as if it were a theological "position paper" intended for the church universal. Inasmuch as Paul has chosen to express himself in the Stoic idiom of his readers, both his logic and the details of his discussion have been shaped by the Corinthians' own moral sensibilities. For an audience elsewhere in Greece, or in Judea, Asia Minor, or Rome, Paul might have couched his understanding of marriage and celibacy in very different terms.

In assessing Paul's position we must, furthermore, take into account that 1 Corinthians 7 is part of an occasional letter written in response to a particular set of circumstances at Corinth. As we have seen, Paul's words presuppose that the Corinthians are in the grips of an economic or political crisis that potentially, at least, has apocalyptic import. Again, to a congregation not beset by these circumstances, or beset by a different set of circumstances, Paul's response may have – most certainly would have – looked substantially different. We are given some indication of this in his letter to the Romans, where apocalyptic expectations play a smaller role than in 1 Corinthians.[1] Here, in contrast to 1 Corinthians 7.8–9, 39–40, Paul's brief remarks on marriage and widowhood lack any preference for the celibate life.[2] We may also point to the letter of 1 Timothy, in which the author, presumably a follower of Paul, actually advises young widows to marry, his concern being the promotion of church order rather than battening down in anticipation of the end time tribulation.[3] To the extent, therefore, that part of what Paul says in 1 Corinthians 7 is eschatologically conditioned, it must be viewed as representing an "interim ethic."

Our investigations in the previous chapter also demonstrate that Paul is dealing with a variety of issues in 1 Corinthians 7. These include, among others, *being* married versus *becoming* celibate, *being* married to a non-Christian versus obtaining a divorce, *remaining* celibate versus *marrying* a Christian, and *marrying* a Christian versus *marrying* a non-Christian. This in turn should alert us, first of all, to the danger of construing any one statement in Paul's discussion as constituting his position "on marriage," as if his subject throughout were the institution of marriage *per se*. It should also alert us to the fact that Paul's treatment of marriage in 1 Corinthians 7 is not designed to cover everything. He gives no ruling, for example, regarding remarriage for Christians whose non-Christian husbands or wives have left them, nor is it clear that

[1] Only Rom. 13.11–14, which is paraenetic and much less urgent than 1 Cor. 1.7–8; 7.26–31; 15.51–8.
[2] Rom. 7.1–3.
[3] 1 Tim. 5.14.

his judgment limiting widows to marriage "only in the Lord" applies to all other Christians as well (see below).

The diversity of issues that Paul addresses in 1 Corinthians 7 has also put limitations on his discussion in another way. Inasmuch as he argues here in favor of marriage, here against it, here in favor of celibacy, here against it, he has effectively tied his hands as to what he can say. He does not want to set the value of marriage too high and thereby discourage all forms of celibacy, nor does he wish to praise celibacy unduly, thereby undermining the institution of marriage. To put the matter in a different light, Paul, as we have seen, selectively uses several arguments from the Stoic–Cynic marriage debate, both for and against marriage. To have availed himself of all the arguments current in this debate, however, would have required him to talk out of both sides of his mouth.

Hence, in 1 Corinthians 7 we find no laudation of the ends of marriage, nor does Paul enumerate for the Corinthians the advantages of having a wife to watch over one's household affairs. This also accounts for the absence of any direct mention of childbearing, a topic dear to many Stoics but anathema to those who took a Cynic stance against marriage.[4] Even though verses 4, 14, and 34 indicate that having children was a concern for the Corinthians, Paul never addresses the matter squarely. He says only that husbands and wives must maintain sexual relations to the degree that it is demanded by either partner – a sure recipe for pregnancy in the ancient world – and that unmarried women have the good fortune of being useful to the Lord with their bodies as well as their spirits. It cannot be simply that Paul considered childbearing a moot point in view of the possible nearness of the End, or that he passes over this subject because it was a Stoic topos directed at citizens for the purpose of increasing the population of their city-states, something for which Paul had little interest. This would not explain why, in promoting celibacy, he forgoes the Cynic argument that raising children is one of the onerous burdens of marriage, which would have coincided nicely with apocalyptic traditions on the hardship of pregnancy and nursing in the end times. Instead, Paul's silence on childbearing must be interpreted as a conscious avoidance of the subject, as its endorsement would have weakened his arguments in favor of celi-

---

[4] This absence has been noted by many scholars, e.g., Weiß, *Korintherbrief*, 172; Schrage, *Die konkreten Einzelgebote*, 220 n. 157; and Ward, "Musonius and Paul on Marriage," 286–7.

bacy, while a statement against it would have undercut what he has to say regarding the necessity of conjugal relations.[5]

Given the task Paul has set for himself, it is not at all surprising that much of what he says in support of marriage in 1 Corinthians 7 draws on the adverse consequences of prolonged celibacy. As Chadwick perceptively reasoned, "the chapter is wholly intelligible as a rearguard action."[6] Understandably, then, if somewhat ironically, the delicate balance of Paul's response to the Corinthians, achieved by so much judicious weighing of argument and counter argument, has been taken by the church fathers and modern interpreters alike as his pronouncement of damnation on marriage through faint praise.

In sum, the forgoing considerations require us to see Paul's statements on marriage and celibacy in 1 Corinthians 7 as the work of a practical church administrator who has entered the fray because certain activities at Corinth appeared detrimental to the Corinthians' faith. It is a mistake, in other words, to interpret his statements as if they were the deliberations of a systematic theologian formulating a general definition of Christian marriage. Although this puts certain limitations on our ability to gage Paul's own understanding of marriage and celibacy, it is nonetheless possible for us to draw conclusions on some specific matters. Let us begin with his understanding of marriage and celibacy for married Christians and then turn to his position on these subjects for single Christians.

### Marriage and celibacy for married Christians

Regarding marriage and celibacy for those already married, Paul assumes, first of all, that Christians will honor all obligations of their marriage relationships to the extent that it is possible. This is true even under the extreme and potentially apocalyptic conditions

---

[5] Cf. Yarbrough, *Not Like the Gentiles*, 107–8; and Chadwick, "'All Things to All Men'," 268: "A remarkable feature of the chapter as a whole is the startling absence of any appeal to the doctrine of Creation. But to have made any such appeal would have put an unmistakable and decisive distance between Paul and the ascetic party at Corinth, and this he was manifestly anxious to avoid."

[6] Chadwick, "'All Things to All Men'," 264. Cf. Heth, "Unmarried 'For the Sake of the Kingdom',"  69, "in all probability 1 Corinthians 7 is primarily a rehabilitation of the marital union in the eyes of the Corinthian ascetics"; and Brown, *Body and Society*, 54–5: "It had not been Paul's concern to praise marriage; he strove, rather, to point out that marriage was safer than unconsidered celibacy. Much of the letter [*sic*: chapter], therefore, consists of blocking moves."

that are presupposed throughout 1 Corinthians 7, whether that means enduring physical or emotional hardship (7.28, 29–31), or being divided in one's allegiances to the Lord (7.32–4). Sexual relations especially must continue so as to avoid unfaithfulness on the part of one of the spouses, even, presumably, if this results in the birth of children (7.3–7). Divorce is impossible, being a violation of Christ's commandment (7.10–11).[7]

On the other hand, Paul recognizes that within the limits of a person's capacity certain forms of devotion to Christ, such as prayer, can take precedence over sexual intercourse (7.5). Because the individual sexual needs of the marriage partners may differ, however, this must be done by mutual agreement for a set period of time. Paul rejects outright the extreme position he cites in 7.1b, that "it is good for a man not to touch a woman." The ability to remain abstinent, according to Paul, is a gift from God. It is not something that one spouse can demand of the other (7.7). Paul is a realist here, and assumes that extra-marital liaisons would be the result of such an ascetic experiment (7.5). Practically speaking, however, Paul also allows for the separation of a couple in order to accommodate the unwillingness of one of the partners (he mentions only the wife) to continue the marriage. But this separation may not evolve into a divorce (7.11).

Although certain members of the Corinthian church evidently maintained that marriages between Christians and non-Christians were a special case, and therefore required separate consideration, Paul contends that the same standards apply here as well. Having an unbelieving spouse is no grounds for divorce, he argues, even in times of hardship (7.12–13). There is nothing morally "unclean" about a non-Christian husband or wife; in fact, their marriage to a Christian has "sanctified" them (7.14). Neither is marriage to a non-Christian a form of slavery in any true, Christian sense (7.15, 17–24), and there is always the possibility that a Christian will convert his or her spouse (7.16). Thus, rather than seeking a divorce, a Christian should work to preserve the couple's original marital peace (7.12–13, 15). This is both a matter of keeping God's commandments and of recognizing the grace inherent in one's Christian

---

[7] Completely unsupported by the text is Brown's contention that "fornication and its avoidance did not preoccupy Paul greatly. He was concerned to emphasize, rather, the continuing validity of all social bonds" (*Body and Society*, 55, citing 1 Cor. 7.17, 21; cf. 54, 56–7).

call (7.15, 17–24). If the non-Christian decides to leave, however, that is his or her prerogative (7.15).

## Marriage and celibacy for single Christians

Just as some married Corinthians had argued that the threat of end time tribulations justified divorce or the cessation of conjugal relations, Paul sees these dire circumstances as an impediment to initiating new marriages. Paul's treatment of whether single Christians should marry or remain celibate is thus based wholly on the expediency of the times – and this cannot be stressed enough. As our investigation in chapter three has demonstrated, what Paul says in 7.27–8, in 7.29–31, in 7.32–5, and in 7.36–40 depends equally on the "necessity" (ἀνάγκη) that he speaks of in 7.26. To overlook this is to overlook the entire rationale of his argument.[8]

To discourage his readers from marrying in this time of crisis, Paul points out that harsh conditions foster material need, or "tribulation in the flesh," among the married (7.28). As a result, the positive aspects of married life such as sexual gratification and the ownership of goods are considerably reduced (7.29–31), while the responsibilities of marriage are made more difficult to fulfill. Those who marry will have concerns that divide their interests and draw them away from the Lord (7.32–4). Given the uncertainty of the times, Paul concludes, devotion to the Lord should take precedence over becoming married (7.35).

Yet Paul exercises caution in advocating this apocalyptically inspired celibacy. His words, he is careful to explain, do not represent a commandment of the Lord but the advice of a church leader who has sought guidance from the Holy Spirit (7.25, 40). If Christians feel that their sexual drives demand it, Paul concedes, they should go ahead with plans to marry, even in adverse circumstances (7.36). Here again Paul shows himself to be something of a realist with regard to sexuality. Nowhere does he make the absolute claim that celibacy under such conditions is "best." Instead, he reasons that while remaining single is "better" than subjecting oneself to almost certain hardship (7.28, 38), marrying is "better" than being overcome with sexual desire (7.9, cf. 7.36). In Paul's opinion, getting married, even in the worst of times, is ultimately an action that is

---

[8] This has been acknowledged by a few scholars, e.g., Schnackenburg, "Die Ehe nach dem Neuen Testament," 21, 23, 24; but it is more often denied, e.g., Niederwimmer, *Askese und Mysterium*, 111–13; Gager, "Functional Diversity," 331, 337.

morally commendable. Both the person who marries and the person who remains single "do well," and both are described as acting wisely (7.36–40).

Lastly, Paul leaves us with an elusive remark on Christians marrying non-Christians. In the case of widows, he says, such a marriage is out of the question. Widows may marry "only in the Lord" (7.39). Whether the same applies for other Christians, however, we cannot be sure. Passages such as 1 Corinthians 5.9–11; 7.12–14; 2 Corinthians 6.14–7.1, and similar texts from Jewish and Stoic authors allow us to speculate as to how some of the Corinthians might have answered this question, but nothing Paul himself says warrants the application of this rule beyond widows. Perhaps, given the opportunity, Paul would have extended this rule to cover other persons. It is also quite possible, however, that he saw widows, or even women in general, as a special case, reasoning that they were particularly susceptible to apostasy once they had been incorporated into a non-Christian household in patriarchal Greco-Roman society.[9]

### 3. Paul in the history of Christian asceticism

Coming finally to Paul's place in the history of Christian asceticism, it is essential for us to be in the clear regarding two findings that have emerged from this study. First, Paul's reason for both condoning and promoting celibacy at Corinth was to keep this congregation, during a period of severe tribulation, as free as possible from the distractions associated with married life in the ancient world. And second, his theological justification for this agenda depends almost entirely on Stoic and apocalyptic traditions of thought, neither of which denigrate human sexuality or espouse the renunciation of sexual relations as the goal of celibacy.[10] This means

---

[9] See, e.g., the discussion in Margaret Y. MacDonald, "Early Christian Women Married to Unbelievers," *Studies in Religion/Sciences Religieuses* 19 (1990) 221–34. For this reason it is also impossible to say whether the mixed marriages described in 7.12–13 were contracted (a) between two pagans, after which one of them converted to Christianity, (b) between a Christian and a pagan, or (c) between two Christians, after which one left the faith – especially since we do not know if the Corinthians had always known and followed Paul's rule.

[10] On this see Schrage, "Die Stellung zur Welt," 149–50 and n. 76; Rosemary Radford Ruether, "Is Celibacy Eschatological? The Suppression of Christian Radicalism," *Liberation Theology: Human Hope Confronts Christian History and American Power* (New York: Paulist Press, 1972) 51–64; cf. Nagel, *Motivierung der Askese*, 20–1. A possible exception is Rev. 14.1–5, although the provenance and

that sexual abstinence was not, as far as Paul was concerned, an aspiration in itself. It was, so to speak, only a secondary feature of celibacy, being the necessary by-product of two things, a desire to live the unencumbered, single life, and the Judeo–Christian prohibition of extra-marital sexual relations.[11] Indeed, Paul advises the Corinthians against the attempt to censure their (God-given) sexual drives, maintaining that if one was unsure of his or her ability to remain continent, then marriage was the better choice. Celibacy, for Paul, was thus not the equivalent of sexual asceticism, a regime that fosters self-induced privation and hardship; and although we are much less informed as to the Corinthians' theology of celibacy, it would appear that they were in basic agreement with Paul on this point.[12]

As Christianity moved into the second century, however, Christian authors began promoting a substantially different understanding of celibacy. As we saw at the end of chapter two, Stoic and Cynic ideals of securing a lifestyle free from marital responsibilities continued to have a following among church leaders. What falls by the wayside, however, is the Stoic argument that adverse circumstances posed an obstacle to marrying, as well as Paul's argument against

intent of this passage is entirely uncertain; for a summary of the various theories see J. Massyngberde Ford, *Revelation*, AB 38 (Garden City, N.Y.: Doubleday, 1975) 234–5.

[11] Cf. Pagels, "Paul and Women," 542, who notes that Paul "refuses to accord religious value to celibacy" (cf. 540). This also applies, I would argue, to the celibacy of Jesus, John the Baptist, and the Essenes. Likewise, Epictetus' Cynic practices abstinence as the result of forswearing marriage while at the same time professing a low opinion of other types of sexual relations – although not human sexuality itself. See Epict. *Diss.* 3.22.13, 95; cf. 4.1.143; 2.18.15–18. Epictetus' view may well reflect his teacher's strict stance against extra-marital relations; see Mus. *frag.* 12, *On Sexual Relations*.

[12] That such a distinction exists between celibacy and asceticism is often overlooked by scholars working on 1 Cor. 7. See, e.g., Balch, "Backgrounds," 351: "There was, at the time of the rise of Christianity, a growing concern for *sexual ascetisism . . . Celibacy* became common enough for Augustus to attempt to correct it from 18 BC to AD 9 through a series of laws" (my emphasis). The Augustan marriage legislation, however, was directed at the refusal of Roman citizens to marry, not their forswearing of sexual relations. By contrast, Schmithals, *Gnosticism in Corinth*, 235 n. 158 writes: "Indeed, fundamentally, Paul does not think ascetically, even when, naturally, he shows no high regard of marriage. Asceticism, however, is opposition to the sexual urge itself, which Paul precisely does *not* command" (his emphasis) – to which Niederwimmer, *Askese und Mysterium*, 84 n. 20 characteristically and quite wrongly replies, "That is a non sequitur."

marrying based on apocalyptic expectations.[13] Instead, many Christians from the second century onward drew their motivations for celibacy from a very different quarter, from the notion of a body–soul dualism. This perspective on human existence maintained that the soul was trapped within the body and was thereby hindered from attaining moral perfection by the constraints of a person's physical nature. In this way, it set the aspirations of the soul in opposition to the needs and desires of the body, among them, the sexual drive. While this body–soul dualism had been a part of Greek philosophical thinking at least since the time of Plato, it takes on new significance in the second century, as if surfacing in the world of ideas for the first time. It was propounded widely by neo-Platonists and neo-Pythagoreans, and many leading Christians incorporated it into their theologies as well.

As a result, Christian discussions on marriage from this period begin to chart a new course. For the first time a negative evaluation of human sexuality enters into the equation. The primary focus of these discussions is no longer the alienation of the individual from the divine will through the social and economic obligations of marriage, but alienation from God on an anthropological level. Unlike Stoics, Cynics, Paul, or the authors of apocalyptic and wisdom literature, all of whom discussed marriage in terms of conflicting allegiances within a person's lifestyle (βίος), this new breed of moralists and theologians saw the problem as one of conflicting allegiances within a person's very being, between the sexual urgings of the body and the soul's yearning for God.[14]

Among leaders of the church, human sexuality came to be seen as part of a fallen creation – a creation, as many would point out, that was brought to its knees by the carnal union of its first man and woman. For the orthodox, the neat dichotomy that Paul had drawn between conjugal relations and *porneia* still held, but the dividing line between them now faded elusively in and out of focus. In turn, the activity of sexual intercourse appeared to many to suggest rebellion against God, surrounding the institution of marriage with

[13] Noted by several scholars: Baltensweiler, *Die Ehe*, 208–9; Cartlidge, "Competing Theologies of Asceticism," 51; Ruether, "Is Celibacy Eschatological?"; and see the references in Allo, *Première épitre*, 178, 180.
[14] Paul, of course, also knows an anthropological alienation from God (e.g., Gal. 5.16–24; Rom. 7.13–25), but this neither involves a rejection of the physical self or human sexuality, nor does it enter into his thinking on marriage; cf. Keck and Furnish, *The Letters of Paul*, 85, "None of Paul's allegedly negative views of sex and marriage . . . is based on either body–soul/spirit dualism or on female inferiority."

inchoate misgivings and suspicions. While they continued to de-
nounce pagan sexual practices as ungodly, unholy, impure,
unrighteous, and sinful, a positive appraisal of Christian sexual
practices as godly, holy, pure, righteous, and sinless came hard to
these fathers, and it chafed. Other Christian groups, by contrast,
such as docetics, Marcionites, Montanists, Encratites, and various
types of gnostics, denounced sexual intercourse altogether, and
consequently forbade marriage.

Despite their strong prejudices against the sexual component of
marriage, however, the orthodox churchmen were unwilling to take
this final step. Unlike their gnostic counterparts, who proclaimed
the material world to be the handiwork of an evil or misguided
Demiurge, and procreation to be the furtherance of his deranged
will, the orthodox continued to affirm the God of the Old Testament, maker of heaven and earth, acknowledging that his first
decree to humanity was the command to "be fruitful and multiply."
If the Creation was in a fallen state, it remained nonetheless God's
creation, and procreation continued to have a part in the divine
plan.[15]

Beginning in the second century, a certain tension thus pervaded
Christian thinking on marriage, the one pole represented by an
aversion to sexuality based on a material dualism, the other by the
belief that procreation was divinely sanctioned. Among the orthodox, a resolution of sorts came in the form of a graded standard of
morality by which theologians declared marriage to be a legitimate,
though lesser manner of life. Although marriage was perhaps necessary for the majority, it nevertheless filled one's life with worldly
concerns, and it involved one in the dangerous and questionable
ordeal of sexual intercourse. Consistent with this, the fathers, as we
have seen, readily joined with the Stoics in demanding that intercourse be performed only for the purpose of procreation. Unlike the
Stoics, however, they did not encourage physical intimacy and large
families, but small families and decreased sexual activity. Celibacy,
on the other hand, was promoted by the fathers as the preferred way
of life for the believer. It not only allowed one to devote him or
herself without distraction to the service of Christ, but it also made
possible the achievement of a goal quite unknown to Paul, namely,

---

[15] Although Jerome and Augustine take the precaution of maintaining that Christ
had rescinded God's command to procreate; for references see Ruether, "Misogynism and Virginal Feminism," 182 n. 49.

the penultimate state of holiness associated with total sexual abstinence.[16]

Returning to the question of Paul's place in the history of Christian asceticism, we see that a significant gulf separates him from
later patristic authors. Paul's statements on marriage and celibacy
belong to an older view of the world, still filled with nostalgia for
traditional life in the Greek city-state. Rather than assuming a place
at the beginning of a supposed trajectory of Christian asceticism, 1
Corinthians 7 is one of the last examples in a series of marriage
discussions whose antecedents are found as far back as the pre-
Socratics. Fully within the parameters of these discussions, Paul
assesses the value of marriage and celibacy with regard to prevailing
circumstances. For him it is not a matter of choosing a lower or
higher standard of morality, but of forestalling important decisions
in life on the basis of expediency. With the church fathers, by
contrast, the focus has shifted to a dualistic understanding of the
world, cleaving the individual into body and soul, and demanding a
choice between sexuality and spirituality. This caesura between Paul
and the fathers cannot be bridged, either by such theories as we
examined in chapter one, or by the insistence of the fathers themselves that their conclusions are fully supported by the Apostle's
writings.[17] It represents the abutting of two great eras in the history
of western thought, the juncture of Hellenism with the world of late
antiquity. While the fathers often appear to speak the same language as Paul, their conceptual world is so different that even the
words "sin," "holiness," "marriage," and "fornication" take on
theological implications quite beyond the scope of anything Paul
imagined.

A revealing, and somewhat entertaining, illustration of this sea-
change in Christian thinking on marriage and celibacy may be had
by comparing Paul and St. Jerome on the subject of whether a
widow can remarry, a comparison that will serve as our epilogue. As
we saw in chapter three, Paul advises against remarriage for widows,
but concedes that it is better for them to marry than to be overcome
with sexual desire. His exact words, perhaps from a popular maxim,

[16] See, e.g., the discussion in Ruether, "Misogynism and Virginal Feminism,"
150–83.

[17] Wilson's warning to those who suggest a gnostic interpretation of 1 Corinthians
is apropos here as well: "The danger which must be avoided is that of reading back,
of interpreting first-century documents in light of second-century texts – which may
themselves actually be reinterpretations of the first-century material" ("How Gnostic
Were the Corinthians?" 68).

are: "It is better to marry than to burn." Writing almost three hundred and fifty years later, St. Jerome also counsels against remarriage for widows. In support of his position he points to the example of the virtuous lady Dido, legendary founder of Carthage. After the death of her husband, it seems, Dido is asked for her hand in marriage by the king of Libya. Knowing that she could hardly refuse the ruler of her land, but not wishing to enter again into carnal union, Dido chose instead to build a funeral pyre in honor of her late husband. Mounting it, she ended her earthly existence. Jerome cites her decision with avid approval, and then remarks, with a sly twist of the Apostle's words, that this widow, in any case, considered it better "to burn than to marry"(*ardere quam nubere*).[18] While Jerome is clearly an extreme case, it is nevertheless this same ascetic mind-set, so foreign to Paul's way of thinking, that time and time again would be read back onto his words in 1 Corinthians 7, thereby serving as the inspiration for generations of Christian theologians from the second century through the Middle Ages and beyond.

---

[18] Jerome *Adv. Jovin.* 1.43. To make the most of his clever insight, Jerome leaves out the fact that Dido was said to have stabbed herself to death on the pyre – see his *Epistle* 123.14.

*Appendix A*

# ANTIPATER OF TARSUS, FROM HIS
# *ON MARRIAGE, SVF* 3.254.23-257.10
# (STOBAEUS 4.507.6-512.7 W.-H.)[1]

The well-born and high-minded youth, being, moreover, a product of civilization and a political being, perceiving that one's home or life cannot otherwise be complete except with a wife and children (for like a city-state it is incomplete,[2] not only one composed [just] of women, but also one composed of single men: just as a flock is not good when it has no increase, nor a herd when it does not thrive, even more so neither a city nor a household) – having observed these things, and, being by nature political, that he must increase the fatherland, the well-born youth < will marry and have children >.[3] For the city-states could not otherwise survive if the children best in nature, being of noble citizens,[4] their predecessors[5] withering and falling off, as it were, just as leaves of a good tree – if these children would not marry in due season, leaving behind, as it were, some noble shoots as successors to the fatherland, making it thrive eternally and protecting its flower forever, at no time leaving it exposed to the enemy

---

[1] The only other complete translation of this text is Eyben, "De latere Stoa," 22–9 (Dutch). Partial translations exist in Max Pohlenz (ed.), *Stoa und Stoiker*, Die Bibliothek der alten Welt: Griechische Reihe (Zurich: Artemis, 1950) 1.185–7 (sometimes lapsing into paraphrase); Konrad Gaiser, *Für und wider die Ehe* (Munich: Heimeran, 1974) 36–9; and Hildegard Cancik-Lindemaier, "Ehe und Liebe: Entwürfe griechischer Philosophen und römischer Dichter," *Zum Thema Frau in Kirche und Gesellschaft*, ed. Hubert Cancik (Stuttgart: Katholisches Bibelwerk, 1972) 58–9. E. Vernon Arnold, *Roman Stoicism* (Cambridge: Cambridge University Press, 1911) 318–19, offers a running paraphrase. None of these translators makes use of Hense's edition of the text. Angled brackets in these appendices indicate a conjecture by editors of the text or by myself. Square brackets indicate a gloss.

[2] I construe ἀτελής with οἶκος καὶ βίος. Von Arnim supplies οἰκία.

[3] This sentence has no finite verb; Hense indicates a lacuna here. Von Arnim's solution of placing *SVF* 3.254.31–255.5 (Stob. 4.507.15–508.2 W.-H.) in parentheses and construing the singular ὁ νέος (*SVF* 3.254.25; Stob. 4.507.7 W.-H.) or ὁ εὐγενής (*SVF* 3.254.30; Stob. 4.507.13–14 W.-H.) with the plural νομίζουσι (*SVF* 3.255.6; Stob. 4.508.3 W.-H.) has been followed by all past translators, but is very implausible. The missing element might be simply, "will marry and have children," as my translation suggests. The entire first paragraph is somewhat convoluted. On Antipater's writing style generally, see Hense, "Zu Antipatros von Tarsos," 302–5.

[4] The text has a ἤ which both von Arnim and Hense bracket out.

[5] Von Arnim writes πατέρων ("fathers") for προτέρων ("forerunners/predecessors").

inasmuch as it depended on them. < Thus, > 6 endeavoring both while alive and after having passed away to protect the fatherland and aid it, they consider joining with a woman in marriage to be among the primary and most necessary of those things which are fitting, being eager to complete every task laid upon them by nature, most especially the duty that concerns the safekeeping and growth of the fatherland, and, even more so, the honor of the gods – for if the race dies out, who will sacrifice to the gods? Some wolves or a race of "bull-killing lions"?[7]

Further, it so happens that he who has not experienced a wedded wife and children has not known the truest and genuine goodwill. For the other friendships and affections of life resemble juxtaposed mixings of beans or other similar things; but those of a husband and wife resemble complete fusions, as wine with water – indeed, this is mixed completely.[8] For not only do they share a partnership of property, and children, who are most dear to everyone, and the soul, but these alone also share their bodies.[9]

And in another way this partnership is reasonably the greatest. For other partnerships are not exclusive,[10] but in this one "it is necessary to focus on one soul,"[11] the husband's. For the wife consents that while his father and mother are still alive[12] and in possession of their faculties she will make this one person both goal and purpose of her life, to please him; [and] that when each of the parents has stepped aside, she and her husband will freely render their foremost consideration to one another,[13] she to her husband, he to his wife. Even Euripides, not inexperienced in married life, observing these matters and putting aside the usual hatred for women he shows in writing, even he said this:

> For in sickness and bad times a wife is sweetest
> To her husband, if she manages the house well.

[6] My addition. I break the preceding sentence after ἐχθροῖς (*SVF* 3.255.4; Stob. 4.507.22 W.-H.), not after βοηθεῖν (*SVF* 3.255.5; Stob. 4.508.2 W.-H.), which is Hense's solution, for which he adds an < οὖν > after τῶν at *SVF* 3.255.5 (Stob. 4.508.2 W.-H.). In my division, the next three sentences (*SVF* 3.255.4–10; Stob. 4.507.22–508.8 W.-H.) form the conclusion to Antipater's first argument.

[7] ταυροκτόνων λεόντων also appears at Sophocles *Philoctetes* 400–1.

[8] The text contains an additional ἔτι μέν, which is corrupt.

[9] Vatin's comment that this paragraph expresses a "veritable biological unity" not based on the husband's authority over the wife but on "mutual love" (*Recherches*, 33), goes beyond the text, as Antipater's following argument and his quotation from the *Medea* indicate.

[10] Lit., "have some other avenues of recourse."

[11] From Euripides *Medea* 247. Medea laments her lot and that of the Corinthian wives, saying that while their husbands may obtain respite from domestic problems by seeking companionship outside the home, "We can seek comfort in only one person," namely, the husband (ἡμῖν δ' ἀνάγκη πρὸς μίαν ψυχὴν βλέπειν).

[12] The text is corrupt here; the translations vary greatly. Hense, who reads σώζουσα, lists the proposals of several editors: ἥ γε οὖσα, σώφρονος οὖσα, and οὕτω ἡ οὖσα. I read σωζομέμου, taking it with πατρὸς καὶ μητρὸς μὴ ἀγνώμονος as part of a genitive absolute construction.

[13] Cf. [Arist.] *Oec.* 3.2 (143.24–5): "[the husband] promising to honor his wife far above all others saving his parents" (*multo magis se post parentes uxori tradidit ad honorem*).

Calming his anger and bad moods,
She turns his disposition around. Even the treachery of friends
becomes sweet.[14]

Indeed, the matter achieves heroic proportions.

But at present, in some cities, along with the other existing laxity and
anarchy, and the inclination toward the degraded and frivolous, even
marriage is reckoned among the most grievous things. They consider the
bachelor's life, since it gives them license for whoring and enjoying various
sordid and cheap pleasures, equal to god,[15] and see the entry of a wife into
their home as if it were some foreign garrison entering a city.[16]

Indeed, it seems that to some people married life appears difficult because
they are unable to take command,[17] being instead slaves to pleasure: some
have been taken captive by beauty, some by the dowry – in some cases,
readily giving the wife a cut![18] And they teach their wives nothing concerning household management, nor concerning the growth of the household, nor for what reason they had married in the first place. Nor do they
instill in them good opinions about the gods, piety and religious sensibilities, nor the destructiveness of lavish living, nor the ill of pleasures. Nor do
they accustom them to reflect on life's former experiences and assess all
future possibilities accurately with good judgement, and further, not to be
blindly and without reflection hopeful that what she longs for can certainly
come about if her husband should be in favor of it, and not to exist for the
present only, but to consider, she herself along with him, the source and the
means, and if something brings security and benefit to the whole.[19]

Whereas, in fact, if someone were able to do these and the other things
which have been duly inspected by the philosophers and are recommended
by them, a wife would seem to be the lightest of all possible burdens.[20] For it
is most similar to when someone, having one hand, adds another one from

[14] A fragment of Euripides extant only here and at Stob. 4.496.16–20 W.-H., under
the lemma Εὐριπίδου Φρίξῳ.
[15] A wordplay: ἤθεον ... ἰσόθεν. (Meineke, followed by von Arnim and Hense,
adds βίον to ἤθεον.) This is perhaps a reference to Epicureans. For a similar wordplay
see Quintilian 1.6.36; cf. Arist. *Pol.* 1.1253a 29; Epict. *Ench.* 15.
[16] On this military metaphor, cf. Antiphon in Stob. 4.521.15–16 W.-H., "For
marriage is a great contest for a man" (μέγας γὰρ ἀγὼν γάμος ἀνθρώπῳ); and *Sent.
of Sextus* 230b: "Marry and have children, knowing each is difficult. But if, knowing
that it is difficult, you would be courageous, as for battle – indeed, marry and have
children" (γάμει καὶ παιδοποιοῦ χαλεπὸν εἰδὼς ἑκάτερον· εἰ δὲ καθάπερ εἰδὼς
πόλεμον ὅτι χαλεπὸν ἀνδρίζοιο, καὶ γάμει καὶ παιδοποιοῦ).
[17] διὰ τὸ μὴ δύνασθαι ἄρχειν, cf. *Sent. of Sextus* 236: "A man who divorces a wife
confesses that he is not able to rule a woman" (μηδὲ γυναικὸς ἄρχειν δύνασθαι).
[18] The text is uncertain here.
[19] Cf. Menander *Sent.* 143 J., "For a wife knows nothing except what she wants"
(γυνὴ γὰρ οὐδὲν οἶδε πλὴν ὃ βούλεται).
[20] Lit., "the lightest burden of the greatest possible number" (ὃ ἂν τῶν πλείστων
καὶ κουφότατον εἶναι βάρος). Since the text here is uncertain, Hense lists the
suggestions of other editors: ἓν ἂν τῶν ἡδίστων "one of the sweetest," and τὸ πάντων
ἥδιστον "the sweetest of all." Cf. above at *SVF* 3.255.28–9 (Stob. 4.509.8–9 W.-H.):
"For in sickness and bad times a wife is *sweetest* to her husband, if she manages the
house well."

somewhere, or, having one foot, gains another from somewhere else.[21] For just as this man would indeed walk and go here and there where he would much more easily, so the man who takes a wife will more easily obtain the necessities that sustain and benefit his life. Indeed, he and his wife have the use of four eyes instead of two, and the same number of hands instead of two – by which, collectively, he would make manual labor easier. Thus, if the one set would become weary, he would be served by the other; and in general, this man would be more successful in life, having become two instead of one.[22]

Therefore, < it seems to me >[23] that the man who thinks the introduction of a woman into his life burdens it and makes it cumbersome is under the same mistaken impression as if someone would prevent us from acquiring more feet so that if it were necessary to walk a lot we would not be dragging many after us – or would censure the man with more hands, for when it is necessary that this man do something, < he thinks >[24] this man will be impeded by their multitude. In the same way, if someone did acquire another like himself (it will make no difference whether this is a female or a male), he would do all the work much more easily and it would be a much lighter task.[25]

Indeed, this is a perfectly settled matter for the man who loves the good and desires to direct spare time either to philosophical discourse or political matters, or both these things. For to the extent that he himself turns more and more aside from the management of his household, it is all the more necessary that he acquire this woman who will take over management, and < that he hold >[26] himself undistracted regarding the necessities of life.[27] Not badly did the comic poet[28] summarize "the man of leisure is ...":

> It seems to me that the man with
> many ongoing concerns and the
> ability to manage great throngs must marry;

having added:

> ... the more carefree man, who desires
> leisure, so that he may go about without anxiety,
> having a manager for his home.

[21] On this argument, cf. Antiphon in Stob. 4.522.15–523.6 W.-H.
[22] δύο γεγονὼς ἀνθ' ἑνός, cf. Plato Symposium 192E, ἀντὶ δυοῖν ἕνα εἶναι.
[23] Hense supplies ἂν οἶμαι, although my choice would be οἶμαι ἄν, since it more closely resembles the preceding ὅμοιον, which might account for the latter's omission from the text.
[24] My addition.
[25] Lit., "much more lightly and easily."
[26] There is a lacuna in the text here. Suggestions by various editors include τηρητέον and ποιητέον.
[27] Cf. Menander *Sent.* 155 J., "A good wife is the rudder of a household" (γυνὴ δὲ χρηστὴ πηδάλιόν ἐστ' οἰκίας); and similarly, *Sent.* 140–1 J.
[28] Aristophanes? These two quotations are extant only here.

*Appendix B*

## [OCELLUS LUCANUS] *ON THE NATURE OF THE UNIVERSE* 43(END)–51[1]

(43, end) Now concerning the genesis of human beings from one another, and how and by whom it will be duly accomplished by law and through the contribution of temperance and holiness – these things I find wonderful. (44) First, however, it is necessary to comprehend this: we have sexual intercourse not for the sake of pleasure, but the procreation of children. For, in fact, the reproductive powers themselves, and the sexual organs, and the yearnings that were given to human beings by God in order to bring on sexual intercourse happen not to have been given for the sake of pleasure, but the everlasting continuation of the race. For since it was impossible that a mortal being share in [immortal] divine life, God supplied each of those who must perish with the immortality of the race, making this genesis of human beings constant and continuous.

(45) Thus it is first necessary to observe this one thing, that sexual intercourse is not for the sake of pleasure, and, thereupon, also the very place of the human being with respect to the Whole[2] – that, being a member of both household and city-state, and, most importantly, of the *kosmos*, he is obligated to replace each person who departs these institutions, if he does not wish to be a deserter either of the ancestral hearth of his household, or the altar of his city-state, or, indeed, the altar of God. For those who have intercourse not at all for the sake of having children do injustice to the most revered systems of partnership.[3] And if, in fact, such persons as these give birth, by means of wantonness and lack of self-control, then those born will

---

[1] This text is available in Thesleff, *Pythagorean Texts*, 135–7; and Richard Harder, *"Ocellus Lucanus": Text und Kommentar*, Neue philologische Untersuchungen 1 (Berlin: Weidmann, 1926) 21–3, with commentary on 120–34. An older English translation is available in Thomas Taylor (trans.), *Ocellus Lucanus, On the Nature of the Universe; Taurus, the Platonic Philosopher, On the Eternity of the World; Julius Firmicus Maternus, Of the Thema Mundi, in Which the Positions of the Stars at the Commencement of the Several Mundane Periods Is Given; Select Theorems, On the Perpetuity of Time, By Proclus* (London: [Richard Taylor], 1831) 21–5.

[2] Cf. Chardonas (third-second century BCE) *Prooemia* 62.30–3 Thesleff:

> Each man should have intercourse with a woman who is lawfully his wife, and from this woman he should have children. For no other reason should he give up sperm of his own children. He should not lawlessly waste and treat with disrespect that which is held in honor by nature and by law. For nature made sperm for the sake of having children, not wantonness.

[3] I.e., marriage, the household, and the city-state.

*230*

be wretched and pitiful, and loathsome in the sight of gods, and divine beings, and men, and households, and city-states.[4]

(46) Therefore, giving thought to these things before hand, it is necessary that we do not enter upon sexual intercourse after the manner of irrational animals, but rather holding as necessary and good that very thing which morally upstanding persons think to be necessary and good, namely, not just that households be filled with people, and most of the earth's surface populated – since of all animals the human is the most civilized and excellent – but, indeed, most importantly, that they be filled and populated with good people. (47) For it is through these means they will inhabit well-governed city-states, and properly manage their own households, and make the gods their friends. It is readily seen that territories both barbarian and Greek grow quite naturally to be most highly esteemed with regard to their forms of government and political practices when they are supplied not only with abundance of people but also with a spirit of fortitude.

(48) Hence, many make a serious mistake by forming marriages without regard for the excellence of a person's soul or for the benefit of the community, fixing their attention on the wealth or prominence of the family. For instead of marrying a young woman in her prime, they married[5] the one too old to have children; and instead of one who is sympathetic in spirit and most like them, one from a distinguished family or one who is very wealthy. (49) For this very reason they bring on disagreement instead of agreement, and division instead of unity of purpose, battling with one another for control. For she, being superior in terms of wealth and family and friends, deliberately chooses contrary to the law of nature to rule over her husband; and he, battling with justice on his side – not wanting to be second but first – is unable to attain control. (50) When these things happen, not only do households turn out to be unhappy, but city-states as well. For the households are the constituent parts of the city-states. Now, the make-up of the whole and the entirety depends on the parts. It is therefore reasonable that whatever happens to characterize the parts also characterizes the whole and the entirety that is composed of such parts. (51) In the crafts, the first beginnings[6] contribute greatly toward a good or a bad completion of the whole work. Just as for building it is laying down a foundation, and for ship building it is a ship's keel, and for musical composition and writing melodies to songs it is choice of the voice's intensity and pitch, so also then for both a well- and an ill-governed political system it is stability and internal harmony of households that contribute the most.

---

[4] The enumeration here is not without rhyme or reason, as Harder claims: failure to continue the sacrificial tradition of one's household or city-state through one's children brings censure from both divine and human realms ("in the sight of gods, and divine beings, and men"), the latter being further described in terms of its two central institutions, household and city-state.

[5] Gnomic aorist.

[6] Harder, followed by Thesleff, replaces the manuscript reading οἰκοδομαί with ἀρχαί. His reasons are twofold: a more general term than οἰκοδομαί is needed with respect to the examples given (building, ship building, musical composition); and, despite author's intentions of treating the relationship between household and city-state as one of a part to the whole (μέρος to τὸ ὅλον), he actually ends up describing this relationship as one of beginning to end (ἀρχή to τέλος).

# BIBLIOGRAPHY

## 1. Editions of Greek and Latin texts, by editor

Arnim, Hans von. *Hierokles ethische Elementarlehre*. Berliner Klassiker-texte 4. Berlin: Weidmann, 1906.

Arnim, Johannes [Hans] von, ed. *Stoicorum Veterum Fragmenta*. 3 vols. Stuttgart: B. G. Teubner, 1903–5. Cited as *SVF*, by volume, page, and line.

Cohoon, J. W., and H. Lamar Crobsy, ed. and trans. *Dio Chrysostom*. 5 vols., LCL. London: William Heinemann, 1932–51; Cambridge: Harvard University Press, 1932–51.

Crönert, Wilhelm. *Kolotes und Menedemos*. Studien zur Palaeographie und Papyruskunde 6. Leipzig: Eduard Avenarius, 1906. 53–67 contain *P. Herculaneum* 339, its columns arranged according to *P. Herc.* 155.

Diels, Herman, ed. and trans. *Die Fragmente der Vorsokratiker*. Vol. 2, 6th edn., ed. Walther Kranz. Berlin-Charlottenburg: Weidmann, 1951.

Dittenberger, Wilhelm. *Sylloge Inscriptionum Graecarum*. Vol. 2, 3rd edn. Leipzig: S. Hirzel, 1917; reprint, Hildesheim/Zurich/New York: Georg Olms, 1982.

Foerster, Richard, ed. *Libanii Opera*. Vol. 8. Leipzig: B. G. Teubner, 1915.

Harder, Richard. *"Ocellus Lucanus": Text und Kommentar*. Neue philologische Untersuchungen 1. Berlin: Weidmann, 1926.

Hense, O., ed. *C. Musonii Rufi Reliquiae*. Leipzig: B. G. Teubner, 1905. Cited by page and line. Note: *frags*. 15A and 15B Hense are *frag*. 15 Lutz.

Hobein, H., ed. *Maximi Tyrii Philosophumena*. Bibliotheca Scriptorum Graecorum et Romanorum Teubneriana. Leipzig: B. G. Teubner, 1910.

Jackel, Siegfried, ed. *Menandri Sententiae, Comparatio Menandri et Philistionis*. Academia Scientiarum Germanica Berolinensis, Bibliotheca Scriptorum Graecorum et Romanorum Teubneriana. Leipzig: B. G. Teubner, 1964.

Körte, Alfred, ed. *Menandri quae supersunt*. Vol. 2: *Reliquiae apud veteres scriptores servatae*. Bibliotheca Scriptorum Graecorum et Romanorum Teubneriana. Leipzig: B. G. Teubner, 1957.

Kroll, Wilhelm, ed. *Vettii Valentis Anthologiarum libri*. Berlin: Weidmann, 1908.

Kühn, Carl Gottlob, ed. *Claudii Galeni opera omnia*. Vol. 8. Leipzig: Carl Cnoblochi, 1824.

Long, A. A., and D. N. Sedley, ed. *The Hellenistic Philosophers*. Vol. 2: *Greek and Latin Texts with Notes and Bibliography*. Cambridge: Cambridge University Press, 1988.

Long, H. S., ed. *Diogenis Laertii Vitae Philosophorum*. Vol. 2, Scriptorum Classicorum Bibliotheca Oxoniensis. Oxford: Clarendon Press, 1964.

Lutz, Cora E. "Musonius Rufus 'The Roman Socrates'". *Yale Classical Studies* 10, ed. Alfred R. Bellinger. New Haven: Yale University Press, 1947, 3–147. Cited by fragment, page, and line.

Malherbe, Abraham J., ed. *The Cynic Epistles*. SBLSBS 12. Missoula, Mont.: Scholars, 1977.

Migne, Jacques-Paul, ed. *Patrologiae cursus completus: Series Latina*. 217 vols. Paris: Migne, 1844–55.

*Patrologiae cursus completus: Series Graeca*. 162 vols. Paris: Migne, 1857–66.

O'Neil, Edward N., ed. and trans. *Teles (The Cynic Teacher)*. SBLTT 11/SBLGRS 3. Missoula, Mont.: Scholars, 1977.

Oldfather, W. A., ed. and trans. *Epictetus: The Discourses as Reported by Arrian, the Manual, and Fragments*. 2 vols., LCL. Cambridge: Harvard University Press, 1959; London: William Heinemann, 1959.

Spengel, Leonard, ed. *Rhetores Graeci*. Vol. 2. Leipzig: B. G. Teubner, 1854. 57–130 contain Aelius Theon, *Progymnasmata*.

Stählin, Otto, ed. *Clemens Alexandrinus*. Vols. 1–4, 3rd edn., Die griechischen christlichen Schriftsteller der ersten Jahrhunderte. Berlin: Akademie, 1960–72.

Thesleff, Holger, ed. *The Pythagorean Texts of the Hellenistic Period*. Acta Academiae Aboensis, Humaniora 30/1. Åbo, Finland: Åbo Akademi, 1965.

Wachsmuth, Curtius [Kurt], and Otto Hense, ed. *Ioannis Stobaei Anthologium*. 5 vols. Berlin: Weidmann, 1884–1912; reprint, 1958. Cited by volume, page, and line.

Wehrli, Fritz, ed. *Die Schule des Aristoteles: Texte und Kommentar*. Vol. 1: *Dikaiarchos*; 2nd edn. Basel/Stuttgart: Schwabe, 1967.

**2. Secondary sources, including translations**

Achelis, Hans. "AGAPĒTÆ." *ERE* 1 (1926) 177–80. This is an English version of "Subintroductae," *Realencyklopädie für protestantische Theologie und Kirche*, 3rd edn., 19 (1907) 123–7.

*Virgines Subintroductae: Ein Beitrag zum VII. Kapitel des I. Korintherbriefs*. Leipzig: J. C. Hinrichs, 1902.

Adam, Alfred. "Erwägungen zur Herkunft der Didache." *ZKG* 68 (1957) 1–47.

Adkins, Arthur W. H. *Merit and Responsibility: A Study in Greek Values*. Oxford: Oxford University Press, 1960.

Allmen, Jean Jacques von. *Pauline Teaching on Marriage*. Studies in Christian Faith and Practice 6. London: Faith, 1963.

Allo, E.-B. *Première épitre aux Corinthiens*. Études Bibliques, 2nd edn. Paris: Librairie Lecoffre, 1934; reprint 1956.

Almquist, Helge. *Plutarch und das Neue Testament: Ein Beitrag zum Corpus*

234    Bibliography

*Hellenisticum Novi Testamenti.* Acta Seminarii Neotestamentici Upsaliensis 15. Uppsala: Appelberg, 1946.

Arai, Sasagu. "Die Gegner des Paulus im I. Korintherbrief und das Problem der Gnosis." *NTS* 19 (1972/73) 430–7.

Arnim, Hans von. "Ineditum Vaticanum." *Hermes* 27 (1892) 118–30.

Arnold, E. Vernon. *Roman Stoicism: Being Lectures on the History of the Stoic Philosophy with Special Reference to Its Development within the Roman Empire.* Cambridge: Cambridge University Press, 1911.

Arthur, Marylin B. "Early Greece: The Origins of the Western Attitude Toward Women." *Women in the Ancient World: The "Arethusa" Papers,* ed. John Peradotto and J. P. Sullivan, SUNY Series in Classical Studies. Albany: SUNY, 1984 7–58.

Attridge, Harold W. *First-Century Cynicism in the Epistles of Heraclitus.* HTS 29. Missoula, Mont.: Scholars, 1976.

Babbitt, Frank Cole, ed. and trans. *Plutarch's Moralia.* Vol. 2, LCL. Cambridge: Harvard University Press, 1962; London: William Heinemann, 1962.

Babut, Daniel. *Plutarque et le Stoïcisme.* Paris: Presses Universitaires de France, 1969.

Bachmann, Philipp. *Der erste Brief des Paulus an die Korinther.* 4th edn., Kommentar zum Neuen Testament 7. Leipzig: A. Deichert, 1936. This is identical to the 3rd edn. of 1921 except for the additional bibliography and notes supplied by Ethelbert Stauffer, 488–514.

Baer, Richard A., Jr. *Philo's Use of the Categories Male and Female.* Arbeiten zur Literatur und Geschichte des hellenistischen Judentums 3. Leiden: E. J. Brill, 1970.

Balch, David L. "Backgrounds of I Cor. vii: Sayings of the Lord in Q; Moses As an Ascetic ΘΕΙΟΣ ANHP in II Cor. iii." *NTS* 18 (1971/72) 351–64.

"Household Codes." *Greco-Roman Literature and the New Testament: Selected Forms and Genres.* Edited David E. Aune, SBLSBS 21. Atlanta: Scholars, 1988 25–50.

*Let Wives Be Submissive: The Domestic Code in I Peter.* SBLMS 26. Chico, Calif.: Scholars, 1981.

"1 Cor 7:32–35 and Stoic Debates about Marriage, Anxiety, and Distraction." *JBL* 102 (1983) 429–39.

Baldry, H. C. "Zeno's Ideal State." *JHS* 79 (1959) 3–15.

Balsdon, J. P. V. D. *Life and Leisure in Ancient Rome.* New York: McGraw Hill, 1969.

Baltensweiler, Heinrich. *Die Ehe im Neuen Testament: Exegetische Untersuchungen über Ehe, Ehelosigkeit und Ehescheidung.* ATANT 52. Zurich/Stuttgart: Zwingli, 1967.

Barns, John. "A New Gnomologium: With Some Remarks on Gnomic Anthologies." *CQ* 44 (1950) 126–37; and n.s. 1 [mistakenly 45] (1951) 1–19.

Barraclough, Ray. "Philo's Politics: Roman Rule and Hellenistic Judaism." *ANRW* 2.21.1 (1984) 417–553.

Barrett, C. K. *A Commentary on the First Epistle to the Corinthians.* HNTC. New York/Evanston: Harper and Row, 1968.

bibliography

Bartchy, S. Scott. *MAΛΛON XPHΣAI: First-Century Slavery and the Interpretation óf 1 Corinthians 7:21*. SBLDS 11. Missoula: University of Montana Press, 1973.

Barwick, Karl. *Probleme der stoischen Sprachlehre und Rhetorik*. Abhandlungen der sächsischen Akademie der Wissenschaften zu Leipzig: Philologisch-historische Klasse 49/3. Berlin: Akademie, 1957.

Basore, John W., ed. and trans. *Seneca: Moral Essays*. Vols. 2–3, LCL. London: William Heinemann, 1932–35; New York: G. P. Putman's Sons, 1932–35.

Baudrillart, André. *Moeurs païennes, moeurs crétiennes*. Vol. 1: *La famille dans l'antiquité païenne et aux premiers siècles du christianisme*. Paris: Librairie Bloud and Gay, 1929.

Bauer, Johannes B. "Was las Tertullian 1 Kor 7₃₉?" *ZNW* 77 (1986) 284–7.

Bauer, Walter. *A Greek-English Lexicon of the New Testament and Other Early Christian Literature*. 2nd English edn. Chicago: University of Chicago Press, 1979.

Baumert, Norbert. *Ehelosigkeit und Ehe im Herrn: Eine Neuinterpretation von 1 Kor 7*. Forschung zur Bibel 47. Würzburg: Echter, 1984.

Baumgarten, Jörg. *Paulus und die Apokalyptik: Die Auslegung apokalyptischer Überlieferungen in den echten Paulusbriefen*. WMANT 44. Neukirchen-Vluyn: Neukirchen, 1975.

Becker, Jürgen. "Erwägungen zur apokalyptischen Tradition in der paulinischen Theologie." *EvT* 30 (1970) 593–609.

*Untersuchungen zur Entstehungsgeschichte der Testamente der Zwölf Patriarchen*. Arbeiten zur Geschichte des antiken Judentums und des Urchristentums 8. Leiden: E. J. Brill, 1970.

Behm, Johannes. "βρῶμα, βρῶσις." *TDNT* 1 (1964) 642–5.

"γλῶσσα, ἑτερόγλωσσος." *TDNT* 1 (1964) 719–27.

Beker, J. Christiaan. *Paul's Apocalyptic Gospel: The Coming Triumph of God*. Philadelphia: Fortress, 1982.

Bengel, Johann Albrecht. *Gnomon of the New Testament*. Vol. 2. Philadelphia: Perkinpine and Higgins, 1864; reprint 1888.

Berger, Klaus. "Gnosis/Gnostizismus I." *TRE* 13 (1984) 519–35.

Betz, Hans Dieter. *Der Apostel Paulus und die sokratische Tradition: Eine exegetische Untersuchung zu seiner "Apologie" 2 Korinther 10–13*. BHT 45. Tübingen: J. C. B. Mohr, 1972.

*Galatians: A Commentary on Paul's Letter to the Churches in Galatia*. Hermeneia. Philadelphia: Fortress, 1979.

"Gottmensch II." *RAC* 12 (1983) 234–312.

"On the Problem of the Religio-Historical Understanding of Apocalypticism." *Journal for Theology and Church* 6 (1969) 134–56.

"2 Cor 6:14–7:1: An Anti-Pauline Fragment?" *JBL* 92 (1973) 88–108.

Bickel, Ernestus. *Diatribe in Senecae philosophi fragmenta*. Vol. 1: *Fragmenta de matrimonio*. Leipzig: B. G. Teubner, 1915.

Bieler, Ludwig. *ΘΕΙΟΣ ΑΝΗΡ: Das Bild des "göttlichen Menschen" in Spätantike und Frühchristentum*. Vol. 1. Vienna: Oskar Höfels, 1935.

Bien, Günther. *Die Grundlegung der politischen Philosophie bei Aristoteles*. 3rd edn. Freiburg/Munich: Karl Alber, 1985.

Billerbeck, Margarethe. *Epiktet: Vom Kynismus*. Philosophia Antiqua 34. Leiden: E. J. Brill, 1978.

*Der Kyniker Demetrius: Ein Beitrag zur Geschichte der frühkaiserzeitlichen Popularphilosophie*. Philosophia Antiqua 36. Leiden: E. J. Brill, 1979.

Billroth, [Johann] Gustav [Friedrich]. *A Commentary on the Epistles of Paul to the Corinthians*. Vol. 1. Edinburgh: Thomas Clark, 1837.

Blass, F., and A. Debrunner. *A Greek Grammar of the New Testament and Other Early Christian Literature*. Trans. and rev. Robert W. Funk. Chicago/London: University of Chicago Press, 1961.

Blau, Ludwig. *Die jüdische Ehescheidung und der jüdische Scheidebrief*. Vol. 2. Strassburg: Karl J. Trübner, 1912.

Blinzler, Joseph. "Zur Auslegung von I. Kor. 7,14." *Aus der Welt und Umwelt des Neuen Testaments: Gesammelte Aufsätze 1*. Stuttgarter Biblische Beiträge. Stuttgart: Katholisches Bibelwerk, 1969 158–84. Replaces the 1963 version.

Bonhöffer, Adolf. *Epiktet und das Neue Testament*. Religionsgeschichtliche Versuche und Vorarbeiten 10. Gießen: Alfred Töpelmann, 1911.

*Epictet und die Stoa: Untersuchungen zur stoischen Philosophie*. Stuttgart: Ferdinand Enke, 1890.

*Die Ethik des Stoikers Epictet*. Stuttgart: Ferdinand Enke, 1894; reprint, Stuttgart-Bad Connstatt: Friedrich Frommann, 1968.

Bornkamm, Günther. *Paul*. New York/Evanston, Ill.: Harper and Row, 1971.

Boswell, John. *The Kindness of Strangers: The Abandonment of Children in Western Europe from Late Antiquity to the Renaissance*. New York: Pantheon Books, 1988.

Bousset, Wilhelm. *Die Religion des Judentums im späthellenistischen Zeitalter*. 3rd edn., ed. Hugo Gressmann. HNT 21. Tübingen: J. C. B. Mohr, 1926.

Braun, Herbert. "Exegetische Randglossen zum 1. Korintherbrief." *Gesammelte Studien zum Neuen Testament und seiner Umwelt.*, 2nd edn. Tübingen: J. C. B. Mohr, 1967, 178–204.

"Die Indifferenz gegenüber der Welt bei Paulus und bei Epiktet." *Gesammelte Studien zum Neuen Testament und seiner Umwelt*, 2nd edn. Tübingen: J. C. B. Mohr, 1967, 156–67, 343–4.

Bréhier, Émile. *Chrysippe*. Paris: Félix Alcan, 1910.

Broek, R. van den. "The Present State of Gnostic Studies." *VC* 37 (1983) 41–71.

Broudéhoux, Jean-Paul. *Mariage et famille chez Clément d'Alexandrie*. Théologie Historique 11. Paris: Beauchesne et ses Fils, 1970.

Brown, Peter. *The Body and Society: Men, Women and Sexual Renunciation in Early Christianity*. Lectures in the History of Religions, n.s. 13. New York: Columbia University Press, 1988.

"The Notion of Virginity in the Early Church." *Christian Spirituality: Origins to the Twelfth Century*, ed. Bernard McGinn and John Meyendorff, World Spirituality: An Encyclopedic History of the Religious Quest. New York: Crossroad, 1985 16:427–43.

Brown, Raymond E. *The Epistles of John*. AB 30. Garden City, N.Y.: Doubleday, 1982.

Bruce, F. F. *Paul: Apostle of the Heart Set Free*. Grand Rapids, Mich.: William B. Eerdmans, 1977.

Bruns, Bernhard. "'Die Frau hat über ihren Leib nicht die Verfügungsgewalt, sondern der Mann . . .': Zur Herkunft und Bedeutung der Formulierung in 1 Kor 7,4." *MTZ* 33 (1982) 177–94.

Brunt, P. A. *Italian Manpower: 225 BC–AD 14*. Oxford: Clarendon Press, 1971.

Brutscheck, Jutta. *Die Maria-Marta-Erzèhlung: Eine redaktionskritische Untersuchung zu Lk 10,38–42*. Bonner Biblische Beiträge 64. Frankfort/Bonn: Peter Hanstein, 1986.

Bultmann, Rudolf. "Ist die Apokalyptik die Mutter der christlichen Theologie? Eine Auseinandersetzung mit Ernst Käsemann." *Exegetica: Aufsätze zur Erforschung des Neuen Testaments*, ed. Erich Dinkler Tübingen: J. C. B. Mohr, 1967 76–82.

"μεριμνάω." *TDNT* 4 (1967) 589–93.

*Der Stil der paulinischen Predigt und die kynisch-stoische Diatribe*. FRLANT 13. Göttingen: Vandenhoeck und Ruprecht, 1910.

*Theology of the New Testament*. Vol. 1. New York: Charles Scribner's Sons, 1951.

Burchard, C. "Joseph and Aseneth." *The Old Testament Pseudepigrapha*, ed. James H. Charlesworth. Garden City, N.Y.: Doubleday, 1985 2.177–247.

Butts, James R. "The Progymnasmata of Theon: A New Text with Translation and Commentary." Ph.D. diss., Claremont Graduate School, 1986.

Caizzi, Fernanda Decleva, ed. *Antisthenis Fragmenta*. Testi e Documenti per lo Studio dell' Antichitá 13. Milan: Istituto Editoriale Cisalpino, 1966.

Cameron, Averil. "The Exposure of Children and Greek Ethics." *Classical Review* 46 (1932) 105–14.

Cancik-Lindemaier, Hildegard. "Ehe und Liebe: Entwürfe griechischer Philosophen und römischer Dichter." *Zum Thema Frau in Kirche und Gesellschaft*, ed. Hubert Cancik. Stuttgart: Katholisches Bibelwerk, 1972 47–80.

Cartlidge, David R. "Competing Theologies of Asceticism in the Early Church." Th.D. diss., Harvard University, 1969.

"1 Corinthians 7 as a Foundation for a Christian Sex Ethic." *Journal of Religion* 55 (1975) 220–34.

Review of *Paul, the Worldly Ascetic* by Vincent L. Wimbush. *JBL* 108 (1989) 355–7.

Chadwick, H. "'All Things to All Men' (I Cor. ix. 22)." *NTS* 1 (1954/55) 261–75.

Cherniss, Harold, ed. and trans. *Plutarch's Moralia*. Vol. 13, pt. 2, LCL. Cambridge: Harvard University Press, 1976; London: William Heinemann, 1976.

Cohen, Boaz. *Jewish and Roman Law: A Comparative Study*. Vol. 1. New York: Jewish Theological Seminary of America, 1966.

Cohn, Hermann. "Antipater von Tarsos: Ein Beitrag zur Geschichte der Stoa." Ph.D. diss., University of Giessen, 1905.

Cohoon, J. W., and H. Lamar Crobsy, ed. and trans. *Dio Chrysostom.* Vols. 1–5, LCL. London: William Heinemann, 1932–51; Cambridge: Harvard University Press, 1932–51.

Colpe, Carsten. "Gnosis II (Gnostizismus)." *RAC* 11 (1981) 537–659.

"Vorschläge des Messina-Kongresses von 1966 zur Gnosisforschung." *Christentum und Gnosis*, ed. Walther Eltester, Beiheft zur ZNW 37. Berlin: Alfred Töpelmann, 1969 129–32.

Colson, F. H., ed. and trans. *Philo.* Vol. 9, LCL. Cambridge: Harvard University Press, 1929; London: William Heinemann, 1929.

Colson, F. H., and G. H. Whitaker, ed. and trans. *Philo.* Vol. 2, LCL. London: William Heinemann, 1929; New York: G. P. Putnam's Sons, 1929.

Conzelmann, Hans. "Zur Analyse der Bekenntnisformel I. Kor. 15,3–5." *EvT* 25 (1965) 1–11.

*1 Corinthians: A Commentary on the First Epistle to the Corinthians.* Hermeneia. Philadelphia: Fortress, 1975.

Countryman, L. William. *Dirt, Greed, and Sex: Sexual Ethics in the New Testament and Their Implications for Today.* Philadelphia: Fortress, 1988.

Coyle, Kevin J. "Empire and Eschaton: The Early Church and the Question of Domestic Relationships." *Église et Théologie* 12 (1981) 35–94.

Crahay, R. "Les moralistes anciens et l'avortement." *L'Antiquité Classique* 10 (1941) 9–23.

Crouzel, Henri. "Marriage and Virginity: Has Christianity Devalued Marriage?" *The Way*, supplement 10 (1970) 3–23. Now in: *Mariage et divorce: Célibat et caractère sacerdotaux dans l'église ancienne.* Études d'histoire du culte et des institutions chrétiennes 2. Torino: Bottega d'Erasmo, 1982, 47–65.

Csillag, Pál. *The Augustan Laws on Family Relations.* Budapest: Akadémiai Kiadó, 1976.

Dahl, Nils A. "Paul and the Church at Corinth According to 1 Corinthians 1:10–4:21." *Christian History and Interpretation: Studies Presented to John Knox*, ed. W. R. Farmer, C. F. D. Moule, and R. R. Niebuhr. Cambridge: Cambridge University Press, 1967 313–35.

Dassmann, Ernst and Georg Schöllgen. "Haus II (Hausgemeinschaft)." *RAC* 13 (1986) 801–906.

Deißner, Kurt. *Das Idealbild des stoischen Weisen: Rede anläßlich der Reichsgründungsfeier der Universität Greifswald am 18. Januar 1930.* Greifswalder Universitätsreden 24. Greifswald: L. Bamberg, 1930.

"Das Sendungsbewußtsein der Urchristenheit." *ZST* 7 (1929/30) 772–90.

Delatte, Armand. *Essai sur la politique pythagoricienne.* Liège/Paris: n.p., 1922; reprint, Geneva: Slatkine, 1979.

Delling, Gerhard. "Ehehindernisse." *RAC* 4 (1959) 680–91.

"Geschlechter." *RAC* 10 (1978) 780–803.

"καιρός." *TDNT* 3 (1965) 455–64.

"Lexikalisches zu τέκνον: Ein Nachtrag zur Exegese von I. Kor. 7,14." *Studien zum Neuen Testament und zum hellenistischen Judentum: Gesammelte Aufsätze 1950–1968*, ed. Ferdinand Hahn, Traugott Holtz, and Nikolaus Walter. Göttingen: Vandenhoeck und Ruprecht, 1970 270–80.

"Nun aber sind sie heilig." *Studien zum Neuen Testament und zum hellenistischen Judentum: Gesammelte Aufsätze 1950–1968*, ed. Ferdinand Hahn, Traugott Holtz, and Nikolaus Walter. Göttingen: Vandenhoeck und Ruprecht, 1970, 257–69.

*Paulus' Stellung zu Frau und Ehe*. BWANT, 4/5. Stuttgart: W. Kohlhammer, 1931.

"Zur Exegese von I. Kor. 7,14." *Studien zum Neuen Testament und zum hellenistischen Judentum: Gesammelte Aufsätze 1950–1968*, ed. Ferdinand Hahn, Traugott Holtz, and Nikolaus Walter. Göttingen: Vandenhoeck und Ruprecht, 1970 281–7.

Deming, Will. "Paul on Marriage and Celibacy: The Hellenistic Background of 1 Corinthians 7." Ph.D. diss., University of Chicago, 1991.

"A Diatribe Pattern in 1 Cor. 7:21–22: A New Perspective on Paul's Directions to Slaves." *NovT* (forthcoming).

Derrett, J. Duncan M. "The Disposal of Virgins." *Studies in the New Testament*. Leiden: E. J. Brill, 1977 1.184–92.

Devine, Richard J. "Holy Virginity: A study of the New Testament Teaching on Virginity and Celibacy." Ph.D. diss., University of Fribourg, 1964.

DeWette, W. M. L. *Kurze Erklärung der Briefe an die Corinther*. 3rd edn., ed. Hermann Messner, Kurzgefasstes exegetisches Handbuch zum Neuen Testament, 2/2. Leipzig: S. Hirzel, 1855.

Di Lella, Alexander A. *The Hebrew Text of Sirach*. The Hague: Mouton, 1966.

Dibelius, Martin. *Der Hirt des Hermas*. HNT Ergänzungsband: Die Apostolischen Väter 4. Tübingen: J. C. B. Mohr, 1923.

Dibelius, Martin, and Hans Conzelmann. *The Pastoral Epistles*. Hermeneia. Philadelphia: Fortress, 1972.

Dihle, Albrecht. "Ethik." *RAC* 6 (1966) 646–796.

Dodd, C. H. *The Apostolic Preaching and its Developments: Three Lectures*. Chicago/New York: Willett, Clark and Company, 1937.

Donahue, John R. "Stoic Indifferents and Christian Indifference in Clement of Alexandria." *Traditio* 19 (1963) 438–46.

Doughty, Darrell J. "Heiligkeit und Freiheit: Eine exegetische Untersuchung der Anwendung des paulinischen Freiheitsgedankens in 1 Kor 7." Ph.D. diss., Göttingen, 1965.

"The Presence and Future of Salvation in Corinth." *ZNW* 66 (1975) 61–90.

Dudley, Donald B. *A History of Cynicism*. London: Methuen, 1937; reprint, Hildesheim: Georg Olms, 1967.

Dungan, David L. *The Sayings of Jesus in the Churches of Paul: The Use of the Synoptic Tradition in the Regulation of Early Church Life*. Philadelphia: Fortress, 1971.

Ebeling, Gerhard. "Der Grund christlicher Theologie: Zum Aufsatz Ernst Käsemanns über 'Die Anfänge christlicher Theologie.'" *ZTK* 58 (1961) 227–44.

Edwards, Thomas Charles. *A Commentary on the First Epistle to the Corinthians*. 2nd edn. New York: A. C. Armstrong and Son, 1886.

Ehrhardt, Arnold. *Politische Metaphysik von Solon bis Augustin*. Vol. 1: *Die Gottesstadt der Griechen und Römer*. Tübingen: J. C. B. Mohr, 1959.

Eijk, Ton H. C. van. "Marriage and Virginity, Death and Immortality." *Epektasis: Mélanges patristiques offerts au Cardinal Jean Daniélou*, ed. Jacques Fontaine and Charles Kannengiesser. Paris: Beauchesne, 1972 209–35.

Elliott, J. K. "Paul's Teaching on Marriage in I Corinthians: Some Problems Considered." *NTS* 19 (1972/73) 219–25.

Elorduy, Eleuterio. *Die Sozialphilosophie der Stoa*. Philologus, supplement 28/3. Leipzig: Dieterich, 1936.

Elze, Martin. *Tatian und seine Theologie*. Forschungen zur Kirchen- und Dogmengeschichte 9. Göttingen: Vandenhoeck und Ruprecht, 1960.

Engberg-Pedersen, Troels. *The Stoic Theory of Oikeiosis: Moral Development and Social Interaction in Early Stoic Philosophy*. Studies in Hellenistic Civilization 2. Aarhus: Aarhus University Press, 1991.

Erdmann, Walter. *Die Ehe im alten Griechenland*. Münchener Beiträge zur Papyrusforschung und antiken Rechtsgeschichte 20. Munich: C. H. Beck, 1934.

Eyben, Emiel. "Family Planning in Graeco-Roman Antiquity." *Ancient Society* 11/12 (1980/81) 5–82.

"De latere Stoa over het huwelijk." *Hermeneus: Tijdschrift voor antieke Cultuur* 50 (1978) 15–32, 71–94, 337–59.

Fahnenbruch, Franz. "Zu 1 Kor 7,36–38." *BZ* (Freiburg i. B.) 12 (1914) 391–401.

Fee, Gordon D. *The First Epistle to the Corinthians*. NICNT. Grand Rapids, Mich.: William B. Eerdmans, 1987.

"1 Corinthians 7:1 in the *N.I.V.*" *Journal of the Evangelical Theological Society* 23 (1980) 307–14.

Feldman, David Michael. *Birth Control in Jewish Law*. New York: New York University Press, 1968; London: University of London Press, 1968.

Ferguson, John. *Utopias of the Classical World*. London: Thomas and Hudson, 1975.

Festugière, André-Jean. *Personal Religion among the Greeks*. Sather Classical Lectures 26. Berkeley: University of California Press, 1954; reprint, Westport, Conn.: Greenwood, 1984.

Ficker, G. Review of *Virgines Subintroductae* by Hans Achelis. *Theologische Rundschau* 8 (1905) 117–18.

Fiedler, Peter. "Haustafel." *RAC* 13 (1986) 1063–73.

Field, James A., Jr. "The Purpose of the *Lex Iulia et Papia Poppaea*." *Classical Journal* 40 (1944/45) 398–416.

Fiorenza, Elisabeth Schüssler. *In Memory of Her: A Feminist Theological Reconstruction of Christian Origins*. New York: Crossroad, 1983. See also under Schüssler Fiorenza, Elisabeth.

Fischel, Henry A. *Rabbinic Literature and Greco-Roman Philosophy*. Studia Post-Biblica 21. Leiden: E. J. Brill, 1973.

"Studies in Cynicism and the Ancient Near East: The Transformation of a Chreia." *Religions in Antiquity: Essays in Memory of Erwin Ramsdell Goodenough*, Numen Supplements 14, ed. Jacob Neusner. Leiden: E. J. Brill, 1968 372–411.

Ford, J. Massyngberde (also Massingberd). *Revelation*. AB 38. Garden City, N.Y.: Doubleday, 1975.

"St Paul, the Philogamist (I Cor. vii in Early Patristic Exegesis)." *NTS* 11 (1964/65) 326–48.

*A Trilogy on Wisdom and Celibacy*. The Cardinal O'Hara Series: Studies and Research in Christian Theology at Notre Dame 4. Notre Dame, Ind./London: University of Notre Dame Press, 1967.

Forschner, Maximilian. *Die stoische Ethik: Über den Zusammenhang von Natur-, Sprach- und Moralphilosophie im altstoischen System*. Stuttgart: Klett-Cotta, 1981.

Foucault, Michel. *The Care of the Self*. The History of Sexuality 3. New York: Pantheon Books, 1986.

*The Use of Pleasure*. The History of Sexuality 2. New York: Pantheon Books, 1985.

Fraade, Steven D. "Ascetical Aspects of Ancient Judaism." *Jewish Spirituality: From the Bible through the Middle Ages*, ed. Arthur Green, World Spirituality: An Encyclopedic History of the Religious Quest 13. New York: Crossroad, 1986 253–88.

Frank, Karl Suso. *Grundzüge der Geschichte des christlichen Mönchtums*. Grundzüge 25. Darmstadt: Wissenschaftliche Buchgesellschaft, 1979.

Frank, Richard I. "Augustus' Legislation on Marriage and Children." *California Studies in Classical Antiquity* 8 (1975) 41–52.

Furnish, Victor Paul. *II Corinthians*. AB 32A. Garden City, N.Y.: Doubleday, 1984.

Gager, John G., Jr. *Kingdom and Community: The Social World of Early Christianity*. Englewood Cliffs, N. J.: Prentice-Hall, 1970.

"Functional Diversity in Paul's Use of End-Time Language." *JBL* 89 (1970) 325–37.

Gaiser, Konrad. *Für und wider die Ehe*. Munich: Heimeran, 1974.

Geffcken, Johannes. *Kynika und Verwandtes*. Heidelberg: Carl Winter, 1909.

Geurts, Nico. *Het Huwelijk bij de Griekse en Romeinse Moralisten*. Amsterdam: H. J. Paris, 1928.

Glotz, Gustave. *The Greek City and its Institutions*. New York: Alfred A. Knopf, 1951; reprint, Ann Arbor: University Microfilms, 1965.

Goessler, Lisette. "Plutarchs Gedanken über die Ehe." Ph.D. diss., Basel University, 1962.

Goodenough, Erwin R. *The Politics of Philo Judaeus: Practice and Theory*. New Haven: Yale University Press, 1938.

Goodspeed, Edgar J. *Problems of New Testament Translation*. Chicago: University of Chicago Press, 1945.

Gottschalk, H. B. "Aristotelian Philosophy in the Roman World from the Time of Cicero to the End of the Second Century AD." *ANRW* 2.36.2 (1987) 1079–1174.

242     *Bibliography*

Gow, A. S. F., and D. L. Page, ed. *The Greek Anthology: Hellenistic Epigrams*. Vol. 2: *Commentary and Indexes*. Cambridge: Cambridge University Press, 1965.

Grafe, Eduard. "Geistliche Verlöbnisse bei Paulus." *Theologische Arbeiten aus dem rheinischen wissenschaftlichen Predigerverein*, n.s. 3 (1899) 57–69.

Grant, Robert M. *Early Christianity and Society: Seven Studies*. San Francisco: Harper and Row, 1977.

"Early Christians and Gnostics in Graeco-Roman Society." *The New Testament and Gnosis: Essays in Honour of Robert McL. Wilson*, ed. A. H. B. Logan and A. J. M. Wedderburn. Edinburgh: T. and T. Clark, 1983 176–83.

*Gnosticism and Early Christianity*. 2nd edn. New York/London: Columbia University, 1966.

Green, Henry A. *The Economic and Social Origins of Gnosticism*. SBLDS 77. Atlanta: Scholars, 1985.

Greeven, Heinrich. "Ehe nach dem Neuen Testament." *Theologie der Ehe: Veröffentlichung des Ökumenischen Arbeitskreises evangelischer und katholischer Theologen*, ed. Gerhard Krems and Reinhard Mumm. Regensburg: Friedrich Pustet, 1969; Göttingen: Vandenhoeck und Ruprecht, 1969 37–79.

*Das Hauptproblem der Sozialethik in der neueren Stoa und im Urchristentum*. Neutestamentliche Forschung 3/4. Gütersloh: C. Bertelsmann, 1935.

Griffin, Miriam T. *Seneca: A Philosopher in Politics*. Oxford: Clarendon Press, 1976.

Grilli, Alberto. *Il problema della vita contemplativa nel mondo greco-romano*. Filologia e Letterature Classiche, 1st series. Milan/Rome: Fratelli Bocca, 1953.

Grosheide, F. W. *Commentary on the First Epistle to the Corinthians*. NICNT. Grand Rapids, Mich.: William B. Eerdmans, 1955.

Grotius, Hugo. *Annotationes in Novum Testamentum*. Vol. 2. Paris: Pelé, 1646.

Gryson, Roger. *Les origines du célibat ecclésiastique: Du premier au septième siècle*. Recherches et synthèses, section Histoire 2. Gembloux: J. Duculot, 1970.

Güttgemanns, Erhardt. *Der leidende Apostel und sein Herr: Studien zur paulinischen Christologie*. FRLANT 90. Göttingen: Vandenhoeck und Ruprecht, 1966.

Gummere, Richard M., ed. and trans. *Seneca: Ad Lucilium, epistulae morales*. 3 vols, LCL. London: William Heinemann, 1930; New York: G. P. Putnam's Sons, 1930.

Guntermann, Friedrich. *Die Eschatologie des Hl. Paulus*. NTAbh 13/4–5. Munster: Aschendorffsche Verlagsbuchhandlung, 1932.

Guthrie, W. K. C. *A History of Greek Philosophy*. Vol. 3: *The Fifth-Century Enlightenment*. Cambridge: Cambridge University Press, 1969.

*A History of Greek Philosophy*. Vol. 5: *The Later Plato and the Academy*. Cambridge: Cambridge University Press, 1978.

Häge, Günter. *Ehegüterrechtliche Verhältnisse in den griechischen Papyri*

*Ägyptens bis Diokletian.* Graezistische Abhandlungen 3. Cologne and Graz: Böhlau, 1968.

Hägg, Tomas. *The Novel in Antiquity.* Berkeley: University of California Press, 1983.

Hamlyn, D. W. *A History of Western Philosophy.* Harmondsworth: Penguin Books, 1987.

Hansen, Günther Christian. "Molestiae nuptiarum." *Wissenschaftliche Zeitschrift der Universität Rostock: Gesellschafts- und sprachwissenschaftliche Reihe* 2/12 (1963) 215–19.

Hauck, Friedrich. "μακάριος D.1." *TDNT* 4 (1967) 367–9.

Hauck, Friedrich, and Siegfried Schulz. "πόρνη." *TDNT* 6 (1968) 579–95.

Heinrici, C. F. Georg. *Der erste Brief an die Korinther.* MeyerK 5, 8th edn. Göttingen: Vandenhoeck und Ruprecht, 1896.

*Das erste Sendschreiben des Apostle Paulus an die Korinthier.* Berlin: Wilhelm Hertz, 1880.

Helm, Rudolf. "Kynismus." *PW* 12.1, half-vol. 23 (1924) 3–24.

Hengel, Martin. *Judaism and Hellenism: Studies in Their Encounter in Palestine during the Early Hellenistic Period.* 2 vols. Philadelphia: Fortress, 1974.

Henrion, Lise. "La conception de la Nature et du rôle de la Femme chez les philosophes cyniques et stoïciens." Ph.D. diss., Université de Liège, 1942/43.

Hense, Otto. "Bio bei Philo." *Rh. Mus.*, n.s. 47 (1892) 219–40.

"Zu Antipatros von Tarsos." *Rh. Mus.*, n.s. 73 (1920/24) 290–305.

Herklotz, Franz. "Zu 1 Kor 7,36ff." *BZ* (Freiburg i. B.) 14 (1916/17) 344–5.

Héring, Jean. *The First Epistle of Saint Paul to the Corinthians.* London: Epworth, 1962.

Heth, William A. "Unmarried 'For the Sake of the Kingdom' (Matthew 19:12) in the Early Church." *Grace Theological Journal* 8 (1987) 55–88.

Hicks, R. D. *Stoic and Epicurean.* Epochs of Philosophy. New York: Charles Scribner's Sons, 1920.

ed. and trans., *Diogenes Laertius: Lives of Eminent Philosophers.* 2 vols, LCL. London: William Heinemann, 1925; Cambridge: Harvard University Press, 1925.

Hierzenberger, Gottfried. *Weltbewertung bei Paulus nach 1 Kor 7,29–31: Eine exegetisch-kerygmatische Studie.* Kommentare und Beiträge zum Alten und Neuen Testament. Düsseldorf: Patmos, 1967.

Hilgenfeld, Adolf. *Die apostolischen Väter: Untersuchungen über Inhalt und Ursprung der unter ihrem Namen erhaltenen Schriften.* Halle: C. E. M. Pfeffer, 1853.

*Die Glossolalie in der alten Kirche, in dem Zusammenhang der Geistesgaben und des Geisteslebens des alten Christenthums: Eine exegetisch-historische Untersuchung.* Leipzig: Breitkopf und Härtel, 1850.

Himes, Norman Edwin. *Medical History of Contraception.* London: Geo. Allen and Unwin, 193–6; Baltimore: Williams and Wilkins, 1936; reprint, New York: Gamut, 1963.

Hock, Roland F., and Edward N. O'Neil, ed. *The Chreia in Ancient*

*Rhetoric.* Vol. 1: *The "Progymnasmata."* SBLTT 27/SBLGRS 9. Atlanta: Scholars, 1986.

Höistad, Ragnar. "Cynic Hero and Cynic King: Studies in the Cynic Conception of Man." Inaugural diss., Uppsala, 1948.

Hofmann, Johann Christian Konrad von. *Die heilige Schrift neuen Testaments: Zusammenhängend untersucht.* Vol. 2/2. Nördlingen: C. H. Beck, 1864.

Holladay, Carl R. *"Theios Aner" in Hellenistic Judaism: A Critique of the Use of this Category in NT Christology.* SBLDS 40. Missoula, Mont.: Scholars, 1977.

Hollander, Harm W. *Joseph as an Ethical Model in the Testaments of the Twelve Patriarchs.* Studia in Veteris Testamenti Pseudepigrapha 6. Leiden: E. J. Brill, 1981.

Hopkins, Keith. "A Textual Emendation in a Fragment of Musonius Rufus: A Note on Contraception." *CQ, n.s.* 15 (1965) 72–4.

Hopkins, M. K. "Contraception in the Roman Empire." *Comparative Studies in Society and History* 8 (1965) 124–51.

Horsley, Richard A. "'How Can Some of You Say That There Is No Resurrection of the Dead?': Spiritual Elitism in Corinth." *NovT* 20 (1978) 203–31.

"Gnosis in Corinth: I Corinthians 8.1–6." *NTS* 27 (1980/81) 32–51.

"Pneumatikos vs. Psychikos: Distinctions of Spiritual Status Among the Corinthians." *HTR* 69 (1976) 269–88.

*Sociology and the Jesus Movement.* New York: Crossroad, 1989.

"Spiritual Marriage with Sophia." *VC* 33 (1979) 30–54.

"Wisdom of Word and Words of Wisdom in Corinth." *CBQ* 39 (1977) 224–39.

Horst, P. W. van der. *The Sentences of Pseudo-Phocylides.* Studia in Veteris Testamenti Pseudepigrapha 4. Leiden: E. J. Brill, 1978.

Humbert, Michel. *Le remariage à Rome: Étude d'histoire juridique et sociale.* Università di Roma: Pubblicazioni dell' Istituto di diritto Romano e dei diritti dell' oriente mediterraneo 44. Milan: A. Giuffrè, 1972.

Hurd, John Coolidge, Jr. *The Origin of I Corinthians.* London: SPCK, 1965; reprint, Macon, Ga.: Mercer University Press, 1983.

Isaac, E. "1 (Ethiopic Apocalypse of) ENOCH." *The Old Testament Pseudepigrapha,* ed. James H. Charlesworth, vol. 1. Garden City, N.Y.: Doubleday, 1983, 5–89.

Jeremias, Joachim. "Die missionarische Aufgabe in der Mischehe (1. Kor. 7,16)." *Abba: Studien zur neutestamentlichen Theologie und Zeitgeschichte.* Göttingen: Vandenhoeck und Ruprecht, 1966 292–8.

"Zur Gedankenführung in den paulinischen Briefen." *Abba: Studien zur neutestamentlichen Theologie und Zeitgeschichte.* Göttingen: Vandenhoeck und Ruprecht, 1966 269–76.

Jonas, Hans. *Gnosis und spätantiker Geist.* Vol. 1: *Die mythologische Gnosis,* 3rd edn. Göttingen: Vandenhoeck und Ruprecht, 1964.

*The Gnostic Religion.* 2nd edn. Boston: Beacon, 1963.

Jones, F. Stanley. *"Freiheit" in den Briefen des Apostels Paulus: Eine historische, exegetische und religionsgeschichtliche Studie.* Göttinger Theologische Arbeiten 34. Göttingen: Vandenhoeck und Ruprecht, 1987.

Jülicher, Adolf. "Die geistlichen Ehen in der alten Kirche." *Archiv für Religionswissenschaft* 7 (1904) 372–86.
"Die Jungfrauen im ersten Korintherbrief." *Protestantische Monatshefte* 22 (1918) 97–119.
Juncker, Alfred. *Die Ethik des Apostels Paulus.* Vol. 2: *Die konkrete Ethik.* Halle a. S.: Max Niemeyer, 1919.
Kahn, Charles H. "Arius as a Doxographer." *On Stoic and Peripatetic Ethics: The Work of Arius Didymus,* Rutgers University Studies in Classical Humanities 1, ed. William W. Fortenbaugh. New Brunswick: Transactions Books, 1983 3–13.
Käsemann, Ernst. "On the Subject of Primitive Christian Apocalyptic." *New Testament Questions of Today,* Philadelphia: Fortress, 1969 108–37.
"Sentences of Holy Law in the New Testament." *New Testament Questions of Today.* Philadelphia: Fortress, 1969, 67–81.
Kaser, Max. *Das römische Privatrecht.* Vol. 1: *Das altrömische, das vorklassische und klassische Recht,* 2nd edn. Handbuch der Altertumswissenschaft, Rechtsgeschichte des Altertums. Munich: C. H. Beck, 1971 10.3.3.1.
Keck, Leander E., and Victor Paul Furnish. *The Letters of Paul.* Interpreting Biblical Texts. Nashville: Abingdon, 1984.
Kee, Howard Clark. "The Ethical Dimensions of the Testaments of the XII as a Clue to Provenance." *NTS* 24 (1978) 259–70.
"Pauline Eschatology: Relationships with Apocalyptic and Stoic Thought." *Glaube und Eschatologie: Festschrift für Werner Georg Kümmel zum 80. Geburtstag,* ed. Erich Gräßer and Otto Merk. Tübingen: J. C. B. Mohr, 1985 135–58.
"Testaments of the Twelve Patriarchs." *The Old Testament Pseudepigrapha,* ed. James H. Charlesworth. Garden City, N.Y.: Doubleday, 1985 1.775–828.
Keyes, Clinton Walker, ed. and trans. *Cicero: De Re Publica, De Legibus.* LCL. Cambridge: Harvard University Press, 1928; London: William Heinemann, 1928.
Kidd, I. G. "Cynics." *Encyclopedia of Philosophy,* ed. Paul Edwards, 2 (1967) 284–5.
"Stoic Intermediates and the End for Man." *Problems in Stoicism,* ed. Anthony Arthur Long. London: University of London Athlone Press, 1971, 216–38.
Kiefer, Otto. *Sexual Life in Ancient Rome.* London: George Routledge and Sons, 1938.
Klassen, William, "Musonius Rufus, Jesus, and Paul: Three First-Century Feminists." *From Jesus to Paul: Studies in Honour of Francis Wright Beare,* ed. Peter Richardson and John Coolidge Hurd. Waterloo, Ontario, Canada: Wilfrid Laurier University Press, 1984 185–206.
Klawiter, Frederick Charles. "The New Prophecy in Early Christianity: The Origin, Nature, and Development of Montanism, AD 165–220." Ph.D. diss., University of Chicago, 1975.
Klein, Günter. "Apokalyptische Naherwartung bei Paulus." *Neues Testament und christliche Existenz: Festschrift für Herbert Braun zum 70. Geburtstag am 4. Mai 1973,* ed. Hans Dieter Betz and Luise Schottroff. Tübingen: J. C. B. Mohr, 1973 241–62.

Kleiner, Diana E. E. "The Great Friezes of the Ara Pacis Augustae: Greek Sources, Roman Derivatives, and Augustan Social Policy." *Mélanges de l'École Française de Rome: Antiquité* 90 (1978) 753–85.

Klijn, A. F. J., trans. "2 (Syriac Apocalypse of) Baruch." *The Old Testament Pseudepigrapha*, ed. James H. Charlesworth. Garden City, N.Y.: Doubleday, 1985 2.615–52.

Kloppenborg, John S. *The Formation of Q: Trajectories in Ancient Wisdom Collections.* Studies in Antiquity and Christianity. Philadelphia: Fortress, 1987.

"Symbolic Eschatology and the Apocalypticism of Q." *HTR* 80 (1987) 287–306.

Koch, Hugo. *Virgines Christi: Die Gelübde der gottgeweihten Jungfrauen in den ersten drei Jahrhunderten.* TU 31/2. Leipzig: J. C. Hinrichs, 1907 59–112.

Koch, Klaus. *The Rediscovery of Apocalyptic: A Polemical Work on a Neglected Area of Biblical Studies and its Damaging Effects on Theology and Philosophy.* Studies in Biblical Theology, 2nd ser. 22. Naperville, Ill.: Alec R. Allenson, (1972).

Koester, Helmut. Review of *Weisheit und Torheit* by Ulrich Wilckens. *Gnomon* 33 (1961) 590–5.

Kretschmar, Georg. "Ein Beitrag zur Frage nach dem Ursprung frühchristlicher Askese." *ZTK* 61 (1964) 27–67.

Kubo, Sakae. "I Corinthians vii. 16: Optimistic or Pessimistic?" *NTS* 24 (1977/78) 539–44.

Kugelmann, Richard. "1 Cor 7:36–38." *CBQ* 10 (1948) 63–71.

Kümmel, Werner Georg. "Verlobung und Heirat bei Paulus (I. Cor 7 36–38)." *Neutestamentliche Studien für Rudolf Bultmann*, ed. Walther Eltester, Beiheft zur ZNW 21. Berlin: Alfred Töpelmann, 1954 275–95. Now in: *Heilsgeschehen und Geschichte: Gesammelte Aufsätze 1933–1964.* Edited Erich Grässer, Otto Merk, and Adolf Fritz, Marburger Theologische Studien 3. Marburg: N. G. Elwert, 1965 310–27.

Labriolle, Pierre de. "Le «mariage spirituel» dans l'antiquité chrétienne." *Revue Historique* 137 (1921) 204–25.

Lacey, W. K. *The Family in Classical Greece.* Aspects of Greek and Roman Life. London: Thames and Hudson, 1968.

Ladeuze, P. Review of *Virgines Subintroductae* by Hans Achelis. *Revue d'Histoire Ecclésiastique* 6 (1905) 58–62.

Lake, Kirsopp. *The Apostolic Fathers.* Vol. 2: *The Shepherd of Hermas, the Martyrdom of Polycarp, the Epistle to Diognetus*, LCL. Cambridge: Harvard University Press, 1913; London: William Heinemann, 1913.

*The Earlier Epistles of St. Paul: Their Motive and Origin.* 2nd edn. London: Rivingtons, 1914.

Lane Fox, Robin. *Pagans and Christians.* New York: Alfred A. Knopf, 1987.

Laub, Franz. *Eschatologische Verkündigung und Lebensgestaltung nach Paulus: Eine Untersuchung zum Wirken des Apostels beim Aufbau der Gemeinde in Thessalonike.* BU 10. Regensburg: Friedrich Pustet, 1973.

Lausberg, Marion. *Untersuchungen zu Senecas Fragmenten.* Untersuchungen zur antiken Literatur und Geschichte 7. Berlin: Walter de Gruyter, 1970.

Legrand, Lucien. *The Biblical Doctrine of Virginity.* London: Geoffrey Chapman, 1963.

"The Prophetical Meaning of Celibacy – I." *Scripture* 12 (1960) 97–105.

"Saint Paul et célibat." *Sacerdoce et Célibat: Études historiques et théologiques,* ed. Joseph Coppens, Bibliotheca Ephemeridum Theologicarum Lovaniensium 28. Gembloux: Duculot, 1971; Louvain: Peeters, 1971 315–31.

Legrand, Ph. E. *Daos: Tableau de la comédie grecque.* Lyon: A. Rey, 1910.

Leipoldt, Johannes. *Griechische Philosophie und frühchristliche Askese.* Berlin: Akademie, 1961.

Léon-Dufour, Xavier. "Mariage et continence selon S. Paul." *A la recontre de Dieu: Mémorial Albert Gelin,* ed. A. Barucq, A. George, and H. de Lubac. Bibliothèque de la Faculté Catholique Théologie de Lyon 8. Le Puy: Xavier Mappus, 1961 319–29.

Lesky, E., and J. H. Waszink. "Embryologie." *RAC* 4 (1959) 1228–44.

"Mariage et virginité selon saint Paul." *Christus* 11 (1964) 179–94.

Lewis, Theodore J. "Belial." *Anchor Bible Dictionary* 1 (1992) 654–6.

Lietzmann, Hans. *An die Korinther I·II.* 5th edn., rev. Werner Georg Kümmel, HNT 9. Tübingen: J. C. B. Mohr, 1969.

Lohse, Bernhard. *Askese und Mönchtum in der Antike und in der alten Kirche.* Religion und Kultur der alten Mittelmeerwelt in Parallelforschungen 1. Munich/Vienna: R. Oldenbourg, 1969.

*Mönchtum und Reformation.* Göttingen: Vandenhoeck und Ruprecht, 1963.

Long, A. A. *Hellenistic Philosophy: Stoics, Epicureans, Sceptics.* 2nd edn. Berkeley: University of California Press, 1986.

Long, A. A., and D. N. Sedley. *The Hellenistic Philosophers.* Vol. 1: *Translations of the Principal Sources with Philosophical Commentary.* Cambridge: Cambridge University Press, 1987.

Lovejoy, Arthur O., and George Boas. *Primitivism and Related Ideas in Antiquity.* Baltimore: John Hopkins University Press, 1935; reprint, New York: Octagon Books, 1973.

Lütgert, W. *Freiheitspredigt und Schwarmgeister in Korinth: Ein Beitrag zur Charakteristik der Christuspartei.* Beiträge zur Förderung christliche Theologie 12/3. Gütersloh: C. Bertelsmann, 1908.

Luther, Martin. *Luther's Works.* Edited Jaroslav Pelikan and Helmut Lehmann, vol. 28: *Commentaries on 1 Corinthians 7, 1 Corinthians 15, Lectures on 1 Timothy,* ed. Hilton C. Oswald. Saint Louis: Concordia, 1973.

Luttikhuizen, Gerard P. *The Revelation of Elchasai: Investigations into the Evidence for a Mesopotamian Jewish Apocalypse of the Second Century and its Reception by Judeo-Christian Propagandists.* Texte und Studien zum Antiken Judentum 8. Tübingen: J. C. B. Mohr, 1985.

Lutz, Cora E. "Musonius Rufus 'The Roman Socrates.'" *Yale Classical Studies* 10, ed. Alfred R. Bellinger. New Haven: Yale University Press, 1947 3–147.

MacDonald, Margaret Y. "Early Christian Women Married to Unbelievers." *Studies in Religion/Sciences Religieuses* 19 (1990) 221–34.

Mack, Burton L. *A Myth of Innocence: Mark and Christian Origins*. Philadelphia: Fortress, 1988.

MacMullen, Ramsay. *Enemies of the Roman Order*. Cambridge: Harvard University Press, 1966.

MacRae, George W. Review of *Gnosticism in Corinth: An Investigation of the Letters to the Corinthians* by Walter Schmithals. *Interpretation 26* (1972) 489–91.

Malherbe, Abraham J. "Cynics." *IDB* supplement vol. (1962) 201–3.

"'Gentle as a Nurse': The Cynic Background to I Thess ii." *NovT* 12 (1970) 203–17.

*Moral Exhortation: A Greco-Roman Sourcebook*. Library of Early Christianity. Philadelphia: Westminster, 1986.

*Paul and the Popular Philosophers*. Minneapolis: Fortress, 1989.

*Paul and the Thessalonians: The Philosophic Tradition of Pastoral Care*. Philadelphia: Fortress, 1987.

"Self-Definition among Epicureans and Cynics." *Jewish and Christian Self Definition*. Vol. 3: *Self-Definition in the Greco-Roman World*, ed. Ben F. Meyer and E. P. Sanders. London: SMC, 1982 46–59.

ed. *The Cynic Epistles*. SBLSBS 12. Missoula, Mont.: Scholars, 1977.

Marrou, H. I. *A History of Education in Antiquity*. Wisconsin Studies in Classics. Madison: University of Wisconsin Press, 1982.

Marshall, Peter. *Enmity in Corinth: Social Conventions in Paul's Relations with the Corinthians*. WUNT, 2/23. Tübingen: J. C. B. Mohr, 1987.

Martin, Hubert, Jr. "Amatorius (Moralia 748E–771E)." *Plutarch's Ethical Writings and Early Christian Literature*, ed. Hans Dieter Betz, Studia ad Corpus Hellenisticum Novi Testamenti 4. Leiden: E. J. Brill, 1978 442–537.

Matura, Thaddée. "Le célibat dans le NT d'après l'exégèse recente." *NRT* 97 (1975) 481–500, 593–604.

Maurer, Christian. "Ehe und Unzucht nach 1. Korinther 6,12–7,7." *Wort und Dienst*, n.s. 6 (1959) 159–69.

Meeks, Wayne A. *The First Urban Christians: The Social World of the Apostle Paul*. New Haven/London: Yale University Press, 1983.

"The Image of the Androgyne: Some Uses of a Symbol in Earliest Christianity." *HR* 13 (1973/74) 165–208.

*The Moral World of the First Christians*. Library of Early Christianity. Philadelphia: Westminster, 1986.

"Social Functions of Apocalyptic Language in Pauline Christianity." *Apocalypticism in the Mediterranean World and the Near East*, ed. David Hellholm. Tübingen: J. C. B. Mohr, 1983 687–705.

Merklein, Helmut. "'Es ist gut für den Menschen, eine Frau nicht anzufassen': Paulus und die Sexualität nach 1 Kor 7." *Die Frau im Urchristentum*, ed. Gerhard Dautzenberg, Helmut Merklein, and Karlheinz Müller. Quaestiones Disputatae 95. Freiburg/Basel/Vienna: Herder, 1983 225–53. Now in: *Studien zu Jesus und Paulus*. WUNT 43. Tübingen: J. C. B. Mohr 1987 385–408.

Meyer, Heinrich August Wilhelm. *Critical and Exegetical Handbook to the Epistles to the Corinthians*. Vol. 1: *First Epistle, Ch. I.–XIII*, rev. William P. Dickson, Critical and Exegetical Commentary on the New Testament 5. Edinburgh: T. and T. Clark, 1892.

Michl, Johann. "Engel II (jüdisch)." *RAC* 5 (1962) 60–97.
Miller, Walter, ed. and trans. *Cicero.* Vol. 21: *De Officiis,* LCL. Cambridge: Harvard University Press, 1913; London: William Heinemann, 1913.
Mitchell, Margaret M. *Paul and the Rhetoric of Reconciliation: An Exegetical Investigation of the Language and Composition of 1 Corinthians.* Louisville, Ky.: Westminster/John Knox, 1991.
Mosheim, Johann Lorenz von. *Erklärung des Ersten Briefes des heiligen Apostles Pauli an die Gemeinde zu Corinthus.* 2nd edn., ed. Christian Ernst von Windheim. Flensburg: Kortem, 1762.
Moulton, James Hope, and George Milligan. *The Vocabulary of the Greek Testament: Illustrated from the Papyri and Other Non-Literary Sources.* Pts. 1–8. London: Hodder and Stoughton, 1915–29; reprint, Grand Rapids, Mich.: William B. Eerdmans, 1980.
Müller, Ulrich B. *Prophetie und Predigt im Neuen Testament: Formgeschichtliche Untersuchungen zur urchristlichen Prophetie.* SNT 10. Gütersloh: Gerd Mohn, 1975.
Mulgan, R. G. *Aristotle's Political Theory: An Introduction for Students of Political Theory.* Oxford: Clarendon Press, 1977.
Murphy-O'Connor, J. "Philo and 2 Cor 6:14–7:1." *RB* 95 (1988) 55–69.
Nadeau, Ray. "The Progymnasmata of Aphthonius." *Speech Monographs* 19 (1952) 264–85.
Nagel, Peter. *Die Motivierung der Askese in der alten Kirche und der Ursprung des Mönchtums.* TU 95. Berlin: Akademie, 1966.
Neuhäusler, E. "Ruf Gottes und Stand des Christen: Bemerkungen zu 1 Kor 7." *BZ* n.s. 3 (1959) 43–60.
Niederwimmer, Kurt. *Askese und Mysterium: Über Ehe, Ehescheidung und Eheverzicht in den Anfängen des christlichen Glaubens.* FRLANT 113. Göttingen: Vandenhoeck und Ruprecht, 1975.
"Zur Analyse der asketischen Motivation in 1. Kor 7." *TLZ* 99 (1974) 241–8.
Nilsson, Martin P. *Geschichte der griechischen Religion.* Vol. 2, 2nd edn., Handbuch der Altertumswissenschaft 5.2. Munich: C. H. Beck, 1961.
Noonan, John T., Jr. *Contraception: A History of Its Treatment by the Catholic Theologians and Canonists,* rev. ed. Cambridge: Harvard University Press, 1965.
O'Neil, Edward N., ed. and trans. *Teles (The Cynic Teacher).* SBLTT 11. Missoula, Mont.: Scholars, 1977.
Oepke, Albrecht. "Ehe I." *RAC* 4 (1959) 650–66.
"Irrwege in der neueren Paulusforschung." *TLZ* 77 (1952) 449–58.
Okin, Susan Moller. *Women in Western Political Thought.* Princeton: Princeton University Press, 1979.
Oldfather, W. A., ed. and trans. *Epictetus: The Discourses as Reported by Arrian, the Manual, and Fragments.* 2 vols, LCL. Cambridge: Harvard University Press, 1959; London: William Heinemann, 1959.
Opelt, Ilona. "Etymologie." *RAC* 6 (1966) 797–844.
Orr, William F., and James Arthur Walther. *I Corinthians: A New Translation.* AB 32. Garden City, N.Y.: Doubleday, 1976.
Oster, Richard E., Jr., "Use, Misuse and Neglect of Archaeological Evidence in Some Modern Works on 1 Corinthians (1 Cor 7,1–5; 8,10; 11,2–16; 12,14–26)." *ZNW* 83 (1992) 52–73.

Oulton, John Ernest Leonard, and Henry Chadwick. *Alexandrian Christianity*. Library of Christian Classics 2. London: SCM, 1954.

Pagels, Elaine H. "Paul and Women: A Response to Recent Discussion." *JAAR* 42 (1974) 538–49.

Painter, John. "Paul and the Πνευματικοί at Corinth." *Paul and Paulinism: Essays in Honour of C. K. Barrett*, ed. M. D. Hooker. London: SPCK, 1982 237–50.

Parente, Margherita Isnardi. "Ierocle Stoico: Oikeiosis e doveri sociali." *ANRW* 2.36.3 (1989) 2201–26.

Parker, Charles Pomeroy. "Musonius in Clement." *Harvard Studies in Classical Philology* 12 (1901) 191–200.

Pautrel, Raymond. "Ben Sira et le stoïcisme." *Recherches de Science Religieuse* 51 (1963) 535–49.

Pearson, Birger Albert "Philo, Gnosis and the New Testament." *The New Testament and Gnosis: Essays in Honour of Robert McL. Wilson*, ed. A. H. B. Logan and A. J. M. Wedderburn. Edinburgh: T. and T. Clark, 1983 73–89.

*The Pneumatikos-Psychikos Terminology in 1 Corinthians: A Study in the Theology of the Corinthian Opponents of Paul and its Relation to Gnosticism*. SBLDS 12. Missoula, Mont.: SBL, 1973.

Pembroke, S. G. "Oikeiōsis." *Problems in Stoicism*, ed. A. A. Long. London: University of London Athlone Press, 1971, 114–49.

Penna, Romano. "San Paolo (1 Cor 7,29b-31a) e Diogene il Cinico." *Biblica* 58 (1977) 237–45.

Pervo, Richard I. "Joseph and Asenath and the Greek Novel." *SBL 1976 Seminar Papers: One Hundred Twelfth Annual Meeting*. SBLSPS 10. Missoula, Mont.: Scholars, 1976 171–81.

Pestman, P. W. *Marriage and Matrimonial Property in Ancient Egypt: A Contribution to Establishing the Legal Position of Women*. Papyrologica Lugduno-Batava 9. Leiden: E. J. Brill, 1961.

Petit, Madeleine, ed. *"Quod omnis probus liber sit": Introduction, texte, traduction et notes*. Les œuvres de Philon d'Alexandrie 28. Paris: Éditions du Cerf, 1974.

Philippson, Robert. "Hierokles der Stoiker." *Rh. Mus*, n.s. 82 (1933) 97–114.

Plooij, D. "Eine enkratitische Glosse im Diatessaron." *ZNW* 22 (1923) 1–16.

Pohlenz, Max. *Freedom in Greek Life and Thought: The History of an Ideal*. Dordrecht, Holland: D. Reidel, 1966; New York: Humanities, 1966.

"Klemens von Alexandreia und sein hellenisches Christentum." *Nachrichten der Akademie der Wissenschaften zu Göttingen, philologisch-historische Klasse* 5.3 (1943) 103–80. Now in: *Kleine Schriften*, vol. 1, ed. Heinrich Dörrie. Hildesheim: Georg Olms, 1965 481–558 (507 is out of sequence).

"Paulus und die Stoa." *ZNW* 42 (1949) 69–104. Also available as: *Paulus und die Stoa*. Darmstadt: Wissenschaftliche Buchgesellschaft, 1964; and in Karl Heinrich Rengstorf, ed., *Das Paulusbild in der neueren deutschen Forschung, Wege der Forschung* 24. Darmstadt: Wissenschaftliche Buchgesellschaft, 1969 522–64.

"Philon von Alexandreia." *Nachrichten der Akademie der Wissenschaften zu Göttingen, philologisch-historische Klasse* 4 (1942) 409–87. Now in: *Kleine Schriften*. Vol. 1, ed. Heinrich Dörrie. Hildesheim: Georg Olms, 1965 305–83.

*Die Stoa: Geschichte einer geistigen Bewegung.* 2 vols, 2nd edn. Göttingen: Vandenhoeck und Ruprecht, 1959.

ed. and trans., *Stoa und Stoiker.* Vol. 1: *Die Gründer, Panaitios, Poseidonios,* Die Bibliothek der alten Welt: Griechische Reihe. Zurich: Artemis, 1950.

Pomeroy, Sarah B. *Goddesses, Whores, Wives, and Slaves: Women in Classical Antiquity.* New York: Schocken, 1975.

Potterie, Ignace de la. "Le titre ΚΥΡΙΟΣ appliqué à Jésus dans l'Évangile de Luc." *Mélanges bibliques: En hommage au R. P. Béda Rigaux,* ed. Albert Descamps and André de Halleux. Gembloux: J. Duculot, 1970 117–46.

Praechter, Karl. *Hierokles der Stoiker.* Leipzig: Dieterich, 1901. Now in: *Kleine Schriften,* ed. Heinrich Dörrie, Collectanea 7. Hildesheim/New York: Georg Olms, 1973, 310–474 (with original pagination in brackets).

Preisker, Herbert. *Christentum und Ehe in den ersten drei Jahrhunderten: Eine Studie zur Kulturgeschichte der alten Welt.* Neue Studien zur Geschichte der Theologie und der Kirche 23. Berlin: Trowitzsch und Sohn, 1927; reprint, Aalen: Scientia, 1979.

"Ehe und Charisma bei Paulus." *ZST* 6 (1928/29) 91–5.

Prete, Benedetto. *Matrimonio e continenza nel cristianesimo delle origini: Studio su 1 Cor. 7,1–40.* Studi Biblici 49. Brescia: Paideia, 1979.

Preysing, Konrad Graf. "Ehezweck und zweite Ehe bei Athenagoras." *TQ* 110 (1929) 85–110.

Puzo, Félix. "Marta y María: Nota exegética a Lc 10,38–42 y 1 Cor 7,29–35." *Estudios Eclesiásticos* 34 (1960) 851–7.

Quispel, G. "The Syrian Thomas and the Syrian Macarius." *VC* 18 (1964) 226–35.

Rabinowitz, Jacob J. *Jewish Law: Its Influence on the Development of Legal Institutions.* New York: Block Publishing Co., 1956.

Rackham, H., ed. and trans. *Cicero: De finibus bonorum et malorum.* LCL. London: William Heinemann, 1914; New York: Macmillan, 1914.

Raditsa, Leo Ferrero. "Augustus' Legislation Concerning Marriage, Procreation, Love Affairs and Adultery." *ANRW* 2.13 (1980) 278–339.

Reitzenstein, Richard. "Etymologika." *PW* 6.1, half-vol. 11 (1907) 808–9.

Rengstorf, Karl Heinrich. "ἀποστέλλω." *TDNT* 1 (1964) 398–447.

"στέλλω." TDNT 7 (1971) 588–99.

Resch, Alfred. *Agrapha: Aussercanonische Schriftfragmente.* TU n.s. 15/3–4. Leipzig: J. C. Hinrichs, 1906.

Rex, Helmut H. "Das ethische Problem in der eschatologischen Existenz bei Paulus." Diss., Tübingen, 1954. Summarized (by editorial staff) in *TLZ* 80 (1955) 240–1.

Richardson, P. "'I Say, Not the Lord': Personal Opinion, Apostolic Authority and the Development of Early Christian Halakah." *Tyndale Bulletin* 31 (1980) 65–86.

Riedel, Manfred. *Metaphysik und Metapolitik: Studien zu Aristoteles und*

*zur politischen Sprache der neuzeitlichen Philosophie.* Frankfort: Suhr-
kamp, 1975.
Rist, J. M. *Stoic Philosophy.* Cambridge: Cambridge University Press,
1969.
Roberts, R. L., Jr. "The Meaning of *Chorizo* and *Douloo* in I Corinthians
7:10–17." *Restoration Quarterly* 80 (1965) 179–84.
Robertson, Archibald, and Alfred Plummer. *A Critical and Exegetical
Commentary on the First Epistle of St Paul to the Corinthians.* 2nd edn.,
ICC. Edinburgh: T. and T. Clark, 1914.
Robinson, James M. "Kerygma and History in the New Testament."
*Trajectories through Early Christianity,* ed. James M. Robinson and
Helmut Koester. Philadelphia: Fortress, 1971 20–70.
Rollins, Wayne G. "The New Testament and Apocalyptic." *NTS* 17
(1970/71) 454–76.
Rousselle, Aline. *Porneia: On Desire and the Body in Antiquity.* New York:
Basil Blackwell, 1988.
Rückert, L. J. *Der erste Brief Pauli an die Korinther.* Die Briefe Pauli an die
Korinther 1. Leipzig: K. F. Köhler, 1836.
Ruether, Rosemary Radford. "Is Celibacy Eschatological? The Suppress-
ion of Christian Radicalism." *Liberation Theology: Human Hope Con-
fronts Christian History and American Power.* New York: Paulist Press,
1972 51–64.
"Misogynism and Virginal Feminism in the Fathers of the Church."
*Religion and Sexism: Images of Women in the Jewish and Christian
Traditions.* New York: Simon and Schuster, 1974 150–83.
Salmon, Pierre. *Population et dépopulation dans l'Empire romain.* Collection
Latomus 137. Brussels: Latomus, 1974.
Sandbach, F. H. *Aristotle and the Stoics.* Cambridge Philological Society,
supplement 10. Cambridge: Cambridge Philological Society, 1985.
Sanders, E. P. *Paul and Palestinian Judaism: A Comparison of Patterns of
Religion.* Philadelphia: Fortress, 1977.
*Paul, the Law and the Jewish People.* Philadelphia: Fortress, 1983.
Schaff, Philip, and Henry Wace, ed. *A Select Library of Nicene and Post-
Nicene Fathers of the Christian Church.* 2nd series, vol. 6: *St. Jerome:
Letters and Select Works.* New York: Christian Literature Co., 1893;
reprint, Grand Rapids: William B. Eerdmans, n.d.
Schilling, Robert. "Vestales et vierges chrétiennes dans la Rome antique."
*Revue de Sciences Religieuses* 35 (1961) 113–29.
Schlatter, Adolf von. *Paulus der Bote Jesu: Eine Deutung seiner Briefe an die
Korinther.* Stuttgart: Calwer, 1934; reprint, 1956.
Schlier, Heinrich. "θλίβω, θλῖψις." *TDNT* 3 (1965) 139–48.
Schmeller, Thomas. *Paulus und die "Diatribe": Eine vergleichende Stilinter-
pretation.* NTAbh, n.s. 19. Münster: Aschendorffsche Verlagsbuch-
handlung, 1987.
Schmidt, Karl Ludwig. "καλέω." *TDNT* 3 (1965) 487–536.
Schmiedel, Paul Wilhelm. *Die Briefe an die Thessalonicher und an die
Korinther.* Hand-Commentar zum Neuen Testament 2/1. Freiburg: J.
C. B. Mohr, 1891.
Schmithals, Walter. *Gnosticism in Corinth: An Investigation of the Letters to
the Corinthians.* Nashville/New York: Abingdon, 1971.

*Neues Testament und Gnosis.* Erträge der Forschung 208. Darmstadt: Wissenschaftliche Buchgesellschaft, 1984.

Schnackenburg, Rudolf. "Die Ehe nach dem Neuen Testament." *Theologie der Ehe: Veröffentlichung des Ökumenischen Arbeitskreises evangelischer und katholischer Theologen*, ed. Gerhard Krems and Reinhard Mumm. Regensburg: Friedrich Pustet/Göttingen: Vandenhoeck und Ruprecht, 1969, 9–36. Now in: *Schriften zum Neuen Testament: Exegese in Fortschritt und Wandel.* Munich: Kösel, 1971 414–34.

Schniewind, Julius. "Die Leugner der Auferstehung in Korinth." *Nachgelassene Reden und Aufsätze*, ed. Ernst Kähler. Theologische Bibliothek Töpelmann 1. Berlin: Alfred Töpelmann, 1952 110–39.

Schottroff, Luise. *Der Glaubende und die feindliche Welt: Beobachtungen zum gnostischen Dualismus und seiner Bedeutung für Paulus und das Johannesevangelium.* WMANT 37. Neukirchen-Vluyn: Neukirchen, 1970.

Schrage, Wolfgang. "Leid, Kreuz und Eschaton: Die Peristasenkataloge als Merkmale paulinischer theologia crucis und Eschatologie." *EvT* 34 (1974) 141–75.

*Die konkreten Einzelgebote in der paulinischen Paränese: Ein Beitrag zur neutestamentlichen Ethik.* Gütersloh: Gütersloh, 1961.

"Die Stellung zur Welt bei Paulus, Epiktet und in der Apokalyptik: Ein Beitrag zu 1 Kor 7,29–31." *ZTK* 61 (1964) 125–54.

"Zur Ethik der neutestamentlichen Haustafeln." *NTS* 21 (1974) 1–22.

"Zur Frontstellung der paulinischen Ehebewertung in 1 Kor 7 1–7." *ZNW* 67 (1976) 214–34.

Schrenk, Gottlob. "ἐντέλλομαι, ἐντολή." *TDNT* 2 (1964) 544–56.

Schürer, Emil. *The History of the Jewish People in the Age of Jesus Christ (175 BC–AD 135).* Vol. 1, rev. and ed. Geza Vermes and Fergus Millar. Edinburgh: T. and T. Clark, 1973.

*The History of the Jewish People in the Age of Jesus Christ (175 BC–AD 135).* Vol. 2, rev. and ed. Geza Vermes, Fergus Millar, and Matthew Black. Edinburgh: T. and T. Clark, 1979.

*The History of the Jewish People in the Age of Jesus Christ (175 BC–AD 135).* Vol. 3.2, rev. and ed. Geza Vermes, Fergus Millar, and Martin Goodman. Edinburgh: T. and T. Clark, 1987.

Schüssler Fiorenza, Elisabeth. *Bread Not Stone: The Challenge of Feminist Biblical Interpretation.* Boston: Beacon, 1984. (See also under Fiorenza, Elisabeth Schüssler.)

Schulz, Siegfried. "Evangelium und Welt." *Neues Testament und christliche Existenz: Festschrift für Herbert Braun zum 70. Geburtstag am 4. Mai 1973*, ed. Hans Dieter Betz and Luise Schottroff. Tübingen: J. C. B. Mohr, 1973 483–501.

Seboldt, Roland H. A. "Spiritual Marriage in the Early Church: A Suggested Interpretation of 1 Cor. 7:36–38." *Concordia Theological Monthly* 30 (1959) 103–19, 176–89.

Sellin, Gerhard. "'Die Auferstehung ist schon geschehen': Zur Spiritualisierung apokalyptischer Terminologie im Neuen Testament." *NovT* 25 (1983) 220–37.

"Hauptprobleme des Ersten Korintherbriefes." *ANRW* 2.25.4 (1987) 2940–3044.

*Der Streit um die Auferstehung der Toten: Eine religionsgeschichtliche und exegetische Untersuchung von 1 Korinther 15.* FRLANT 138. Göttingen: Vandenhoeck und Ruprecht, 1986.

Sevenster, J. N. *Paul and Seneca.* NovT Supplement 4. Leiden: E. J. Brill, 1961.

Shaw, Brent D. "The Divine Economy: Stoicism as Ideology." *Latomus* 44 (1985) 16–54.

Sickenberger, Joseph. "Syneisaktentum im ersten Korintherbriefe?" *BZ* 3 (1905) 44–69.

Skehan, Patrick W., and Alexander A. Di Lella. *The Wisdom of Ben Sira.* AB 39. New York: Double Day, 1987.

Smend, Rudolf. *Die Weisheit des Jesus Sirach.* Berlin: Georg Reimer, 1906.

Smith, Jonathan Z. "Wisdom and Apocalyptic." *Map is Not Territory: Studies in the History of Religions,* Studies in Judaism in Late Antiquity 23. Leiden: E. J. Brill, 1979 67–87.

Soden, Hans von. "Sakrament und Ethik bei Paulus: Zur Frage der literarischen und theologischen Einheitlichkeit von 1 Kor. 8–10." *Urchristentum und Geschichte: Gesammelte Aufsätze und Vorträge,* vol. 1: *Grundsätzliches und Neutestamentliches,* ed. Hans von Campenhausen. Tübingen: J. C. B. Mohr, 1951 239–75.

Spanneut, Michel. *Permanence du stoïcisme: De Zéno à Malraux.* Gembloux: J. Duculot, 1973.

*Le stoïcisme des Pères de l'Eglise de Clément de Rome à Clément d'Alexandrie.* Patristica Sorbonensia 1. Paris: Éditions de Seuil, 1957.

Speyer, Wolfgang. *Naucellius und sein Kreis.* Munich: C. H. Beck, 1959.

Spicq, Ceslas. *Notes de lexicographie néo-testamentaire.* Vols. 1–2, with supplement, Orbis Biblicus et Orientalis 22/1–3. Fribourg: Éditions Universitaires 1978–82; Göttingen: Vandenhoeck und Ruprecht, 1978–82.

Spittler, R. P. "Testament of Job." *The Old Testament Pseudepigrapha,* ed. James H. Charlesworth. Garden City, N.Y.: Doubleday, 1983 1:829–68.

Spörlein, Bernhard. *Die Leugnung der Auferstehung: Eine historisch-kritische Untersuchung zu 1 Kor. 15.* BU 7, Münchener Universitäts-Schriften, Katholisch-Theologische Facultät. Regensburg: Friedrich Pustet, 1971.

Städele, Alfons. *Die Briefe des Pythagoras und der Pythagoreer.* Beiträge zur klassischen Philologie 115. Meisenheim am Glan: Anton Hain, 1980.

Stauffer, Ethelbert. "γαμέω, γάμος." *TDNT* 1 (1964) 648–57.

Steck, Rudolf. "Geistliche Ehen bei Paulus? (I. Kor. 7,36–38.)." *Schweizerische Theologische Zeitschrift* 34 (1917) 177–89.

Stegemann, Willy. "Theon, 5." *PW* 2nd series 5.2, half-vol. 10 (1934) 2037–54.

Steinthal, Heymann. *Geschichte der Sprachwissenschaft bei den Griechen und Römern mit besonderer Rücksicht auf die Logik.* 2nd edn., vol. 1. Berlin: Ferd. Dümmler, 1890.

Stelzenberger, Johannes. *Die Beziehungen der frühchristlichen Sittenlehre zur Ethik der Stoa.* Munich: Max Hueber, 1933.

Stone, Michael Edward. *Fourth Ezra.* Hermeneia. Minneapolis: Augsburg Fortress, 1990.

Stowers, Stanley Kent. "The Diatribe." *Greco-Roman Literature and the New Testament: Selected Forms and Genres*, ed. David E. Aune, SBLSBS 21. Atlanta: Scholars, 1988 51–83.

*The Diatribe and Paul's Letter to the Romans*. SBLDS 57. Chico, Calif.: Scholars, 1981.

Strack, Hermann L., and Paul Billerbeck. *Kommentar zum Neuen Testament aus Talmud und Midrash*. 4 vols. Munich: C. H. Beck, 1956.

Strugnell, John. "Flavius Josephus and the Essenes: *Antiquities* XVIII.18–22." *JBL* 77 (1958) 106–15.

Sullivan, Clayton. *Rethinking Realized Eschatology*. [Macon, Ga.]: Mercer University Press, 1988.

Tarn, W. W., and G. T. Griffith. *Hellenistic Civilization*. 3rd edn. London: Edward Arnold, 1959.

Taylor, Thomas, trans. *Ocellus Lucanus, On the Nature of the Universe; Taurus, the Platonic Philosopher, On the Eternity of the World; Julius Firmicus Maternus, Of the Thema Mundi, in Which the Positions of the Stars at the Commencement of the Several Mundane Periods Is Given; Select Theorems, On the Perpetuity of Time, By Proclus*. London: [Richard Taylor], 1831.

Thackeray, Henry St. John. *The Relation of St. Paul to Contemporary Jewish Thought*. London: Macmillan, 1900.

Theissen, Gerd. *Psychological Aspects of Pauline Theology*. Philadelphia: Fortress, 1987.

*The Social Setting of Pauline Christianity: Essays on Corinth*, ed. and introduction by John H. Schütz. Philadelphia: Fortress, 1982.

*Sociology of Early Palestinian Christianity*. Philadelphia: Fortress, 1977.

Thesleff, Holger. *An Introduction to the Pythagorean Writings of the Hellenistic Period*. Acta Academiae Aboensis, Humaniora 24/3. Åbo, Finland: Åbo Akademi, 1961.

ed., *The Pythagorean Texts of the Hellenistic Period*. Acta Academiae Aboensis, Humaniora 30/1. Åbo, Finland: Åbo Akademi, 1965.

Thiselton, Anthony C. "Realized Eschatology at Corinth." *NTS* 24 (1977/78) 510–26.

Tholuck, A. *Exposition, Doctrinal and Philological, of Christ's Sermon on the Mount According to the Gospel of Matthew*. Vol. 1, 2nd edn., The Biblical Cabinet 6. Edinburgh: Thomas Clark, 1843.

Thraede, Klaus. "Ärger mit der Freiheit." *"Freunde in Christus werden...,"* ed. Gerta Scharffenort and Klaus Thraede. Gelnhausen: Burckhardthaus, 1977 31–182.

"Zum historischen Hintergrund der 'Haustafel' des NT." *Jahrbuch für Antike und Christentum*, supplement 8: *Pietas: Festschrift für Bernhard Kötting*, ed. Ernst Dassmann and K. Suso Frank. Münster: Aschendorffsche Verlagsbuchhandlung, 1980 359–68.

Thrall, Margaret E. *Greek Particles in the New Testament: Linguistic and Exegetical Studies*. NTTS 3. Grand Rapids, Mich.: William B. Eerdmans, 1962.

"The Problem of II Cor. vi. 14–vii. 1 in Some Recent Discussion." *NTS* 24 (1977/78) 132–48.

Tischleder, P. *Wesen und Stellung der Frau nach der Lehre des heiligen*

*Paulus: Eine ethisch-exegetische Untersuchung.* NTAbh 10/3–4. Münster: Aschendorffsche Verlagbuchhandlung, 1923.

Trenchard, Warren C. *Ben Sira's View of Women: A Literary Analysis.* Brown Judaic Studies 38. Chico, Calif.: Scholars, 1982.

Trendennick, Hugh, and G. Cyril Armstrong, eds. and trans. *Aristotle.* Vol. 18: *Metaphysics: Books X-XIV, Oeconomica, and Magna Moralia,* LCL. Cambridge: Harvard University Press, 1935; London: William Heinemann, 1935.

Trevett, Christine. "Apocalypse, Ignatius, Montanism: Seeking the Seeds." *VC* 43 (1989) 313–38.

Trillitzsch, Winfried. "Hieronymus und Seneca." *Mittellateinisches Jahrbuch* 2 (1965) 42–54.

*Seneca im literarischen Urteil der Antike: Darstellung und Sammlung der Zeugnisse.* 2 vols. Amsterdam: Adolf M. Hakkert, 1971.

Tuckett, C. M. "1 Corinthians and Q." *JBL* 102 (1983) 607–19.

Valckenaer, Lodewijk Kasper. *Selecta e scholis Lud. Casp. Valckenarii in libros quosdam Novi Testamenti,* ed. Everwijn Wassenbergh, vol. 2. Amsterdam: Petri den Hengst et filii, 1817.

Vatin, Claude. *Recherches sur le mariage et la condition de la femme mariée à l'époque hellénistique.* Bibliothèque des Écoles Françaises d'Athènes et de Rome 216. Paris: E. de Boccard, 1970.

Verner, David C. *The Household of God: The Social World of the Pastoral Epistles.* SBLDS 71. Chico, Calif.: Scholars, 1983.

Veyne, Paul. "La famille et l'amour sous le Haut-Empire romain." *Annales: Économies, Sociétés, Civilisations* 33 (1978) 35–63.

"The Roman Empire." *A History of Private Life,* ed. Paul Veyne. Vol. 1: *From Pagan Rome to Byzantium.* Cambridge: Harvard University Belknap Press, 1987 5–233.

Viller, Marcel, and Karl Rahner. *Aszese und Mystik in der Väterzeit: Ein Abriß.* Freiburg: Herder, 1939. A free reworking of Marcel Viller, *La spiritualité des premiers siècles crétiens* (Paris: Bloud et Gay, 1930).

Voelke, André-Jean. *Les rapports avec autrui dans la philosophie grecque: D'Aristote à Panétius.* Bibliothèque d'histoire de la philosophie. Paris: J. Vrin, 1961.

Völker, Walther. *Der wahre Gnostiker nach Clemens Alexandrinus.* TU 57. Berlin: Akademie, 1952; Leipzig: J. C. Hinrichs, 1952.

Vööbus, Arthur. *History of Asceticism in the Syrian Orient.* Vol. 1, CSCO 184. Louvain: Secrétariat du CSCO, 1958.

Vogt, Joseph. "Von der Gleichwertigkeit der Geschlechter in der bürgerlichen Gesellschaft." *Akademie der Wissenschaften und der Literatur: Abhandlungen der Geistes- und Sozialwissenschaftlichen Klasse* 2 (1960) 209–55.

Wahl, Christian Abraham. *Clavis Novi Testamenti Philologica.* 3rd edn. Leipzig: Joh. Ambros. Barth, 1834.

Waltz, Pierre, and Guy Soury. *Anthologie grecque, première partie: Anthologie Palatine.* Vol. 3. Paris: Société d'édition «Les belles lettres», 1974.

Ward, Roy Bowen. "Musonius and Paul on Marriage." *NTS* 36 (1990) 281–9.

Waszink, J. H. "Abtreibung." *RAC* 1 (1950) 55–60.

Webster, T. B. L. *Hellenistic Poetry and Art.* London: Methuen, 1964.
*An Introduction to Menander.* Manchester: University of Manchester, 1974; New York: Barnes and Noble, 1974.
*Studies in Menander.* 2nd edn., Publications of the University of Manchester 309, Classical Series 7. Manchester: Manchester University Press, 1960.
Wedderburn, A. J. M. *Baptism and Resurrection: Studies in Pauline Theology against Its Graeco-Roman Background.* WUNT 44. Tübingen: J. C. B. Mohr, 1987.
Wehrli, Fritz, ed. *Die Schule des Aristoteles: Texte und Kommentar.* Vol. 4: *Demetrios von Phaleron,* 2nd edn. Basel/Stuttgart: Schwabe, 1968.
Weiß, Hans-Friedrich. "Paulus und die Häretiker: Zum Paulusverständnis in der Gnosis." *Christentum und Gnosis,* ed. Walther Eltester, Beiheft zur ZNW 37. Berlin: Alfred Töpelmann, 1969 116–28.
Weiß, Johannes. *Beiträge zur Paulinischen Rhetorik.* Göttingen: Vandenhoeck und Ruprecht, 1897.
*Der erste Korintherbrief.* MeyerK 5. Göttingen: Vandenhoeck und Ruprecht, 1925.
*The History of Primitive Christianity.* Completed following author's death by Rudolf Knopf, ed. Frederick C. Grant. Vol. 2. New York: Wilson-Erickson, 1937.
Weiss, Konrad. "φέρω." *TDNT* 9 (1974) 56–87.
Weizsäcker, Carl. "Die Anfänge christlicher Sitte." *Jahrbücher für Deutsche Theologie* 21 (1876) 1–36.
*Das apostolische Zeitalter der christlichen Kirche.* 1st edn. Freiburg im Breisgau: J. C. B. Mohr, 1886.
Wendland, Paul. "Philo und die kynisch-stoische Diatribe." *Beiträge zur Geschichte der griechischen Philosophie und Religion,* ed. Paul Wendland and Otto Kern. Berlin: Georg Reimer, 1895 3–75.
*Quaestiones Musonianae: De Musonio Stoico Clementis Alexandrini Aliorumque Auctore.* Berlin: Mayer und Mueller, 1886.
"Die Therapeuten und die philonische Schrift vom beschaulichen Leben." *Jahrbücher für classische Philologie,* supplement vol. 22 (1896) 693–771.
Review of *C. Musonii Rufi reliquiae,* ed. O. Hense. *Berliner philologische Wochenschrift* 26 (1906) 197–202.
Wettstein, Johann Jakob. *Novum Testamentum Graecum.* Vol. 2. Amsterdam: Dommerian, 1752; reprint, Graz, Austria: Akademische Druck- und Verlagsanstalt, 1962.
Wilhelm, Friedrich. "Die Oeconomica der Neopythagoreer Bryson, Kallikratidas, Periktione, Phintys." *Rh. Mus.* 70 (1915) 161–223.
"Zu Achilles Tatius." *Rh. Mus.* n.s. 57 (1902) 55–75.
Wilkinson, L. P. *Classical Attitudes to Modern Issues: Population and Family Planning, Women's Liberation, Nudism in Deed and Word, Homosexuality.* London: William Kimber, 1978.
Wilson, Jack H. "The Corinthians Who Say There Is No Resurrection of the Dead." *ZNW* 59 (1968) 90–107.
Wilson, R. McL. "Gnosis at Corinth." *Paul and Paulinism: Essays in Honour of C. K. Barrett.* London: SPCK, 1982 102–44.

"Gnosis/Gnostizismus II." *TRE* 13 (1984) 535–50.

"How Gnostic Were the Corinthians?" *NTS* 19 (1972/73) 65–74.

Wimbush, Vincent L. *Paul the Worldly Ascetic: Response to the World and Self-Understanding according to 1 Corinthians 7*. Macon, Ga.: Mercer University Press, 1987.

Winston, David. *The Wisdom of Solomon: A New Translation with Introduction and Commentary*. AB 43. Garden City, N.Y.: Doubleday, 1979.

Witherington, Ben, III. *Women in the Earliest Churches*. SNTSMS 59. Cambridge: Cambridge University Press, 1988.

Wolbert, Werner. *Ethische Argumentation und Paränese in 1 Kor 7*. Moraltheologische Studien, systematische Abteilung 8. Düsseldorf: Patmos, 1981.

Wolff, Hans Julius. *Written and Unwritten Marriages in Hellenistic and Postclassical Roman Law*. Philological Monographs 9. Haverford, Penn.: American Philological Association, 1939.

Wood, Neal. *Cicero's Social and Political Thought*. Berkeley: University of California Press, 1988.

Yamauchi, Edwin M. *Pre-Christian Gnosticism: A Survey of the Proposed Evidences*. London: Tyndale, 1973.

Yarbrough, O. Larry. *Not Like the Gentiles: Marriage Rules in the Letters of Paul*. SBLDS 80. Atlanta: Scholars, 1985.

Zeller, Eduard. *Die Philosophie der Griechen in ihrer geschichtlichen Entwicklung*. Vols. 2–3, 5th edn. Leipzig: Fues (O. R. Reisland), 1922–3.

Zucker, Friedrich. "Socia unanimans." *Rh. Mus.* n.s. 92 (1944) 193–217.

# INDEX OF SELECTED NAMES
# AND SUBJECTS

# INDEX OF SELECTED SCRIPTURE REFERENCES

264     *Index*

# INDEX OF SELECTED GREEK WORDS